Frederick Do
A Critical R

𝔹

BLACKWELL CRITICAL READERS

Blackwell's *Critical Readers* series presents a collection of linked perspectives on continental philosophers, and social and cultural theorists. Edited and introduced by acknowledged experts and written by representatives of different schools and positions, the series embodies debate, dissent, and a committed heterodoxy. From Foucault to Derrida, from Heidegger to Nietzsche, *Critical Readers* also address figures whose work requires elucidation by a variety of perspectives. Volumes in the series include both primary and secondary bibliographies.

Althusser: *A Critical Reader*
Edited by Gregory Elliott

Bataille: *A Critical Reader*
Edited by Fred Botting and Scott Wilson

Baudrillard: *A Critical Reader*
Edited by Douglas Kellner

Deleuze: *A Critical Reader*
Edited by Paul Patton

Derrida: *A Critical Reader*
Edited by David Wood

Frederick Douglass: *A Critical Reader*
Edited by Bill E. Lawson and Frank M. Kirkland

Fanon: *A Critical Reader*
Edited by Lewis R. Gordon, T. Denean Sharpley-Whiting and Renée T. White

Foucault: *A Critical Reader*
Edited by David Hoy

Heidegger: *A Critical Reader*
Edited by Hubert L. Dreyfus and Harrison Hall

Kierkegaard: *A Critical Reader*
Edited by Jonathan Ree and Jane Chamberlain

Nietzsche: *A Critical Reader*
Edited by Peter Sedgwick

Frederick Douglass:
A Critical Reader

Edited by
Bill E. Lawson and Frank M. Kirkland

Copyright © Blackwell Publishers Ltd 1999

First published 1999

2 4 6 8 10 9 7 5 3 1

Blackwell Publishers Inc.
350 Main Street
Malden, Massachusetts 02148
USA

Blackwell Publishers Ltd
108 Cowley Road
Oxford OX4 1JF
UK

All rights reserved. Except for the quotation of short passages for the purposes of criticism and review, no part of this publication may be reproduced, stored in a retrieval system, or transmitted, in any form or by any means, electronic, mechanical, photocopying, recording or otherwise, without the prior permission of the publisher.

Except in the United States of America, this book is sold subject to the condition that it shall not, by way of trade or otherwise, be lent, resold, hired out, or otherwise circulated without the publisher's prior consent in any form of binding or cover other than that in which it is published and without a similar condition including this condition being imposed on the subsequent purchaser.

Library of Congress Cataloging-in-Publication Data
Frederick Douglass / edited by Bill E. Lawson and Frank M. Kirkland.
    p. cm.—(Blackwell critical readers)
    Includes bibliographical references and index.
    ISBN 0-631-20577-2 (hb : alk. paper).—ISBN 0-631-20578-0 (pbk. : alk. paper)
    1. Douglass, Frederick, 1817?–1895—Political and social views.
I. Lawson, Bill E., 1947– . II. Kirkland, Frank M. III. Series.
E449.D75F738 1999
973.8′092—dc21   98–24582
                                                                              CIP

British Library Cataloguing in Publication Data

A CIP catalogue record for this book is available from the British Library

Typeset in 10 on 12 pt Plantin
by SetSystems Ltd, Saffron Walden, Essex
Printed in Great Britain by MPG Books Ltd, Bodmin, Cornwall.

This book is printed on acid-free paper

*This book is dedicated to my aunt Nannie Arnold,
and in memory of her twin sister,
my mother, Annie J. Lawson, and my father,
Edmond Daniel Lawson*

B. E. Lawson

*This book is dedicated to my mother,
Arcadia Canales Kirkland, and, in memory
of my father, Frank Kirkland*

F. M. Kirkland

Contents

List of Contributors	ix
Preface	xiii
Acknowledgments	xv
Introduction	1

Part I: Racial Assimilation and Emigration 19

1. Douglass Against the Emigrationists 21
   Bernard R. Boxill
2. Douglass on Racial Assimilation and Racial Institutions 50
   Howard McGary
3. Douglass's Assimilationism and Antislavery 64
   John P. Pittman

Part II: Natural Law and America's Founding Documents 83

4. Natural Law in the Constitutional Thought of Frederick Douglass 85
   David E. Schrader
5. Whose Fourth of July? Frederick Douglass and "Original Intent" 100
   Charles W. Mills

Part III: Enlightenment and Enslavement 143

6. The Claims of Frederick Douglass Philosophically Considered 145
   Roderick M. Stewart

7	The Grammar of Civilization: Douglass and Crummell on Doing Things with Words *Stephen L. Thompson*	173

Part IV: Moral Suasion and Rebellion — 205

8	Douglass as an Existentialist *Lewis R. Gordon*	207
9	Honor and Insurrection or A Short Story about why John Brown (with David Walker's Spirit) was Right and Frederick Douglass (with Benjamin Banneker's Spirit) was Wrong *Leonard Harris*	227
10	Enslavement, Moral Suasion, and Struggles for Recognition: Frederick Douglass's Answer to the Question – "What is Enlightenment?" *Frank M. Kirkland*	243

Part V: Incarcerating and Lynching Black Bodies — 311

11	Frederick Douglass on the Myth of the Black Rapist *Tommy L. Lott*	313
12	From the Prison of Slavery to the Slavery of Prison: Frederick Douglass and the Convict Lease System *Angela Y. Davis*	339

Part VI: Douglass (1818–95): One Hundred Years Later — 363

13	Frederick Douglass and African-American Social Progress: Does Race Matter at the Bottom of the Well? *Bill E. Lawson*	365

Selected Bibliography — 392
Index — 395

Contributors

Bernard R. Boxill is Professor of Philosophy at the University of North Carolina at Chapel Hill. He has published extensively in the areas of ethics, social justice, and political theory regarding the black American experience. He is the author of *Blacks and Social Justice* and of several recent articles on Frederick Douglass, including "Fear and Shame as Forms of Moral Suasion in the The Thought of Frederick Douglass," *Charles S. Pierce Society Proceedings*, Fall 1995, and "The Fight with Covey," in Lewis R. Gordon, ed, *Existence in Black*.

Angela Y. Davis is Professor of Philosophy in the History of Consciousness Program at the University of California, Santa Cruz. She is the editor of the volume *If They Come in the Morning: Voices of Resistance* and the author of *Angela Davis: An Autobiography, Women, Race, and Class, Women, Culture, and Politics*, and the current critically acclaimed work *Blues Legacies and Black Feminism: Gertrude "Ma" Rainey, Bessie Smith, and Billie Holiday*.

Lewis R. Gordon is Professor of Afro-American Studies, Contemporary Religious Thought, and Modern Culture and Media at Brown University. He is author of many articles in philosophy of existence, phenomenology, Africana philosophy. His books include *Bad Faith and Antiblack Racism, Fanon and the Crisis of European Man: An Essay on Philosophy and the Human Sciences*, and *Existence in Black: An Anthology of Black Existential Philosophy*.

Leonard Harris is Professor of Philosophy at Purdue University. He is also the Director, African-American Studies and Research Center, Purdue University. He has published scholarly articles on the history of blacks in Philosophy and normative ethical theory. He has edited and authored a number of books including *The Concept of Racism*, *Alain Locke and Values*, *The Philosophy of Alain Locke: Harlem Renaissance and Beyond*, and *Philosophy Born of Struggle: Anthology of Afro-American Philosophy from 1917*.

Frank M. Kirkland is Associate Professor of Philosophy at Hunter College and the Graduate Center, both of the City University of New York. He is editor of the volume *Phenomenology: East and West* and has written articles on Kant, Hegel, and Husserl as well as on the theme of modernity and African-American intellectual life. He is currently writing a book provisionally entitled *Hegel and Husserl: Idealist Meditations*.

Bill E. Lawson is Professor of Philosophy at Michigan State University. He has published articles on political obligation, crime victimization, and jazz. He is the editor of *The Underclass Question* and co-author with Howard McGary of *Between Slavery and Freedom: Philosophy and American Slavery*.

Tommy L. Lott is Professor of Philosophy at the University of Missouri at St Louis. He is the editor of *Subjugation and Bondage: Critical Essays on Slavery and Social Philosophy*, co-editor of *A Companion to African-American Philosophy*, and author of *Like Rum in the Punch: Alain Locke and the Theory of African-American Culture*.

Howard McGary is Professor of Philosophy at Rutgers, The State University of New Jersey. He has published widely in the areas of African-American Philosophy and Social and Political Philosophy. He is the author of *Race and Social Justice* and has co-authored with Bill E. Lawson *Between Slavery and Freedom*.

Charles W. Mills is Associate Professor of Philosophy at the University of Illinois at Chicago. He works in the area of oppositional political theory, and has recently published two books on race, *The Racial Contract* and *Blackness Visible: Essays on Philosophy and Race*.

John P. Pittman is Associate Professor of Philosophy at John Jay College of Criminal Justice, CUNY. He edited the anthology, *African-American Perspectives and Philosophical Traditions*, and is currently co-editing, with Tommy L. Lott, the *Blackwell Companion to African-American Philosophy*.

David E. Schrader is Professor of Philosophy at Washington and Jefferson College. He has published in the areas of philosophy of religion, philosophy of economics, and applied ethics. He is author of *The Corporation as Anomaly*.

Roderick M. Stewart is Associate Professor and Chair of Philosophy and Religion at Austin College in Sherman, Texas. His special research interests are in continental philosophy and multiculturalism, with publications on Nietzsche and Heidegger in *American Philosophical Quarterly, Philosophy and Phenomenological Research, Nous,* and *Man and World*.

Stephen L. Thompson is Assistant Professor of Philosophy at Howard University. He is the author of several articles in the philosophy of language as well as the forthcoming book *Talking about Thinking about Feeling: Alain Locke on the Norming of Everyday Life*.

Preface

The idea for this book was formed about ten years ago at the Eastern Division Meeting of the American Philosophical Association. As was normally the case at these meeting, the black philosophers would spend at least one afternoon/evening "catching up" on research, promotions, and other news of interest to them. At this meeting, the discussion turned to the writings of nineteenth-century Black Nationalist thinkers in the United States. Citing persons like Douglass, Stewart, Delany, and Garnet, the general consensus was that these thinkers were very insightful in their thinking and writing about the problems of race and racism.

It was agreed by all of those gathered at this meeting that it would be interesting and worthwhile to put together a volume that examines the writings of these thinkers. The years passed but the idea stayed with Bill and when Steve Smith of Blackwell Publishers called to discuss book ideas, he suggested the nineteenth-century volume. After much discussion, it was decided to begin by focusing on Frederick Douglass. In retrospect, that was a good choice. Douglass's written work deserves examination by philosophers. Not because he was a philosopher, but because of the philosophical insights he brought to his writings. Douglass was also committed to presenting his positions in the form of arguments. Thus, his writings provide a fertile ground for philosophic examination. We are proud to present this philosophic examination of Douglass's thought and writings.

This work has been a labor of love. The contributors were responsive and timely. We have enjoyed working on this project. Steve Smith remained committed, although there were geographical moves, deaths, and other events over the past year and a half that slowed the progress of publication. Thanks Steve. We also want to thank all of those persons who helped make this volume possible. We hope that volumes on Martin Delany, Maria Stewart, Henry Highland Garnet, and others will follow. Their work is also worthy of philosophical examination.

Bill E. Lawson and Frank M. Kirkland

Acknowledgments

We have been very fortunate to have the support of some wonderful people at Blackwell Publishers. We want to thank Steve Smith and Mary Riso for their support. We also want to give our heartfelt appreciation to Debbie Seymour. Her initial proofing of the manuscript was exceptional. We must thank Mary Imperatore and Gail Ross for their work on the originally submitted essays. Howard McGary made very important critical suggestions throughout the process, for this we are grateful.

We would like to thank members of the Society for the Study of African Philosophy (SSAP) as well as CUNY's Institute for Research on the African Diaspora in the Americas and the Caribbean (IRADAC) for their suggestions and support during the editing of this book.

Finally, we would like to thank LaVern and Gaston McGary for their support. A heartfelt thanks also goes to William Lance Lawson and Renee Sanders-Lawson for their patience, comments, and support during the editing of this work.

Strange things have happened of late and are still happening. Some of these tend to dim the luster of the American name, and chill the hopes once entertained for the cause of American liberty. He is a wiser man than I am, who can tell how low the moral sentiments of the Republican may yet fall. When the moral sense of a nation begins to decline, and the wheels of progress to roll backward, there is no telling how low one will fall or where the other will stop. The downward tendency, already manifest, has swept away some of the most important safeguards. The Supreme Court has surrendered. State Sovereignty is restored. It has destroyed the civil rights Bill, and converted the Republican Party into a party of money rather than a party of morals, a party of things rather that a party of humanity and justice. We may well ask what next?

Frederick Douglass, *Lessons of the Hour*, 1894

Introduction

Bill E. Lawson and Frank M. Kirkland

Nearly two centuries from his birth – one hundred and eighty years – and barely a century after his death, philosophy has finally come to the work and thought of Frederick Douglass. Has it arrived on the scene too late? Has philosophy's tardiness brought it to a scene where Douglass's reflections have now become cut and dried after the historians and literary theorists have made fresh interpretive work of his intellectual legacy? Or is its tardiness simply another example of, say, "the owl of Minerva" again unfolding its wings with the onset of nightfall, promulgating "untimely meditations" on Douglass? Or is its tardiness due to its participation in what Charles Mills has recently called "The Racial Contract"[1] in which "black/colored" voices and texts are to be regarded as philosophically "dumb" and "whited out" respectively?

Fortunately, for the discipline of philosophy, Douglass's work can never be rendered cut and dried, despite the richly textured, highly nuanced, and scholarly detailed interpretations recently produced by historians (Blassingame, Blight, Martin, McFeely, Preston) and literary theorists (Andrews, Gates, Sundquist, Walker) over the past twenty years. Historians and biographers have essentially concentrated on the life of Douglass as a major advocate of social reform, as a patron of black social upward mobility and, most importantly, as a leader in and of the antislavery crusade. They have disclosed previously unexplored facets of his life to reconstruct the integrity of it as one of the most exemplary on the nineteenth-century American scene.

Literary theorists have focused on the literary genre in which Douglass's life has been framed. They have fleshed out the narrative and rhetorical strategies of his speeches and texts to claim for Douglass an exemplary ability to "represent" himself to an audience as a "self-made man" and to claim for his speeches and texts an exemplary relationship to other texts in the American or African-American intellectual and literary traditions.

Ultimately the work of all three groups converge in their disciplinary considerations of Douglass as the "Representative Colored Man of the United States," in which "representative" conveys three meanings: (1) Douglass's ability to describe, explain, depict (represent) clearly to the mind the terms and effects of racial enslavement, (2) Douglass's credentials to speak and act on behalf of (represent) free and enslaved black people by virtue of (1), and (3) Douglass's personal qualities enabling others to regard his character as exemplifying, embodying (representing) someone ennobling, extraordinary by virtue of (1) and (2).[2]

Yet, recently, a noted historian of Douglass, David Blight, has observed that, although much scholarly attention has been paid to Douglass as "Representative Man," as the sterling icon of his age, little regard has been given him as a thinker.[3] *Frederick Douglass: A Critical Reader* attempts to start the process of filling that gap. In the spirit of interpreting Douglass as a "thinker," what philosophers have found in Douglass is the wealth of arguments he offers throughout his texts and speeches that bear philosophical importance. Douglass participates in the enterprise of philosophy because of his commitment to argument. This commitment, however, does not solely reflect a dedication to chains of inference, let alone an allegiance to some specific philosophical doctrine or method, which are usually construed as the "scholastic" and technical criteria for identifying a person as a thinker or philosopher. Nor does it detract from his commitment to activism. *It rather reflects Douglass's concern with systematically (and not just rhetorically) engaging discursively amplified ways of thinking, i.e., cogently sustaining chains of reasoning in conjunction with responsible envisioning of the manner in which we ought to live our lives with our concepts and judgments.* And, on this matter, the fecundity of his reflections is boundless.

Still the incredulous amongst us would express doubt regarding Douglass the "thinker." Douglass was never a philosopher in solely the above-mentioned technical sense of that term. Nor did he ever claim to be one. Furthermore, he never crossed professionally, the more doubtful could assert, the boundary into the academic discipline of philosophy. Such incredulity would indeed resound with blaring absurdity, if not blatant insensitivity, when placed against the life of Douglass or of any black person in American thralldom. But, although a skeptical person could be sympathetic to the problems being racially designated as black and being enslaved have wrought in socially excluding non-white people from all substantial and significant areas of American life, it would still be a fact, such a person would contend, that Douglass does not satisfy that sole technical sense most would believe defines a philosopher.

Nonetheless, Douglass's commitment to argument, we believe, turns him toward the enterprise of philosophy, because it reflects his ongoing advocacy of intellectual honesty and his willingness to live up to its demands consistently, exposing his reflections to intellectual and political risks and living through existential tensions passionately. It embodies his (1) pursuit for clarity in analysis, (2) attempt to attune our judgments to the ends of human reason and to cultivate a confidence in bringing those ends to our structures of human interaction, and finally (3) attempt to examine ourselves critically as being constituted by our own history and the historical present we live in. So Douglass's commitment to argument, as we are here presenting it, moves on a variety of philosophical-political levels than just simply that of dedication to inference and allegiance to doctrine and method. Moreover, Douglass inserts a genuinely philosophical problem like a detonator into this many-leveled enterprise, viz., *the dualistic and duellistic American experiment of constitutional democracy and slavery or tyranny.*

How is intellectual honesty to be maintained in the face of the incongruence and duplicity of this American experiment? What are the intellectual and political risks to exposing one's reflections in the face of this American experiment? How is clarity of our concepts and judgments to be maintained in the light of this American experiment? How are the ends of human reason brought with confidence to this American experiment of political rule and social interaction? How does a person responsibly envision the manner in which she should live her life with her concepts and judgments with consistency under this American experiment? How are our social identities and sense of humanity shaped by this American experiment and how are they to be transformed? In short, how are discursively amplified ways of thinking to counteract the experiment in a context of social space and historical time that the experiment defines and pervades?

Responses to questions of this sort permeate the writings and speeches of Douglass, responses that are culturally and socially embedded, entangled in power and interest, yet whose truth content must carry universal significance. This is the philosophical dimension in which the complexity of Douglass as "thinker" is set.

On this note, this volume is disposed to the view that Douglass's commitment to argument is a fidelity more to the truth content of his speeches than simply to the persuasive character of them, especially in the light of his deliberations about our genuine humanity and autonomy, about the revisioning of constitutional democracy, and about the legitimacy of resistance, all of which are discursively forged in the blaze and light that comprise his experience in and struggle against the "peculiar institution" of the American experiment. Discursively amplified ways of thinking are, then, also not regarded as synonymous with Douglass's extraordinary mastery of oratory and expression. But they are embodied in his oratorical excellence or powers of expression.

In addition, they are important for what they show us of Douglass's venture in (1) critically addressing the contradictions and invalidity of pro-slavery claims, (2) critically affirming the sense and validity of principles of autonomy and equality, (3) strongly advocating against slavery's institutional deficits which nullify the fulfillment of justice, freedom, and human solidarity, and (4) strongly recognizing the limits of argumentation against slavery by promoting the importance of acts of resistance to it for the sake of one's humanity.

For the most part, this anthology concentrates on an examination of the arguments of the historical Douglass. However, in recent years, aspects of Douglass's thought have been parlayed to defend two intriguing contentions, viz., the critique of racial (black) kinship and loyalty and the "end of racism" thesis. Can Douglass's thought be so parlayed? In order to address this question, we will examine the positions of two gentlemen who have recently made Douglass a supporter of one or the other contention. The Harvard law professor, Randall Kennedy, is representative of the first; the research fellow at the American Enterprise Institute, Dinesh D'Souza, representative of the second. Kennedy is of the view that "neither racial pride nor racial kinship offers guidance that is intellectually, morally, or politically satisfactory," that "the sentiments and conduct of racial kinship are morally dubious" and that "the basis of our feelings of pride and kinship" need to be reconsidered and reconstructed non-racially.[4] And Kennedy rightly finds strong support for his critique in Douglass.[5] Both Douglass and Kennedy would agree, for example, that a person cannot feel pride in a state of affairs separate from one's own contribution to it and that a person cannot have feelings of attachment to another based solely on blood/skin ties alone regardless of the other's deeds. Race, for them, falsely leads people to take pride in matters independent of their own contribution to it and to give loyalty to "like-colored" others regardless of their actions.

In his rejection of racial pride and loyalty, Kennedy believes he is able to assume what the Harvard political theorist Michael Sandel has called the "unencumbered self."[6] For Sandel, the "unencumbered self" is a self-conception "freed from the sanctions of custom and tradition and inherited status, unbound by moral ties antecedent to choice, [and] installed as sovereign, cast as the author of the only obligations that constrain." Although, on the one hand, Sandel is highly critical of this self-conception that he believes must be operative in all contract-based political liberalism, Kennedy, on the other hand, wholeheartedly embraces it. He regards it as a strong alternative, if not corrective, to a self-conception accorded moral weight by virtue of its racial commitments and attachments and, hence, to ties and obligations antecedent to one's own individual choices and contributions. Moreover he adopts the conception of the "unencumbered self," because it would avail a person a self-identity unburdened counterfactually with racially conventionalist or role-conformist attitudes and dependent on an uncritical acceptance of one's loyalty to a racialized cultural form of life. Kennedy believes that he has found ready support for this conception of the "unencumbered self," as it pertains to race, in Douglass's thought. But, unknownst to him, this is the point where he and Douglass part company.

Douglass is indeed critical of race pride and loyalty. But his criticism of them is not proferred in behalf of upholding or seeking anything like the "unencumbered self." Rather it allows him to concede, although with some theoretical difficulty, the importance of what he calls "institutions of a complexional character,"[7] i.e., the building of, say, black institutions and practices. (Most people will be surprised that Douglass also acknowledges the importance of affirmative action, i.e., giving special consideration for offices or positions to qualified black persons over qualified white persons, in the light of the legacy of slavery, all else about them being equal. He would, nonetheless, not regard it as a "complexional institution" contemporary and past public opinion notwithstanding.)[8] Douglass, however, sees these institutions as having a provisional or interim status, because their *raison d'être* is to serve the "idea of a single human brotherhood"[9] whose realization would ultimately make such institutions unnecessary and transient. They would not for Douglass serve the values, interests, and needs plausible only in and pertinent only to a particular yet enduring form of life. It seems then they only have an instrumental, rather than an intrinsic, significance. Whether such institution building can have instrumental significance alone, separate from any intrinsic one, is an intriguing question. Nonetheless, provisional and instrumental as "complexional institutions" may be, Douglass could never endorse them if he were to subscribe to the "unencumbered self" as Kennedy maintains, since such a self would be defined apart from racial attachments, provisional or otherwise. Furthermore, provisional and instrumental as "complexional institutions" may be, he still grants them some moral pertinence, although without any acknowledgment of theoretical difficulty, because he regards them as contributing to the protection of the rights of black people as something worthy of respect and to the protection against better advantaged black people personally doing nothing for their least advantaged racial brethren. But these contributions do not have intrinsic moral worth. They are adjunct to the end of enabling blacks to participate in the work of fulfilling the idea of human brotherhood in the form of racial assimilation.

The primary task of "complexional institutions" is not to foster race pride. Rather it is to foster, according to Douglass, the morally preeminent aim of enabling blacks, socially disfavored through enslavement and racism, to affirm their moral worth as persons and thereby enabling them to be more willing to engage in and struggle for the social cooperation necessary to appreciate members of any racial group in terms of their competencies and achievements alone. To be sure, the rights of black people are not underwritten by "complexional institutions." But the documents and institutions that do had not served, according to Douglass, to safeguard those rights from the violation of others. As a consequence, "complexional institutions" enable black people themselves to set about protecting their rights. Moreover, according to Douglass, "complexional institutions" work against impediments to the self-reliance of black people and counteract the inaction, idleness, and indifference of black people toward the uplift and improvement of the group's social condition and welfare. Nonetheless, these aims and values ultimately, not immediately, take a moral backseat, if not assume a moral dubiety, because of his commitment to the idea of human brotherhood and racial assimilation and the "non-complexional" institutions needed to sustain the realization of that idea. For Kennedy, they immediately are morally dubious. Moreover, unlike Kennedy, Douglass does not deny that the provisional "institutions of complexion" he promotes are for a time morally germane. Yet they are always adjunct to racial assimilation as the morally preeminent idea.

Douglass, then, could never endorse the "unencumbered self," given his claims, rightly or wrongly, about the limited moral relevance of provisional "complexional institutions." Although Douglass is persistent throughout his life in his calls for racial assimilation and against race pride, those calls are not as straightforward and consistent in ways Kennedy would have us believe or in ways Kennedy himself would so rigorously and stringently frame the matter. But what self-conception would allow Douglass to maintain a racially assimilationist commitment while endorsing the temporary moral relevancy of "complexional institutions" of a provisional kind? Everyone is familiar with Douglass's self-conception as the "self-made" man and as "the unassailable and integral black self." In the literary-autobiographical tradition, Douglass's self-conception is "non-existent as an entity, but [characterized] as a coded system of signs, arbitrary in reference,"[10] allowing for the coordinations and contradictions of a plurality of selves expressed, for example, in Douglass's three autobiographies. With the exception of the third, none of these conceptions could address the question raised above. Yet the third conception could confront it only by representing Douglass in the light of a "fictive self in language marked from the start by burdensome ironies."[11] No self-conception of the moral- and political-philosophical import Kennedy seeks with the "unencumbered self" could be generated about Douglass along that literary-autobiographical route.

Douglas himself makes the principle of self-reliance very conspicuous in his thought, but it could not be the self-conception needed to address the above-mentioned question. What does answer the question is a self-conception that, unfortunately, Douglass uses quite sparingly. The self-conception, which enables him to support "complexional institutions" and their moral relevancy provisionally while embracing their transcendence for the sake of racial assimilation (and hence downplaying those institutions and their relevancy ultimately,) is the ability of a person to distance herself wittingly from racial (complexional) or racialized roles. A person critical of race pride and loyalty, identifying herself as free of racial sentiments and duties, does not need to imagine herself in a manner extremely counterfactual to who she is, i.e., to think of herself as "unencumbered." She must rather be able and willing to assume reflectively a distance from social roles, racial and otherwise, in order to challenge, in this case, attitudes or behaviors stemming from either an uncritical/naive or a racist endorsement of *prima facie* duties and obligations a socially racialized form of life would impose.[12]

Such a person would be challenging racial or racist role-conventionalism that makes that endorsement possible. But the capacity of, say, a black individual, in this instance, to distance herself wittingly from racial or racialized roles would not entail a challenge to the significance of her fidelities to complexional (black) institutions instrumental to the development of her wherewithal and self-reliance, so long as her fidelities do not become blind or, better said, formulaic ones. And, for Douglass, these formulaic fidelities to "complexional institutions" yield uncritical racial pride in and solidarity with racially based economic, political, and cultural endeavors indefinitely, functioning as if they are intrinsically binding on a racial group.

Outside of these "strong" or formulaic fidelities, evidence of Douglass's support of "weak" fidelities to "complexional institutions" would be his advocacy for black newspapers, not only to advance black viewpoints and attitudes on matters such as the slavery question and racial elevation, generating to some degree racial pride, but to advance "an able, sound, and decent journal, conducted in the spirit of justice. . . . and an able and influential public journal that removes popular prejudice [and secures] the judgment of those whose good opinion is worth having."[13] Another piece of evidence would be his supportive argument for linking free and enslaved "Negroes" to the high civilizational legacy of ancient Egypt not simply for the sake of their racial pride, but primarily for their ethnological inclusion in the single human race and family in his commencement address. "The Claims of the Negro Ethnologically Considered," at Western Reserve College in 1854.[14]

But embracing these views does not compromise Douglass's moral sense of worth or his moral autonomy. It is not necessary for Douglass to be morally autonomous by defining himself independently of the attachments that make him what he is, as Kennedy seems to suggest. That is to say, it is neither morally nor hypothetically imperative for Douglass to assume the "unemcumbered self" in order to have a sense of moral worth or be morally autonomous.

When we turn to the "end of racism" thesis, the idea of blacks contributing to the material advancement of civil society is the major theme. And Thomas Sowell, senior research fellow at the Hoover Institution, Stanford University, has been the "Rock of Gibraltar" to a growing number of scholars, politicians, and citizens who respectively have hung their research, agendas, and needs around that thesis and, hence, that idea. For the thesis to make sense, proponents need a minimalist, not an elaborate, definition of racism. So a presupposition of the thesis is a definition of racism stating that it is simply an irrational belief in an inherent inferiority and superiority among so-called races.[15] If an act of racial discrimination is a racist act, then that act must exhibit or foster this belief. But, Sowell contends, all acts of racial discrimination do not carry this belief. Since all acts of racial discrimination neither reflect nor encourage this belief, discrimination against members of specific racial groups, Sowell argues, does not have to be necessarily founded on racist beliefs.

For example, underrepresentation of American racial minorities in the student body and faculty of colleges or among the recipients of business contracts would not be necessarily the result of racism. Empirical generalizations unbecoming of racialminorities, D'Souza would testify, may reflect factual group tendencies rather than racist belief. So racial discrimination, in cases like these, may simply be "rational discrimination."[16] And, for D'Souza, most cases of racial discrimination in contemporary United States are rational and, hence, do not harbor racist beliefs.

But there are, according to Sowell and others, two visible and eminently qualified acts of racial discrimination that sustain and promote racism or racial injustice. The first is governmental laws that discriminate against or oppress people on the grounds of race. The second is governmental intervention into the market economy that engenders racism and unjust double standards in the form of racial preference. Racism is brought to an end in the first with the removal of race-based legal barriers preventing a person to be recognized as free and equal under the law. Only recently has this removal taken place with the elimination of *de jure* racial segregation. Racism is brought to an end in the second with the removal from the market economy of all governmental regulation, especially policies establishing equal opportunity through preferential treatment policies for "socially protected" groups, inclusive of racial minorities. Currently this matter has reached some political success among supporters of the "end of racism" thesis. Nonetheless whereas the first item establishes formal equality under the law, the latter seeks to establish merit-based opportunity through a fully deregulated market economy, not equal opportunity through the race-based preferential treatment policies of the government. And, in this instance, as long as black people, so say supporters of the thesis, are self-reliant, help themselves, assume the orientation to succeed in the market economy, and work hard in it to obtain material success, opportunities for such success as well as psychological well-being will ensue. If they are not self-reliant, do not help themselves, and the orientation is not assumed, and the hard work is not done to obtain success, then black people, so say supporters of the thesis, only have themselves to blame not racism, for their relative "failure" in civil society in general and in the market economy in particular. Blacks would also have themselves to blame for their underrepresentation in many prominent arenas of social life and for the rational discrimination extended against them by others. In this context, racism would not be the rational discrimination extended toward racial or "racialized" groups based on their imprudent recalcitrance to the free market orientation. But it would be any governmental policy modifying such discriminations on the grounds of race and for the sake of benefiting (supposedly non-deserving) members of a racial group over members of other racial groups.

It is not our intention to discuss here the merits or demerits of the "end of racism" thesis, although our intellectual proclivities would be to argue against it. Be that as it may, our intention is to discuss the manner in which the thought of Douglass has been used to support the thesis. For example, D'Souza asserts that "Frederick Douglass, who better than anyone else understood the lasting harms inflicted by slavery, argued that it entitled blacks to nothing more than the freedom to help themselves."[17] He further states that "the most telling refutation of racism, as Frederick Douglass once said about slavery, 'is the presence of an industrious, enterprising, thrifty and intelligent free black population.'"[18]

Indeed Douglass makes his life a "striking example of the American ideal of pulling oneself up by his bootstraps."[19] In many places and throughout his career, Douglass exhorts African Americans to make freedom their own by initiating a constant pattern of achievement for themselves and their children with the commitment to hard work and to the appropriate measures of perseverance, frugality, and sobriety.[20] Yet, despite the strong similarity, Douglass's views concerning the need for blacks to be economically independent and industrious cannot be used legitimately to endorse the "end of racism" thesis for the following two reasons.

First, the "end of racism" thesis is part of a larger (neo-conservative) critique directed against the political authority of the welfare state. There is nothing in the arsenal of Douglass's thought that could allow anyone even to hint that he would be either critical or supportive of that kind of institutionalized political authority.[21] In the context of the larger critique, supporters of the thesis seek to replace the political authority characteristic of the welfare state with that characteristic of a traditional liberal state. In the latter, political authority is self-restricting and partial from which citizens and the space of civil society are exempted, thereby enabling social peace through a kind of "passive" citizenship, i.e., through the citizen's enjoyment in the free use of her property or fruits of labor without any interference from others, including the state itself. In a more modern form, it tends to extol civil privatism in order to insulate itself, if not militate, against any approval of "excess" demands of the population as democratically legitimate. And demands for the political and social support of racial equality would be regarded as "excessive."

This conception of political authority, however, is not Douglass's. In the light of American slavery, it ought not be surprising that he would be supportive of blacks to continue working hard and being industrious so to engage in the free use of their hard-earned property without private or state sanctioned "interference." But, for Douglass, that would never be at odds with a conception of political authority wherein the equality of rights, including the, right to participate, actively in the porocess by which that authority is established, is the norm. This bespeaks Douglass's endorsement of an "active" citizenship, i.e., citizens recognizing and pressing their democratic entitlement to political rights. The most famous quotation of Douglass makes this point quite clear:

> If there is no struggle there is no progress. Those who profess to favor freedom yet deprecate agitation, are men who want crops without plowing up the ground; they want rain without thunder and lightening. They want the ocean without the awful roar of its many waters . . . Power concedes nothing without demand. It never did and it never will. Find out just what any people will quietly submit to and you have found out the exact measure of injustice and wrong that will be imposed upon them and these will continue till they are resisted with either words or blow, or with both. The limits of tyrants are prescribed by the endurance of those whom they oppress.[22]

Second, since supporters of the "end of racism" thesis, like Douglass, claim to be advocates of racial assimilation, perhaps the views of Douglass on this point can legitimately serve as evidence that they are the precursor to similar ones articulated in the thesis. To address this point, let us separate hypothetically the "end of racism" thesis from the larger neo-conservative critique directed against the political authority of the welfare state and allow the thesis to stand on its own. Let us also separate hypothetically Douglass's advocacy for racial assimilation from his advocacy for provisional "institutions of complexion."

Supporters for the "end of racism" thesis champion a society in which "race ceases to matter."[23] They call for race-neutral (colorblind) laws and public policy to extend ubiquitously into all areas of social life. Laws and public policy are neither to benefit nor to harm, for example, black people on the grounds of race. They are, D'Souza contends, to be "strictly indifferent to race."[24]

But these points simply address bringing racism or the governmental use of race in law and public policy to an end. They neither promote nor prompt racial assimilation. Indeed even the government according to the thesis, is to be indifferent regarding that end. Racial assimilation occurs only on the condition that an economically floundering racial group absorbs the habits, lifestyle, and values conducive of and serviceable for success in the free market economic arrangement of modern civil society by emulating economically thriving racial groups. If that condition is not satisfied, not only will racial assimilation not occur but, as stated previously, racial discrimination, supposedly based on empirical generalizations of factual group tendencies, would be allowed to proliferate as rational. Since black people in the United States are not regarded generally as an economically advanced racial group, the onus for initiating and establishing racial assimilation, as D'Souza tells it, would fall squarely on the shoulders of African Americans alone.[25] Douglass never mounts his argument for racial assimilation in this manner. Racial assimilation is not posed as a desirable end, because it is in the economic self-interest of a racial group. Even if a racial group's economic self-interest were to be best satisfied in a racially assimilationist environment, it would never serve as the basis of Douglass's arguments for racial assimilation. As we know, Douglass is of the mind that racial assimilation is (1) a matter of morality, enabling us to understand persons, regardless of racial background, as fundamentally equal in the most important regards; (2) the responsibility of government to promote and to guarantee in the face of racist barriers (past and present; institutional and personal) its attainment; and (3) the responsibility of the citizenry to show its fellow citizens of different racial groups that a society is desired in which members of all racial groups contribute favorably to its life and are potentially social exemplars for all.

These three points show why Douglass's call for racial assimilation cannot be used legitimately to support the "end of racism" thesis. Regarding the first point, racial assimilation for Douglass does not mean a racial group's self-immersion into the habits, skills, and values of other racial groups thriving in a market economy. Rather it rests on the moral dedication of the goal of rendering racial distinctions in our social interactions morally dubious, save for those distinctions provisionally instrumental in establishing that goal. As Douglass states, "Never refuse to act with a white society or institution because it is white, or a black one, because it is black. But act with all men without distinction of color. By so acting, we shall find many opportunities for removing prejudices and establishing the rights of all men."[26] In Douglass's eyes, a racial group's dedication to and achievement of economic success would not be the predominant measure of that group's racial assimilation in a society, but they would be criterial for evaluating that group's conviction of what it takes to be successful and how prudent that group is in following that conviction. Furthermore, under the auspice of the "end of racism" thesis, racial discrimination would be a matter of prudence or rational; for Douglass, it would ultimately be morally impermissible.

Regarding the second point, Douglass does not believe, unlike supporters of the "end of racism" thesis, that the government is indifferent to the prospect of a racially assimilationist society. Douglass is of the mind "that the interests of all the people would be promoted by the full participation of colored men in the affairs of government ... The American government rests for support ... upon the loyalty and patriotism of all its people. The friendship and affection of her black sons and daughters, as they increase in virtue and knowledge, will be an element of strength to the Republic too obvious to be neglected and repelled."[27] Moreover, since Douglass believes the American government is to be held accountable for the legacy the injustice of enslavement and color prejudice have wrought, it appears that Douglass would have to hold onto a more elaborate conception of racial injustice and racism than the "end of racism" thesis would permit.

Regarding the final point, the onus for inaugurating and enacting racial assimilation, contrary to the supporters of the "end of racism" thesis, does not fall upon African Americans alone. The struggle for racial integration, Douglass maintains, is not the "Negro's problem," but the "nation's problem":

> It is not the, Negro, educated or illiterate, intelligent or ignorant, who is on trial or whose qualities are giving trouble to the nation. The real problem lies in the other direction. It is not so much what the Negro is, what he has been, or what he may be that constitutes the problem ... The Negro's significance is dwarfed by a factor vastly larger than himself. The real question, the all-commanding question, is whether American justice, American liberty, American civilization, American law, and American Christianity can be made to include and protect alike and forever all American citizens in the rights which, in a generous moment in the nation's life, have been guaranteed to them by the organic and fundamental law of the land. It is whether this great nation shall conquer its prejudices, rise to the dignity of its professions, and proceed in the sublime course of truth and liberty marked out for itself since the late war, or shall swing back to its ancient moorings of slavery and barbarism ... It is not what [the Negro] shall be or do, but what the nation shall be and do, which is to solve this great national problem.[28]

As can be seen, the struggle for racial integration in the United States, according to Douglass, includes the work of African-American citizens, but never at their expense and never apart from fellow-citizens. It is only in this vein that racial assimilation could ever be, in Douglass's mind, morally, socially, and politically satisfying. To solicit Douglass for the conception of racial assimilation endorsed by supporters of the "end of racism" thesis is to reveal ignorance of Douglass's thought, or to take advantage of Booker T. Washington's interpretation of Douglass,[29] or to be disingenuous in the employment of his thought.

In any case, Douglass's commitment to argument is the view that resonates in the essays written by the contributors to this anthology. The result, we hope, is a critical anthology of note, giving more than ample demonstration of the philosophical magnitude of Frederick Douglass's work.

Bill E. Lawson and Frank M. Kirkland

Notes

1 See Charles W. Mills, *The Racial Contract* (Ithaca: Cornell University Press, 1997).
2 See the literary theorist Henry L. Gates, Jr, *Figures in Black: Words, Signs, and the "Racial" Self* (New York: Oxford University Press, 1987), p. 108. Gates argues that "Douglass was Representative Man because he was Rhetorical Man, black master of the verbal arts." He further claims in the same context that "the act of writing for the slave constituted the act of creating a public, historical self, not only the self of the individual author but also the self, as it were, of the race." We find Gates's remarks compatible with our claim about the three aspects of Douglass being "representative" and about the convergence of Douglass-scholars on this point. See also the historian John Blassingame, ed, *The Frederick Douglass Papers*, vols I–IV (New Haven: Yale University Press, 1979–91), vol. I, p. xi. Blassingame states that "contemporary Americans and most historians generally recognize Frederick Douglass as the representative black man of the nineteenth century."
3 See David W. Blight, *Frederick Douglass' Civil War: Keeping Faith in Jubilee* (Baton Rouge: Louisiana State University Press, 1989), p. xii. Blight's work as well as the work of Waldo Martin also takes the path of looking at Douglass as a "thinker." See Waldo Martin, *The Mind of Frederick Douglass* (Chapel Hill: The University of North Carolina Press, 1984).
4 See Randall Kennedy, "My Race Problem – And Ours" in *The Atlantic Monthly*, vol. 279, no. 5, May 1997, pp. 55 and 66.
5 Ibid., pp. 56 and 66.
6 See Michael Sandel, *Liberalism and the Limits of Justice* (New York: Cambridge University Press, 1984). See also his "The Procedural Republic and the Unencumbered Self," in *Political Theory*, vol. 12, no. 1, (1984), pp. 81–96.
7 See Frederick Douglass, "An Address to the Colored People of the United States," September 1848, in Howard Brotz, ed, *African-American Social*

and Political Thought (New Brunswick: Transaction Publishers, 1992), p. 211.
8   See Frederick Douglass, "We Need a True, Strong, and Principled Party," March 1871, in John Blassingame and John R. McKivigan, eds, *The Frederick Douglass Papers*, vol. 4 (New Haven: Yale University Press, 1991), p. 284. Douglass states: "that while I am in favor of no distinctions on account of color, remembering the stripes, remembering the 250 years of bondage in this land, through which the colored man has been dragged, remembering that 250 years he has not had the right to *learn to read* the name of the God that made him, and that every man in the land has been at liberty to kick him, and to disregard his rights, he having no rights which a white man was bound to respect – I say, in view of that history, and the history of stripes, of tears, and of blood for the black man's track through this country for two hundred years . . . I say, whenever the black man and the white man, equally eligible, equally available, equally qualified for an office, present themselves for that office, the black man, at this juncture of our affairs, should be preferred. That is my conviction."
9   Brotz, ed, *African-American Social and Political Thought*, p. 211.
10 See Gates, *Figures in Black*, pp. 115 and 123 (our addition).
11 Ibid., p. 123.
12 The only place we have found Douglass articulate this self-conception is in a passage from his essay entitled "Prejudice against Color." "Just here is our sin: we have been a slave; we have passed through all the grades of servitude, and have, under God, secured our freedom; and if we have become the special object of attack, it is because we speak and act among our fellow-[persons] without the slightest regard to their or our own complexion; – and further, because we claim and exercise the right to associate with just such persons as are willing to associate with us, and who are agreeable to our tastes, and suited to our moral and intellectual tendencies, without reference to the color of our skin, and without the slightest trouble to inquire whether the world [is] pleased or displeased by our conduct." See Philip Foner, ed, *Life and Writings of Frederick Douglass*, vol. 2 (New York: International Publishers, 1950), pp. 129–30. Words in brackets are our emendations.
13 See Frederick Douglass, "The Nation's Problem," April 1889, in Brotz, ed, *African-American Social and Political Thought*, p. 320 (our additions).
14 See Frederick Douglass, "The Claims of the Negro Ethnologically Considered," July 1854, in John Blassingame, ed, *The Frederick Douglass Papers*, vol. 2 (New Haven: Yale University Press, 1982), pp. 497–525.
15 See Thomas Sowell, *Race and Culture: A World View* (New York: Basic Books, 1994), p. 154. Compare this minimalist definition of racism to the more elaborate ones of Derek Bell, David Theo Goldberg, Amy Gutmann, Charles W. Mills, and Toni Morrison. "Racism is an integral, permanent and indestructible component of this society. Americans achieve a measure of social stability through their unspoken pact to keep blacks at the

bottom." See Derek Bell, *Faces at the Bottom of the Well: The Permanence of Racism* (New York: Basic Books, 1992), p. 152. "[Racism] rests on an underlying picture of rationality that is equally blinding [as irrational prejudice.]" See David Theo Goldberg, *Racist Culture: Philosophy and the Politics of Meaning* (Oxford: Blackwell Publishers, 1993), p. 120, (our addition). "Racial injustice may be the most morally and intellectually vexing problem in the public life of this country . . . The issue of racial injustice toward black Americans is certainly among the most long-standing, systematic, and vexing examples of racial injustice in our society." See Amy Gutmann, "Responding to Racial Injustice" in Kwame Anthony Appiah and Amy Gutmann, *Color Conscious: The Political Morality of Race* (Princeton: Princeton University Press, 1996), p. 107. "The heart of white supremacy is the acceptance of and reluctance to give up differential racial privilege, manifested morally in a Herrenvolk ethics that changes form according to the evolution of the system, originally overtly racist, later not." See Charles W. Mills, *Blackness Visible: Essays on Philosophy and Race* (Ithaca: Cornell University Press, 1998), p. 146. "[Racism] has assumed a metaphorical life so completely embedded in daily discourse that it is perhaps more necessary and more on display than ever before." See Toni Morrison, *Playing in the Dark: Whiteness and the Literary Imagination* (Cambridge: Harvard University Press, 1992), p. 63.

16 See Dinesh D'Souza, *The End of Racism* (New York: Free Press, 1995), pp. 286–7.
17 Ibid., p. 113.
18 Ibid., p. 556.
19 See Benjamin Quarles, "Frederick Douglass, Bridge-Builder in Human Relations," in *Negro History Bulletin*, vol. 29, no. 5, February 1966, p. 100.
20 For a representative piece of Douglass's position on this point, see Frederick Douglass, "An Address to the Colored People of the United States, on September 1848", in Brotz, ed, *African-American Social and Political Thought*, pp. 211–13. "Understand this, that independence is an essential condition of respectability. To be dependent is to be degraded . . . Now it is impossible that we should ever be respected as a people, while we are so universally and completely dependent upon white men for the necessaries of life. We must make white persons as dependent upon us, as we are dependent upon them . . . We beg and intreat you, to save your money – live economically – dispense with finery, and the gaieties which have rendered us proverbial . . . save your money, that you may be able to educate your children, and render your share to the common stock of prosperity and happiness around you."
21 However, for a fascinating and brilliant discussion of the controversy over Civil War pensions, a controversy contributing to the embryonic stages of the American version of the welfare state during the later years of Douglass's life (1889 and onward), prior to the era of Roosevelt's "New Deal," see Theda Skocpol, *Protecting Soldiers and Mothers: The Political Origins of*

Social Policy in the United States (Cambridge: Harvard University Press, 1992).
22 See Frederick Douglass, "West India Emancipation," August 1857, in Foner, ed, *Life and Writings*, vol. 2, p. 437.
23 D'Souza, *The End of Racism*, p. 551.
24 Ibid., p. 551.
25 Ibid., p. 551.
26 See Frederick Douglass, "An Address to the Colored People of the United States," p. 211.
27 See Frederick Douglass, "The Present and Future of the Colored Race in America," June 1863, in Brotz, ed, *African-American Social and Political Thought*, p. 272. In the same essay, Douglass also states: "Can the white and colored people of this country be blended into a common nationality, and enjoy together, in the same country, under the same flag, the inestimable blessings of life, liberty, and the pursuit of happiness, as neighborly citizens of a common country? I answer most unhesitatingly, I believe they can." Ibid., p. 271.
28 See Frederick Douglass, "The Nation's Problem," April 1889, in ibid., p. 314.
29 See Booker T. Washington, *Frederick Douglass* (New York: New York University Press, 1968).

Part I

Radical Assimilation and Emigration

1
Douglass Against the Emigrationists

Bernard R. Boxill

Derrick Bell's allegory of the USA making a lucrative deal with "Space Traders" to carry off its black population recapitulates an old American fantasy of ridding the country of black people; proposals to send "Negroes back to Africa," had begun to surface as early as the beginning of the eighteenth century.[1] Thomas Jefferson was, however, the first important American statesman to urge the "colonization" of black Americans, though he was by no means the last; almost a century after Jefferson made his case Henry Clay and Abraham Lincoln were still scheming to get blacks out of the country.

White people were not the only ones to urge black emigration. Some blacks did too. Henry Highland Garnet, Alexander Crummell, J. M. Whitefield, James Holly, and above all, Martin Robson Delany, called on blacks to go to countries where they could enjoy the advantages of full and equal citizenship, insisting that they would never enjoy these advantages in the country of their birth. These black emigrationists were not popular leaders of the black population. Most free blacks rejected all schemes to "colonize" African Americans, whether these schemes originated from white statesmen like Clay and Lincoln, or from black people like themselves. Frederick Douglass was the most uncompromising. He dismissed Jefferson's arguments, denounced Clay's schemes, and relentlessly attacked the vision of the black emigrationists. Although he admitted that there could come a time when he would be driven to recommend that blacks emigrate, and was himself once on the point of traveling to Haiti to explore its possibilities as a refuge, he never conceded that the time had come to give up on America.[2] It may seem that his optimism was only a heroic determination to make the best of a bad situation, and that he opposed black emigrationism because he thought that its propaganda exacerbated the black American's sense of alienation and "homelessness" in his own homeland, while its utopian and grandiose schemes gave him false hopes that were bound to be dashed. In fact Douglass's opposition to black emigrationism went deeper. Although he agreed with its view that citizenship was vitally important in the modern world, he believed that its pessimism about the prospects for black citizenship in the US stemmed from a misunderstanding of the nature of national feeling. His own experience convinced him blacks could acquire the moral power to compel whites to accept them as full and equal members of the nation. The heart of my argument is in section III. But we must begin with the case his opponents made for emigration.

I

Jefferson wanted to "colonize" blacks because while he admitted that slavery was a great evil, and ought to be abolished, he also argued that there were decisive reasons why black and white people should not live as free people in the same society.[3] Lincoln's schemes were based on very similar considerations, though he was more sensitive to the rights of black people than Jefferson, for while Jefferson wanted to deport blacks whether they liked it or not, Lincoln always thought that he had to persuade them to leave.[4] Lincoln claimed in his eulogy on Henry Clay that Clay "ever was, on principle and in feeling opposed to slavery," and that he had helped create the American Colonization Society in 1816 in order to eradicate slavery.[5] The free black population disagreed, arguing that Clay helped created the Society to protect and perpetuate slavery because he realized that it was endangered by the presence of free blacks in the US.[6] They were probably closer to the truth than Lincoln since the Society's main activity seemed to be trying to get free blacks out of the US to Liberia, and to raise funds to transport them there.[7]

As one might expect, most black emigrationists tried to have as little to do as possible with the American Colonization Society. Their proposals also differed from those of Jefferson and Lincoln. Jefferson and Lincoln wanted to get blacks out of the country because they thought this would be good for whites, and they gave little thought to how blacks would fare once they were somewhere else. The black emigrationists on the other hand wanted to get blacks out of the country because they thought this would be good for blacks, and they spent a lot of time thinking about what blacks should do when after they had emigrated. To understand the deep humanity of their schemes we must understand how they conceived of the problems that blacks faced in mid-nineteenth-century America. I focus here on the views of Martin Delany because they are representative, and because he wrote with the greatest clarity and sophistication.

Delany noticed that human beings were normally motivated mainly by ambition and self-interest. But he also noticed that they usually pursued their ambitions and interests with unrestrained rapaciousness only when this was at the expense of those they considered to be foreign, alien, and dissimilar to themselves; here the case that most impressed Delany was the fact that the European invaders of North America enslaved Indians and blacks rather than each other.[8] He therefore inferred that human beings possessed a disposition to identify with, and to feel compassion or pity for those they felt to importantly similar to themselves, and that this disposition, which he called sympathy, explained the difference between the way people treated those they identified with and those they felt to be foreign. Thus on Delany's account, Europeans enslaved Indians and blacks rather than each other because, having determined that a "subservient class" was in their interests, they naturally chose to enslave those most "foreign to their sympathies."[9] Generalizing from these observations Delany argued that national similarities were particularly potent in moving people to identify and sympathize with each other, while national dissimilarities were particularly potent in moving people to consider each other foreign and consequently to fail to feel sympathy for each other. It followed, on this account, that the people of the stronger nations would tend to take advantage of people of weaker nations. Particularly vulnerable were the people of nations that failed to be independent and self-governing. These were the national minorities found in most nations, or in Delany's preferred expression, the "nations within nations."[10] And he thought that their history amply illustrated his theory. Both in ancient and in modern times, Delany claimed, all such "nations within nations," the "Israelites in Egypt," the "Gipsics in Italy and Greece," the "Cossacs in Russia and Turkey," the "Sclaves and Croats in the Germanic States," the "Hungarians in Austria," the "Scotch, Irish, and Welsh in the United Kingdom," and the "Jews, scattered throughout not only the length and breadth of Europe, but almost the inhabitable globe," have been deprived of the "political, religious, and social" privileges the majority enjoyed.[11] Moreover, given that nations within nations were invariably subjected to such "cruel and unjust" treatment, "especially in the nations laying the greatest claim to civilization and enlightenment," Delany drew the further conclusion that "civilization and enlightenment," did not make human beings more likely to restrain their rapaciousness because of strictly moral considerations.[12] However civilized and enlightened people became they continued to be motivated mainly by ambition, self-interest, and sympathy, and strong nations would continue to take advantage of weak nations. The only recourse left to weak nations was therefore to become strong, and the first step to securing this end was to become self-governing and independent. And all nations recognized this basic fact. As Delany observed, all the nations within nations that he listed looked forward with "high hopes," to securing positions of "self-government and independence."[13]

Delany's diagnosis of the cause of black problems follows from these general views if we put them together with his view that blacks in America were "a nation within a nation."[14] The US violated blacks' natural rights to freedom and property because it was in its interest to do so, because it was more powerful than the black nation within it, and because its members were not restrained in their dealings with blacks by that sympathy they felt for each other.[15] Further, in order to continue to violate blacks' natural rights with impunity, the US also violated their political rights to vote, and to participate in the affairs of the country, and prevented them from acting on their desire to become independent and self-governing.

These violations of rights are the first tier of problems Delany thought that blacks faced in the US. A second tier of problems followed. Like all nations that oppressed the nations within them, the US added insult to injury, and "actually asserted blacks' inferiority by nature," and their "incapacity for self-government."[16] The object of this assertion was to defuse the complaint that the US violated blacks' rights to participate in the affairs of the state, and to govern themselves, and consequently to eliminate any sympathy their neighbors might be disposed to feel for them; if blacks were incapable of self-government they would have rights neither to govern themselves as an independent and self-governing nation, nor to participate in the political affairs of the US.[17]

Delany's arguments presuppose the distinction between a state and nation.[18] Delany does not make the distinction explicitly himself, following the usual practice of using "nation" to refer to both a nation and a state, but the distinction is implicit in his discussion. Our previous analysis suggests that Delany thought that a number of people constituted a nation if they satisfied two conditions: (1) they were moved by certain similarities, called national similarities, to identify with and sympathize with each other, and (2) they aspired to be self-governing and independent. His claim that all nations within nations "looked forward" to the day when they could be self-governing and independent clearly implies that he thought that not all nations were self-governing and independent. However, he also clearly implied that some nations, specifically nations like ancient Egypt, Turkey, Greece, and the United Kingdom were independent and self-governing. When a nation realizes its hope to be self-governing and independent it is what we would call today a state, and since a body of people cannot be self-governing and independent unless it controls a territory, a state has been famously defined as a body of people that successfully claims a monopoly of legitimate force in a given territory.[19] Delany was, of course, fully aware that a nation had to control a territory in order to be self-governing and independent, noting that the various "nations within nations," wanted to be independent and self-governing in "whatever part of the habitable globe it may be."[20] Finally, the existence of nations like the United Kingdom that had nations within them implies that nations that were states could contain several nations. Indeed, Delany seemed to think that such "multinational" states were the usual and perhaps inevitable case, though his view that nations within nations were likely to be exploited suggests that he thought that the best arrangement would be for every state to contain only one nation, and to be what is nowadays called a "nation-state."

On Delany's account, black people in America were members of the black nation within the US, and also morally and legally citizens of the American state, having as he put it, "a birthright citizenship," although the US violated their citizenship rights to vote, to participate in its political affairs, and to share in ruling the country.[21] But although Delany thought that blacks in America were citizens of the American state, he did not believe that they were members of the American nation. This does not follow from his claim that blacks in America were a "nation within a nation"; as some have pointed out dual nationality is possible.[22] But it follows from his claim that despite having "merged in the habits and customs" of their "oppressors," black people in America, being "distinguished by complexion," are "still singled out . . . as a distinct nation of people."[23] On Delany's account, being thus singled out as alien and foreign put blacks in a very vulnerable position in America, for it meant that their white neighbors did not feel the sympathy for them that they felt for each other, and consequently that they were particularly liable to take advantage of blacks when this seemed to serve their interests. Nor would it help much if blacks' rights as citizens were legally recognized. Delany believed that the main bulwarks against injustice were power and the sympathy of one's neighbors, and since the mere legal status of citizenship would give blacks neither of these advantages, they would continue to be repulsed and exploited whatever their legal status.[24] It was imperative therefore that blacks emigrate to some country where they could become members of the nation that comprised the state, or to "some part of the habitable globe" where they could set themselves up as a self-governing and independent nation-state.

In the body of his book on black emigration Delany endorses the first alternative urging black Americans to emigrate either to Canada or to various countries in Central and South America and the West Indies.[25] He was particularly enthusiastic about Central and South America and the West Indies. Brazil, he claimed, was "the only nation that can be termed white, and the only one that is a real slave holding nation in South America."[26] And more expansively he declared that the people of Central and South America and the West Indies "are precisely the same people as ourselves and share the same fate with us, as the case of numbers of them have proven, who have been adventitiously thrown among us – stand ready and willing to take us by the hand – nay, are anxiously waiting, and earnestly importuning us to come, that they may make common cause with us, and we all share in the same fate. There is nothing under heaven in our way – the people stand with open arms ready to receive us."[27] And it is clear that he expected that blacks would become full-fledged citizens of these countries. As he put it with respect to emigration to Central and South America, "In going, let us have but one object – to become elevated men and women, worthy of freedom – the worthy citizens of an adopted country. What to us will be adopted – to our children will be legitimate."[28]

But despite his brave words Delany was in two minds about black emigration to these places. In the Appendix to his book, the proposed destination for African-American emigrants is not Canada, and Central and South America, but Eastern Africa.[29] And there were other differences. In the body of the book, one gains the impression that Delany was envisaging a general exodus of the black population of the US. In the Appendix, however, Delany seemed to be envisaging only "enlightened freemen," and "colored and adventurers from the United States," going to Eastern Africa.[30] Finally, whereas in the body of the book Delany's aim is for blacks to become immigrants to, and eventually citizens of already existing countries in Latin America, his aim in the Appendix is for his "colored adventurers" and "enlightened freemen" to create a "powerful nation" in East Africa.[31] These changes mark an important development in Delany's thought, and it is important to explain them.[32]

Delany's reasons for doubting that Canada was a suitable destination for black emigrants from the US are pretty clear. He had always had reservations about that country as a refuge for blacks because he feared it would be annexed by the US, and that American policies of black slavery and racial subordination would be extended into it.³³ And apparently he believed that Canada was in some ways already worse than the US. As he noted in his novel *Blake*, blacks were denied privileges in Canada that were "common to the slave in every Southern State."³⁴ The reasons for his uncertainties about Central and South America as destinations for black emigration are less obvious, and he never states what they were. But I hazard the guess that he must have begun to get an inkling of some facts about South and Central America that were later to frustrate Lincoln's colonization schemes. These schemes called for sending American blacks to various "Spanish-American" republics in Central America, but as Lincoln admitted in a message to Congress, these republics "protested against the sending of [black] colonies to their respective territories."³⁵ What their reasons were is not clear, but since they too had enslaved blacks, it would not be surprising if they shared Lincoln's doubts about the advisability of mixed race societies. If Delany became aware of their attitudes about black colonies from the US he would have, I assume, rethought his plans for a black exodus to Latin America.

These considerations explain why Delany would have wanted to substitute Africa for Canada and Central and South America as the appropriate destination for black emigration from the US; and presumably he picked Eastern Africa instead of West Africa to make sure that everyone would be clear that he had nothing to do with the American Colonization Society, which, of course, had established its colony, Liberia, in West Africa. To explain the other two changes in his ideas about black emigration that we noted earlier – that only a few "colored adventurers" and "enlightened freemen" were expected to emigrate, and that their task was to create a powerful black nation-state in Africa – takes us to a deeper and theoretically more interesting assumption in his thought.

Delany often deplored the fact that black Americans for the most part showed little interest in going to Central and South America or anywhere else white Americans were not taking them.³⁶ Delany put this down to African Americans' "deep degradation" and "servility" which he thought was the result of slavery and subordination. "A continuance in any position," he wrote, "becomes what is termed 'Second Nature;' it begets *an adaptation and reconciliation of mind* to such conditions." As a result, because black people have been so long in positions of oppression, "we have learned to love them."³⁷ But if black people could not be persuaded to emigrate, Delany's plan for a black exodus out of the country – whatever the destination – was doomed. At best he could expect positive results only from those few black people, who out of luck or extraordinary strength of character, had managed to escape the effects of the degrading environment of the US. This explains why in the Appendix to the book, the plea for a general black exodus is muted, and the appeal is only for "enlightened freemen" and "colored adventurers" to go to East Africa.[38]

But if only "enlightened freemen," and "colored adventurers" departed for Africa, what was to be the fate of those too degraded or timid to follow? And what of the slaves who might have had a mind to follow, but whose masters would presumably not permit them to do so? Had Delany abandoned them? And if he had not abandoned them how would his plan help them?

The answers to these questions lay in Delany's assumption that the powerful black independent and self-governing black nation-state in Africa would represent the claims of all members of the black nation wherever they happened to be, including the black minority left behind in the US. That minority was therefore not abandoned. As Delany had promised in *Blake*, to effectively free the slaves, he had to take them, "not as we wish them to be, but as we really find them to be."[39] And he was taking the bulk of the black inhabitants of America as he found them to be – benighted and degraded enough to be afraid to strike out for themselves. Nevertheless they would be freed and their claims protected by the nation-state the "enlightened freemen," and "colored adventurers," had set up in Africa.[40]

Delany was not merely appealing to the fact that a beleaguered minority within a state could sometimes hope for help from the international community. That fact was well understood in his day. Many abolitionists, including Douglass, had traveled to England to urge it to put moral and economic pressure on the US to abolish slavery. And I think that Delany was not only expecting that a black nation-state would take a greater interest in the well being of blacks in the US than the white nations of Europe, and consequently would be more inclined to intercede on their behalf; his view that this nation-state would "present" the claims of blacks in the US in a "national capacity" suggests that he expected that it would be the legal and formal representative to the US of the black nation within its borders. Delany's plan would thus radically alter the traditional view that it is illegal for one state to intervene in the domestic affairs of another state, even to assist a persecuted minority. Whether such a system could work is not now the issue. But Delany and the emigrationists who agreed with him seemed to believe that if it could be implemented then despite the misgivings of Jefferson and

Lincoln, black and white people could live as free and equal members of the same society.

II

Douglass always emphasized that he did not object to individual blacks exercising their rights to emigrate. He also made it clear that he had no objection to black missionary work in Africa. His objections, he insisted, were to a general policy of black emigration or colonization as the only satisfactory means to the elevation of the black population in the US. Some of these objections can be set aside quickly. For example, perhaps for rhetorical purposes, Douglass liked to point out that schemes to take eight million black people out of America were hopelessly impracticable, sometimes adding that the country would not consent to the loss of so large a part of its labor force. This objection was decisive against schemes like Jefferson's that were based on the assumption that black and white people could not live as free and equal citizens of the same country, and that consequently all blacks had to leave.[41] But most black emigrationists rejected that assumption, and designed their emigrationist schemes on considerations like those in the Appendix to Delany's book. As J. M. Whitefield put it, black emigrationists considered the total emigration of the black population to be "absolutely impossible" and the whole issue "a tissue of nonsense."[42] And Jefferson had anticipated the alleged worry the nation would have over the loss of so large a part of its labor force, arguing that white immigration could be encouraged to replace the loss of the deported blacks.[43] I also set aside Douglass's criticism of the emigrationists' argument that cotton cultivation in Africa would undercut and destroy the slave economy in the American South. Douglass argued that slaveholders would put the slaves to do other profitable work even if American cotton was undersold, but his own escape from slavery should have suggested to him that there were limits to the kind of profitable work that the slaveholders could put the slaves to do.[44]

Douglass's complaint that emigrationism encouraged the majority to "hope that by persecution or by persuasion the Negro can finally be dislodged and driven from his natural home,"[45] takes us closer to his real differences from the emigrationists. Douglass believed that emigrationism had that effect because it encouraged the false belief that black and white people could not live peacefully together in the same society. Again, this complaint may seem to be fairly directed only at emigrationist schemes like Jefferson's that assumed that blacks and whites could not live peacefully together in the same society, but to be irrelevant to the schemes of the black emigrationists, who were clear that this assumption was false. But Douglass was making two serious objections against the black emigrationists. The first was that since most colonization schemes were based on the assumption in question, all policies urging black emigration would likely encourage people to believe it. The second objection went deeper. In a way the emigrationists' plan did assume that blacks and whites could not live in peace in the same society. Although that plan allowed that many blacks would remain in America, it also claimed that their white neighbors would never accept them as fellow nationals, and that their rights would only be protected from white persecution by the intercession of an alien power. Douglass's worry was that even if this arrangement established a kind of peace between blacks and whites in America, it would be the tense and precarious peace secured by a balance of power, and that the emigrationist position made it difficult for blacks to ever enjoy the better and more stable peace based on sharing a common nationality with their neighbors.

This leads to a further point, which is I think, the crux of Douglass's case against emigrationism. The emigrationist position, Douglass complained, forced on the Negro "the idea that he is forever doomed to be a stranger and a sojourner in the land of his birth."[46] This complaint goes beyond the objection that the emigrationists' plans gave blacks hope only for the precarious peace secured by a balance of power. It calls attention to the fact that these plans do nothing to overcome, and indeed are likely to exacerbate, the black American's feeling that he is a stranger in a place that he should not be a stranger – the land of his birth. Blacks born in America, Douglass was saying, were not foreign nationals who happened to be living in America, and who were seeking citizenship rights, though they had some other place they could call home; blacks born in America were thoroughly American, and had and knew no other home but America. They had "copied" the majority's "manners and customs"; preferred "American institutions as against those of any other country"; wished to remain in the country; desired her "safety and welfare"; and in general were American in "sentiment, in ideas, in hopes, in aspirations, and in responsibilities."[47] Douglass's complaint was therefore that insofar as the emigrationists' plan accepted the majority's claim that blacks were strangers in the land they identified with and called home, it would perpetuate the sense of alienation and homelessness that he thought already devastated the black population, even if a balance of power secured by a black nation-state in Africa gave them some protection from their white neighbors. And Douglass thought that the sense of having a home and a country was essential to morality and progress. He wrote, "home is the fountain head, the foundation, and main support, not only of all social virtue, but of all motives to human progress . . . To have a home the Negro must have a country, and he is an enemy to the moral progress of the Negro . . . who calls on him to break up his home in this country, for an uncertain home in Africa."[48]

The force of Douglass's point is all the greater because Delany conceded it. Notice that although Delany insisted that blacks were denied an American nationality, he also insisted that they satisfied most of the conditions for having it. Certainly he wanted to distinguish their status from the status of naturalized citizens – people who had legal rights of citizenship – but who might not have the kind of emotional ties to the country that come from being born and raised in it, and from knowing that one's ancestors were buried in it. As Delany observed of blacks in America, "Here we were born, here raised and educated; here are the scenes of childhood; the pleasant associations of our school going days; the loved enjoyments of our domestic and fireside relations, and the sacred graves of our fathers and mothers."[49] It may be objected that although the feelings of being attached to a certain territory that Delany alludes to are often part of a national feeling, it does not follow that Delany cited them to show that blacks felt themselves to be American. Many different nations can occupy the same territory and be emotionally attached to it; indeed a nation can be attached to a territory even if it does not occupy that territory, and has not occupied it for centuries, and even if some other nation now occupies it. Consequently we cannot conclude that all people who are strongly attached to a given territory also feel that they share a common nationality. They may be members of two or several nations, and feel themselves to be bitter national enemies. In particular, since Delany thought that the black nation within the US occupied the same territory as the US, we cannot conclude that he thought that blacks felt themselves to be part of the American nation just because they were emotionally attached to the territory the American nation occupied. But Delany did not only say that black Americans were attached to the territory that the US occupied. He also emphasized their similarity to other Americans. Almost echoing Douglass, Delany wrote that black Americans' "feelings, tastes, predilections, wants, demands and sympathies, are identical, and homogenous with those of all other Americans."[50]

Again, although this claim indicates that blacks satisfied many of the conditions for being American, it does not prove that they were American, or even that they felt themselves to be American. Nations occupying the same territory may to a considerable degree adopt each others' habits, customs, and ways of thinking and feeling and yet remain distinct nations if their members do not feel that peculiar sympathy for each other that is an essential part of a national feeling. But Delany believed that blacks felt themselves to be American. His claim that, "Our common country is the United States," and "We are Americans, having a birthright citizenship"[51] was not meant to simply make the legal point that black Americans had citizenship rights. Consider too the dedication of his book. Delany dedicated his book to "the American people, North and South," describing himself as "their most devout and patriotic fellow-citizen." It should be noted that he did not describe himself simply as a citizen – this might have suggested only his legal relationship to the state; he described himself as a "fellow-citizen" of the "American people," suggesting thereby that he felt that there were bonds of national fellowship between himself and other members of the nation-state of America. And he emphasized his identity as an American by calling himself a "patriotic" fellow-citizen of the American people. This went far beyond noting that others could identify him as an American because they could notice that he possessed traits characteristic of most Americans. Since a patriot is one who feels that he is a part of his country it indicates that he identified himself as so much American as to be part of America.

One may be tempted, at this point, to conclude that Delany believed that blacks were part of the American nation. (As well, of course, as being members of the black nation within America.) But this would undercut his assumption that the peculiar cause of black's problems in the US was that they were not part of the American nation. And indeed there was a crucial condition for being a part of the American nation – as distinct from feeling one to be a part of that nation – that black Americans did not satisfy. For a person to be a part of a nation the other members of the nation must recognize him to be a member of the nation. If they do not, they will not feel that peculiar sympathy for him that is a part of national feeling – though he may feel that sympathy for them – and he and they will not be mutually bound by the feeling that make people into a nation. Indeed, if, as E. Renan put it in the most famous essay on nationality ever written, a nation is "a daily plebiscite" in which people commit themselves to continue their lives together, then the conditions usually cited as constitutive of nationality – that people share a common language, culture, customs, memories, sentiments, birthplace, blood, race, and ancestry – are not sufficient or even necessary conditions of a common nationality, but only supportive.[52] That is, they may only serve to support peoples' commitment to continue their lives together, making it reasonable, understandable, and likely that they will recognize each other as fellow nationals and will continue to do so despite the difficulties that are certain to arise. If so, mutual recognition of a common nationality is a sufficient – and necessary – condition for a common nationality, and all the familiar facts that support blacks' American nationality, that they were born and raised in the country, that their ancestors made contributions to it and were buried in its territory, that they felt a bond between themselves and the other Americans, even that they identified themselves as American, and were prepared to die for America, do not prove that they are Americans, given that Americans did not recognize them to be Americans. Delany saw this with unblinking clarity. Although having "merged in the habits and customs," of the majority, he noted, blacks "being distinguished by their complexion" are still "singled out as a distinct nation."[53] And he acknowledged the pain of this alienation. "We love our country, dearly love her," he wrote, " but she don't love us – she despises us, and bids us begone, driving us from her embraces"; and it is clear, of course, that the country he is here claiming that he loves is not the black nation within the US but the US itself.[54]

We should pause to notice the radical nature of the alienation that Douglass and Delany agreed was the fate of blacks in America. This alienation went beyond the alienation that W. E. B. DuBois believed moved every thoughtful black American to ask himself, "Am I an American or am I a Negro? Can I be both?"[55] DuBois would have admitted that the black person's uncertainty about her identity was prompted by white America's insistent claim that she was not an American. But he assumed that one of its necessary conditions was the fact that she possessed both American and Negro national traits – American national traits because she lived in the great national community of America, and Negro traits because she also lived in the black community in America.[56] If I am right about Douglass and Delany, however, they believed that the black American suffered from a more radical uncertainty about her identity; on their account the black American possessed no Negro national traits that could make it possible for her to wonder whether she was Negro. For her, the question was not "Am I an American or am I a Negro?" but, "If I am not an American, what am I, because I know nothing else that I can be?"

Delany, for example, is clear that the black population in the US had been stripped of its positive national characteristics and consequently was anomalous among other "nations among nations."[57] Other "nations among nations," Delany writes, people like the "Poles, Hungarians, Irish, and others . . . still retain their native peculiarities, of language, habits, and various other traits."[58] But, "We," meaning black people in America, "have been, by our oppressors, despoiled of our purity, and corrupted in our native characteristics, so that we have inherited their vices, and but few of their virtues, leaving us in character, really a broken people."[59] On Delany's account, black people in America had "merged in the habits and customs," of their oppressors, and were "singled out" as a "distinct nation of people" solely because they were "distinguished by complexion."[60] Consequently they were a nation only in the minimal sense that their common complexion and suffering gave them the basis for a special sympathy for each other; they were not a nation in the fuller sense that they wanted to be governed together. Although their reluctance to answer his call to accompany him to Africa forced Delany to accept this implication, as we have seen he believed that their claims would be represented and protected by the powerful black nation in Africa. But even if this scheme was successful, and the black nation compelled the US to respect the rights of its black residents, it would not follow that they would enjoy the blessings of citizenship because it would not follow that their neighbors would accept them as full and equal fellow citizens. This was Douglass's decisive objection against the emigrationists. Their schemes included no provision for overcoming the homelessness and alienation that troubled black Americans.

Everything Delany said and did indicates that he would have agreed that the ideal solution would be for the white majority to accept blacks as fellow citizens and nationals.[61] The problem, on his account, was that this did not seem likely to happen. This may suggest that Douglass and Delany simply disagreed about the likelihood of whites accepting blacks as fellow citizens and nationals. In fact their disagreement went deeper. They disagreed about the likelihood of whites accepting blacks as equal fellow citizens and nationals because they disagreed about what this would involve, that is, they disagreed about the nature of national feeling.

III

As we have seen, Delany identified national feeling as sympathy for others based on shared national characteristics combined with a desire to be governed with them. Delany felt that such sympathy was an important part of national feeling because it restrained fellow nationals from harming each other. Specifically it led fellow nationals to feel pity for each others' misfortunes, and consequently to be moved to assist each other, or at least to restrain their pursuit of their self-interest when doing so would harm fellow nationals. I argue that Douglass was dubious of supposing sympathy to be such an important part of national feeling. My argument is based on his view that pity for others tended to change into an inability to honor them. "A man without force," Douglass wrote, "is without the essential dignity of humanity. Human nature is so constituted that it cannot honor a helpless man, although it can pity him; and even that it cannot do long, if signs of power do not arise."[62] Douglass's insight here was that although pity makes us sorrow for and reach out to the helpless, it also inclines us to feel superior to them, if only for our good fortune at having escaped their predicament. But feeling superior to the helpless makes our pity for them short lived, because it tends to make us feel that we cannot be in their predicament, while to pity them we must feel that we can be in their predicament. Further, feeling superior to them we begin to think of them as inferior, and feeling that we cannot be in their predicament we begin to lose the ability to identify with them, and these evolutions of our initial pity for them saps our ability to honor them. And indeed when Delany calls his less fortunate fellow nationals "degraded," and "servile," and compares them to fawning "spaniels," one cannot help feeling that this process was well at work in him.[63] But if sympathy is an important part of national feeling, and sympathy for others leads to pity for them if they are helpless, and such pity changes quickly to dishonor, national feeling may lead the powerful classes of a nation to dishonor their less powerful fellow nationals. The incongruity of supposing that national feeling can instigate dishonor among fellow nationals suggests that even if it includes sympathy, it must also include something else to counteract the tendency of sympathy to instigate dishonor. If Douglass was right about the consequences of force or power that other ingredient could very well be force or power. If force or power gives one the essential dignity of humanity, then if fellow nationals all have force or power, they would have the "essential dignity of humanity," and presumably this would make it difficult, if not impossible, for them to dishonor one another.

It may be objected that Delany would have agreed with Douglass that national feeling must help motivate fellow nationals to honor or respect each other, and that such honor or respect is based on their having force or power. In defence of this objection it may be argued that he called for the creation of a powerful black nation precisely because he understood that black honor and respect depended on black power. But this argument faces two difficulties: first, even if a powerful black nation-state would win the respect of whites, its members might not honor and respect blacks in America; second, the respect that Delany thought that the powerful black nation was likely to win for blacks was not the honor that Douglass implied that fellow nationals should have for each other.

The first difficulty follows from the fact that Delany's argument supposes that blacks in America will need the protection of the black nation, and consequently will be a permanently helpless class, and from the argument presented above that the strong tend to dishonor the permanently helpless that sympathy binds them to. The second difficulty depends on a more extended argument. Let us begin with Delany's apparent belief that only a powerful black nation could guarantee that the US would not violate the valid claims of their black residents. The emphasis Delany places on the economic and presumably military capacity of such a state suggests that he assumed that states reason almost wholly prudentially. A black nation without considerable economic and military capability could not guarantee the protection of black claims in the US because even if sympathy moved it to intervene to protect such claims, it would probably refrain, being wisely unwilling to risk the considerable losses it knows it would suffer if it did. However, a black nation with considerable economic and military capability would be more likely to guarantee the protection of black claims in the US because it would be more likely to intervene to protect such claims, confident that it would risk little if it did. Or if it did risk much, its opponent would too, which would motivate its opponent to prudently avoid provoking it to intervene.

This reliance on the prudential reasoning of states in their relations with one another suggests that the respect Delany expected the black state to gain internationally as a result of its power is the respect accorded to anything that can cause trouble. This is an acceptable use of the word "respect" especially in international affairs. Realists speak of the respect that power can bring, and there is no doubt that such respect, based on a "balance of power" can also secure peace. More generally we also speak of respecting the power of a boxer's punch, because he can knock you out with it, and even of respecting a hurricane's power because it can do so much damage. But this is not the sense in which Douglass felt that fellow citizens and nationals should respect each other. He said or implied that power was a condition of "honor" or "dignity" and this suggests that fellow nationals should respect each other in the sense that they respect each others' equal moral standing.

This claim may seem implausible since Douglass and Delany both based honor and respect on power. Does it not follow that they meant the same thing by honor and respect? I argue that it does not. Notice first that Delany's view that a powerful black nation is a state with considerable economic and presumably military capability relies on the false assumption that power depends almost wholly on the ability to cause trouble. Power depends on other things besides an ability to cause trouble. To see this suppose that the black nation lacked considerable economic and military capabilities, and would lose in a conflict with a rival state that violated black claims, although it would still be able to inflict enough damage on the rival state to make it regret that it provoked the conflict. Clearly the black nation would have the power to defend black claims against its rival, if it was willing to use its ability to cause trouble to defend such claims, and if its rival reasoned prudentially. It may be objected that this attitude would hardly be reasonable given the risks the black state would have to be prepared to take; the rival state may be reckless and proud, and even if it reasons prudentially it may miscalculate. But this objection depends on the assumption that the black state values avoiding the risks in question more than fighting for and possibly succeeding in defending black claims. If the black state took a different view of what was valuable, specifically if it supposed that fighting for and possibly succeeding in defending black claims was more valuable than avoiding the risks of the losses in question, it could conclude that its attitude was the only one it could reasonably take.

This argument does not depend on any ambiguity in the word "power." To have the power to do something a person must be able to do it, if he chooses to; he must be undeterred from doing it; and doing it must secure what he takes to valuable, or at least must not detract from it.[64] The first of these factors, what we may term ability, is uncontroversial. But perhaps the second and third need comment. Even if a person is able to do something, and doing it secures what he takes to be valuable, he lacks the power to do it if he is deterred from doing it; nerve or daring is therefore an essential part of power. But what about the third condition? It may seem that if a person is able to do something, and is undeterred from doing it in the sense that he has the nerve or daring to do it, then he necessarily has the power to do it. But this is a mistake. Suppose that someone rashly violates the law and is now languishing in jail and bitterly regretting his action. It seems false to say that he had the power to do what he did; truer to say that he might have falsely believed that he had the power to do it. If I am right about this a person's power is a function not only of his ability and daring or nerve, but also of his values; two persons or nations can have different and unequal abilities to cause trouble and yet have the same power, if they differ in daring or in what they value. In particular, the power to defend one's rights does not depend only on one's ability to cause trouble and one's daring or nerve, it also depends on what one values. If one values fighting for one's rights even if one is not certain to win, and can suffer considerable losses if one loses, then as long as one is able to inflict some losses on the potential violator one may have the power to defend one's rights; indeed one may have more power in this respect than others who have greater ability to cause trouble, but who suppose that fighting for their rights is worth the trouble only if the gains are certain to outweigh the costs.

I suggest that when Douglass claimed that a man without power was without "the essential dignity of humanity" he was relying on the fact that a person's power does not only depend on her ability to cause trouble, but also, and perhaps and more crucially, on her firm conviction that there is value in risking her life in fighting for her rights. Since Douglass states that a person without force is without the essential dignity of humanity, this suggestion implies that practically everyone, even the physically weak, can have power and the essential dignity of humanity, as long as he values his rights enough to be willing to risk his life to defend them, and as long as he has some capacity to cause potential violators trouble. Two examples from Douglass support the suggestion, his account of his fight with Covey, and his account of the fight of the slave woman Nellie Harris against the proud and cruel overseer Sevier.[65]

The main points about Douglass's fight with Covey are as follows: the slavebreaker Edward Covey had broken Douglass with constant whippings, and was trying to whip again, presumably to put the finishing touches on his work; on this occasion, however, Douglass fought back and successfully resisted Covey; surprisingly Covey did not have Douglass punished or hanged as the law provided; further, apparently as a result of the fight, Covey never tried to whip Douglass again.[66] In his autobiographies Douglass speculated that Covey did not have him hanged or punished because he would then have to admit that a boy of seventeen had successfully resisted him, and this would ruin his reputation as a slavebreaker, and destroy his livelihood. This may suggest that Douglass fought Covey calculating carefully and prudently that things would work out as they did. It may also suggest, assuming that Covey never tried to whip Douglass again because Douglass had successfully resisted him, that the fight was an exercise of Douglass's power, and that this power lay in his being strong enough to fend off Covey. But this interpretation of the sources of Douglass's power and motivation faces an insuperable difficulty: Douglass hazarded the explanation mentioned above why Covey did not have him hanged or punished only *after he fought Covey*; before he fought Covey he did not know that he was strong enough to fend him off, and he had proof, in the cold-blooded shooting of Denby, a rebellious slave, that slavemasters were quite prepared to kill slaves who resisted.[67] This suggests a different explanation of why Douglass fought Covey, and a different account of his power: perhaps Douglass fought Covey because of a conviction that it was worthwhile to risk his life in defense of his rights, even if he lost the fight and was killed; and perhaps his power lay more in that conviction and less in his physical ability and daring.

The same emphasis on the possibly moral sources of power and dignity emerges more clearly in the example of Harris's fight with Sevier.[68] As in the case of Covey and Douglass, Sevier tried to whip Harris, and Harris resisted. Unlike Douglass, Harris was not strong enough to fend off her tormentor and was whipped cruelly after she was overpowered. However, just as Covey never tried to whip Douglass after their fight, Sevier never again tried to whip Harris after their fight. Now it is implausible to suppose that Harris fought Sevier from a prudential calculation of the costs and benefits of doing so. It is far more plausible to suppose that she fought Sevier from the conviction that it was morally contemptible to allow him to whip her without resisting. If this is correct, her fighting Sevier was an exercise of power, at least if it was the reason why he never tried to whip her again. Further since, unlike Douglass, she lost her fight, her case illustrates more clearly how lack of physical ability may not prevent a person from having power and dignity.

It may be objected that Douglass's moral convictions had nothing to do with his fighting Covey, and that he fought Covey simply because he was desperate and daring. And it may similarly be objected that Harris fought Sevier simply out of anger and desperation, like an animal that fights its tormentor. It is impossible to absolutely rebut this objection, since it is impossible to be absolutely sure what peoples' motivations are. But the objection is irrelevant. Douglass's point, I take it, is not to maintain absolutely that he and Harris defended themselves out of moral conviction, but that moral conviction can motivate even the physically weak to defend themselves and consequently to have dignity.

But even if I am granted that moral conviction, and in particular, a willingness to risk and suffer losses in defense of one's rights can give even a physically weak person the essential dignity of humanity and the power to defend his rights, my argument still falls far short of what I have to show. I have to show why Douglass was optimistic that white Americans would honor black Americans as equal and full-fledged fellow citizens. My argument so far has shown at best that moral conviction may give black Americas the power to compel white Americans to respect their rights. Even if we acknowledge the important moral source of that power and call it dignity, the respect it may get from others may be no more than the circumspection accorded to anyone who is able and willing to cause more damage or inconvenience to the potential violator than the violator is willing to accept. But this respect seems to be no different from the respect the emigrationists settled for, and the power that compels it may, despite its moral sources, secure only the precarious peace of a balance of ability and willingness to cause trouble. Perhaps Douglass's moral convictions gave him power, and perhaps this power gave him dignity. But it is still possible that Covey refrained from trying to whip him simply because he calculated that it was not worth the trouble; it may not have been because he came to honor Douglass or respect his dignity. Similarly, although Sevier never tried to whip Harris after the fight, it need not have been because he came to honor her; it might have been because he calculated that whipping her was too much trouble, much as he might have calculated that whipping a mettlesome horse was too much trouble.

What then is Douglass's argument that moral power can not only give a person dignity, but that it can also move others to honor him and respect his dignity? Let us be clear first that his considered view was not that moral conviction and a willingness to risk one's life in defense of one's rights were enough to win the honor of others. At one time he might have taken that view; it is possibly suggested in his important essay, "Is it Right and Wise to Kill a Kidnapper?"[69] In that essay Douglass maintained that slave resistance was wise because it would rebut the public's argument that enslaving blacks was acceptable because they failed to peril their lives for their freedom, thus showing that they did not love freedom, and consequently had no right to it. It is probably not a sound argument that people who are unwilling to peril their lives for their freedom do not love freedom and have no right to it. But even if that argument were sound it would not follow that slave resistance would move the public to honor the slaves and demand their release. This is because even if the slaves' resistance gave indisputable evidence of their love of liberty, and of their right to liberty, the public might choose to ignore or misinterpret that evidence. Douglass seemed to have become more clearly aware of the possibility, and indeed the likelihood that the public might react to slave resistance in this fashion, and in a later essay on John Brown he suggested that slave resistance that made the slaveholders fear for their lives would have a better chance of reaching their consciences.

I emphasize the advance this argument makes on the argument in the "Is it Right and Wise to Kill a Kidnapper?," essay. That essay said nothing about arousing the slaveholders' fear; it urged resistance but only to give the public evidence of the slaves' love of freedom. By contrast the argument in the essay on John Brown implies that it is not enough for the slaves to give evidence of their love of freedom; to reach the consciences of their tormentors, to make these tormentors pay attention to the evidence of their dignity that they give by risking their lives for their freedom, they must also arouse their tormentors' fear. This development reflects Douglass's considered view that while moral conviction and a willingness to risk one's life for one's rights may give one dignity, it is generally not enough to move others to acknowledge that dignity; to move others more reliably to acknowledge one's dignity one must have power, and this means one must have the ability and nerve to cause trouble. As my account of power indicated power necessarily includes an ability to cause potential violators trouble and the nerve or daring to use it. I have been careful to emphasize this point in my analyses of Douglass's fight with Covey, and of Harris's fight with Sevier. The characteristic of Douglass and Harris that set them apart from most other slaves was their willingness to risk their lives in defense of their rights. But it was not enough to give them power. To have power they also had to have the ability to give their potential violators trouble, and the nerve to use it. If Douglass had not been physically strong enough to successfully resist Covey's attempt to whip him, his attempt at resistance might have been heroic, but it might not have been an exercise of power because it might not have induced Covey to never try to whip him again. Similarly, if Harris's heroic resistance gave Sevier no trouble at all, she would have had little power, and he would have whipped her again and again.

Elsewhere I have tried to defend Douglass's view that arousing the slaveholders might be a way to reach their consciences by forcing them to pay attention to the slaves' dignity that they might otherwise have ignored.[70] But it need not be necessary in all cases to arouse the fear of potential violators. Sometimes it may be sufficient to give them enough trouble to induce them to pause and reflect on their behavior. If they have a sense of justice this may be enough to lead them to acknowledge the moral standing of those whose rights they would violate. It is possible to interpret Sevier's reluctance to whip Harris, and Covey's reluctance to whip Douglass or have him hanged in this way. For example, Sevier's pride would move him to whip Harris while his desire to avoid trouble would move him not to, and the reflection these contrary desires could lead him to could move him to an awareness of her equal moral standing. This process assumes that Sevier has a sense of justice, but this is an advantage since it is more plausible to suppose that functioning members of a society have a sense of justice, though they may not consult it often and appropriately, than to suppose that they have no sense of justice at all.[71]

These considerations explain Douglass's response to the emigrationists' contempt for moral suasion. Douglass agreed with them that subtle arguments and elaborate presentations of the evidence of black humanity were silly and demeaning. This was not because he depreciated the role of reason in morality and human affairs generally, or because he denied that people sometimes make moral mistakes because they commit subtle errors of logic or are ignorant of the relevant facts. It was because he believed that the basic moral mistakes whites made with respect to blacks did not stem from committing subtle logical errors or from ignorance of the relevant facts, but from failing to pay attention to the transparently bad reasons they had for the way they treated blacks. The emigrationists understood this as well as Douglass and they inferred that moral suasion was therefore useless. But they were mistaken because they misunderstood the nature of moral suasion. Sometimes, often with our connivance, our feelings enable us to ignore that we are acting for transparently bad reasons.[72] Moral suasion involves techniques for manipulating these feelings and consequently for redirecting our attention to the obvious errors that we contrive not to see. Such techniques include eloquence, sarcasm, wit, mockery, and mimicry, and in the pacific part of his career as orator and abolitionist Douglass used them all to try to embarrass and shame his audiences and to manipulate their feelings to make them see the plain moral truths that their pride and greed and vanity had enabled them to ignore. Later on, after he abandoned pacifism, he saw that resistance could arouse certain feelings – fear especially – that could clear the moral vision, and consequently that resistance, properly executed, could be a part of moral suasion; and, as his account of Harris's fight with Sevier suggests, he also seems to have concluded that resistance could sometimes have this useful effect even when it did not arouse fear. Some years later Douglass made this point when he defended the exodus of blacks from the South to the North after the Civil War. According to Douglass, "the exodus had done valuable service," as an "assertion of power by a people hitherto held in bitter contempt," an "emphatic and stinging protest against highhanded, shameless and greedy injustice to the weak and defenseless," and a "means of opening the blind eyes of the oppressors to their folly and peril."[73]

The mutual respect for dignity that the exercise of moral power can win is not the whole of national feeling. That respect should hold between all human beings; national feeling creates a special bond between citizens of the same country. Even if people are inclined to respect each other's rights and humanity, their political views may be so different that they cannot easily be governed together. If national feeling involves a reasonable desire to be governed together, the fact that people are culturally similar, and share political views would also be essential. National feeling would then be the respect fellow nationals had for each other's humanity, together with a sympathy based on a common language, traditions, culture, and political views, in short, the things I referred to earlier as the supporting conditions for nationality. Douglass believed that the emigrationists were pessimistic about the prospects of black citizenship in the US because they mistakenly supposed that the characteristics that created bonds of sympathy between people are fixed by instinct or nature rather than being picked out and made salient by reason. This led them to falsely conclude that since sympathy is part of national feeling, instinct or nature limits national feeling to those of the same skin color, when in fact it is reason, looking for a way to serve pride and greed that fastens on skin color and makes it the basis of an exclusive sympathy and national feeling. Here too then, Douglass could hope that blacks could use their moral power to manipulate the feelings of the white majority to enable it to see the obvious fact that their black neighbors shared all the supporting conditions for a common nationality with other Americans, and thus to create a more inclusive sympathy and national feeling.

Douglass's view of the kind of power that supports respect supports his general egalitarian and populist position, and his frequent complaint that the emigrationists' plan to save blacks in America by establishing a black nation-state in Africa relied too much on "indirect" methods, and that a forthright "direct" opposition to slavery and racial oppression was far preferable. He meant that clearcut, unequivocal denunciation of and opposition to injustice ought to accompany efforts to undo it, and that any pretence to go along with, or to acquiesce or even tolerate injustice, even if the object of that pretense is to eventually undo the injustice, is always a second-best solution.[74] There are solid arguments that "direct" ways of dealing with injustice are likely to be more effective than "indirect" ways, especially in the long run, but the decisive consideration from Douglass's point of view was that to exercise the power and sustain the mutual respect that was a part of national feeling, the people had to participate in projects for their own elevation. Direct methods, like the forms of moral suasion he urged against slavery and racial subordination, activate and train the sense of justice, develop the virtues of courage and patience, and in general encourage an active citizenry. However, the indirect method preferred by the black emigrationists dulls the sense of justice, is content with leaving citizens ignorant, passive, and dependent on the elite for their salvation, and may encourage both hypocrisy and servility.

IV

Today, more than a hundred years after Delany and Douglass debated where black people stood and were likely to stand in the US, the issue is still with us. Delany's prescriptions have not come to pass. Although Derrick Bell once claimed that the US Supreme Court ordered schools desegregated in 1954 in order to win the US respect in several states in Africa that had recently become independent, no great black African state has arisen to present and protect black claims in America. However, Delany's diagnosis of the structure of American society has been adopted and radicalized. Although Delany thought that the US contained a variety of nations, he seemed clear that it was itself also a nation. But many of today's multiculturists and multinationalists maintain that while the US is composed of a variety of nations, it is not and never was itself a nation, and that it is held together simply by its citizens' commitment to the political ideas of the Constitution and Bill of Rights. These views are descriptively false and prescriptively suspect. More importantly from our perspective is they do not suggest how blacks are to avoid being shoved aside by the racism of the other nations or cultural groups that occupy the state. There are suggestions of a kind of balance of power among these nations. This may be deemed a version of Delany's prescription, though without the weight of a powerful black nation-state it still leaves the status of black Americans unclear, given their continuing minority status.

If Delany's prescriptions have not come to pass neither have Douglass's. Perhaps his call for the kind of power and political participation required a greater degree of the civic virtues than it is reasonable to expect in the average person, although Martin Luther King's theory of civil disobedience bears some resemblance to it. In any case, blacks are still not accepted as full-fledged fellow nationals by the rest of the citizens. The distinguished historian Ronald Takaki recounts how a taxicab driver in Virginia did not recognize him as an American, when in fact Takaki was born in the US, his grandfather having migrated here from Japan in the 1880s. Takaki's chagrin is understandable, but the case of the black American is more poignant. The taxicab driver at least thought Takaki was from abroad. But no American would ever mistake a black American as coming from any other country but America. The black American is the most recognizably American of all Americans. But he remains an outsider in the country whose national character he epitomizes. So what is to be done? Is the solution to be found in some entirely new ideas, or in the ideas of Delany or Douglass in some of their contemporary reincarnations? Or must the black American always ask, in W. E. B. DuBois's words, "Why did God make me an outcast and a stranger in mine own house?"[75]

Notes

1 John Hope Franklin, *From Slavery to Freedom* (New York: Alfred A. Knopf, 1974), p. 184. Bell's allegory appears in his essay, "The Space Traders," in his book, *Faces at the Bottom of the Well* (New York: Basic Books, 1992), pp. 158–94. I thank Bill Lawson for drawing my attention to this troubling essay.
2 See, for example, Philip S. Foner, ed, *Life and Writings of Frederick Douglass* (New York: International Publishers, 1950), vol. 2, pp. 252, 253. For his proposed trip to Haiti, see *Life and Writings of Frederick Douglass*, vol. 3, pp. 85–8.
3 Thomas Jefferson, *Notes on the State of Virginia*, edited by William Peden (Chapel Hill: University of North Carolina Press, 1982), pp. 137–43.
4 For discussion of Lincoln's views of black "colonization" see Benjamin Quarles, *Lincoln and the Negro* (New York: Da Capo Press, 1990). And David Herbert Donald, *Lincoln* (New York: Simon and Schuster, 1995).
5 David Herbert Donald, *Lincoln*, p. 165.
6 The point was made most strongly by Delany. In his words, the object of the society was "the removal of the free colored people from the land of their birth, for the security of the slaves, as property to the slave propagandists." See Martin Robson Delany, *The Condition, Elevation, Emigration, and Destiny of the Colored People of the United States* (Salem: Ayer Company, 1988), p. 30. Henceforth referred to as *The Condition*. See also, Philip S. Foner's introduction to his edition of *Life and Writings of Frederick Douglass* (New York: International Publishers, 1950), vol. I, p. 31. For Frederick Douglass's interpretation of Clay's schemes and motives, see *Life and Writings*, vol. I, pp. 387–90. The suspicions of the free black population about the Society's motives are supported by William Lloyd Garrison. In his book denouncing the society Garrison admitted that he had "formerly supposed" that it was "a praiseworthy association." See William Lloyd Garrison, *Thoughts on African Colonization* (New York: Arno Press, 1968). On the other hand it is fair to say that the black Episcopalian priest, Alexander Crummell, whose probity and intelligence cannot be doubted, started as a firm opponent of the Society, but eventually became one of the spokesmen and supporters, and spend twenty years in Liberia. See Wilson

Jeremiah Moses, *Alexander Crummell* (New York: Oxford University Press, 1989), p. 135.
7   See *From Slavery to Freedom*, p. 184.
8   *The Condition*, pp. 21, 22.
9   Ibid., pp. 21, 22.
10 Ibid., pp. 11, 12.
11 Ibid., pp. 11, 12.
12 Ibid., pp. 11, 12.
13 Ibid., pp. 11, 12
14 Ibid., p. 210, 212.
15 Ibid., pp. 14, 19–21.
16 Ibid., p. 13.
17 Ibid., p. 13. This assumes that people of different nations are capable of feeling some sympathy for each other. Delany does not deny this. His point is that sympathy is more easily aroused, and more keenly felt, for people of the same nation than for people of other nations.
18 See, for example, David Miller, *On Nationality* (Oxford: Oxford University Press, 1995), pp. 18, 19.
19 M. Weber, "Politics as a Vocation," in H. H. Gerth and C. W. Mills, eds, *From Max Weber* (London: Routledge and Kegan Paul, 1970), p. 78.
20 *The Condition*, p. 12.
21 Ibid., p. 48, 49.
22 On the possibility of dual nationality, see, Miller, *On Nationality*, pp. 45, 46.
23 *The Condition*, p. 209.
24 Delany thought that the Fugitive Slave Law amply proved his point. See, *The Condition*, pp. 147–58.
25 See *The Condition*, chapters XX and XXI.
26 Ibid, pp. 179, 180.
27 Ibid., pp. 189, 181.
28 Ibid., p. 187.
29 Ibid., pp. 209, 211.
30 Ibid., pp. 211, 213.
31 Ibid., pp. 209–15.
32 I discuss these changes with a somewhat different emphasis in "Two Traditions in African American Political Thought," *Philosophical Forum*, Fall-Spring 1992-3, vol. XXIV, pp. 119–35.
33 *The Condition*, p. 174.
34 Martin Delany, *Blake*, ed. Floyd J. Miller (Boston: Beacon Press 1970), p. 153.
35 *Lincoln and the Negro*, p. 113. Some countries in Latin America were interested in black immigration from the US. Significantly these are the countries we would recognize as unambiguously black. For example, Haiti welcomed black immigrants and Jamaica and British Guinea were interested. See, *Lincoln and the Negro*, pp. 108–23.

36 *The Condition*, pp. 184–6.
37 Ibid., pp. 206, 207.
38 One problem with this interpretation is that in the book's Preface Delany claims that he wrote the Appendix before the book when he was 24, and that its plan had "been abandoned for a far more glorious one," p. 10.
39 *Blake*, p. 126.
40 Evidently Delany was anticipating actual developments. Thus Kymlicka notes that in Europe early in the twentieth century states made bilateral treatises with other states to assure the fair treatment of fellow nationals in those states. See *Multinational Citizenship: A Liberal Theory of Minority Rights* (New York: Oxford University Press, 1995), p. 2.
41 Of course, another solution would be for all whites to leave, but this was assumed to be out of the question because whites were "more powerful." Douglass commented that this was "a little grating." *Life and Writings*, vol. 3, p. 285.
42 J. M. Whitefield, letter to Frederick Douglass, in *Life and Writings*, vol. 5, p. 294.
43 *Notes on the State of Virginia*, p. 138.
44 For the concession see *Life and Writings*, vol. 3, p. 288. The objection is vulnerable because it overlooks the possibility that some kinds of work may be such that it is very difficult or impossible to have people do that kind of work while holding them as slaves. Douglass should have been aware of this point since his own escape from slavery was facilitated by the fact that he was a slave doing skilled work in an urban environment. See, Frederick Douglass, ed. William L. Andrews, *My Bondage and My Freedom* (Urbana: University of Illinois Press, 1987), chapter XXI.
45 Frederick Douglass, "The Folly of Colonization," in Howard Brotz, ed, *African American Social and Political Thought: 1850–1920* (New Brunswick: Transaction Publishers, 1992), p. 330.
46 Ibid., p. 330.
47 *Life and Writings*, vol. 3, pp. 213, 286.
48 "The Folly of Colonization," p. 330. It is worth noting that Douglass did not always admit to feeling attached to America. In a letter written to Garrison in 1846 Douglass wrote that although he could concede that patriotism was "perfectly natural," and that he could give it "intellectual recognition" as a "philosophical fact," he himself felt no patriotism. "If ever I had any patriotism, or any capacity for the feeling," Douglass wrote, "it was whipped out of me long since by the lash of the American soul drivers," *Life and Times of Frederick Douglass* (New York: Collier Books, 1962), p. 242. See also his famous, "What to the slave is the Fourth of July?," in William L. Andrews, ed, *Frederick Douglass Reader* (New York: Oxford University Press, 1996), pp. 109–30. Even in passages where he tries to emphasize his differences with America, however, one can detect the ambivalence in his feeling. In the letter to Garrison, for example, he wrote, "America will not allow her children to love her. She seems bent on

48 compelling those who would be her warmest friends to be her worst enemies. May God give her repentance before it is too late, is the ardent prayer of my heart." I would also argue that Douglass's opposition to Southern secession, which abolitionists like Garrison welcomed, was driven, at least in part by his attachment to the Union. And that he eventually decided that the Constitution was opposed to slavery in order to vindicate his attachment to America.
49 *The Condition*, pp. 209, 49.
50 Ibid., pp. 8.
51 Ibid., p. 48.
52 Ernest Renan, "What is a Nation?," in Omar Dahbour and Micheline R. Ishay, eds, *The Nationalism Reader* (New Jersey: Humanities Press, 1995), p. 154.
53 *The Condition*, p. 209.
54 Ibid., p. 203.
55 W. E. B. DuBois, "The Conservation of Races," in Eric J. Sundquist ed, *W. E. B. DuBois Reader* (New York: Oxford University Press, 1996), p. 43.
56 The DuBois of the "Conservation of Races," at any rate. By the time he wrote the *Souls of Black Folk* (New York: Library of America, 1990) DuBois had come to a more complex view of the uncertainty of black identity that he described as "double consciousness." I have explored this latter view in "DuBois on Double Consciousness," unpublished manuscript.
57 In an essay published after *The Condition*, however, Delany took a position somewhat similar to the position DuBois would later take, suggesting that blacks in America had retained some distinctive cultural traits. All nations, he declared in that essay, had "native or inherent peculiarities," and since blacks were a nation, they too had "inherent traits" and "native characteristics." Further anticipating DuBois he wrote that if blacks were able to "cultivate and develop" these traits and characteristics they would "instruct the world" in the "true principles of morals, correctness of thought, religion and law or civil government." See, Martin Delany, "The Political Destiny of the Colored Race," in *The Ideological Origins of Black Nationalism* (Boston: Beacon Press, 1971), p. 203.
58 *The Condition*, p. 210.
59 Ibid., p. 209.
60 Ibid., p. 209.
61 During and after the Civil War Delany jumped at the chance to be accepted as a fellow national by other Americans. See a discussion of his life in Victor Ullman, *Martin R. Delany*, (Boston: Beacon Books, 1971).
62 *My Bondage and My Freedom*, p. 151.
63 Delany's elitism has often been noticed. See especially Nell Painter account in "Martin R. Delany: Elitism and Black Nationalism," in Leon Litwack and August Meier, eds, *Black Leaders of the Nineteenth Century* (Urbana: University of Illinois Press, 1988). As Painter notes, on p. 156, "intelligent"

was "the most common adjective in Delany's vocabulary. Crummell's contempt for those of his own race that he considered benighted was more extreme." See, for example, his "Our National Mistakes and the Remedy for Them," in *Destiny and Race*, pp. 175–93.

64 I have explored these questions more fully in "Frederick Douglass's Two Transformations." Unpublished manuscript.

65 *My Bondage and My Freedom*, pp. 144–53.

66 I have considered Douglass's fight with Covey at greater length in "The Fight with Covey," in Lewis R. Gordon, ed, *Existence in Black* (New York: Routledge, 1997).

67 Ibid., p. 79.

68 Ibid., pp. 62, 63.

69 Frederick Douglass, "Is it Right and Wise to Kill a Kidnapper?," in *Life and Times of Frederick Douglass*, vol. 2, pp. 284–9.

70 I have developed this argument in "Fear and Shame as Forms of Moral Suasion in the Thought of Frederick Douglass," in *Transactions of the Charles S. Peirce Society*, XXXI (4) 1993, pp. 713–44.

71 I have developed this argument in "Washington, DuBois and Plessy v. Ferguson," *Law and Philosophy*, vol. 16 (3), 1997.

72 I defend these claims at some length in "Fear and Shame as Forms of Moral Suasion in the Thought of Frederick Douglass."

73 Frederick Douglass, *Life and Times of Frederick Douglass*, p. 438. It should be noted that Douglass opposed a "wholesale exodus of colored people from the South to the northern state." On his account the exodus that did occur should have been enough to give the white planters a sense of the blacks' power. As Douglass acknowledged, in opposing black emigration from the South to the North, he never found himself "more widely and painfully at variance with leading colored men of the country," p. 428.

74 Douglass held this position quite generally. See, for example, his comment that, when he was a slave, he was "not only ashamed to be contented in slavery, but ashamed to seem to be contented." *My Bondage and My Freedom*, p. 167.

75 W. E. B. DuBois, "Of Our Spiritual Strivings," in W. E. B. DuBois, *The Souls of Black Folk*, p. 8.

2
Douglass on Racial Assimilation and Racial Institutions

Howard McGary

Frederick Douglass is famous for his eloquent defense of the dignity of human beings, but he did not believe that all humans act in dignified ways. His point was that every human being is deserving of rights and respect irrespective of characteristics like race, religion, and gender.[1] Furthermore, Douglass firmly believed that political and social policies must have a moral foundation. For Douglass, morality sets the bounds of political and social action, and thus it should govern the means and strategies adopted by political and social activists.[2]

It should be noted, however, that Douglass recognized that justice is an important part of what we mean by morality, but it does not exhaust the concept. So even though a political leader may not be required by the constraints of justice to show compassion and generosity, more general moral requirements may obligate him to do so. But Douglass's position raises an interesting question. If justice does not exhaust the demands of morality, can a person distribute social benefits and burdens by using race as a criterion of distribution?

Douglass does not give a blanket condemnation of racial classifications. He writes: "we shall undoubtedly for many years be compelled to have institutions of a complexional character, in order to obtain this very idea of human brotherhood."[3] As a racial assimilationist, Douglass condemns distinctions on the basis of race, but he reluctantly accepted voluntary self-segregation of the races in certain institutions as a possible step to a racially assimilated society.[4] By a racially assimilated society, he meant a society where a person's race is legally, morally, politically, and socially irrelevant. According to Douglass, the ideal of the morally good society is racial assimilation.[5]

In this essay, I begin with a statement of Douglass's views on racial assimilation and the value of racial institutions. Then I examine whether Douglass's commitment to African-American institutions violates an important moral requirement: the "universality constraint." Finally, I consider whether Douglass's provisional commitment to racially defined institutions is consistent with his racial assimilationist position.

I

Douglass was extremely cautious about making racial distinctions, because race had been used to cause so much pain and suffering to innocent human beings. He rejected racial divisions in society, but he stopped short of claiming that race is never a relevant characteristic of persons. While Douglass clearly believed that people made too much of race, he refused to completely reject the significance of race.

There is clearly some ambivalence about the significance of race in Douglass's thought. As I quoted earlier, Douglass saw a need for black institutions as a means for navigating between a racist society and the racially assimilated society. Even though it is clear that he believed this, he still spoke in a mocking manner of people who took pride in their race. According to Douglass, it is a mistake to take pride in one's race, because to do so is to take pride in something over which one has no control.[6]

Douglass's argument against racial pride is controversial. If I understand his position, African Americans for a time will need institutions organized on the basis of race, but they should not be proud of the need to organize and support these institutions. Their attitude should be one of a person who takes an awful-tasting medicine, because it is the most effective means of curing some ailment. It is not done out of a sense of pride or delight, but necessity.

Clearly in practice this is not an easy posture for any group of people to take, especially a group that has been despised and oppressed over a long period of time. The task of organizing and supporting black institutions is very different from taking distasteful medicine. In order for institutions to be effective, the people who populate them (as a matter of motivation) often feel that there is something of value in the institutions themselves. Frequently they reject the view that the value of these institutions strictly lies in the ends to be achieved.

As an intellectual exercise, Douglass's view does make sense. People can in thought see black institutions as a necessary evil. However, in practice, it is hard to build and support institutions that you think only have instrumental value. I don't think that there is any conceptual confusion in Douglass's position nor am I sure that his view is psychologically impossible to achieve. However, I don't think that most people will be able, in a racist society, to do what is required to build and support such institutions, if they cannot claim that such institutions have some intrinsic value that can serve as a source of pride for the parties involved.

More generally, Douglass's argument against racial pride is very controversial. Bernard Boxill has given us fairly compelling reasons for thinking that it is unsound.[7] My purpose, however, is not to challenge the soundness of Douglass's argument against racial pride, but merely to explore some of the consequences of Douglass's reluctance to rule out the significance of racial identity in decision making. Douglass's views about the relevance of race in decision making came under attack from a variety of sources. Antiassimilationists[8] argued that he failed to appreciate the importance of race, and some racial assimilationists flatly denied that race should have any significance.[9] Who is right?

Douglass's position was clearly influenced by his own slavery experience. Slavery in the United States presented a stark example of how race could be misused. American slavery was clearly an institution that denied certain human beings their rights because of their race. But we should be careful here. The basic wrong of slavery is not that it makes some people slaves and others not. The moral wrongness of slavery is that it makes any human being a slave. Even if slaves were not singled out for slavery because of their racial identity, slavery would still be a profound wrong. The case of American slavery does not show that distributing benefits on the basis of race is, in itself, wrong. Or, put in another way, the case of slavery does not show that race is never morally relevant in making moral and political judgments. But one thing is clear: Douglass was extremely reluctant to accept race as a morally relevant characteristic.

Douglass's reluctance to see race as morally relevant seems to be based upon something like the following principle – likes should be treated alike unless there is some morally relevant reason(s) for treating them differently. Of course, Douglass would add that race is rarely, if ever, a morally relevant difference between persons. Since Douglass did not take a categorical stance against the relevance of race, how does he justify the use of race in our moral decision-making? Douglass tells us that for a period of time we must make decisions on the basis of race in order to reach a time where such decisions are unnecessary. But what is the structure of his argument?

It might appear that Douglass is giving a utilitarian argument in support of his position. According to such an argument, we use race as a means for creating a future good or to avoid some future harm for the society as a whole. On this view, it is not the individual good but the aggregate good that matters. The rights of individuals matter only to the extent that respect for these rights promote greater good for society as whole than any of the other available alternatives. However, there is strong reason for thinking that this was not the structure of Douglass's argument. Over and over again, Douglass tells us that slavery and racial discrimination are wrong because they violate the natural rights of human beings, not because these practices fail to promote the greatest good for society as a whole.

Douglass uses a natural rights argument to defend the position that we can use race as a means to secure the racially assimilated society.[10] In other words, acknowledging race as relevant in decision making is necessary to secure equal human rights for all. So, for Douglass, ex-slaves could self-segregate or build African-American institutions as a kind of self-defense against the denial of their humanity. As is normally the case with self-defense, the potential victim is justified in causing harm to another person if there is no other recourse open to him. This is most apparent when the victimization is due to wrongdoing.

However some theorists believe that we have a right to defend ourselves against innocent threats.[11] If they are correct, Douglass may be on firm footing if he maintains that ex-slaves and their descendants have a moral right to make racial characteristics relevant provided that doing so is the only way to defend their natural rights as equal human beings against innocent and non-innocent threats.

But does this self-defensive account of the moral relevance of racial classifications violate any important moral constraints? Is it moral to include or exclude people for certain benefits and burdens, because they have been designated as members of certain groups that have a particular political and social history? If we say that race is sometimes morally relevant, can we give a consistent account of this relevancy? If we answer no to the first question and yes to the other two questions, then we must explain why our answers are consistent with widely acknowledged moral constraints. One such constraint on moral judgments that is often seen as a barrier to considering race as a relevant characteristic in making moral judgments is the "universality constraint."[12]

II

Immanuel Kant's categorical imperative represents what many philosophers believe to be an important condition for turning judgments into moral judgments. According to Kant, a moral judgment or rule prescribes what we ought to do without appeal to any purpose or end. This type of judgment is categorical and is in contrast to a hypothetical imperative, which tells us what we ought to do given that we have particular ends.

But how do we apply Kant's categorical imperative as a test of moral judgments? Kant provides his readers with three formulations of his categorical imperative, which are intended to shed light on how we apply the test. The first formulation mandates that a moral rule or judgment must consistently be prescribed as a guide to everyone's conduct. The second formulation claims that a moral judgment or rule must be such that if all persons followed it, they would treat each other as ends in themselves and never as mere means. The third and final formulation says that, for a judgment or rule to be moral, a person who imposes upon herself an obligation to follow it must be willing to impose the same obligation on all others. The import of these formulations is that no person is exempt from the requirements of morality, and no person should have a moral obligation that is not the result of the free exercise of his will. In addition, no person or group should have special privileges unless these things are granted to all. If universality is indeed a constraint on moral judgments, then Douglass's account of the relevance of race should be consistent with it. In what follows, I will explain why using race in certain circumstances does not violate this alleged constraint on moral judgments.

Universalizability is a feature of moral judgments that is endorsed by many moral philosophers in the Western tradition. However, there is disagreement about what this endorsement entails. On the one hand, some believe that universalizability is purely a logical feature of moral judgments.[13] Or, put in another way, a judgment must have the feature of universalizability, if it is to count as a moral judgment. While, on the other hand, others deny that universalizability is a part of what it means to be a moral judgment. For these theorists, to say that a moral judgment is universalizable is to say more than something about the judgment's logical structure. The claim that moral judgments are universal is not analytic, but a substantive claim that requires a commitment to specific moral principles. According to this view, universalizability reveals something about our moral preferences, not just something about the logical structure of moral judgments.[14]

It is important at this juncture to note that both sides of the debate over the universalizability requirement believe that universality is not identical to generality. Generality is seen as the opposite of specificity. But the universal is compatible with the general as well as the specific. As R. M. Hare[15] tells us, principles like "one ought not to kill" is general and universal. While a principle like: "one ought never to kill someone who is young and defenseless" is specific, it is still universal. The second principle, although specific, is still universal because it applies to all cases that fall under the description provided by the principle. Put another way, the predicates contained in the judgment are all universal and the subject-terms are all universally quantified variables. These subject-terms are never individual constants. For example, the principle: "for all (X) and (Y) if (X) is stronger than (Y) then (X) ought not to take advantage of (Y)" is a universal principle, while David ought not to take advantage of Howard is a specific non-universal principle.

Let us suppose for the purposes of this essay that moral judgments are universal. What does this assumption tell us about using race as a subject-term in our moral judgments? Does using race as a subject-term violate the universalizability constraint on what can count as a moral judgment? In other words, expressions like "blacks ought not kill other blacks" or "whites are obligated to help other whites" are specific judgments that fail to satisfy the universality constraint on moral judgments. The universalizability constraint is seen as an adequacy test for moral principles or judgments.

The idea here is that people cannot be said to have made a moral judgment if they intend their judgments to apply only to members of their family, religious sect, or race. On this view, there is no moral basis for the claim that it is wrong to harm members of one's own race, but not wrong to harm members of other races in the same circumstance.[16] According to this account, such judgments might be religious, political, and prudential, but not moral. Let us be clear about what is being said here. When Johnny's mother says: "Johnny you should not hit your sister." Is she uttering a moral judgment? According to the view above, she is not if she is not willing to endorse the view that for all brothers and all sisters, brothers should not hit sisters. But if we say that moral judgments should be universalizable, why should we limit the domain to brothers and sisters? Why wouldn't the appropriate domain be all persons rather than brothers and sisters?

In response to this question the supporters of the universalizability constraint maintain that we don't always have to appeal to the most general subject-terms possible in our moral judgments in order for them to qualify as moral judgments. They believe that husbands can have moral duties to wives, and parents can have moral duties to their children, provided that we are willing to say that any parent and child or husband and wife who were similarly situated would have the same duties.

But if we admit that wives can have moral duties to husbands and parents to their children, then why can't members of one race have universal specific moral duties to members of their race? The typical answer that is given by universalists who oppose the use of race as a subject-term is that we can only have this duty, if we are willing to recognize that we should feel the same sense of moral duty to person's of other races, if the relevant circumstances are the same. But what does this mean? In order to shed some light on this question, let us briefly return to our case involving parents and children. Do we mean that everyone should have the same obligations to any child who is brought into their home under their care? Does the universalizability condition deny any special obligation to one's natural offspring? On one reading, it seems as though it should. For to answer "no" would seem to require that the relevant domain that is to be universalized is one's natural offspring rather any child for which one acts as a parent. This is wrong. If we restrict the subject-terms in our judgment to natural offspring, then we seem to rob the judgment of its moral nature. But if we are willing to say that the proper subject-terms are any parent or child (natural or adopted), then this allows the judgment to pass the universalizability test.

An interesting question is: why are we open to recognizing specific universal moral judgments when it comes to husbands and wives and parents and children, but we are not open to specific universal moral judgments for races? I think it is because we think that race in some way is an illegitimate or at best a suspect moral characteristic of persons. When it comes to race the belief is that we cannot employ racial subject-terms in our judgments without violating the universalizability test. Remember this test requires that if we treat people in the same circumstances differently, then we must have a good moral reason for doing so. And race is thought by many to never be such a reason. As Joel Feinberg puts it, likes should be treated alike unless we can show that they are different in morally relevant ways.[17] But cannot a person's race be a morally relevant reason for making a moral difference? A part of the reluctance to saying that it should can be traced to how race has been used to cause great harm to innocent human beings. But I do not think that we should conclude from this that racial subject-terms are always morally inappropriate. At best, we are warranted in concluding that racial characteristics are suspect. Or, put in another way, racial subject-terms may be morally justifiable, but they require very close scrutiny.

Why isn't this reply satisfactory? Some have not been persuaded by this response because they have a difficult time accepting that a characteristic that a person has no control over can be used to mark a moral distinction between persons. I guess the idea is that if I am not responsible for being a member of a particular race, then how can my race be morally relevant? But if this is their worry, then they must explain why other characteristics of persons that we are not responsible for are thought to be morally relevant, e. g., native intelligence. Why pick on race?

Perhaps their worry is not that we lack responsibility for our racial identities, but that we have no control over them. And something we have no control over should not be used to mark a moral difference between persons. Race as a characteristic of persons is thought to be different from I.Q., because some psychologists believe that we can boost our intelligence quotients through study and experience and thus we have some control over them, while the critics of using racial distinctions would deny that we have any control over our racial identities. But is this true?

It might be true if we define race in biological terms. However, many who believe that race is a morally relevant characteristic of persons also believe that race should be defined in social and historical rather than biological terms. On this understanding of race, a person's racial identity is tied to their experiences and not in some strict way to biology. W. E. B. DuBois endorsed this conception of race in his classic paper "The Conservation of Races."[18] If we accept DuBois's conception of race, our racial identities are not biologically determined.

But will this move satisfy those who believe that race always violates the universalizability constraint on moral judgments? Wouldn't they reply that institutions like American slavery and Jim Crow laws were morally wrong not because they singled out blacks, but because they treated persons in ways that a person should not be treated. As I said earlier, American slavery was not wrong because it only picked out blacks to be held as slaves. It was wrong because it held persons as slaves. These critics claim that a focus on race causes us to miss what is really wrong with such practices. It is their contention that the universalizability test is a powerful tool that will allow us to understand what is truly required by morality as opposed to focusing on irrelevant characteristics like a person's race.

However, their opponents believe that race can be morally relevant if understood in social and historical terms. They insist that race can be relevant without violating the universalizability test. Their argument is that we cannot capture the important features of certain group-based experiences without referring to concepts like race. Attempts to give race-neutral descriptions of these experiences fail to capture the true nature of these experiences. And if we cannot capture the true nature of this experience, we will not be able to adequately access their moral relevancy. For example, to replace the expression black oppression with human oppression would fail to adequately describe how the oppression of black people has differed from other forms of human oppression.[19] The worry is that it would be impossible or next to impossible to construct a racially neutral description that does justice to the experiences of blacks in America. Even if this neutral description is carefully crafted it will still create problems that will in the end undermine the goal we are attempting to achieve by avoiding making race morally relevant. On this view, race is relevant because it is the best means of describing and referring to certain human experiences. Race does not refer to biology, but lived experiences.

On this way of viewing race and morals, the universality constraint is understood in hypothetical terms. We still have to ask ourselves what if I was a member of that race, would I still endorse this moral judgment? If I cannot answer "yes," then the judgment fails to satisfy one important requirement of morality. The move to the hypothetical is thought to be legitimate because we frequently apply our moral terms to hypothetical cases. Even though we have not experienced what it is like to be a member of another racial group, and even though we doubt that we will ever have this experience, we can pass the universalizability test if we are willing to honestly consider what it would be like to extend our judgments to all races. The move to the hypothetical in this case is less controversial than the move that R. M. Hare makes. Hare wonders whether it would be morally right for a human being to hang a cat up by its tail just for fun but deny that it would be right to hang a human being up by its tail if it had one.[20] In this case, in order to satisfy the hypothetical universality test one has to be able to imagine if, in identical circumstances, someone were to hang a human being up by its tail if it had one, whether the human suffering would be the same as the cat's suffering? This hypothetical is a difficult thing to imagine. Thus it has lead these people to question whether the hypothetical universalizability test would be of any use to us in such cases.

Some animal rights supporters argue that our inability to imagine what it would be like to be a non-human animal is what allows us to morally ignore the suffering of animals. Animal rights supporters maintain that even the most adamant human rights supporters fail to be able to apply the universalizability test to animals. Their species bias blocks their ability to see the commonality of the human and animal experiences.

However, when we make the hypothetical move in the case of races, we maintain that we can imagine what it is like to be a member of another race, although we cannot fully imagine what it is like to be a member of another species. To imagine what it is like to be a member of another race is clearly not beyond human imagination. As such, it is reasonable to think we can recognize different racial identities, and use these moral identities as subject-terms in our moral judgments without violating the universalizability test. According to this view, races can be morally deserving because of their experiences and not their biology. Racial difference is a contingent fact about the experiences of human beings and not a logical claim about what follows from the biological nature of persons.

III

If the arguments that I have offered above are sound, Douglass can justify the following two judgments: (1) African Americans should have their own institutions as a means of insuring that their rights are respected; and (2) middle-class African Americans have a special obligation to help members of their racial group that are less fortunate without violating the universalizability constraint. These judgments are not rooted in biology or genetics, but in the social and historical experiences of a nation that has a long history of describing events and people in racial terms. Race, in this sense, is clearly a social construction. But to say this in no way implies that it has no reality. This reality has often been painful, but it has also been the source of pride, inspiration, and creativity.

Douglass, unlike DuBois, believed that our ultimate goal should be to completely rid our society of racial classifications, but we may have to use these classifications for a time in order to reach this goal. Basically, he believed that racial classifications were a hindrance to the individual and the society. Although I think I have shown that race can be used as a subject-term in moral judgments without violating the universalizability condition, Douglass's provisional reliance on institutions of a complexional character is still the source of a great deal of controversy. One wonders how long institutions of a complexional character will be needed. Are they needed until all the laws that prohibit African Americans from participating are wiped from the books? Or perhaps they are needed until the spirit as well as the letter of civil rights laws have been achieved.

Answers to these questions are not simple. A system of prolonged racial oppression like the one in the United States had profound effects. It not only assigned positions and roles in society, but it shaped the way we think about others and ourselves. It produced harmful stereotypical attitudes and beliefs, and it bred deep-seated distrust and suspicion between people perceived to be of different races. If it is reasonable to believe that the harmful consequences cited above did occur, and that they were an assault to the human dignity of African Americans, then we need to have a clear account of why Douglass felt that African-American institutions were necessary to avoid these harmful effects and to secure the rights of African Americans.

When African Americans were legally barred from participating in important institutions that were necessary for their development and self-respect, it is clear why there was a need for separate institutions of a complexional character. Because they were legally prevented from participating in white institutions that were crucial for their self-development, they needed their own institutions to fill this void. But what about after Jim Crow laws were formally abolished? Did this eliminate the need for African American institutions? I think not. Even though segregation laws were no longer on the books, this was a far cry from opening up American institutions to all under conditions of fair equality of opportunity. The repeal of Jim Crow did not eliminate the need for African-Americans to struggle to become true participants. Even today, many would argue that African Americans still have a second-class status when it comes to participating in American life.

Would Douglass urge African Americans today to abandon institutions of a complexional character or would he think many of the current cultural, economic, and political obstacles still make such institutions necessary? Perhaps Douglass's views on African-American emigration proposals after the Civil War can be of some use to us here. Martin Delany and other African-American activists urged African Americans to leave the United States and to establish residency in Africa and other places.[21] Douglass vigorously opposed these proposals.[22]

Douglass believed that the emigrationist's position was based upon an unwarranted pessimism about the future of race relations in the United States. According to Bernard Boxill, the primary reason for

Douglass's optimism was his confidence in the power of moral suasion.[23] In other words, Douglass believed that white racists could be convinced that African Americans were deserving of human rights. In fact, Douglass believed the legitimacy of the claim by African Americans for human rights was so self-evident that the denial of such rights would eventually become a source of shame for white people. And this shame would lead them to change their behavior.[24]

Should Douglass's optimism be applied to the present situation of African Americans? If we do, what should follow from such optimism? Should this optimism lead us to embrace a racially assimilationist ideal which requires that we reject all racial classifications, including those of a transitional sort? Remember in Douglass's argument against African-American emigration proposals, he urged African Americans to stay in the United States to struggle to achieve their rights as American citizens. He felt that their resistance would serve to confirm their humanity to themselves and others. But if we employ this reasoning in the case of present-day race relations in the United States, an assimilationist like Douglass would not endorse the creation of institutions of a complexional character. He would urge people to be optimistic about eliminating racial distinctions instead of forming racially defined institutions. Given that there has been some progress in race relations, the assimilationist recommendation would be to fight for the opportunity for all to participate in common institutions rather than any kind of separation based on race.

All racial assimilationists who share Douglass's belief about racially defined institutions will face the pain of inconsistency, if they defend racially defined institutions as a provisional means to achieve a racially assimilated society. These provisional institutions cannot be defended without giving race a significance that assimilationists claim that they are unwilling to give it. Although this racial significance need not be understood in biological or genetic terms, it must be acknowledged, if racially defined institutions are to be sustained in the present cultural, economic, political, and social climate.

If racialized institutions, even ones of a temporary nature, are to be defended, then any such defense will require an account of the significance of race that is socially viable and consistent with democracy and justice. Whether or not such an account can be provided is a matter of controversy.[25] My aim here has not been to enter this debate, but to point to some of the interesting consequences of Douglass's racial assimilationist views on the need for racially defined institutions.

Notes

1 Fredrick Douglass, "The Claims of the Negro Ethnologically Considered," in Howard Brotz, ed, *African-American Social and Political Thought, 1850–1920* (New Brunswick: Transaction Publishers, 1992), pp. 226–41.
2 Douglass, "Love of God, Love of Man, Love of Country: An Address Delivered in Syracuse, New York, On September 24, 1847," in John W. Blassingame, ed. *The Frederick Douglass Papers, vol. 2* (New Haven: Yale University Press, 1982), p. 105; Frederick Douglass, "Of Morals and Men: An Address delivered in New York, New York, On 8 May 1849," in Blassingame, ed, *The Frederick Douglass Papers, vol. 2*, pp. 170–4; Frederick Douglass, "The Color Question: An Address Delivered in Washington, D.C., on 5 July 1875," in John W. Blassingame and John R. McKivigan, eds, *The Frederick Douglass Papers, vol. 4* (New Haven: Yale University Press, 1991), pp. 420–1.
3 Douglass, "An Address to the Colored People of the United States," in Brotz, ed, p. 211.
4 Douglass, "Letter to Harriet Beecher Stowe," in ibid., pp. 222–6.
5 Douglass, "The Future of the Colored Race," in ibid., pp. 308–10.
6 Douglass, "The Nation's Problem," in ibid., pp. 316–17.
7 Bernard Boxill, *Blacks and Social Justice*, revised edition (Lanham, MD: Rowman and Littlefield, 1992), pp. 176–7.
8 See, e.g., Martin R. Delany, "The Condition, Elevation, Emigration, and Destiny of the Colored People of the United States," in Brontz, ed, *African-American social and Political Thought*, pp. 37–111.
9 See Henry Highland Garnet, "The Past and the Present Condition, and the Destiny of the Colored Race," in Brotz, ed, *African-American Social and Political Thought*, pp. 199–202.
10 Douglass in Philip S. Foner, ed, *Life and Writings of Frederick Douglass, vol. 4* (New York: International Publishers, 1975), pp. 136, 147, 162–4.
11 This argument is often made in the case of abortion. Some pro-abortionists believe that even if the fetus is an innocent person, the woman has a right to defend herself against it if it threatens her life.
12 Immanuel Kant, *Groundwork of the Metaphysics of Morals*, trans. by H. J. Paton (New York: Harper and Row, 1964) especially chapter 2.
13 R. M. Hare, *Freedom and Reason* (London: Oxford University Press, 1970), pp. 10–29.
14 See, e.g., W. Rabinowicz, *Universalizability* (Dordrecht: Reidel, 1979).
15 R. M. Hare, "Principles," *Proceedings of the Aristotelian Society*, 72, 1972–3, pp. 1–18.
16 The controversy over whether African Americans have special obligations to each other is discussed in Kwame Anthony Appiah, "Racisms," in David Theo Goldberg, ed, *Anatomy of Racism* (Minneapolis: University of Minnesota Press, 1990), pp. 3–17 and Bill E. Lawson, "Uplifting the Race:

Middle-Class Blacks and the Truly Disadvantaged," in Bill E. Lawson, ed, *The Underclass Question* (Philadelphia: Temple University Press, 1992), pp. 90–113.
17 Joel Feinberg, *Social Philosophy* (Englewood Cliffs, NJ: Prentice Hall, 1973), pp. 99–103.
18 W. E. B. DuBois, "The Conservation of Races," in Brotz, ed, *African-American Social and Political Thought*, pp. 483–92.
19 For such an attempt see Bill E. Lawson, "Oppression and Slavery, in Howard McGary and Bill E. Lawson, *Between Slavery and Freedom: Philosophy and American Slavery* (Indianapolis: Indiana University Press, 1992), especially chapter 1.
20 R. M. Hare, *Moral Thinking* (Oxford: Oxford University Press, 1981).
21 Delany, "The Condition" and Alexander Crummell, "The Race Problem in America," in Brotz ed, *African-American Social and Political Thought*, pp. 180–90.
22 Douglass, "African Civilization Society," in ibid., pp. 262–6.
23 Bernard R. Boxill, "Two Traditions in African-American Political Philosophy," *The Philosophical Forum*, 1–3 (24) 1992–3, pp. 125–31.
24 See Foner, ed, *Life and Writings of Frederick Douglass*, pp. 162–4.
25 See Lucius T. Outlaw, *On Race and Philosophy* (New York: Routledge, 1996), especially chapters 6 and 7.

3
Douglass's Assimilationism and Antislavery

John P. Pittman

Frederick Douglass has often been called an "assimilationist"; the significance of this characterization, and how it relates to his thought and practice generally and its historical occasions are less often explored. In what follows I want to discuss the import of this characterization of Douglass's thought. In the first two sections I relate what has been called Douglass's assimilationism to the self-understanding projected in his own narratives. In the third section I shift gears to consider an attempt by a contemporary of Douglass, Karl Marx, in another arena and with respect to another social situation, to give an account of the demand for the emancipation of another oppressed group – the European Jews – in relation to the putative modernity of European society. Returning to Douglass's work in section four, I discuss his account of the slave system and offer an analogy between Douglass's and Marx's accounts of the character of the oppression of African Americans and European Jews respectively. Then in section five I return to the issue of "assimilationism," suggest two distinct versions of that view, and try to locate the versions which Douglass and Marx affirm on the continuum from revolutionary to individualistic.

I

What is called Douglass's "assimilationism" could be described as his insistence that the achievement and exercise of full and effective citizenship rights always take priority over – or be the end toward which is aimed – any particularist cultural or social manifestations of African-American solidarity. Bernard Boxill, who describes Douglass as "the most consistent and thorough-going assimilationist," characterizes assimilationism elsewhere as governed by the belief that "a society in which racial differences have no moral, political, or economic significance – that is, a color-blind society – is both possible and desirable in America."¹ What Douglass emphasizes over and over is the demand for recognition expressed in the struggle for citizenship rights for black folk. Douglass contrasts that struggle and its object positively with any "separatist" solutions or ends for black folk that do not involve their full, expanded, participation in American society. Although Douglass understood and accepted the – strategic – need for what he called "institutions of a complexional character," he regarded these as means that sometimes had to be resorted to "in order to attain this very idea of human brotherhood." That ideal was always his goal, both for himself and for the African people in America.

The issue of assimilationism is fairly closely connected not only with the ideal of a colorblind society but also with the idea of a modern one. One way of understanding modernity is as "an epoch wherein legitimate structures of human interaction are those informed by a conception of the person whose social significance is no longer defined by natural determinations such as race, sex, etc., but by a person's self-determination."² And one very big element of Douglass's understanding of his life and times – the element most evident in his narrative self-descriptions – was the significance he placed on self-determination as essential to the actual achieved humanity of the citizen of a modern republic. And I want to suggest that it was this significance he ascribed to self-determination in his own self-conception, and writerly self-description, that helped shape Douglass's point of view on the social prospects of black folk – the point of view often characterized as "assimilationist."

Self-determination is inherently a social process. But Douglass begins, rhetorically, from the standpoint of a God-given humanity. He was thrown back on this purely abstract identity conferred through inclusion in "the circle of human brotherhood" precisely by slavery's attempts to deny to the slave that humanity achieved through self-determination within the sphere of civil society. Because of that attempted denial, because of the height of the barriers placed against the development of his humanity and the energy he had to expend to overcome those obstacles personally, his humanity, and the abstract humanity of the African people in America, became a principle on which he rested everything. But for the black slave's humanity to be a principle, humanity itself had to be a principle in the first place. The ideological principle of humanity that Douglass embraced was that of the natural rights of man, more specifically the principle of respect for the moral personality that is each human being's God-given inheritance:

> I want no better basis for my activities and affinities than the broad foundation laid by the Bible itself, that "God has made of one blood all nations of men to dwell on all the face of the earth." This comprehends the Fatherhood of God and the brotherhood of man.[3]

The basis of Douglass's "activities and affinities" was thus distinctively and decisively biblical, and in two related senses. The bible represented, first, not only nor even primarily the revelation of the "will of God to man"; but also, and in virtue of that, the crucial site of sectarian contention, which takes the form of a "confusion of tongues" and "endless contradictions" of interpretation. This contention is, on Douglass's view, essentially political, focused as it is on revealed truth. For:

> that truth is the power of God for the salvation of the world, and I do not limit truth to mere spiritual matters, but to man in all his relations in the family, in the church, in the government, in the world.[4]

Thus any account of God's will, and hence of salvation, must be of what is in part an essentially political and social, this-worldly salvation.

Second, and more basically, such an account must be an interpretation or reading – that is, a literate discourse oriented toward the determination of "truth," while also cognizant of a practical context of political contention amid a "confusion of tongues." Thus Douglass's use of a Biblical basis for his activities underscores that for him literacy is a crucial condition for the full achievement of humanity or moral personality itself. Literacy is not only the first step in the "improvement" and "elevation" of the oppressed, of their escape from a condition of enslavement, but of their full inclusion in the "circle of humanity," as well as within the ambit of "civil society" itself. Thus we should not allow Douglass's repeated reliance on religious rhetoric in his oratory and writing to obscure the deeply secular and modern aims of the two closely connected aspects of his activity. First, salvation is a this-worldly, specifically political process demanding the mobilization and concerted action of all those opposed to the depredations of the "slave system." But this political struggle must be waged concurrently with and through the actual intellectual autonomy – that is to say literary self-determination – of black folk in positions of practical leadership of that political struggle.

Politically, Douglass began from the assumption that the abolition of slavery was the crucial condition that would set the stage for the elevation of black folk and their overcoming of the inferior position assigned to them in American society. For Douglass conceived of that inferior position as being a more or less direct product of the ascendancy of the slave system and its political hegemony. That conception was consolidated and articulated, both during the course of the antebellum period and during and after the war as well, through two further theses. First, the historical result of the social processes of the slave system – perpetuated even after its abolition – is a condition (both a structural position and a social identity) Douglass characterized alternately as a kind of semi-slavery (free blacks in the north before the war being "slaves of the community") as well as with the oft-employed term "degradation." Second, the political abolition of slavery was not an irreversible and final triumph over and dispatch of the forces of the "slavocracy" but only the first of many battles against those forces, who persist in throwing up obstacles to the achievement of full freedom for black folk.

II

Douglass identified himself as a "fugitive slave," years after his fame as an abolitionist orator and writer had been won. This may have been an ironic gesture toward his initial role as living witness to the abominations of slavery, some of which were written across his back. But it also was a significant indication of his own recognition of the major part played in the formation of his own self-consciousness and identity by his experiences under the slave system. That is, the fact of his having been a slave – of his having suffered under its brutalities and indignities; of his having educated himself clandestinely and at his own peril in spite of it; of his having gained his own manhood, as it were, by challenging and overcoming its attempts to degrade him; his having finally planned and executed his own escape from it – all these were decisive in his coming to be Frederick Douglass. In some sense, Douglass developed a social personality that was self-determined; nonetheless, he was ever so conscious of his personal ties to slavery.

"Personal" needs stressing in that last remark: it was his personal ties to slavery that were decisive for Douglass's identity and for his understanding of the oppression(s) to which the slave was subject. I don't mean simply that Douglass personally experienced the oppressions of the slave, though that obviously is true. More fundamentally, Douglass understood that the subjections of the slave were based on bonds of *personal* dependency: he was Thomas Auld's chattel, who had to undergo the lashings of Edward Covey, and had to turn over his entire week's wages earned as a caulker to Hugh Auld. This is decisive because it gave the struggle and resistance by which Douglass distinguished himself also a personal character. That is to say, Douglass as the resisting slave, rebellious slave, and ultimately fugitive slave was able to experience – and, decisively, literally recreate – each moment, each step of that struggle as a *personal* affirmation, in opposition to the *personal* power of another. It was thus his *concrete, personal* individuality that was asserted, affirmed, and ultimately recognized in his acts of resistance to, and steps out of slavery.

Consider the famous fight with Covey. It was Frederick Bailey's sheer physical strength and determination that laid Covey low. I want to focus on the identity of the humanity he affirmed – not a self-identical, abstract humanity as in the "brotherhood of man" discussed above – but the concrete human identity of Frederick Bailey, rebellious slave. It was *his* humanity because of who he was as an individual and what he had done. As Douglass wrote:

> This battle with Mr. Covey was the turning point in my career as a slave. It rekindled the few expiring embers of freedom, and revived within me a sense of my own manhood . . . I now resolved that, however long I might remain a slave in form, the day had passed forever when I could be a slave in fact. I did not hesitate to let it be known of me, that the white man, who expected to succeed in whipping, must also succeed in killing me.[5]

Douglass writes his confrontation with Covey as a drama of *personal* redemption and spiritual resurrection. It is the moment at which Douglass as "self-made man" begins his life and Douglass as slave is overcome. It's worth noting that, even in Douglass's own telling, Covey was overcome by *united* resistance, the collective resistance of the several slaves at hand, who witnessed the fight and refused Covey's demands for help, and not by Douglass's own efforts alone. But the narrative of Douglass's life is a story of self-constitution and self-determination; what is foregrounded is the personal struggle for freedom. Douglass's confrontation with Covey earns him freedom of a sort – freedom from the kind of personal dependence that slavery is classically regarded as embodying. Douglass was able to free himself largely of this kind of subjection even while still enmeshed in the slave system.

Douglass became engaged in the activities of a "self-made man" over the course of the next ten years, during which he attempted to escape, was returned to Baltimore, became a caulker, as well as a wage-laborer, became involved in Baltimore's free colored society, met Anna Murray, planned and executed his own escape, married, became a lay preacher, a manual laborer, a father, an abolitionist orator, an author. Each of these steps was a move away from and out of, the bonds of personal dependency, and a move away from the conditions of slavery. Precisely because he was able to come so far out of slavery without state-sanctioned political emancipation, by dint of a personal struggle, the humanity Douglass personified – by becoming in his writing (and speaking) representative of – was not the merely abstract humanity of the citizen, nor the egotistical "human nature" of the bourgeois. But also, it was not the abstract humanity of the black man, of the Negro, of the colored man. For Douglass, to be a man is to be a self-made man, in the style of American (mythical) civil society.

Thus the social basis of Douglass's assimilationism can be seen as deriving from the trajectory of his *personal* struggle – which only later became a social and political struggle – for recognition of his "manhood." While a people's struggle for its recognition must necessarily be a social struggle, the slave's struggle for the recognition of his/her humanity is a struggle against a personal antagonist, a moral/physical struggle between individuals. As a concrete being, the slave's humanity can only be recognized by another concrete being. That fight for the recognition of manhood/humanity must therefore be a fight against Covey, that particular person. That struggle, being won, as it was by Douglass, represented an achievement that, ironically, constituted a bar against any significant identification with a racial party on Douglass's part – that is, with a particularist cultural or racial identification. For the struggle for recognition, conducted by the slave, can only be successful to the extent that there is no essential distinction between the slave as self-consciousness and the master as self-consciousness. That struggle is one for the recognition of a fully achieved and concrete humanity, and can only be successful to the extent that one has burst asunder every given social particularity defined through slavery and race.[6]

III

Karl Marx's article "On the Jewish Question," written in 1843 and printed the next year in the *Deutsch-Französische Jahrbücher*, was a response to and critique of a pair of articles published somewhat earlier by Bruno Bauer, one of the leading "Young Hegelians." For Bauer, "the Jewish Question" is the question of the Jews' emancipation from Judaism given a modern state. Marx's treatment of the Jewish question goes beyond Bauer's in two important respects: first, Marx criticizes Bauer's implicit limitation of emancipation to that possible within the confines of the modern state. Bauer also limits himself to considering the question merely from the religious standpoint itself, that is, immanently: in contrasting the two religions, he considers only the religious manifestations of Christianity and Judaism in his analysis. In terms of critical theory this represents Bauer's refusal to examine the secular basis of the social lives of Jews and Christians in German society. Marx employs the Feuerbachian method, criticizing religion by holding up for examination the secular basis of religious practices and institutions. Marx then turns to an analysis of the Jew as a "particular secular" character:

> Let us consider the actual, worldly Jew, not the *Sabbath Jew*, as Bauer does, but the *everyday Jew*; Let us not look for the secret of the Jew in his religion, but let us look for the secret of his religion in the real Jew. What is the secular basis of Judaism? *Practical* need, *self-interest*. What is the worldly religion of the Jew? *Huckstering*. What is his worldly God? *Money*. Very well then! Emancipation from *huckstering* and *money*, consequently from practical, real Judaism, would be the self-emancipation of our time.[7]

Thus Marx sets out what he calls "the special position of Judaism in the contemporary enslaved world." By that, I take it, he means himself to be describing the social position of the Jew, whose employment – defined and circumscribed by a historically anti-Semitic Christian European society – as moneylender and trader (huckster) reveals precisely the limitations of political emancipation. To free the Jew – in this sense – from domination by the Christian state is to liberate the state from the social role of the Jew. That is, the emancipation of the Jew, as envisioned by Bauer, preserves the necessity for *man*, as distinct from *citizen*, to practically worship the secular god of bourgeois society – money.

Marx reformulates the demand for the emancipation of the Jew as a demand to eliminate or "abolish" the social conditions that constitute a particular and oppressive social role – or perhaps set of such roles – for "the Jew." ("For us the question of the Jew's capacity for emancipation becomes the question: What particular *social* element has to be overcome in order to abolish Judaism?"[8]) That (set of) social role(s) should not be seen as distinct from a preexisting and settled (cultural or religious) identity for the Jew within that social system; rather, the social role comes to provide the basis for a (distinctive) social identity – a social identity which is, at least in part – a locus of oppressive social relations.

Marx's response to Bauer relies on finding the secular basis – that is to say, the basis in socio-economic relations – of the special position of the Jew and Judaism in Christian society. This allows Marx to show the basis of the oppression of the Jew in the conditions underlying both civil society and the state. Marx is thus able to infuse the demand for the abolition of religious sectarianism, an Enlightenment political demand that Bauer takes more or less as given, with a more radical, social content. But he does this by formulating the relation of Jew and Christian in terms of social roles and social identities which are themselves substantially the products of a history of oppression, while also being the current forms that oppression takes. This theoretical socializing of the issue does not circumvent or abandon the cultural or ideological representations, but aims to uncover their actual ground in oppressive social relations. Marx's demand for "the abolition of Judaism" is the demand, posed in a disturbing shorthand manner, for the abolition of an oppressive system of social identity. (Who can hear that demand today, at the end of the twentieth century, and not fall under a shadow of horror, given what happened through German culture less than a century after that demand was voiced?)

That demand can and has been seen as a rejection not only of the social identity of the Jew as a function of the role prescribed for him by an oppressive social system, but also as signifying an assimilationist urge, a rejection of any cultural ties to Judaism, by Marx. Whether and to what extent it makes sense to characterize Marx, as an assimilationist will be discussed below in section five of this essay. For now I want to turn back to Frederick Douglass and consider whether anything like Marx's argument about the emancipation of the Jews can be found in Douglass's writings about the prospects of black folk in the United States.

IV

Douglass identifies the historical oppressor of African Americans as the "slave system," and often insists on the systematic character of slavery as it existed in the southern states. It was a civilization unto itself, with its own laws, and its own religion, customs, and morals. Even many years after the victorious outcome of the civil war against the secessionist slavocracy, Douglass continued to describe the obstacles confronting blacks both north and south in broad terms connected to the slave system:

> the irrepressible conflict of which we heard so much before the war of the rebellion and during the war, and which we supposed was ended by the war, is still in progress. It is still the battle between two opposite civilizations – the one created and sustained by slavery and the other framed and fashioned in the spirit of liberty and humanity.[9]

This system, he thought, existed in various forms at different historical times and in various regions of the world, but with its last major institutional incarnation in America. The slave system, oppressive in itself, tended to the promotion of cruelty and brutality in its effort to perpetuate and maintain itself. Douglass often described the effects of the slave system on the slave, and revealed it as subject to moral condemnation because of these effects. But he also pointed out that the slave system has other victims beside the slave, that it was engaged in the oppression of other strata of society as well.

Douglass was in a very good position to understand the systemic character of slavery – not merely because he had been a slave, but because he was well-placed in the sense of having experienced first-hand the many incarnations and articulations that slave labor took in the "rational" system of American slavery. Because he experienced and was subject to so many of the varied relations that the slave system was exemplified in, he was in a unique position to come to separate conceptually the bonds of personal dependence – slavery narrowly conceived – from the much broader complex of variegated relations that constituted the core and margin of the slave system. Douglass came to identify that system with the generalized condition of his race, both north and south. He described that condition as one of *degradation*, even as he described the condition of those persons of color in antebellum America who were not chattel slaves themselves as "slaves of the community":

> In the Northern states, we are not slaves to individuals, not personal slaves, yet in many respects we are the slaves of the community . . . It is more than a mere figure of speech to say that we are as a people, chained together. We are one people – one in general complexion, one in a common degradation, one in popular estimation. As one rises, all must rise, and as one falls all must fall.[10]

Douglass identifies *complexion* as a mark of the degradation of *slavery*, or at least, with the residual effects of the slave system. Consequently, he also equates the actual, effectual (rather than political) abolition of slavery with freedom from those but also *colorblindness* – the absence of socially significant color distinctions. For Douglass, color had become metonymic for slavery, the condition of enslavement. Just as the slave can only make himself – and achieve freedom – in opposition to, in the struggle against, the personal bonds of slavery itself, so black people generally could only emancipate themselves and become fully self-determining by waging determined struggle against the ramified effects of the slave system.

It is important that Douglass recognized the slave system, as distinct from the slaveowner or master, as the force or entity that is the source and basis of the oppression of the slave particularly, and of black people generally. It is important as well that he identified other strata of the population as victims of the slave system – even when they were not victims of the racism that is its most distinctive ideological mainstay and product. This represents an identity of interests that can be – which Douglass thought of as – the basis for alliances and coalitions in the practical political struggle to overthrow the slave power. But also this coincidence of oppressors pointed beyond the abstract criterion of humanity (as the political criterion for inclusion within the purview of "the state") and toward the social struggle between contending interests and classes (of "civil society") as the crucial locus for the formation of social identity:

> The slaveholders, with a craftiness peculiar to themselves, by encouraging the enmity of the poor, laboring white man against the blacks, succeeds in making the said white man almost as much a slave as the black slave himself. The difference between the white slave, and the black slave, is this: the latter belongs to *one* slaveholder, and the former belongs to *all* the slaveholders, collectively. The white slave has taken from him by indirection, what the black slave has taken from him directly, and without ceremony. Both are plundered, and by the same plunderers . . . The competition, and its injurious consequences, will, one day, array the non-slaveholding white people of the slave states, against the slave system, and make them the most effective workers against the great evil. At present, the slaveholders blind them to this competition, by keeping alive their prejudice against the slaves, *as men* – not against them *as slaves*.[11]

This kind of status – the status of being "a slave of the community" of slaveowners – is one he also ascribes to the white working man who, under slavery, is pitted against the slave by the slaveowners. The white worker is forced to compete with slaves, and this competition continually threatens the living standard and security of the white worker. But while objectively the white worker's interests are threatened by the slave system, this competition becomes a competition between white workers and the black men who, as slaves, are used and exploited by that system. The racist prejudice of the white workers leads them to oppose themselves to the black men *as black men* rather than as slaves. Here again the "complexion" of the slaves becomes identified with both their degraded condition and a form of oppression that Douglass attributes to the slave system. Thus the kinds of circumstances Marx and Engels attributed to the proletarian condition generally, Douglass attributed to the peculiar distortion that the slave system effected on American civil society.[12]

This distortion, as Douglass seems to conceive it, involves the skin color of the slaves, or degraded workers, serving as a sign of that degradation itself. Generalized, this relation is between the "complexion" of the black worker and the degraded condition in which that worker has been put, a condition harboring considerable dangers for humanity. This relation is constituted by/represents a kind of social role similar to that analytically identified by the young Marx as grounding the condition of the Jews in the European society of the second quarter of the nineteenth century. This suggests an analogy between the respective analyses of the oppression faced by black folk in the United States and the Jews in Europe offered respectively by Douglass and Marx and the attitudes regarding the prospects of these groups within the larger society – attitudes often characterized as assimilationist – that Douglass and Marx are both taken to have embraced.

V

Let me first distinguish a number of senses which the term "assimilationism" has been used to convey, both in reference to Douglass and more generally. In the influential book-length study of *Assimilation in American Life*, published in 1964, Milton M. Gordon presents a model of assimilation as a social process of "adaptation" of a minority "subsociety" to the "subculture" of a "core subsociety" of a society, e.g., in the case of the United States the adaptation of ethnic and racial minorities and immigrant groups to the dominant cultural patterns of the "middle-class, white, Anglo-Saxon Protestants."[13] After isolating and identifying seven subprocesses constitutive of assimilation, Gordon formulates and contrasts three distinct normative theories or "central ideological tendencies" concerning assimilation, which he calls Anglo-conformity, the Melting Pot theory, and cultural pluralism (p. 85). Anglo-conformity's "central assumption [is] the desirability of maintaining English institutions (as modified by the American Revolution), the English language, and English-oriented cultural patterns as dominant and standard in American life" (p. 88). According to Gordon, this is the oldest and "most prevalent ideology of assimilation in America throughout the nation's history" (p. 89).

Gordon's analysis has played an important role in the debate about assimilationism as such, and Douglass's alleged advocacy of it particularly. It's worth noting in this connection that while Gordon discusses three different "tendencies" or "ideologies" within assimilationism, it is the ideology of "Anglo-conformity" that has generally been given pride of place in discussions about assimilation. Thus Harold Cruse, who identifies Frederick Douglass as "the prototype leader" of the "racial integration strain" of Negro intellectuals, quotes Gordon at length, beginning with his characterization of Anglo-conformity cited above. Cruse, who tends to use "integration" and "assimilation" interchangeably, at one point refers to the "assimilationist worship of the WASP ideal."[14] More recently Tommy Lott, in an article about "Black Urban Youth Culture and Social Pathology" traces accusations about the "social pathology" of the "black underclass" to "the dominant group's one-way assimilationist ideology," which presupposes "the legitimacy of the American capitalist social order." In a note Lott specifies his use of assimilationist: "the claim that black people ought to acquire the values, that is, cultural practices, of the dominant European group at the expense of retaining any such values . . . that are derived from their own African heritage." He then goes on to ascribe to Douglass the "assimilationist view" that "the notion of elevation meant the acculturation of black people into the American mainstream." [15]

Now I want to argue that, though in one sense the label "assimilationism" may be justly used to characterize some of the impetus behind the policies and goals Douglass advanced and worked for, that characterization cannot be made as simply as it generally has been. Thus both of the last-quoted writers seem to have taken something like Gordon's Anglo-conformity and attributed it to both the "dominant group" and specific ideological tendencies among historical formations of black intellectuals, and, in this case, Douglass in particular. Such an approach runs the risk of obscuring the particular historical context that Douglass was addressing as well as the distinctive modalities through which he advanced his agenda. Given the connected yet disparate projects of Douglass's antebellum radical abolitionist agitating on the one hand and his literary and particularly autobiographical writing on the other hand, the notion that Douglass advocated the continuance of "English-oriented cultural patterns" and the acquisition by blacks of the "values of the dominant European group" is unhelpful at best. It seems that a reconception of the "assimilation" concept, at least, is called for.

As a first provisional step toward such reconception, I want to stipulate a distinction between two senses of assimilation:

(1) the conception of a people giving up one established identity or culture, which is distinctive and autonomous or self-determined – determined independently of a dominant culture – as the condition of taking on another identity that makes it possible for them to be absorbed, as individuals, into that dominant culture. I call this *immigrant-assimilationism*.

(2) the conception of a people throwing off an identity that is predominantly the effect of a system of oppression through the radical or revolutionary overthrow of that system and consequent transformation of society. I call this *social-assimilationism*.

The difference between these two conceptions of assimilation can be formulated in a number of ways. Immigrant-assimilationism is an individualist version since it seems grounded in the paradigm case of the individual immigrant (or small group of such) who is able to "pass" into a society without making any impression or difference in the system of identities/culture into which they move. By contrast, social-assimilation not only brings in its wake profound changes in the socially constituted system of identities, but involves the wholesale transformation of identities of entire peoples, of cultures of entire societies. On the social-assimilationist conception, assimilation is the product of a fundamental social transformation that leaves no one – that is, no set of social roles or social identity – unchanged. A question might be raised, at this point, as to why this second conception should be called assimilationism at all. There doesn't seem to be any assimilating going on. One answer to this objection is that it represents the shedding of an identity, and a reconciliation or resolution of a social opposition or division that marks and is the effect of the dichotomy of identities or cultures. These features it has in common with immigrant-assimilation, though the opposition in the immigrant case may not be a systemic one in the way that it is in the social case. Although social-assimilation as an ideal often provokes in people who embrace it a personal change that appears in many ways similar to that involved in immigrant-assimilation, the basic perspective is one of global social transformation, and not American-style individual social mobility.

Another difference between these two is that immigrant-assimilation is not likely to be connected to an account of the social structure as inherently oppressive, or at least as involving deep and persistently oppressive features. An immigrant-assimilationist may seek entrance into the "core subsociety" as a way of escaping oppression, but any identification of the "core subsociety" as the locus of persistently oppressive features is likely to elicit a social critique significantly in tension with the goal of absorption. An immigrant-assimilationist more likely simply wishes to adopt the mainstream culture because she finds it more congenial or superior, for any number of reasons, to what has until now been her own. A social-assimilationist is one who rejects a social identity that is seen as rooted in an oppressive system; what is rejected is the social identity as part of the social system that, from this standpoint, is itself in need of transformation. Social-assimilationism thus demands an account of social particularity, that is, of the social identity that is inherently wedded to social structure, and, indeed, to oppressive social structure at that. This is not to say that all forms of social particularity are seen as inherently oppressive, but only that, in general, particularity cannot be simply a matter of "natural difference" or "religious faith" unarticulated/unmediated through social structure. Because social identity is grounded in social structure, identity can only be transformed through and by transforming social structure. On this view, then, "the Negro" (as personification of the social identity of race) or "the Jew" (as personification of the social identity of (other) religion) cannot be a matter of brute contingent natural or cultural/religious determination; rather, it must be a function of the structural position of what is identified as the "racial" ((other) cultural/religious) group within the social formation. A social transformation which eliminates the structural position is therefore the condition for the elimination of the oppressive social identity, such that persons previously oppressively identified as members of the "racial" ((other) cultural/religious) group are no longer so distinguished and are free to choose a social identity in the same manner as other citizens. That is, an entire dimension along which social identity had previously been defined is no longer socially available or has disappeared; with respect to that dimension, social identities are now "blind."

The discussion of the last three sections explored an analogy between a conception of social identities as sets of social roles grounded in or constituted by oppressive social relations. This conception locates social identities in what is sometimes called, in the language of sociology, social structure. To the extent that one is prepared to operate with such a schema, and the conception of social identity at its core – and it bears emphasis that this sort of analysis would represent only one phase or moment of inquiry into the social problem – the conception of social-assimilationism represents a normative (and revolutionary) account of assimilation with which it can be aligned. I can only say at this point that this conception of social-assimilationism seems at least as good an account as those rivals canvassed in the preceding section. If one wants to use the concept of assimilation, the conception of social-assimilationism is as plausible, as a normative-analytic tool, as the others.

I also think the account I gave of the young Marx's article on the Jewish question lends some plausibility to the further suggestion that the related conceptions of social identity and social-assimilationism constructed here has some claim to represent the views about the prospects for the emancipation of the Jewish people that Marx put forward there. Of course that was only a brief moment in Marx's rapid theoretical and political development in the 1830s and 1840s. Marx did not return to reconsider the topic of the Jewish question after the 1843 article. Of course, that is in itself a significant fact, but its exploration has not been and cannot be my concern here. Suffice to say that Marx, at the time of the 1843 article, could be characterized as a social-assimilationist.

Where, finally, does all this get us in attempting to characterize Douglass's assimilationism? Let me suggest the following points.

Frederick Douglass did not formulate, with anything close to the explicitness attempted here, either a conception of social identity or one of assimilation. These words do not appear in his writings. I have tried to suggest that something analogous to the conception of social identity advanced in sections three and four can be helpful to make sense of some of the things Douglass said about the slave system and its connection to the "degradation" of black folk in nineteenth-century America. But I do not claim that the conception of social-assimilationism captures fully the sense in which Douglass could most appropriately be called an assimilationist. Rather I hold that if it makes sense at all to characterize Douglass as an assimilationist, his assimilationism must be seen to contain a substantial admixture of social-assimilationism. The conception of social identity is a way to think about one element or "strain" of Douglass's thinking about the slave system; to that extent social-assimilationism suggests an element of his strategic and normative thinking about the future of social relations in the United States. The conception of social-assimilationism, combined with the conception suggested by Bernard Boxill in the passage quoted in section one, makes much more sense of the overall tendency of Douglass's thought than the rival conceptions discussed in section four. I am only too aware at this point of how preliminary and incomplete the resulting account of Douglass's social views is.

A final suggestion concerns the provenance of those elements of Douglass's thinking that resonate to the social-assimilationist model. Something like the immigrant-assimilationist conception should be visible in outline prefigured in Douglass's autobiographical account of his self-creation as a fully achieved member of America's mythical civil society. Correlatively, a social-assimilationist Douglass would emerge more sharply delineated from a consideration of his activity as radical abolitionist agitator and journalist.[16] Particularly relevant here is Douglass's break with the Garrisonians as he came to see the interpretation of the Constitution as a field of political contestation. This decisive move strengthened rather than compromised Douglass's sense of the anti-slavery struggle as one between social systems or civilizations, that is, as one whose successful conclusion would involve a radical and complete rupture with the fundamental structures and relations definitive of the social situation in America from the 1840s on. That there were profound transformations in American society during that period can hardly be denied; that Douglass as radical abolitionist played a significant role in identifying and addressing the character of those transformations seems equally beyond dispute. At least, then, our characterization of Douglass as assimilationist should express the decisively revolutionary element in Douglass's thought and action.

Notes

1 This characterization of assimilationism is in his "Two Traditions in African-American Political Philosophy," in John P. Pittman, ed, *African-American Perspectives and Philosophical Traditions* (New York: Routledge, 1997), p. 119.

2 This characterization is Frank Kirkland's, from his "Modernity and Intellectual Life in Black," in Pittman, ed, *African-American Perspectives*, pp. 140–1.

3 "The Nation's Problem" (Speech delivered April 16, 1889), in Howard Brotz, ed, *Negro Social and Political Thought 1850–1920* (New York: Basic Books, 1966), p. 317.

4 Douglass to Theophilus Gould Steward, July 27, 1886, reprinted by William L. Andrews, ed, *The Oxford Frederick Douglass Reader* (New York:

Oxford University Press, 1996), pp. 312–14. This letter contained Douglass's reply to a pastoral inquiry concerning Douglass's rumored infidelity from the pastor of the church Douglass regularly attended in Washington, D.C.

5 David W. Blight, ed, *Narrative of the Life of Frederick Douglass, An American Slave, Written by Himself* (Boston: Bedford Books, 1993), p. 79.

6 In a letter to James Redpath of July 29, 1871, Douglass acknowledged with resignation that "[i]t is too late now to do much to improve my relation to the public. I shall never get beyond Frederick Douglass the self-educated fugitive slave." Perhaps this should be read as recognition of the absolute historical limit of the mythical American civil society. Quoted in Waldo E. Martin, *The Mind of Frederick Douglass* (Chapel Hill: University of North Carolina Press, 1984), p. 251.

7 Karl Marx and Frederick Engels, *Collected Works* (New York: International Publishers, 1975), vol. 3, pp. 171–2.

8 Ibid., p. 171.

9 "The Nation's Problem," p. 325.

10 "Address to the Colored People of the United States," September 29, 1848, in Philip S. Foner, ed, *The Life and Writings of Frederick Douglass* (New York: International Publishers, 1950), vol. 1, p. 333.

11 *My Bondage and My Freedom*, in Henry Louis Gates, Jr, ed, *Frederick Douglass: Autobiographies* (New York: Library of America, 1994), p. 330.

12 Answering his own question – "In what way does the proletarian differ from the slave?" – Engels writes:

> The slave is sold once and for all, the proletarian has to sell himself by the day and by the hour. The slave is the property of one master and for that very reason has a guaranteed subsistence, however wretched it may be. The proletarian is, so to speak, the slave of the entire bourgeois *class*, not of one master, and therefore has no guaranteed subsistence, since nobody buys his labor if he does not need it. The slave is accounted a *thing* and not a member of civil society. The proletarian is recognized as a *person*, as a member of civil society. The slave *may*, therefore have a better subsistence than the proletarian but the latter stands at a higher stage of development. The slave frees himself by *becoming a proletarian*, abolishing from the totality of property relationships *only* the relationship of *slavery*. The proletarian can free himself only by abolishing *property in general*.

Frederick Engels, *Draft of a Communist Confession of Faith*, written as the draft program for the first Congress of the Communist League, held in London June 2–9, 1847. (It was at that Congress that the League was renamed the Communist League – it had been called the League of the Just. Another act of the Congress was to adopt a new slogan, "Working Men of All Countries, Unite!" which replaced "All Men are Brothers.") Marx and Engels, *Collected Works*, vol. 6, pp. 96–103.

13 Milton M. Gordon, *Assimilation in American Life: The Role of Race, Religion,*

and National Origins (New York: Oxford Univeristy Press, 1964), p. 72–3. Further references to this work are given in parentheses in the text.

14 Harold Cruse, *The Crisis of the Negro Intellectual* (New York: William Morrow, 1967), pp. 4, 506.

15 See his article "Marooned in America: Black Urban Youth Culture and Social Pathology" in Bill E. Lawson, ed, *The Underclass Question* (Philadelphia: Temple U P, 1992), pp. 72, 74, 86.

16 See for example the article "The Various Phases of Anti-Slavery," in Foner, ed, *Life and Writings*, vol. 5, pp. 366–71.

Part II

Natural Law and America's Founding Documents

4
Natural Law in the Constitutional Thought of Frederick Douglass

David E. Schrader

Frederick Douglass developed his understanding of the United States Constitution in a context very different from that in which most other constitutional theorists develop their positions. Douglass was not a trained philosopher, a judge, a law professor, or an attorney. Rather, Frederick Douglass was an escaped slave and an activist in the abolitionist movement in the 1840s and 1850s. For Douglass, the central issue that led to questions of constitutional interpretation was how the United States Constitution might affect the strategies required for the abolition of slavery. My purpose in this essay is to show how Douglass's mature views on constitutional interpretation came to reflect an understanding of natural law that provided a basis for a constitutional critique of the institution of American slavery. This understanding of natural law and its role in legal interpretation placed Douglass squarely at odds with the brand of strong legal positivism shared by both William Lloyd Garrison, the dominant figure in the abolitionist movement, and the United States Supreme Court under the leadership of Chief Justice Roger Taney.

The collected writings of Frederick Douglass give us a kind of record of the dispute on constitutional interpretation within the abolitionist movement. For the first decade of his involvement with the movement Douglass was solidly within the Garrisonian camp. Garrisonians held political control in both the American Anti-Slavery Society and the Massachusetts Anti-Slavery Society, in which Douglass first became involved with the abolitionist movement. Douglass expressed clearly the Garrisonian interpretation of the Constitution immediately following his concession in 1849 that, "if strictly 'construed according to its reading,' [the Constitution] is not a pro-slavery instrument." Douglass continued:

> I now hold, as I have ever done, that the original intent and meaning of the Constitution (the one given to it by the men who framed it, those who adopted, and the one given to it by the Supreme Court of the United States) makes it a pro-slavery instrument – such an one as I cannot bring myself to vote under, or swear to support.[1]

The understanding of the Constitution expressed here is that the Constitution was a social contract intended to express the will of those that framed and adopted it. It was, as Chief Justice Taney was later to point out in *Dred Scott v. Sanford*, framed and adopted by people of European descent. Some of those people intended that it should protect the institution of slavery. Others, while perhaps opposing slavery, acquiesced in the constitutional protection of slavery for the sake of political union. For those who viewed the Constitution in this manner, the sole question was whether they should be party to that social contract. The answer of the Garrisonian abolitionists was unequivocally negative. The social contract was a contract with slavery, a contract with the devil. The only morally acceptable thing to do was to have nothing to do with any union formed by that contract. As a result, Garrisonians did not vote under the Constitution, they did not seek or hold office under the Constitution, they would not swear to uphold the Constitution. Instead, they sought to have the northern states, whose inhabitants they saw as generally opposed to the institution of slavery, sever their ties with the American union and secede.

The Garrisonian view, however, did not go unopposed within the abolitionist movement. Among the chief advocates of a different view of constitutional interpretation, a natural law view of constitutional interpretation, according to which the political union based on the Constitution was not irredeemably corrupt, were Gerrit Smith, William Goodell, and Lysander Spooner. When Douglass left Massachusetts and found himself a part of an abolitionist community not under the domination of William Lloyd Garrison, he started to read the works of these men and to engage, at first critically, the views that they held. The result of that engagement was a change in Douglass's position on the Constitution.

A good point from which to start to unfold the mature constitutional thought of Douglass is with a claim made in Spooner's book, *The Unconstitutionality of Slavery*, a claim with which Garrison might well have agreed:

[T]hose contracts of government, state and national, which we call constitutions, are void, and unlawful, so far as they purport to authorize, (if any of them do authorize,) anything in violation of natural justice, or the natural rights of any man or class of men whatsoever.[2]

Garrison clearly thought that the United States Constitution did purport to authorize such violations, and was by that fact fundamentally voided for men and women of conscience. The question then became for Douglass, as it was for Spooner, can the United States Constitution be read as a document supporting the natural rights of all human beings?

Both at the time of Douglass and even at present, as the Senate hearings on the Supreme Court nomination of Judge Robert Bork a few years ago would indicate, the "original intentions" of the framers has been a fairly widely accepted principle of constitutional interpretation. At one level, both Douglass and Spooner agreed with the claim that the Constitution should be interpreted according to the "original intentions" of the document. At one level, in fact, it is certainly a commonplace of the entire history of common law understanding that, as Chief Justice Flemming of the Court of King's Bench pointed out as early as 1611, "as touching the construction of words, they shall be taken according to the . . . intent of the parties."[3] The problem, of course, is that there are several ways of understanding the "intent of the parties." Similarly, with the United States Constitution, there is the additional problem of determining exactly who the relevant "parties" were.

On the one hand, the early so-called "Republicans," followers of Thomas Jefferson, generally maintained that the "parties" to the Constitution were the several sovereign states that composed the United States. The early "Federalists," on the other hand, generally took the people to be the primary "parties" to the Constitution. While the "republican" understanding held political dominance from the time of the 1800 election up to the Civil War, the "federalist" understanding maintained considerable influence in the Supreme Court through the leadership of Chief Justice Marshall, and continued through the work of Justice Joseph Story. Justice Story's *Commentaries on the Constitution of the United States*, probably the most important of all the early treatises on constitutional interpretation, states the federalist position with uncompromising clarity:

> The language is, "We the *people* of the United States," not, We the *states*, "do *ordain* and *establish*;" not, do *contract* and enter into a *treaty* with each other; "this *constitution* for the United States of

America," not this *treaty* between the several states. [Story's emphases][4]

It should, of course, be clear that Garrison held to the republican position on this issue. Douglass, by contrast, maintained the federalist position.

Perhaps, however, the most fundamental element in Douglass's dispute with the Garrisonians (and with the Taney Supreme Court) came to focus on whether those "original intentions" should be limited to the intentions identified in the Constitution itself, perhaps along with those declared in some of the other "founding documents," or whether those intentions should be understood to include the full range of social views alleged to have been held by those who drafted the Constitution. In support of the former, the narrower, construal of "original intention," Douglass gave what I have long regarded as a decisive and devastating criticism of the broader interpretation held by Garrison, the Taney court and, more recently, Judge Bork:

> The rule here laid down ["Promises are to be performed in that spirit in which the promiser apprehended at the time the promised received it"] . . . is wholly without pertinence in the administration of the powers granted by the federal Constitution; first, because the Constitution is the record of its own intention; and second, because outside of that instrument we shall find conflicting and irreconcilable intentions. One state may have adopted the Constitution, intending that it should serve one end; while another may have adopted it intending that it should serve another quite different end.[5]

Douglass notes here, surely correctly, that any political document is the result of a compromise wherein the parties, who regularly disagree in many of the details of their intentions, settle on a set of words that they find mutually satisfactory. The argument was not altogether original with Douglass, however. In advancing this line of argument, Douglass echoed the argument of Justice Story's *Commentaries* on the same point:

> [T]he text was adopted by the people in its obvious, and general sense. We have no means of knowing, that any particular gloss, short of this sense, was either contemplated, or approved by the people; and such a gloss might, though satisfactory in one state, have been the very ground of objection in another. It might have

formed a motive to reject it in one, and to adopt it in another. The sense of a part of the people has no title to be deemed the sense of the whole.[6]

In an 1860 speech in Glasgow, Scotland, Douglass repeated this argument, and advanced a different, this time a historically-based argument for the same conclusion.

> Again, it should be borne in mind that the mere text, and only the text, and not any commentaries or creeds written by those who wished to give the text a meaning apart from its plain reading, was adopted as the Constitution of the United States. It should also be borne in mind that the intentions of those who framed the Constitution, be they good or bad, for slavery or against slavery, are to be respected so far, and so far only, as we find those intentions plainly stated in the Constitution. It would be the wildest of absurdities, and lead to endless confusion and mischiefs, if, instead of looking to the written paper itself, for its meaning, it were attempted to make us search it out, in the secret motives, and dishonest intentions, of some of the men who took part in writing it. It was what they said that was adopted by the people, not what they were ashamed or afraid to say, and really omitted to say. Bear in mind, also, and the fact is an important one, that the framers of the Constitution sat with closed doors, and that this was done purposely, that nothing but the result of their labours should be seen, and that result should be judged of by the people free from any bias shown in the debates. It should be borne in mind, and the fact is still more important, that the debates in the convention that framed the Constitution, and by means of which a pro-slavery interpretation is now attempted to be forced upon that instrument, were not published till more than a quarter of a century after the presentation and adoption of the Constitution. These debates were purposely kept out of view, in order that the people should adopt, not the secret motives or unexpressed intentions of any body, but the simple text of the paper itself. Those debates form no part of the original agreement.[7]

We see a nice turn of argument here, as Douglass makes the case that it was the "original intention" of the framers (understood narrowly and according to their explicit enactments) that their "original intentions" (understood broadly) should not even be known, to say nothing about being used as a canon for the interpretation of what they wrote.

It is important to note that Douglass advanced two quite distinct arguments against the expansive understanding of "original intent" here. The first argument, the one that Douglass shared with Justice Story, is an argument based on rational politics. An expansive understanding of "original intent" leads invariably in the direction of political incoherence, as different people and groups involved in the framing and adoption of the Constitution presumably held different, and even incompatible intentions about what kind of social order they might have wished to see develop out of the Constitution.

The second argument, by contrast, is purely a historical argument. It looks at what the historical record indicates about the wishes of those who participated in the original drafting of the Constitution, and concludes that they wished to have the Constitution understood apart from any indication of their broader views and disputes on the shape of society. While the first argument is far more fundamental to Douglass's own views on jurisprudence, the second is certainly a beautiful rhetorical response to a legal community in which the historical wishes of the founders of the past had replaced considerations of rational politics as a canon of constitutional interpretation.

Douglass's rejection of an expansive understanding of constitutional "original intention" in favor of a narrower understanding by which the "original intention" of the Constitution was limited to the Constitution's own declaration of its intentions did, of course, raise its own set of problems. The Constitution's own declaration of intentions, the "Preamble," is filled with extremely general language. How is this language to be understood with sufficient precision to serve as a canon of interpretation? The answer to this question carries us into the dispute over whether the law is a creature only of will or of reason as well.

As what I have said above might suggest, the dispute between Douglass, Spooner, et al., on the one hand, and Garrison, the Taney Court, at al., on the other, falls along lines admirably laid out by Paul Kahn:

> The founders believed in the possibility of molding political order on the basis of political science, and more importantly, they believed that the unique meaning of the constitutional founding lay in successfully obtaining popular consent to scientifically correct political order. By the time of Dred Scott, these beliefs had essentially disappeared. The scientific element within the general understanding of the constitutional foundation had dropped out. Constitutional order, instead, came to be understood solely within the framework of consent.[8]

If, as Douglass and, as Kahn maintains, the American founders believed, there is such a thing as "scientifically correct political order," an order expressed in natural law, and if the United States Constitution can be seen as an expression of such correct political order, then the "original intent" of the Constitution can and should be viewed as the elaboration of such an order. The sources for discovering that "original intent" accordingly should be seen as those places in which we find the founders attempting to set out those "scientifically correct" principles of political order.

By contrast, if, as Chief Justice Taney and such modern-day "intentionalists" as Judge Bork maintain, there is no such thing as "scientifically correct political order," if law is simply the brute will of the lawgiver, then it becomes appropriate to view the Constitution in light of the full range of social views held by those who were instrumental in its enactment. Accordingly, the sources for discovering the "original intent" of the Constitution, on this latter view, would expand to whatever discussions and debates may have been involved in the historical process through which the Constitution was enacted.

Douglass, Spooner, and all the other participants in the legal controversies of the first half of the nineteenth century were, of course, well aware of Noah Webster's definition of "law." "Law is a rule of civil conduct, prescribed by the supreme power of the state, commanding what its subjects are to do, and prohibiting what they are to forbear."[9] Note that Webster defined law simply in terms of the will of the "supreme power of the state." Spooner noted, quite rightly, that such a definition reduces law to mere force.[10]

By contrast with Webster's view of law, however, there was also a well-established understanding of law according to which law is a creature at least in part descended from reason. Sir William Blackstone (1723–80), in his classic eighteenth-century *Commentaries on the Laws of England*, characterized law as "a rule prescribed by the supreme power of the State commanding what is right and forbidding what is wrong."[11] According to Blackstone, and a long tradition of earlier English legal theorists, some such characterization of law followed simply from the very nature of law. Influenced by this tradition, Spooner defined "law" as, "an intelligible principle of right, necessarily resulting from the nature of man; and not an arbitrary rule, that can be established by mere will, numbers or power."[12] From this it follows that if the Constitution is genuinely to be law, it must be construed as an instrument promoting the ends announced in its "Preamble," understood in light of law's natural purpose in securing the natural rights of all people. Spooner, in fact, found additional support for this understanding of law in the United States Supreme Court's decision in *United States v. Fisher*:

> Where rights are infringed, where fundamental principles are overthrown, where the general system of law is deparated from, the legislative intention must be expressed with irresistible clearness, to induce a court of justice to suppose a design to effect such objects.[13]

In sum, if there is a way of interpreting the text of the law so as to make it consistent with the idea of law, with principles of natural justice and the natural rights of human beings, then the law must be interpreted in that manner. If there is no such way of interpreting the text of the law, then the law is, by its very nature, void. Applied to the Constitution, this meant that if there was a way of interpreting the Constitution that did not commit the Constitution to the support of slavery, which even most of the supporters of the legality of slavery agreed was contrary to the demands of natural justice, then the anti-union and antipolitical commitments of the Garrisonians would not follow.

In Douglass's own view, it was clear that there were ample resources in the Constitution to warrant an antislavery reading of that document. In a speech on the Dred Scott decision, Douglass identified those resources with admirable clarity:

> I base my sense of the certain overthrow of slavery, in part, upon the nature of the American Government, the Constitution, the tendencies of the age, and the character of the American people; and this, notwithstanding the important decision of Judge Taney. I know of no soil better adapted to the growth of reform than American soil. I know of no country where the conditions for affecting great changes in the settled order of things, for the development of right ideas of liberty and humanity, are more favorable than here in these United States. The very groundwork of this government is a good repository of Christian civilization. The Constitution, as well as the Declaration of Independence, and the sentiments of the founders of the Republic, give us a platform broad enough, and strong enough, to support the most comprehensive plans for the freedom and elevation of all the people of this country, without regard to color, class, or clime.[14]

Note that Douglass identifies three sources here that might be taken to help supply the principles of "scientifically correct political order:" the

Constitution, the Declaration of Independence, and the sentiments of the founders.

In Douglass's view of constitutional interpretation, perhaps the most basic canon of interpretation is internal consistency. This, I take it, is the most minimal condition of natural law. While advocates of natural law over the course of history, from St Thomas Aquinas, to John Locke, to contemporary jurisprudential theorists like Lon Fuller and Ronald Dworkin would disagree over many alleged implications of natural law, they would one and all agree that two components of a legal system that contradict one another cannot both carry the force of genuine law. As Douglass pointed out:

> To suppose that one portion of this instrument sanctions Slavery, and another sanctions liberty, is to array the Constitution in conflict with itself. And this brings us to the consideration of another rule of interpretation, which is, that one part of an instrument must not be allowed to contradict another unless the language be so explicit as to make the contradiction inevitable.[15]

It was, of course, important to Douglass that the Constitution never mentions slavery explicitly. Neither the word, 'slave', nor the word 'slavery' ever appears in the text of the Constitution. The so-called "Fugitive Slave Clause" and the infamous "3/5 Clause" are both written in such a manner as to carefully avoid any explicit mention of slaves or slavery. Because of this, the literal text of the Constitution is open to interpretation in the light of its self-proclaimed intentions in the Preamble. Douglass appealed to the intentions stated in the Preamble frequently. The following is typical of these appeals:

> Much has been said concerning the limited powers of the Federal Government; but certainly these powers are not so limited as to prevent it from performing what it is expressly required to perform. We must ever remember that if the Constitution calls upon the Federal Government, to "secure the blessings of Liberty" – "to establish justice" – "insure domestic tranquility" – "provide for the common defense," and "promote the general welfare," and the powers of the General Government are too limited to "interfere" with a "State Institution," which is a fruitful source of all manner of Despotism, of injustice, of wars, &c., &c., then the State Governments *virtually abolish the General Government*, as their powers are supreme, and the General Government *is a nullity*. [Douglass's emphases][16]

Douglass argued often and powerfully that the Preamble's expression of the intention to "secure the blessings of liberty," and to "promote the general welfare," force us to interpret the Constitution as a document intended to do precisely those things; and that the lack of any explicit mention of slaves or slavery permits us to see the institution of slavery as contrary to expressed constitutional purposes.

Again, in his use of the Preamble as a guide to the intent of the Constitution, Douglass was far from being a radical innovator. Rather he again drew on well-established principles of interpretation. Again I cite Justice Story's *Commentaries*:

> The importance of examining the preamble, for the purpose of expounding the language of a statute, has been long felt, and universally conceded in all juridical discussions. It is an admitted maxim in the ordinary course of the administration of justice, that the preamble of a statute is a key to open the minds of the makers, as to the mischiefs, which are to be remedied, and the objects, which are to be accomplished by the provisions of the statute . . . There does not seem any reason why, in a fundamental law or constitution of government, an equal attention should not be given to the intention of the framers, as stated in the preamble. And accordingly we find, that it has been constantly referred to by statesmen and jurists to aid them in the exposition of its provisions.[17]

Douglass also appealed to the Declaration of Independence as an expression both of the natural rights of human beings and of the commitment of the founders to establish government on the basis of a commitment to those rights:

> Your fathers have said that man's right to liberty is self-evident. There is no need of argument to make it clear. The voices of nature, of conscience, of reason, and of revelation, proclaim it as the right of all rights, the foundation of all trust, and of all responsibility. Man was born with it. It was his before he comprehended it.[18]

This kind of appeal to the Declaration of Independence illustrates an important difference between the constitutional thought of Douglass and that of Justice Story. I noted earlier that Douglass's understanding of the Constitution was guided by a commitment to a rationally correct view of political order, the principles of which constituted a natural law.

While Justice Story both lectured and wrote on natural law as a professor at Harvard University, Story adhered to a rational enterprise of constitutional interpretation that was substantially independent of rational politics.[19] Story's understanding of constitutional interpretation was limited to an elaboration of text, where Douglass saw the text itself as an expression of rational political order. To the extent that the Declaration of Independence, as well as other founding documents, served to elaborate that vision of rational political order, those documents became suitable tools in the task of clarifying the intent of the Constitution.

Finally, Douglass's third level of appeal was to the intentions of the founders, arguing that in their most general intentions these founders were committed to the natural rights of all people in ways denied by both Garrison and Chief Justice Taney. In his speech on the Dred Scott decision, for example, Douglass quoted George Washington, himself a slave-owner:

> There is not a man living, who wishes more sincerely than I do, to see some plan adopted for the abolition of slavery; but there is only one proper and effectual mode by which it can be accomplished, and that is by Legislative authority; and this, as far as my suffrage will go, shall not be wanting.[20]

In speaking of the three sources noted above – the intentions of the Constitution as stated in the Preamble, the Declaration of Independence, and the sentiments of the founders – Douglass was working at two different hermeneutical levels. Clearly only the "Preamble" to the Constitution was actually adopted by the people as a part of the Constitution. As an interpretive vehicle, therefore, it clearly had a primacy that the other two sources lacked. At the same time, however, there are two important facts about the Preamble. First, the Preamble is written in highly general language. It has a vagueness about it that simply requires additional interpretation. At the same time, the Preamble's reference to such political ideals as liberty, justice, and the general welfare, point to a vision of a well and rationally ordered society. The notion of law as pure fiat or will is surely foreign to the expression of ideals given in the Preamble. To this extent, then, the Preamble points to a vision of rational political order. Such a vision must be sought to resolve the obviously open-textured language of the Preamble. It was the need to elaborate that vision that carried Douglass to the second hermeneutical level that included the Declaration of Independence and "the sentiments of the founders of the Republic."

As well as playing a role in Douglass's view of constitutional interpretation, helping to provide keys to the genuine intentions expressed in the Constitution of the United States, the Declaration of Independence and "the sentiments of the founders" played a valuable rhetorical role in Douglass's work to end slavery in America. Beyond their role in constitutional interpretation, Douglass appealed to those sources to show that the American tradition of government rests on a commitment to natural rights, and that his use of a doctrine of natural law and natural rights as a vehicle for constitutional interpretation was fully consonant with those American traditions. In the battle between a will-centered understanding of law and a reason-based understanding of law, Douglass wanted to maintain that the intentions of the founders, at their most basic level, were that law be understood not as brute will, but that it be understood as protecting something of the basic nature of humanity, a vision of "scientifically correct political order." In short, it was Douglass, not Taney, who was being most faithful to the intentions on which American government was founded. It allowed Douglass to claim that he was not only correct in his disagreement with the Garrisonians and the supporters of the Taney Court as to interpretation of the Constitution, but that he was truer to American traditions as well.

There is a final, and somewhat different role that natural law plays in Frederick Douglass's views on the issue of slavery. Douglass and Spooner were both very explicit in viewing natural law as a law that is rooted in the nature of things. As a result, insofar as the institution of slavery is contrary to the natural order of things, there is a natural tendency of history in the direction of its extinction. Slavery can have no place in a "scientifically correct political order." Douglass traced out what he saw as the direction in which history was moving and, in fact, had to move in his Dred Scott speech:

> Loud and exultingly have we been told that the slavery question is settled, and settled forever. You remember it was settled thirty-seven years ago, when Missouri was admitted into the Union with a slave-holding constitution, and slavery prohibited in all territory north of thirty-six degrees of north latitude. Just fifteen years afterwards, it was settled again by voting down the right of petition, and gagging down free discussion in Congress. Ten years after this it was settled again by the annexation of Texas, and with it the war with Mexico. In 1850 it was again settled. This was called the final settlement. By it slavery was virtually declared to be the equal of Liberty, and should come into the Union on the same terms. By it the right and the power to hunt down men, women, and children,

in every part of this country, was conceded to our southern brethren, in order to keep them in the Union. Four years after this settlement, the whole question was once more settled, and settled by a settlement which unsettled all the former settlements. The fact is, the more the question has been settled, the more it has needed settling. The space between the different settlements has been strikingly on the decrease. The first stood longer than any of its successors. There is a lesson in the decreasing spaces. The first stood fifteen years – the second, ten years – the third, five years – the fourth stood four years – and the fifth has stood the brief space of two years. This last settlement must be called the Taney settlement. We are now told, in tones of lofty exultation, that the day is lost – all lost – and that we might as well give up the struggle . . . If it were at all likely that the people of these free States would tamely submit to this demoniacal judgment, I might feel gloomy and sad over it, and possibly it might be necessary for my people to look for a home in some other country. But as things stand, we have nothing to fear.[21]

This last argument of Douglass is, of course, an historical and not a constitutional argument. Douglass believed that there is a natural law. He believed this because he believed that there is a natural moral order to the universe. The existence of such a natural moral order is both a necessary and sufficient condition for the existence of a "scientifically correct political order." Thus, Douglass's understanding of the operation of natural law in history is inextricably connected with his understanding of the place of natural law in constitutional interpretation. In believing these things, he was clearly at one with John Locke, Washington, Jefferson, and a whole host of luminaries. Douglass believed that this natural moral order of the universe governs both the nature of law and the course of history. In governing the nature of law, it must play a role in any understanding we might have of law. If the Constitution of the United States is in fact genuine law, then, like any law, it must fall subject to the constraints imposed by the nature of law itself.

At the same time, the natural moral order must also be effective in history. There are certain sorts of social relationships that simply cannot coexist with certain other forms of social relationships. Douglass maintained most adamantly that slavery and liberty are forms of social life in natural opposition to each other. As such, a society which attempts to maintain a commitment to principles of liberty cannot at the same time maintain a commitment to the institution of slavery. One of the two opposites must extinguish the other.

Douglass's criticism of the view that the "original intentions" of the framers (understood broadly) must govern constitutional interpretation was based on solid, and I think decisive argumentation. Douglass maintained that the law must have at least some rudimentary basis in the nature of human moral relationships. While it may run counter to twentieth-century sensibilities to say that there is such a thing as "scientifically correct political order," that claim at bottom amounts to no more than the claim that some sets of political arrangements are objectively better than others. If you find yourself thinking that such a claim is too dogmatic for twentieth-century minds, you might consider whether you really want to maintain that a political order that includes slavery is as good as one which lacks slavery. Frederick Douglass clearly believed that slavery was objectively bad. This provided one of the underpinnings of "scientifically correct political order." It also led him to hold the correct position in the debates on constitutional interpretation in the 1850s. Moreover, the view that he defended then remains correct in the debates on constitutional interpretation in the 1990s and beyond.

Notes

1. Frederick Douglass, "The Constitution and Slavery," Philip S. Foner, ed, *Life and Writings of Frederick Douglass*, vol. *1* (New York: International Publishers, 1950), p. 353.
2. Lysander Spooner, *The Unconstitutionality of Slavery* (New York: Burt Franklin, n.d.), pp. 9–10. [first published, Boston: B. Marsh, 1845]
3. *Hewet v. Painter*, 1 Bulstrode 174, 175, 80 Eng. Rep. 864, 865, (1611); cited in H. Jefferson Powell, "The Original Understanding of Original Intent," *Harvard Law Review*, 98 (5) (March 1985), p. 894.
4. Joseph Story, *Commentaries on the Constitution of the United States*, vol. I, 3rd edition (Boston: Little, Brown and Company, 1858), p. 328. [First published, 1833.]
5. Frederick Douglass, "Is the United States Constitution for Or Against Slavery?" *Frederick Douglass' Paper*, July 24, 1851, in Foner, ed, *Life and Writings of Frederick Douglass*, vol. 5 (New York: International Publishers, 1975), p. 198.
6. Story, *Commentaries*, vol. *I*, pp. 300–1.
7. Frederick Douglass, "The Constitution of the United States: Is it Pro-Slavery or Anti-Slavery?," in Foner, ed, *Life and Writings of Frederick Douglass*, vol. *2*, (New York: International Publishers, 1950), p. 469.
8. Paul W. Kahn, "Reason and Will in the Origins of American Constitutionalism," *The Yale Law Journal*, 98 (3), January 1989, p. 450.

9 Cited in Spooner, *The Unconstitutionality of Slavery*, p. 11.
10 Spooner, *The Unconstitutionality of Slavery*, p. 12.
11 Sir William Blackstone, *Commentaries on the Laws of England*, vol. I (Philadelphia: Childs and Peterson, 1860), p. 1. [First published, 1765.] Cited in Douglass, "The Constitution of the United States: Is It Pro-Slavery or Anti-Slavery?," p. 476.
12 Spooner, *The Unconstitutionality of Slavery*, p. 1.
13 *United States v. Fischer*, 2 Cranch, 390, cited in Spooner, *The Unconstitutionality of Slavery*, pp. 18–19.
14 Douglass, "The Dred Scott Decision," speech delivered before the American Anti-Slavery Society, New York, May 11, 1857, in Foner, ed, *Life and Writings of Frederick Douglass*, vol. 2, pp. 414–15.
15 Douglass, "Slavery Unconstitutional," *Frederick Douglass' Paper*, February 1, 1856, Foner, ed, *Life and Writings of Frederick Douglass*, vol. 5, p. 376.
16 Douglass, "The Republican Party – Our Position," *Frederick Douglass' Paper*, December 7, 1855, in Foner, ed, *Life and Writings of Frederick Douglass*, vol. 2, p. 381.
17 Story, *Commentaries*, pp. 326–7.
18 Douglass, "The Dred Scott Decision," p. 411.
19 See Kahn, "Reason and Will in the Origins of American Constitutionalism," pp. 487–90.
20 Cited in Douglass, "The Dred Scott Decision," p. 423.
21 Douglass, "The Dred Scott Decision," pp. 410 and 412.

5

Whose Fourth of July? Frederick Douglass and "Original Intent"

Charles W. Mills

On July 5, 1852, Frederick Douglass delivered a speech in Rochester, New York, titled "The Meaning of July Fourth for the Negro."[1] An oratorical masterpiece, "the most famous antislavery speech Douglass ever gave,"[2] it focuses on the dualisms and (apparent) contradictions that marked the founding of the republic, and that unresolved, continue to haunt us today, a century and a half after he spoke. The central themes of Douglass's mature thought are all present: the scornful exposure of the gap between the noble ideals and the actual reality of the American polity; the insistence on black personhood and the (supposed) fact of slavery's violation of natural law morality; the corresponding appeal to his audience's moral sense; and above all the optimistic faith in the original Constitution and the original intent of the Framers as a vehicle of eventual change. As such, the speech reveals both the strengths and the weaknesses of Douglass's critique of white oppression. Read now, in a period seen by many African Americans as characterized by the betrayal of the "Second Reconstruction," in a United States still segregated by the legacy of the 1896 *Plessy v. Ferguson* decision, approaching a twenty-first century evidently as likely as the twentieth to be divided by W. E. B. DuBois's "color line," it seems simultaneously inspiring and naive. The debate between the two traditions in African-American political philosophy, assimilationism, and separatism,[3] has still not been settled, polarizing black Americans between hope and despair, the dream of national unity and the ongoing nightmare of division into two nations.[4] I want to look at some of the key assumptions of Douglass's political thought, as shown both in this speech and in his other writings, and ask what they might reveal to be problematic about the analysis of the assimilationist tradition.

I The Speech

Let me start with a synopsis of the speech itself.[5] Douglass begins by expressing his "astonishment as well as . . . gratitude" that he, a former slave, should be addressing such an audience. He notes that the Fourth of July is the birthday of national independence and political freedom, and recapitulates the history of American resistance to British tyranny. But there is something odd about the language of these opening pages whose full rhetorical significance the reader may not immediately grasp. Douglass both *identifies* himself with, and *distances* himself from, his audience, on the one hand addressing them as "fellow-citizens," on the other hand talking about "your National Independence," "your political freedom," "your fathers," and "your nation." He points out that while it is easy in retrospect to applaud the goals of the Revolution, it took courage to do so in 1776: "They who did so were accounted in their day plotters of mischief, agitators and rebels, dangerous men. To side with the right against the wrong, with the weak against the strong, and with the oppressed against the oppressor!" He describes how the colonists "sought redress" from the home government: "They petitioned and remonstrated; they did so in a decorous, respectful, and loyal manner. Their conduct was wholly unexceptionable. This, however, did not answer the purpose. They saw themselves treated with sovereign indifference, coldness and scorn."

Nonetheless, convinced of the justice of their cause, they persevered, framing at the Continental Congress in 1776 the resolution that the united colonies should be free. Douglass praises the "fathers of this republic" for their "admiration of liberty": "They were peace men; but they preferred revolution to peaceful submission to bondage. They were quiet men; but they did not shrink from agitating against oppression. They showed forbearance; but that they knew its limits. They believed in order; but not in the order of tyranny . . . With them, justice, liberty and humanity were 'final'; not slavery and oppression." With these familiar words of praise for the Founders and the auspicious occasion of the birth of the republic, Douglass puts his audience off guard. One imagines them relaxing in their seats, concluding that they are, after all, just going to be treated to the standard encomium to American greatness.

But then there is a crucial segue. Douglass comments that "I need not enter further into the causes which led to this anniversary," since they "have never lacked for a tongue. They have all been taught in your common schools, narrated at your firesides, unfolded from your pulpits, and thundered from your legislative halls, and are as familiar to you as household words . . . Americans are remarkably familiar with all facts which make in their own favor . . . I think the American side of any question may be safely left in American hands." In recounting the official white narrative, Douglass may, if only for the duration, pretend to an honorifically colorless civic status. But the problem is that he is both a part of, and apart from, his "fellow-citizens," being a *black* American, a walking oxymoron, an unacknowledged child from the slave quarters who cannot legitimately speak of *our* white fathers. So suddenly there is a switch, and another voice begins to speak, unfolding the tale of a repudiated son that *cannot* be safely left in (white) American hands, that *has* generally lacked for an official tongue, and that involves embarrassing facts with which white Americans are not, and do not *want* to be, familiar. The significance of the earlier "fellow"/"your" split now becomes clear. "Fellow-citizens, pardon me, allow me to ask, why am I called upon to speak here to-day? What have I, or those I represent, to do with your national independence? Are the great principles of political freedom and of natural justice, embodied in that Declaration of Independence, extended to us?" And the answer is, of course, no. In a blistering passage, Douglass goes on to lambaste the hypocrisy of the divided independence:

> I am not included within the pale of this glorious anniversary! Your high independence only reveals the immeasurable distance between us. The blessings in which you, this day, rejoice, are not enjoyed in common. The rich inheritance of justice, liberty, prosperity and independence, bequeathed by your fathers, is shared by you, not by me. The sunlight that brought light and healing to you has brought stripes and death to me. This Fourth of July is *yours*, not *mine*. *You* may rejoice, *I* must mourn.

The illusory inclusiveness of abstract colorless "citizens" is thus thrown off, and Douglass unequivocally adopts what, in a contemporary vocabulary, would be called the "epistemological standpoint" of race – "I shall see this day and its popular characteristics from the slave's point of view." And from this demystificatory perspective, the proceedings are revealed as a fraud – "What, to the American slave, is your 4th of July? I answer; a day that reveals to him, more than all other days in the year, the gross injustice and cruelty to which he is the constant victim. To him, your celebration is a sham; your boasted liberty, an unholy license; your national greatness, swelling vanity; your sounds of rejoicing are empty and heartless; your denunciation of tyrants, brass fronted impudence; your shouts of liberty and equality, hollow mockery; your prayers and hymns, your sermons and thanksgivings, with all your religious parade and solemnity, are, to him, mere bombast, fraud, deception, impiety, and hypocrisy." The conceptual inversion, the rhetorical turning of the tables on the audience, is therefore complete. Douglass, the former slave meant for illiteracy, the piece of "speaking property" meant to speak only when spoken to, has learned (dangerously) well from his oratorical models – Caleb Bingham's 1797 *The Columbian Orator*, *The Bible*, the Enlightenment rhetoric of Locke and the Founding Fathers, the cadences of William Lloyd Garrison and Daniel Webster, the "antithetical prose style" of eighteenth-century England.[6] Moreover, it is not merely a matter of style and oratorical flourishes, but of calculated dialogical "techniques of reversal," whose conceptual purpose is to "subvert the official monologic discourse of the dominant class" through simultaneously employing and *reversing* its categories.[7] The painful but epistemically privileged bifocal black vision that DuBois would later term "double-consciousness" is seeking to educate a myopic white vision to the injustice of the split tiers, slave and free, of Lincoln's "house divided." Douglass is trying to remove the moral scales from the white eye. His initial description of the heroic struggles of the colonists in the previous century against oppression and for freedom has been carefully designed so as to be equally applicable to the abolitionist cause of his own century, so that white Americans must, on pain of inconsistency, applaud the latter as heartily as the former. He wants to put his audience in a moral and conceptual bind, by which they are forced to acknowledge that one cause is no less noble than the other. The points made about the commitment of the Founding Fathers to justice, liberty, and humanity; the description of their patient attempts to achieve a peaceful solution, but, failing this, to call for revolution; the praise of their courage and adherence to principle; the reminder that what comes to be seen as morally right may once have seemed morally controversial; can all be applied equally well to the abolitionists in their struggle against slavery. So if one believes in "natural justice," if one agrees with Locke that "man is entitled to liberty" and "that he is the rightful owner of his own body," then – since blacks are equally "men" who should be self-owning – there must be an end to the "dividing" and "subdividing" of the "discourse" of liberty that the countenancing of slavery requires. It is a call for universalization in the classic humanist tradition, for an end to the color-coding of moral principles and the pattern of "national inconsistencies": "The existence of slavery in this country brands your republicanism as a sham, your humanity as a base pretense, and your Christianity as a lie."

Finally, and crucially, Douglass claims that this universalization is one to which the Framers themselves were committed. It is important to appreciate that the irony and doubleness of his account were never meant to be targeted against the "Fathers of this Republic" themselves.[8] Rather, he sees the accusation that slavery is "guaranteed and sanctioned by the Constitution of the United States" as a "base . . . slander upon their memory." "[I]nterpreted, as it ought to be interpreted, the Constitution is a glorious liberty document . . . I defy the presentation of a single pro-slavery clause in it. On the other hand, it will be found to contain principles and purposes, entirely hostile to the existence of slavery." The significance of an earlier remark – "America is false to the past, false to the present, and solemnly binds herself to be false to the future" – now emerges more clearly. For Douglass, slavery is a *betrayal* of the Revolutionary past; it is an institution "false" to original intent. Thus he concludes on a positive note, rejecting despair, "drawing encouragement from 'the Declaration of Independence,' the great principles it contains, and the genius of American Institutions." Because of what he sees as this initial commitment to universal equality, there is reason for optimism that upon these foundations a new non-racial America can and will eventually be built.

II Four Theses of Douglass's Assimilationism

I want now to turn to the examination of the background assumptions of Douglass's argument, and his resulting conclusions. To this end, I will draw not only on the speech itself but on other statements he makes elsewhere. I suggest that the following four theses (comprising what can illuminatingly be seen as two roughly-linked enthymematic arguments, [1] and [2] implying [3], [3] implying [4]) are central:

(1) Natural law is the appropriate framework for considering moral and jurisprudential issues.
(2) The "original intent" of the Framers is crucial, and this intent was antislavery and anti-white supremacy.
(3) There is, therefore, an inconsistency between the actuality and the founding principles of the American polity, which, through using moral suasion on white Americans, can be exploited by those agitating for racial equality.

(4) So grounds for optimism exist that blacks will eventually be accepted as full citizens in the American polity.

Douglass is thus a classic representative in the black American political tradition of the dominant assimilationist view.[9] Embodying "both militant protest and integrationism," he has in fact been seen as the "patriarch," the "nineteenth-century father," of the twentieth-century black civil rights movement.[10] Waldo Martin's biography characterizes his guiding assumptions as universal and egalitarian humanism, Protestant and Enlightenment optimism, reformist and idealist social meliorism, combined in a "fundamental Americanism."[11] There have always been opposing separatist currents in black political theory, from Martin Delany in the nineteenth century through Garveyism in the early twentieth century to the more recent radical nationalist groups of the 1960s and 1970s. Skeptical that blacks will ever really be accepted as equals in America, they have agreed with the negative diagnoses of nineteenth-century white colonizationists, and have historically advocated such solutions as emigration to Africa, or the formal partitioning of the US to create the "two nations" that informally already exist. But the mainstream movement, as represented by Douglass, by the NAACP, by Martin Luther King, Jr, has been integrationist.[12] The Constitution has been viewed more ambivalently than in Douglass's portrayal and few blacks today would endorse his interpretation of "original intent." But there *has* been a religious commitment to a Christian moral objectivity (if not to an articulated notion of natural law) by which black subordination is clearly wrong, and a confidence that "the genius of American institutions" contained the potential for changing America through a moral and constitutional appeal to white Americans to eradicate this "inconsistency." Douglass's integrationism, anti-emigrationism Americanism, and overt hostility in the last years of his life to the "positive evil" of "race pride," which made him insufficiently radical – a "reformist" figure, or even (remarkably) a "good nigger" – for some of the black nationalists of the 1960s and 1970s, establish him as a pre-eminent standard-bearer of the optimistic assimilationist school.[13]

The overturning of Jim Crow legislation in the 1950s and 1960s seemed to vindicate assimilationists, since it was precisely the principles in the founding documents that were being appealed to. Thurgood Marshall argued that if blacks had been enslaved, disenfranchised, and segregated by law, it was also true that they had been emancipated and had begun to win equality by law.[14] But as noted, the setbacks of the 1980s and 1990s have ushered in a more somber mood, giving a renewed credibility to the radical analysis. While there is no mass separatist movement today – where would one go? – the sentiment that would support it has revived, manifesting itself now not in emigration schemes but in a deep pessimism about the possibility of change. In a bitter recent memoir, Kenneth Clark, the black psychologist whose testimony about the harmful effects on black children of segregated education was so pivotal to the 1954 *Brown v. Board of Education* decision, and who in the 1960s derided Black Power as "a sour grapes phenomenon,"[15] looks back at his life: "I write these words in my seventy-sixth year. My beloved wife is dead and my career is nearing an end. Reluctantly, I am forced to face the likely possibility that the United States will never rid itself of racism and reach true integration. I look back and I shudder at how naive we all were in our belief in the steady progress racial minorities would make through programs of litigation and education . . . I am forced to recognize that my life has, in fact, been a series of glorious defeats."[16]

What, then, was the cause of these defeats? If the promise of *Brown* was illusory, or at least overstated, it is obviously important to understand why. To the extent that Douglass's progressivism and social optimism may be taken as emblematic of the mainstream integrationist position, investigating his own views may then be more broadly enlightening about possible weaknesses in this position. If he is wrong – if this tradition is wrong – then where exactly does the mistake lie?

III Thesis I: Natural Law as the Appropriate Theoretical Framework

Let us begin with the theoretical framework. Like most political and legal theorists of the mid nineteenth century, and like the Founding Fathers themselves, Douglass believed in natural law.[17] Natural law theory has its origins in the classical world, the nomos/physis distinction of Ancient Greece, the writings of Plato and Aristotle, and the Greek and Roman Stoics.[18] It evolves and changes over the next two millennia; Christianized by Aquinas, shifting in emphasis from natural duties to natural rights by the time of the Enlightenment. But throughout these changes, its distinctive feature remains the identification of law with morality. In the words of A. P. d'Entreves: "The relation between law and morals is the crux of all natural law theory . . . Law is an indication of what is good and evil . . . Thus the doctrine of natural law is in fact nothing but an assertion that law is a part of ethics."[19] And ethics is conceived of not merely in objectivist, but absolutist, terms: "[Natural law theorists] believed in absolute values, and they conceived of law as a means to achieve them."[20] In the Stoic philosopher Cicero's *De Republica*, for example, we find the statement that "True law is right reason in agreement with Nature; it is of universal application, unchanging and everlasting; it summons to duty by its commands, and averts from wrong-doing by its prohibitions . . . [O]ne eternal and unchangeable law will be valid for all nations and for all times."[21] Natural law is universal and unchanging, and reflects the immanent moral structure of the universe. And for the Stoics, "Human equality is the direct consequence of natural law, its first and essential tenet."[22]

The notion of natural law thus contains several distinct theses, which need to be separated: the view sometimes called moral realism, that morality is objective, so that there are moral facts independently of what moral agents actually deem to be moral; the stronger thesis of moral absolutism, that moral principles are exceptionless and eternal; the commitment to human equality as the first and foundational element of these principles; and the notion that there is a natural law embodying these principles to which human law must conform to be valid.

The reasons for Douglass embracing a natural law position should therefore be obvious, apart from the fact that it was, in any case, the dominant viewpoint of the time. The great virtue of natural law and natural rights theory, as it became in the modern period, is that it provides one with a preexisting and enduring Archimedean moral vantage-point from which to denounce actually existing human laws and practices. Its commitment to moral realism and jurisprudential denial of the validity of immoral positive law make it immensely attractive to a political dissenter opposing an immoral but institutionalized system. Might, even when legally backed, does not make right; a crime is still a crime though it may have the support of the highest court in the land.

The uncompromisingly absolutist character of natural law prohibitions precludes any appeal to contingent circumstances (for example, that retaining slavery was justified to keep the union together). Moreover, the Framers were themselves natural lawyers, and the tradition, as noted, has a weight and ideological authority that goes back through Locke and Aquinas all the way to classical civilization. So Douglass is thereby enabled to locate himself in the jurisprudential discourse central to the intellectual history of the West, appealing, in addition, to a Christianized version that his fellow-citizens and co-religionists had (theoretically) no choice but to recognize. By their own standards, his fellow white Americans, fellow Christians, were guilty of ignoring the implications of the truth that all men were created equal. Finally, there is an undeniable rhetorical grandeur to this tradition – compare Cicero with Bentham – that fits well with the pulpit, the political platform, the abolitionist speech. The eternal rights of man, the contemptible violation of God's principles, the sacredness of human freedom – these are far more inspirational and likely to set the heart pounding than the niggling plusses and minuses of the felicific calculus.

Nevertheless, it needs to be emphasized that, even given his political and moral commitments, there was no conceptual necessity for Douglass to have adopted this framework. The legal positivism initiated in Europe by Bentham and Austin was not in Douglass's America an influential presence, but there would have been no inconsistency in a political abolitionist and moral realist endorsing its competing approach. Positivism is sometimes associated with a conventionalist view of morality, but this is in fact a misrepresentation, since there are several varieties of positivism, not all of which are committed to such a position. The essential positivist thesis is simply that law and morality ought to be separated, that, as Austin originally pointed out, the task of analytical jurisprudence needs to be distinguished from the task of normative jurisprudence. The question of whether a law is valid should be disentangled from the question of whether a law is morally good.[23] So Douglass could theoretically have taken a positivist position, concede that pro-slavery legislation was *legally* valid, while still condemning it from a *moral* point of view.

Now obviously it is far easier for us, with the benefit of more than a century of intervening legal theory, to appreciate the wide range of possible positions, and their respective implications, on the relationship between morality and law. But the point is important because Douglass ends up endorsing some strange interpretations and arguments, and I think this is because he believes they follow from natural law. His train of reasoning seems to run something like this. Natural law links law to morality; natural law upholds human equality and opposes slavery; the Founders were natural lawyers; therefore the Declaration and the Constitution that the Founders wrote must also have been intended to uphold human equality and oppose slavery. So any appearance that it does not must be illusory.

What has gone wrong here? The problem is that natural law theory, with its rationalist and realist emphasis on the eternal character of natural law and its relatively slight interest in historical causes, is going to be singularly unhelpful on the *social* sources of law. As d'Entreves points out, "Natural law theorists would never have admitted that law is merely the expression of the standards of a particular group or society."[24] By contrast, the great virtue of positivism, which opens the conceptual door to more politically sophisticated and sociologically informed variants like the American legal realism of the 1920s, and the critical legal studies and critical race theory of the present,[25] is its demystified focus on actual laws and law-making, and their embeddedness in social context and power relations. Douglass understandably wants to retain the moral high ground from which to launch thunderbolts of condemnation. But one can reject the amoralist position that power determines justice, that might makes right, while still accepting the unhappy truth that power and might often determine what is legal and what is *taken* to be right. And one can concede the natural law insight that there is a relation between law and morality, between the laws people accept and the laws they see as morally right, without ignoring the fact that moral views may themselves be socio-historically determined. The points of value in naturalism can be retained in a more sophisticated contemporary framework without the implausibilities that Douglass takes to follow from natural law theory itself.

IV Thesis II: Original Intent as Anti-white Supremacy

These implausibilities emerge most clearly in his views on "original intent," views which put him sharply at odds with most contemporary African-American legal thinkers, and in the embarrassing company of, *inter alia*, Reagan's Attorney General Edwin Meese and his defeated Supreme Court nominee Judge Robert Bork.[26] Douglass saw "original intent" as crucial; he saw this intent as antislavery; and – I think it can be more generally extrapolated from what he says – he saw it as anti-white supremacy. (As will become clearer below, I think this is really the more significant question.) So I suggest there are three issues here: (1) what and whose "original intent" is important? (2) what are the different ways in which it could be important? (3) what evidence is there for this intent being antislavery, and anti-white supremacy?

(1) What is called "originalism" (and also "intentionalism," "preservatism," "historicism," and other terms) was the accepted, axiomatic model of constitutional interpretation from the birth of the republic to the New Deal in the 1930s, before it suffered an apparent demise at the hands of legal realists like Oliver Wendell Holmes. In the last quarter-century, however, it has undergone a surprising resurrection through the writings of Judges Bork and Rehnquist.[27] The simple guiding principle, which comes down from the medieval juristic tradition, is that "all legal instruments should be construed in accordance with the intent of their makers."[28] When constitutional scholars talk about "original

intent," it is usually the original intent of the Framers that they have in mind, and this is what Douglass meant also. But there are numerous ambiguities and alternative possibilities, both in the nature of the intent and in the pertinent "intending" population, that need to be taken into account (and whose breadth contributes to the *anti*-intentionalist case). Bruce Ledewitz, for example, distinguishes between "original intent" and "textual intent," and between the "general intent" of the Constitution and the "specific intent" with respect to blacks.[29] Even more complicatedly, Gregory Bassham differentiates under the category of intent "scope beliefs, counterfactual scope beliefs, semantic intentions, and constitutionalized *extratextual* intentions," and under the category of intenders "the drafters, the Framers, the ratifiers, the people of the United States, or some combination of the preceding four."[30] So there are different varieties of originalism, according to which permutation of these is chosen, and a case has to be made for one's particular choice. It is by no means a simple matter of pointing uncontroversially to an unequivocal statement made by a unanimously designated speaker.

Because of these and other problems, anti-originalists argue that the search for "original intent" is pointless. For example, Cass Sunstein suggests that the notion of a pristine, apolitical, uninterpreted text, which we can recover through the sanding away of the accumulated layers of subsequent readings and reviews, is a myth. "Constitutional interpretation inevitably requires us to use principles external to the Constitution. There is no such thing as interpretation without interpretive principles, and these cannot be found in the Constitution."[31] The words actually written down obviously exercise some semantic constraint, but the text is not foundational, since its meaning will be partially given through the shifting readings, the evolving consensual (or hegemonic) conceptual frameworks, and the changing and unchanging value commitments of the interpreters. Unlike conventionalists or deconstructionists, however, who would infer from this indeterminacy that meaning is *completely* open-ended, determined simply by power or whim, Sunstein insists that rational criteria in legal argument can still be reconstructed. I would agree with this, but my claim would be that this rationality is a *raced* rationality that reflects the normative structure of the actual polity, a structure that Douglass denies. And once one recognizes this, it becomes clear that the "original intent" of the official white citizenry, or the reading of that intent by the Supreme Court, may be just as important as, or more important than, the Framers' own views.

(2) My meaning will become clearer if we ask why "original intent" should be seen as important in the first place. I suggest that there are

two basic (but not mutually exclusive) alternatives: (i) original intent is important simply as a *normative* foundation (moral/juridical) for evaluating the character of the polity, and/or (ii) original intent is important as part of a larger *descriptive* causal story ("idealist" or "materialist") about the evolution of the character of the polity.

(i) The first claim is that original intent should be the normative reference point for adjudication of possible changes in the polity. In the Western Enlightenment tradition, the ideal liberal state is the *Rechtsstaat*, the morally and juridically bound state, committed to protecting the rights and liberties of its citizens. The Constitution then sets the moral tone, acting as a normative beacon, making a statement about what the polity essentially should be. The presumption is, of course, that the founding principles can in fact themselves be given an independent moral justification. But this may not necessarily be the case. Note, then, what should be the obvious point that a moral objectivist should not automatically feel bound by original intent even if it can be unambiguously determined, since if original intent was unjust to begin with, the mere fact that it becomes constitutionally enshrined does not make it any the less wrong. Douglass reads original intent as antislavery and anti-white supremacy, and on this basis seeks to indict his fellow-citizens and the government itself for straying from its prescriptions. But if original intent is actually pro-slavery and pro-white supremacy, then his appropriate response as a natural lawyer, and thus a moral objectivist, should have been to condemn it. Original intent should not in that case be what is normatively most important for him, or for us.

(ii) The second claim needs to be clearly differentiated from the first, since it is a *causal* claim about social dynamics. Original intent is seen as important in the historical evolution of the polity, not just as a basis for evaluating it. The contrast standardly invoked in socio-historical theorizing is between "idealist" theories of history, that take ideas and moral values to be decisive in determining social evolution, and "materialist" theories, according to which the causal hierarchies run the other way, so that group interests and power politics are more important. (It is, of course, also possible to see them as equally significant, or as so intertwined that the categories become inapplicable.) Suppose there really were an original intent for the creation of a colorblind America. If it is true that moral motivation generally overrides countervailing group interests, or (not always the same thing) perceived group interests, then campaigns of moral suasion appealing to this original intent will be able to bring about radical changes, despite a preponderance of vested material interests in the established racial order.

On the contrasting materialist view, of course, this will not be the case. A plausible materialist theory will not consign morality to the epiphenomenal (that is, zero causal efficaciousness), but it will make it secondary, subordinate to (perceived) group interests, so that when they come into conflict, it is the latter that are likely to triumph. Note that this position by no means commits one to amoralism, though it is sometimes interpreted that way. Rather, it is simply pointing out that the issue of the objectivity of moral judgments needs to be separated from the issue of the social efficaciousness of moral motivation. One can judge a society to be oppressive without also believing that the fact of this oppressiveness will itself lead to social change. Nor, of course, does sociological materialism imply (what a glance at world history would show to be clearly false) that moral progress is impossible. Oppressed groups seeking to advance their own interests may become strong enough to force change; technological progress and socioeconomic shifts may alter the cost/benefit balance sheet of an unjust social order; and, as noted, moral motivation may play a real, if secondary, role. The claim is simply that such progress will not for the most part be the result of a self-contained moral dynamic. In this framework, the character of the Framers' original intent will itself be shaped by the imprinting of group interests on dominant moral conceptions. Its significance will then inhere less in its putative role as a detached and independent moral vector lifted above the political fray, than in its epistemic role as an indicator of the balance of underlying social forces.

(3) With that said, let us now turn to Douglass's claims about what original intent actually was. It needs to be emphasized, to begin with, that the mature position articulated in his July 5, 1852 speech, which he promulgated for the rest of his life, was by no means his original view, but reflects a famous *reversal* of his previous position. Previously he had endorsed the orthodox view of the William Lloyd Garrison abolitionists that the Constitution was a "pro-slavery document," a "compromise with tyranny." The masthead of Garrison's abolitionist weekly, the *Liberator*, bore the resolution "Resolved, That the Compact which exists between the North and the South is a 'covenant with Death, and an agreement with hell,' – involving both parties in atrocious criminality, – and should be immediately annulled."[32] As late as 1851, Douglass is still agreeing that the slaveholders "are doubtless right so far as the intentions of the framers of the Constitution are concerned," though wondering "may we avail ourselves of legal rules which enable us to defeat even the wicked intentions of our Constitution makers . . . Is it good morality to take advantage of a legal flaw and put a meaning upon

a legal instrument the very opposite of what we have good reason to believe was the intention of the men who framed it?"[33]

This *strategic* use of the Constitution would have brought him closer to twentieth-century African-American legal activism, where the question of original intent is subordinated to the notion of a living and evolving document whose meaning alters over time. Thus one author points out that to the extent that racial progress has been made, it has been "because of fundamental changes in the *interpretation* and implementation of that Constitution."[34] Or in the blunt words of Thurgood Marshall: "'We the People' no longer enslaved, but the credit does not belong to the framers. It belongs to those who refused to acquiesce in outdated notions of 'liberty,' 'justice,' and 'equality,' and who strived to better them."[35]

But Douglass came to disagree, bringing upon himself the fury of the Garrisonians, as well as the puzzlement of some later generations. What are his arguments? Over the next few years, he would give several different considerations as decisive. In his "change of opinion" statement itself, he cited a "careful study of the writings of Lysander Spooner, of Gerrit Smith, and of William Goodell" as having brought him to this conclusion.[36] In the July Fourth speech, as earlier noted, he argues that "the Constitution is a glorious liberty document," that he "[denies] the presentation of a single pro-slavery clause in it," indeed "neither slavery, slaveholding, nor slave can anywhere be found in it."[37] In a July 1853 address, he says that the word "citizen" is unqualified by the word "white": "The word 'white' was unknown to the framers of the Constitution of the United States in such connections . . . It is a modern word, brought into use by modern legislators, despised in revolutionary times."[38] Similarly, he would later claim that the "constitution knows no man by the color of his skin. The men who made it were too noble for any such limitation of humanity and human rights. The word white is a modern term in the legislation of this country. It was never used in the better days of the Republic, but has sprung up within the period of our national degeneracy."[39] In a later speech, he argues that the Constitution must recognize slaves either as persons or as beasts of burden – "It cannot regard them as men and regard them as things at the same time" – and repeats that there is not a "word, sentence or syllable" about slavery in the Constitution.[40] Replying to the 1857 *Dred Scott* decision, he insists that the "well known rules of legal interpretation" bear him out in the fact that slavery is not formally recognized, reiterates the natural law position that "Law is in its nature opposed to wrong, and must everywhere be presumed to be in favor of the right," and rejects the interpretation of Chief Justice Roger Taney as "discrediting and casting away as worthless the most beneficent rules of legal interpretation; by disregarding the plain and common sense reading of the instrument itself; by showing that the Constitution does not mean what it says, and says what it does not mean."[41]

So Douglass's evidence involves several claims: (1) there is no explicit reference in the Constitution to slaves and slavery; (2) there is no explicit distinction in the Constitution between blacks and whites – indeed such a distinction is a modern one; (3) it would be contradictory both to recognize black manhood ("personhood" for us) and relegate blacks to the status of property, since they must either be men or things, but cannot be both; (4) law must be morally right, so the Framers as natural lawyers could not have intended something clearly wrong.

Now it should be obvious that these claims are at best problematic, and at worst obviously false. Consider, to begin with, points (1) and (2). Constitutional scholars such as William Wiecek have pointed out that there was a deliberate decision on the part of the Framers to use circuitous and euphemistic language so as to avoid formal reference to slavery, but that in practice everybody knew what was being talked about. This was recognized at the time by anti-Federalist critics such as "Brutus," who in his "Essay #3" comments sarcastically on the "strange and unnecessary accumulation of words" being used "to conceal from the public eye" what could be expressed more concisely.[42] As Wiecek puts it: "To evade introducing the words 'slave' or 'slavery' into the document, they chose ambiguous and inelegant phrases that clouded their meaning . . . Repeatedly in the ratifying conventions they stated that 'in plain English' the euphemisms referred to slaves . . . Why then the muddy language if everyone knew what was meant? . . . [One contemporary commentator] explained that the framers avoided 'expressions which might be odious in the ears of Americans, although they were willing to admit into their system those things which the expressions signified.' "[43]

In fact, "the Philadelphia Convention inserted no less than ten clauses in the Constitution that directly or indirectly accommodated the peculiar institution." Wiecek cites the following: Article I, section 2: the three-fifths clause; Article I, section 2 and Article I, section 9: taxation on this basis; Article I, section 9: prohibition till 1808 of abolition of the international slave trade to the US; Article IV, section 2: fugitive slaves; Article I, section 8: states' militias to suppress insurrections, including slave uprisings; Article IV, section 4: Federal protection against domestic violence, again including slave uprisings; Article V: insulation of certain clauses involving slavery; Article I, section 9 and Article I, section 10: prohibition of indirect taxation of slavery.[44] So though slaves and slavery are not referred to directly, there were expressions which everybody knew had that denotation. A ready parallel can be discerned here with the emergence in recent decades of many terms in white American public discourse – "law and order," the "underclass," "welfare queens" – that are essentially coded references to blacks and black-related problems. What needs to be appreciated, obviously, is that such racial cryptography goes back a long way, indeed all the way to the founding of the republic.

Similarly, the fact that the Declaration refers to "all men" does not prove that the implicit reference was not exclusively to white men, nor is it remotely true that "white" is a modern "degenerate" term previously unemployed. Judge A. Leon Higginbotham, Jr, has demonstrated that from the mid-seventeenth century onwards, a pattern began to develop throughout the colonial period of formally distinguishing juridically between blacks and whites, with correspondingly differentiated rights and criminal penalties.[45] And in 1790, certainly squarely within the Revolutionary period, Congress made whiteness a prerequisite for naturalization, which could hardly be a clearer statement of the connection in the legislators' minds between race and civic virtue.[46]

So what Douglass says here is quite wrong, and seems to rely on a naive textual formalism (what the text says) that ignores the standard principles of *interpretation* of the text that would have obtained at the time, and which would have given it its actual contextual meaning. But the very banality of these rejoinders, the obviously dubious character of Douglass's claims, raised the question of whether something more interesting might not be going on, especially since in an earlier (1849) article he had pointed out some of these clauses himself (identified at the time by the abolitionist Wendell Phillips), and commented on how "cunning" the Constitution's framing was.[47]

One possible solution would be the "masking," the calculated two-facedness, that is part of the subversive strategy of the slave in dealing with white power.[48] Thus in Paul Laurence Dunbar's famous poem: "We wear the mask that grins and lies/It hides our cheeks and shades our eyes/This debt we pay to human guile."[49] On this reading, Douglass would be perfectly well aware that the Constitution sanctioned slavery, but consciously decided to adopt the straightfaced/blackfaced literal-mindedness that, with a sophisticated "naiveté," refused to see any exclusionary racial subtext in its moral guarantees, thereby enabling him to ask, in deadpan puzzlement, what had happened – if indeed all men were created equal – to the rights of black citizens. ("But Massa, dis-here paper says I'se created equal . . .?!") The 1851 quote cited above would point in this direction, the instrumentalist deployment of a document one realized actually had quite different goals. But Douglass's anti-Garrisonian conversion, his impassioned defense of original intent in the 1852 "July Fourth" speech and elsewhere, seem completely genuine. Whatever he is doing, he is not playing a part. A more straightforward answer might simply be, then, that his growing opposition to Garrisonian principles – nonresistance, political quietism, exclusive reliance on moral suasion, and disunionism ("Come-outism": the demand to dissolve the union with the slaveholders) – led him to repudiate the analysis of the Constitution he associated with the upholders *of* these principles.[50] This would by no means be a matter of logical necessity, since in fact the connection between principles and analysis is very loose indeed, and certainly twentieth-century black activists, as indicated, have had no difficulty in combining political militance with a rejection of original intent. But there are situational as well as formal logics, and given the existing politico-ideological positions of the time, this may have seemed the best strategic choice. If one is already because of race and abolitionist conviction outside the pale of respectability, why add to one's moral blackness by seeming to oppose the Constitution as well? Yet, though I think there is something to this, Douglass's insistence goes beyond a pragmatic adjustment to political realities. It seems to me that there is a genuine puzzle here, whose elucidation is useful not merely for understanding Douglass (as indicated, his idiosyncratic interpretation is not itself a black mainstream position), but, more interestingly, for the light it sheds on the general assumptions of the integrationist view. I think that to understand his misrepresentation of the factual record, and the seeming bizarreness of his arguments, we need to see Douglass as having been captured by a genuine insight that, given the available conceptual frameworks and the scholarship of the time (or the present – see the discussion below), led him in dubious directions, making him distort the facts to fit the theory. We need to focus on the significance of points (3) and (4): that recognizing blacks as both men and property would have been a contradiction, and that the Founders as natural lawyers could not have intended something wrong. And these, I will suggest, are of broader significance because of what they say about the conceptual apparatus of liberalism and its blocking from sight of certain embarrassing historical truths.

V Thesis III: The "Contradiction" of Black Subordination

The notion (sometimes dubbed the "anomaly thesis")[51] that there is a "contradiction," an "inconsistency," an "anomaly," in the founding ideals of the republic has been widespread, and has historically been the occasion of much irony from critics both black and white. Samuel Johnson asked, "how is it that we hear the loudest yelps for liberty among the drivers of negroes," and Abigail Adams wrote to her husband John that "it always appeared a most iniquitous scheme to me to fight ourselves for what we are daily robbing and plundering from those who have as good a right to freedom as we have."[52] The claim has also been central to the optimistic integrationist case. Douglass himself speaks, as we have seen, about the "national inconsistencies" in American practices. A hundred years later, the idea would be at the heart of the single most influential study of race in America, Gunnar Myrdal's *An American Dilemma*, whose introduction describes the status of blacks as "an anomaly in the very structure of American society," and glosses the eponymous dilemma as the "ever-raging conflict" in the white citizenry between the general evaluations of the American Creed and the specific evaluations with respect to blacks.[53] Since eliminating inconsistencies is a basic prerequisite for rational discourse, it has therefore not seemed unreasonable for social reformers to expect that the demands both of rationality and morality will converge on the elimination of racism.

But what exactly is the putative inconsistency? It is supposedly centered on Jefferson's famous proclamation in the opening paragraph of the Declaration of Independence that "We hold these truths to be self-evident, that all men are created equal, that they are endowed by their Creator with certain unalienable Rights." Since this statement is standardly taken to govern the provisions of the Constitution also, there is an apparent tension between the Declaration and the latter's (coded) acceptance of the enslavement of some men. Note, however, that because of his views on original intent, *Douglass's* version of the inconsistency is actually significantly different from what most black intellectuals would believe today. Douglass reads "all men" in the *inclusivist* colorblind sense, so that what is involved is an inconsistency between the Framers' original intent, as revealed both in the Declaration and the Constitution, and the institution of slavery. His apparent train of reasoning here has been sketched earlier: natural law is committed to moral law, and universal human equality is the central principle of morality, so the Framers, as natural lawyers, would not have countenanced any violation of this principle. By contrast, most black intellectuals today, more cynical, would read "all men" in the *exclusivist* color-coded sense, so that what is involved is an inconsistency between the Framers' original intent and the moral facts of black personhood. Nevertheless, I will try to show that understanding the logic that leads to Douglass's position can still be more broadly illuminating.

The divergence between the two possible interpretations of the Declaration, inclusivist and exclusivist, was historically most clearly articulated in the notorious 1857 *Dred Scott v. Sanford* Supreme Court decision of Chief Justice Roger Taney.[54] Dred Scott was a slave who petitioned for his freedom on the basis of his residence on free soil (Missouri). Taney denied it on the grounds that the scope of the Declaration manifestly did *not* extend to blacks, who in the Revolutionary period were seen as an inferior race not part of the citizenry. His reasons are worth citing at length:

> It is difficult at this day to realize the state of public opinion in relation to that unfortunate race, which prevailed in the civilized and enlightened portions of the world at the time of the Declaration of Independence, and when the Constitution of the United States was formed and adopted. But the public history of every European nation displays it in a manner too plain to be mistaken.
>
> They had for more than a century before been regarded as beings of an inferior order, and altogether unfit to associate with the white race, either in social or political relations; and so far inferior, that they had no rights which the white man was bound to respect; and that the negro might justly and lawfully be reduced to slavery for his benefit. He was bought and sold, and treated as an ordinary article of merchandise and traffic, whenever a profit could be made by it. This opinion was at that time fixed and universal in the civilized portion of the white race. It was regarded as an axiom in morals as well as in politics, which no one thought of disputing, or supposed to be open to dispute . . .
>
> [I]f the language, as understood in that day, would embrace them, the conduct of the distinguished men who framed the Declaration of Independence would have been utterly and flagrantly inconsistent with the principles they asserted . . .
>
> Yet the men who framed this declaration were great men – high in literary acquirements – high in their sense of honor, and incapable of asserting principles inconsistent with those on which they were acting. They perfectly understood the meaning of the

language they used, and how it would be understood by others; and they knew that it would not in any part of the civilized world be supposed to embrace the negro race, which, by common consent, had been excluded from civilized Governments and the family of nations, and doomed to slavery.[55]

Douglass was outraged at the Taney decision, seeing it as a violation of the natural law commitment to human equality (and a slander on the Framers): "The Supreme Court of the United States is not the only power in this world. It is very great, but the Supreme Court of the Almighty is greater. Judge Taney can do many things, but he cannot perform impossibilities . . . He may decide, and decide again; but he cannot reverse the decision of the Most High. He cannot change the essential nature of things – making evil good, and good evil. Happily for the whole human family, their rights have been defined, declared, and decided in a court higher than the Supreme Court . . . Man was born with [the right to liberty] . . . To decide against this right in the person of Dred Scott, or the humblest and most whip-scarred bondman in the land, is to decide against God. It is an open rebellion against God's government. It is an attempt to undo what God has done, to blot out the broad distinction instituted by the *Allwise* between men and things."[56] And in an 1861 article, he asserts that: "By that law [of natural justice], universal, 'unchangeable and eternal,' every man is the rightful owner of his own body, and to dispossess him of this right, is, and can only be, among the highest crimes which can be committed against human nature. The only foundation for slavery is positive law against natural law."[57]

Now the interesting issue for us here is not, of course, whether Taney was morally wrong, but whether his assessment of white opinion of the time, and the Framers' moral perceptions, is factually right. For Taney, the seeming inconsistency between Declaration and Constitution is eliminated through reading "all men" exclusively, as white, and committing the Framers to slavery and white supremacy; for Douglass, it is eliminated through reading "all men" inclusively, as colorblind, and committing the Framers to antislavery and anti-white supremacy. Both men rely on the premise of the honorable moral character of the Framers, but come to different conclusions. For Douglass, Taney's assessment of Revolutionary white opinion is factually wrong, and in any case irrelevant since the Framers' moral natural law commitments would *a priori* have precluded their endorsing the obvious immorality of depriving self-owning men of their liberty and treating them as things. Only "positive law" and conventionalist morality could permit this.

Douglass's position here is convergent with contemporary conservative constitutional scholar Harry Jaffa, also a natural law theorist and a believer in original intent.[58] So I am going to use Jaffa's more developed argument to explicate Douglass's views, since the *Dred Scott* decision is a crucial reference point for both men. In my opinion, they both misrepresent Taney, a misrepresentation enlightening for what it says about the restricted set of theoretical options they consider. Like Douglass, Jaffa sees the Founders as natural lawyers for whom blacks must "obviously" be men. Unlike Douglass, however, Jaffa does not deny that there are many clauses related to slavery in the Constitution. His is rather the most plausible version of this position: the argument that the concessions to slavery reflect a compromise with the South, a necessary evil that would eventually be eliminated, rather than a principled position resting on the restrictive interpretation of "men." He takes Taney to be endorsing a positivist thesis by which the moral status of blacks is conventionally determined. But this, he argues, is clearly wrong: "That the Negro is a human being is a matter of fact and not of opinion . . . Fundamental to the law of the Constitution was the fact of the Negro's personality – in short, his humanity . . . That the Negro belongs to the species *homo sapiens* is as undeniable as that any white (or yellow, red, or brown) individual belongs to this species. His rationality . . . is indicative of the essence of his humanity; the color of his skin, a mere accident."[59] And the Framers, he claims, would, of course, have been equally aware of this: "For Jefferson and his contemporaries, there was no question but that the differences in natures, differences inherent in the distinctions the Bible itself draws between man and beast, had implications (as in the Bible) that were no less moral than metaphysical . . . The equality of man proclaimed by the Declaration of Independence is to be understood first of all by comparison with the inequality that characterizes man's relationship with the lower orders of living beings."[60]

Jaffa therefore presents us with the following two alternatives: (1) his own interpretation of original intent as committed in the Declaration, within a natural law framework, to the morally objectivist, "obvious" truth of human equality, including black equality, and a constitutional compromise with the slaveowners to save the union; (2) the (alleged) Taney interpretation of original intent as committed in the Declaration, within a positivist framework, to a conventionalist moral division between the human population, whites being equal and blacks being unequal, with the pro-slavery clauses then being a reflection of the historical and conjunctural consensus on the moral status of blacks.

Douglass's dichotomization is similar, except that, as we have seen, he *denies* the existence of any pro-slavery clauses.

But, as Jaffa and Douglass both point out, we know the Framers were natural lawyers, and that natural law, from the Stoics down through the Lockean inspiration for Jefferson, is committed to human equality. It is an obvious moral and metaphysical truth that blacks are human, therefore rational, and so clearly self-owning, to be distinguished from "the lower orders of living beings." But then the Framers could *not* have had a principled position committed to white supremacy and black inferiority, and Taney's restrictive interpretation has to be a mistaken positivist one.

Now what I want to suggest is that Jaffa and Douglass are both wrong on this, and that Taney is right. For the choice is not between the mutually exhaustive alternatives of a naturalist commitment to an inclusive human equality and a positivist conventionalist moral division in the human population: this is a false dichotomization. There is a third alternative, which is that at least some (and maybe the majority) of the Framers were convinced of the *objective moral truth*, as *part* of natural law, of black inequality, so that excluding them from "all men" was principled rather than pragmatic. (For our purposes, it does not matter whether or not this naturalism was Taney's own position, rather than the positivism Jaffa and Douglass attribute to him, though I think a case for naturalism can certainly be made.) In their own eyes, these Framers would *not* then have been doing something wrong in codifying black subordination (if not necessarily slavery itself), since blacks were in fact lesser beings of a "lower order," and this had both "moral and metaphysical" implications. It was by no means merely a matter of (white) human convention and positive law.

Why do Jaffa and Douglass not consider this obvious alternative? They are both taking for granted – Jaffa with far less excuse, as a professional scholar with the advantage of a century of research to draw on – the supposed absurdity of the notion that any Enlightenment figure could ever have regarded blacks as less than human. Modernist Enlightenment liberalism operates with the (seemingly) simple category of "men," with moral egalitarianism taken as the ground floor, and no formal markers to indicate differential moral/ontological standing.[61] Blacks are obviously "men"; "men" is a univocal homogeneous term, without qualification or degree; so once it has been established that blacks are "men," all the natural law provisions must apply in full force to them also. There is supposed to be no conceptual room for the idea that if all men are equal, nonetheless some men are more equal than others. And this is what traps Douglass into concluding, against the evidence, that the Framers must have meant the term inclusively. The feminist exposure of the gender-specificity of these "men" is by now a familiar story.[62] But the facially raceless appearance of the category better conceals its *racial* specificity. Yet this claim of racial neutrality is quite false. The classic contractarians, I suggest, were really expounding a *racial* contractarianism, where racial exclusion is not a matter of contingent prejudice but part of the architecture of the theory. The modern natural law tradition that provides the normative background for liberalism evolves in a period of European encroachment upon the rest of the world, and is shaped accordingly. And the prerequisites for being a "man" in the full rational sense that entitles one to natural law protection are constructed so as to exclude non-Europeans. Thus "men" is by no means an unambiguously inclusive category, but one that is internally divided, tacitly contrasted with "savages." A conceptual space opens up in European thought for entities who are humanoid but not fully human, men who are not men – seen variously as beasts in human form, lesser humans of a different species and a different genesis, or admitted yet inferior members of the same species – but in all cases sub-persons rather than persons. *And for these beings, a different set of normative rules applies; natural law speaks differently.*

This reasoning should be less surprising once one recognizes that there is a precedent in the vaunted legacy of the ancient world. It is a familiar fact that Aristotle thought that some men were biologically destined to be natural slaves (though there were epistemic problems in identifying them), but as Anthony Pagden has pointed out, even Cicero, the egalitarian Stoic cited at the start, tied full humanity to cultural membership in the Roman Empire.[63] The modern period brings "race" into existence as the infallible epistemic marker conveniently linking inferior biology *and* inferior culture, thereby dividing the population covered by the natural law framework into persons and sub-persons. The result is that in most of the classic contractarians there is a dichotomized racial logic in the text. In the non-mainstream prudential contract of Hobbes's *Leviathan*, Native Americans are the only examples cited of the real-life, literal state of nature, Europeans by contrast being sufficiently rational to institute the absolutist sovereign necessary to avoid the bestial state of war.[64] And in the mainstream morally objectivist contract, whether Lockean or Kantian, there is a racial partitioning in different peoples' ability to perceive the prescriptions of natural law. Locke's unenlightened Native Americans are not sufficiently "industrious and rational" to appropriate and add value to the land God has given them, unlike hardworking day laborers in England;[65] so their later expropriation by European settlers is clearly justifiable. Kant, the preeminent Enlightenment theorist of personhood, is also, as has recently been revealed, the founder of the modern concept of race, and thus in a sense, fittingly, the preeminent theorist of *sub*-personhood also. He maps a natural racial hierarchy of degrees of human rationality and moral educability, in which it turns out that Native Americans are at the bottom, being completely impervious to such education, while blacks, one rung above, have innate abilities no more extensive than would equip them for slavery or servanthood.[66] Finally, Vattel, the natural law theorist whose work was to provide the authoritative juristic framework for international relations, explicitly endorsed the moral rightness of the civilized taking possession of "lands which the savages have no special need of and are making no present and continuous use of," thereby giving general normative backing to the process of European expansionism and settlement.[67]

So if the leading Enlightenment theorists of the age had no difficulty in racing and partitioning personhood, no embarrassment in reconciling an ostensibly general commitment to universal human equality with non-white subordination, why should the Framers have been any more conceptually discommoded? Indeed one of the ironies of Douglass's complaints about white moral blindness is the myopia arising from his own (at least partial) identification with the white West. In protesting his exclusion from full American citizenship, he fails to see that the same Jeffersonian Declaration of Independence he is citing as evidence of *his* personhood distinguishes the "men" in whose ranks he wants to be included from the "merciless Indian Savages" who are clearly relegated to a separate category. Douglass satirizes the ironies and contradictions of "white doublethink," insisting that he is part of the human community and that this country is legitimately his also, while not recognizing that to a certain extent he is practicing the same exclusionary logic as they are.[68]

Once one recognizes that such a category exists, then, the whole notion of a "contradiction"/"inconsistency"/"anomaly" becomes much fuzzier and more problematic. And this will have implications not merely for Douglass's peculiar version of the "inconsistency" (that absolves the Framers themselves), but the general claim that there is a deep "American Dilemma" over race, a cognitive dissonance between norms for blacks and whites. The assimilationist school, even when more negative about the Framers than Douglass, has generally conceptualized race within the framework of prejudice, bigotry, etc., attitudes and practices seen as a "deviation" from a raceless democratic ideal taken to be central to the European tradition. What I am suggesting by contrast is that we need to see European expansionism as rewriting that tradition, and bringing into existence in America a *new kind* of political system, a racial polity, that is misleadingly conceptualized within orthodox categories. The division of the human population generates what could be regarded as a racial liberalism and a *Herrenvolk* ethics, intellectual systems that are structured precisely around the differential treatment of the non-white population, and conceptually shaped accordingly. It is not a matter of black subordination coming into straightforward and clear-cut conflict with abstract raceless normative principles, but rather of encountering principles that have themselves historically been rewritten by race, so that white moral consciousness is used to negotiating and accommodating differentiated treatment.

Morality is then racialized. Contemporary naturalists like Ronald Dworkin argue against positivists that while it is certainly logically possible for any set of formally valid laws to be issued as commands, in practice a background sense of justice and fairness plays a role in determining what laws will become acceptable to the population. Thus he designates as "principles" those moral appeals that are part of the discursive moral logic of the system and that are crucial to decision making.[69] So it is not a matter of crass power politics, with the simple imposition of the will of the stronger. Rather there is a genuine internal moral logic present, which will assert itself like a normative lodestone, guiding judgments of correctness.

And the point is that this set of background principles, this deeply "felt" sense of what is right and wrong, will in a racial polity itself be racially normed. The "original intent" that is both morally and causally important will, as I have suggested earlier, be the majoritarian white intent that both historically and currently has been committed to white domination, originally more openly proclaimed, now more usually concealed under the cloak of an ostensibly "neutral" baseline that is not to be tampered with. What is obfuscated in the original documents is made clear in the Taney decision, so that this undeservedly calumniated figure is really being excoriated for his plain speaking, for spelling out what is hidden by constitutional circumlocution and racial cryptography. The "virtual disappearance from most contemporary constitutional law case books" of the decision conceals the embarrassing reality that it was "a fair reflection of geographically unqualified values and attitudes," comporting "not only with the imperatives of slavery but also with the priorities of general society which by law had pervasively and overtly expressed its racism."[70] Thus while Don Fehrenbacher points out the many mistakes in the decision, he emphasizes nonetheless that "the racial theory underlying his opinion was majoritarian . . . although the principal conclusions of Taney's opinion were soon wiped away by the

Civil War and subsequent constitutional amendments, the spirit of the opinion survived for a century in the racial sequel to emancipation."[71] Taney was wrong on the details, but right on the principle. His central underlying rationale is basically entirely correct: that blacks were seen as an inferior race who could – normatively, legitimately, morally – be subordinated by the white majority.[72] *Taney is the indiscreet speaker who blurts out in public what is only supposed to be mentioned privately: that the polity is a racial one.* What accounts for his banishment from case history is not his *falsehoods*, but his *truth*.

Douglass's wrath is therefore misdirected, and his (and Jaffa's) claims of original Revolutionary racelessness unfounded. What is involved is not a degeneration from an original, all-encompassing, colorless humanism to a novel nineteenth-century racism but rather a shift from a racial "common sense" without scientific backing, and in uneasy tension with lingering Enlightenment environmentalism, to a gradually hardening, *scientifically*-rationalized racism. George Fredrickson characterizes the former period as one of "proto-racism" rather than racism proper, but he concedes that this is a semantic stipulation.[73] In the broader sense useful for our purposes, racism – the conviction of the inferiority of blacks – was already widespread in the white population, and seen as an objective moral/political/metaphysical truth. Obviously if there had not been some degree of bad conscience about slavery, it would not have been necessary to resort to constitutional circumlocution in the first place. And undoubtedly there was a range of positions, with some Framers genuinely concerned about what they were doing. Jefferson's *Notes on Virginia* (1784) would advance black inferiority "as a suspicion only," and leave room for non-biological explanations.[74] But as indicated, the view of black inferiority, theologically or culturally if not biologically explained, and the conviction that they were "a permanently alien and unassimilable element of the population,"[75] had been around for more than a century by the time of the Philadelphia congress, and was already reflected in pre-Revolutionary practices of discrimination.[76] As Reginald Horsman has argued, the notion of an Anglo-Saxonist "manifest destiny," by which race is the basis of the nation, became central to the conception of the American polity.[77] Blacks and Indians were seen as lacking the civic virtues requisite to be good citizens of the new republic, so that fitness for entry into the realm of the political was explicitly racially normed.[78]

Thus, as Fredrickson concludes elsewhere, natural rights were codified in a white social contract from which slaves were excluded, the Declaration, *pace* Douglass, not being universalistic but intended "more to assert the right of a particular 'homogeneous' community to self-determination than to establish a haven of freedom and equality for all types and varieties of people . . . [A]ll nonwhites were, from the beginnings of nationhood, commonly regarded as 'aliens' of the unassimilable kind."[79] Majoritarian original intent though somewhat divided on the issue of slavery itself was racial, committed to white domination and by Douglass's time had hardened with the rise of racist theory to a point where the inequality of races was scientifically rationalized. This would be true for the rest of the century: across the political spectrum – liberals and conservatives, abolitionists and anti-abolitionists – and across the country – North and South – virtually all whites would assume the premise of black inferiority, whatever their differences as to its implications.[80] Thus one could speak of a national "consensus in favor of white supremacy, although at times the proper mechanism to ensure white domination might be in dispute."[81] If there was controversy over whether slavery was wrong, there was no controversy over the political axiom that, emancipated or not, blacks were not to be social equals.

VI Thesis IV: Optimism about Black Inclusion

It will be obvious, then, that once one faces this fact, the whole concept of a "contradiction" or "inconsistency" becomes much more dubious. If the US was intended to be, and is basically, a non-racial liberal democracy in which racism is a "deviation" from the ideal norm, since the Framers' and the white majority's "original intent" was to include all races, then there is indeed a clear-cut internal contradiction with which one can work. But if the US was intended to be, and is basically still, a white republic (Saxton), a *Herrenvolk* democracy (Van den Berghe), a caste society (Myrdal), a white supremacist state (Fredrickson),[82] a racial polity (me), in which the Framers' and the white majority's original intent was to privilege whites, then if there is a contradiction, its nature is quite different, being an external contradiction between the system as a whole and the facts of black personhood. The socioeconomic changes that would have to be made are much more radical, and the obstacles to be overcome in the white psyche are much more formidable, since the white citizenry have historically benefited from, and been cognitively and affectively molded by, their entitlement to differential treatment. This is in fact what whiteness comes to *mean*, so that it is embedded at the deepest level of one's identity, locating one in the superior tier in this new type of *polis* not to be found in the classical taxonomies of the Old World. The category of "prejudice" is inadequate to capture this relation, since what is really involved is a system of racially determined structural advantage and handicap. Douglass, as an adherent of the "anomaly" view, took the polity to be essentially non-racial. For the alternative perspective, however (what is sometimes called the "symbiosis thesis"),[83] race is built-in to the structure of the polity itself. So there is no real "American Dilemma" (though there might be an "un-American Dilemma"),[84] and to think that there is just shows that the nature of the polity has been misunderstood.

The symbiosis view (according to which liberalism for whites and racism for blacks are in symbiosis rather than contradiction) has traditionally been associated with separatist prescriptions, and sometimes also a biologistic understanding of race. But neither of these associations is conceptually necessary. Race can be seen as "constructed" but nonetheless real (the inference that the non-biological character of race implies its unreality has recently earned its own pejorative: "vulgar anti-essentialism").[85] And symbiosis theorists can still advocate integrationism as an ideal, while being far less optimistic about its likelihood. The defining feature of this alternative view is simply what Gary Peller calls its "race-consciousness," its emphasis, in defiance of the official myth of race-neutrality and a "colorblind" Constitution, that race has been central to the makeup of the American polity, and that this needs to be faced in any viable set of proposals for reform.[86]

Separatists have always had a much keener appreciation of these realities than assimilationists, and if their own resulting prescriptions have not always been realistic, one has to bear in mind the restricted menu of available options. From this perspective, white racial privilege – whether or not it is termed "white supremacy" – is really the fundamental overarching political category, with black slavery just being *one* form of non-white disadvantage. Douglass and many other black abolitionists mistakenly identified all white moral opposition to slavery with a white moral commitment to black equality, and assumed that with Emancipation racism would soon wither away. But one can oppose slavery as wrong while still being convinced of black inferiority, and one can recognize slavery as unfair while denying that other systems of racial disadvantage are unfair, or indeed without conceding that they *are* systems of disadvantage in the first place. The "contradiction," if there is one, becomes much more easily negotiable. A transcendence of the traditional terms of the debate (assimilationist/separatist) would incorporate the separatist insight of the centrality of race to critique the assimilationist dream of integration of the "races" as they are into existing America. Since that "America" has been constructed precisely *on* racial exclusion, transformation of the polity would require the genuine transcendence of race, not through an evasive "colorblindness" that encodes and perpetuates white privilege without naming it, but through the dismantling of the objective structures and subjective psychology of racial subordination.

So the criticism is not that Douglass was a theorist so impressed with the power of moral suasion that he thought it would be sufficient to overcome the vested interests that whites had in the racial structure. After all, part of his reason for breaking with the Garrisonians was precisely because he realized that political activism would also be necessary. Rather, it is that he failed to fully recognize this structure itself, to realize how deeply race and racial self-interest had entered into the creation of the polity and its citizens' identities, so that he would later underestimate, and be astonished by, the extent of white resistance to racial equality. Like many others of the period, Douglass saw "color prejudice" as arising *from* the degradation of slavery – recall his mistaken claim that "race" did not become a significant category until the mid-nineteenth century – so that with Emancipation, it would soon disappear.[87] George Fredrickson comments on the prevalence in black antislavery thought of a failure to perceive "that more than two hundred years of slavery and discrimination had planted the notion of black 'otherness' and inferiority so deeply into the white psyche that liberation of blacks from bondage could not remove it." The polity becomes a racial one, predicated on a white race consciousness that "maintained and reinforced the positive self-image and status pretensions of white Americans vis-à-vis inferior blacks.[88]"

There are some hints in Douglass's writings that race may become more deep-rooted and autonomous, shaping white psychology in such a way as to make black equality threatening to white self-respect. "My *crime* is," he says disgustedly at one point, "that I have assumed to be a man, entitled to all the rights, privileges and dignity, which belong to human nature."[89] And elsewhere: "Properly speaking, *prejudice against color* does not exist in this country . . . While we are servants, we are never offensive to the whites . . . In these conditions, we are thought to be in our place; and to aspire to anything above them, is to contradict the established views of the community – to get out of our sphere, and commit the provoking sin of *impudence*."[90] But these insights are scattered and not integrated into any larger theory. Had they been followed up, and systematized, they might have led to a more realistic sense of race as a global system of self-definition with respect to a non-white other that could survive the demise of slavery. But for Douglass, the Constitution, original intent, and the Enlightenment polity itself, were all colorblind. How, then, could it not soon be made obvious to whites

– appealing to their Enlightenment rationality – that blacks, like themselves, were self-owning Lockean persons? A leading official of the Republican Party after the war, he became in later life a strong opponent of independent black political action, in keeping with his faith in a raceless Constitution that, the very year after his death in 1895, would accommodate the *Plessy v. Ferguson* decision that formally legitimated "separate but equal."

Douglass's idealism and misconception of the nature of the polity thus discounted, or at least seriously undercounted, what W. E. B. DuBois would later term "the wages of whiteness,"[91] the multi-dimensional payoff from whiteness – economic, juridico-political, social, cultural, somatic, "ontological" – in a white-supremacist system.[92] (Whites themselves offer a more realistic accounting. Andrew Hacker, author of *Two Nations*, routinely asks the white students in his course on race how much compensation they would require to be turned into blacks; the standard figure given is a million dollars a year for the rest of their lives.)[93] This investment in whiteness, not merely one's own but for one's children's future, constitutes a formidable barrier to be overcome by morality-based accounts of social change. Moreover, apart from the resistance arising from straight interest-based motivation, there are cognitive problems inherent in the demonstration of the "contradiction" itself, and that would become manifest in the disappointments of the aftermath of the 1950s–60s victories over *de jure* segregation. Twentieth-century civil-rights activists, following in Douglass's footsteps, have in some respects recapitulated his stumbles.

Proponents of the anomaly thesis like Douglass and his later heirs often seem to be assuming the following simple model: whites believe in a moral code, M; there is a clear contradiction between the prescriptions of this code and the treatment of blacks; so whites can be enlightened to recognize this contradiction. But to begin with, insofar as moral prescription arises out of a combination of normative commitment and *factual* assessment, certain empirical claims *about* the treatment of blacks, E, have to be accepted before the existence of a contradiction is conceded. So it is not a straightforward matter of the implications of the moral code, M, but rather of the implications of M *in conjunction with* empirical claims, of M + E. If one's model of discrimination is slavery and Jim Crow, if one's conceptualization of white domination is based on the plantation and the formal demarcations of "White" and "Colored" signs, one will find it much more difficult to "see" these realities in the present period. They are no longer as empirically visible, but require theoretical labor. Indeed, the same dominant American Creed being appealed to has descriptive as well as normative implications, shaping people's consciousness with a naive but hugely influential individualist folk sociology, on which it is basically up to the person to succeed or fail. There is little grasp of the global workings of a class and racial system, especially when whites' education largely deprives them of a historical appreciation of the full extent of black subordination, and imprints on their minds a conceptual framework (the US as a liberal democracy) refractory to understanding these realities.

Thus most whites, even apart from motivational factors, will be cognitively disadvantaged both experientially, through their segregated sheltering in a white lifeworld distant from the hard empirical facts, and discursively, by the theoretical framework into which they have been socialized. A few high-profile black success stories (a Colin Powell, an Oprah Winfrey, a Michael Jordan) will for many whites be more cognitively salient, sticking in the mind as evidence of the diminution or non-existence of racial barriers for those willing to work hard. The fate of their more representative black brothers and sisters will then be explained otherwise than through race. There are many very respectable, apparently non-racist theories to account for continuing black problems – variants of the "culture of poverty," the claim of too much dependence on Big Government, black clinging to the "myth of victimization" – made even more respectable by the fact that they are endorsed by some black conservatives. Whites can (and do) say to themselves, and others, that they have never owned slaves, they have never oppressed anybody, that all of that was the dead ancient past, whatever compensation was required was done years ago, and it is now time to move on. "The idea of making special investments in blacks so that they could be brought to the starting line of a fair race is now dormant or dead, and affirmative action increasingly has come to imply reverse discrimination . . . [I]f whites ever felt any guilt about their treatment of blacks and a need to make recompense, the civil rights revolution relieved them of it. Changes in the law seemingly removed all barriers to equal opportunities for blacks, thereby giving whites moral absolution and a certainty that discrimination, if it were ever directed against blacks, was a practice of the distant past . . . [W]hites realize that blacks have worse jobs, lower incomes, and less desirable housing, but racial discrimination is not seen as the primary cause of these inequities. Lack of motivation and lack of ability are cited by whites as the explanation for the status of blacks. Whites, in general, believe that opportunities are open to blacks."[94] As a result, the white population is able to think of themselves as "innocent," since the notion that they are collectively the group beneficiaries of a system of domination is alien to the individualist framework that writes race out of the polity.⁹⁵ As Benjamin DeMott has recently argued, one then demonstrates one's antiracist commitments through individual acts of sympathy and friendship, which, however morally praiseworthy and well-intentioned, do not address the legacy of structural disadvantage itself.⁹⁶ So even where whites do *not* have racist views, the "contradiction" can easily be negotiated around rather than activated, since auxiliary factual claims need to be accepted for a contradiction to be perceived in the first place. But the second point, of course, is that the picture of an abstract moral code, M, prescribing black equality, is questionable to begin with. In the years immediately following the appearance of Myrdal's book, several sociologists did empirical testing of his thesis that the supposed contradiction would generate tensions leading to a favorable resolution, and what they found was that this notion was naive because it ignored the many alternative mechanisms for reducing cognitive dissonance on the issue.⁹⁷ People may shift back and forth between the abstract code and versions customized for local realities. Or, as I have argued in section V above, one might suggest that the abstract code M never really existed in the first place, being reshaped by race from the beginning into RM – a racial morality, a *Herrenvolk* ethics – in which there are elaborate internal conceptual mechanisms to sidestep apparent inconsistencies, algorithms for specifying racially-concrete instantiations of general abstractions, and empathic buffers to mute the impact of black suffering. "It is possible to assert, in contrast to Myrdal's profile of American values, that racism is not a 'lower' and 'local' set of attitudes, but rather a complex value orientation equal in every respect (except that of a humanistic morality) to that of the [ostensible] American creed."⁹⁸ And considering the long-enduring character of this "contradiction," considering that whites have lived with it for several hundred years, would the *opposite* not be far more surprising? Cheryl Harris has argued that whiteness as entitlement to differential privilege itself becomes property in the evolution of the American polity, so that a line of normative consistency can be traced out by which, through the various shifts in race relations, this baseline of differential white privilege is maintained, and norms for action and inaction constructed accordingly to guarantee its protection.⁹⁹

Morality and racism, then, do not collide as separate externals; rather they interpenetrate one another. Even under slavery and Jim Crow, a racial moral economy was able largely to reconcile the American Creed with formal black subordination. How much easier will this be now that such subordination has apparently been eradicated by a colorblind Constitution? The optimistic integrationist position would then have to face a scenario involving not an ideal morality set in clear opposition to (and expected to triumph over) interest-based motivation, but the worst-case outcome where perceived interest *and* a sensed moral entitlement *converge* on the preservation of the existing racial system.

This more pessimistic, but arguably more realistic, analysis is supported by the actual historical record. The three great moments of possibility for transforming the republic are the Founding, postbellum Reconstruction, and the ending of Jim Crow. In all three cases, there was an opportunity to write blacks fully into the polity and end its racial nature. And all three were missed, the first clearly and completely, through the constitutional sanctioning of slavery, the second and third partially, through constitutional and juridical change unsupported by majoritarian white moral transformation and commitment to black equality. The outcome was that legal advances were later reversed, the 14th and 15th amendments remained "a dead letter" for a century, and post-*Brown* antidiscrimination, desegregation and affirmative action law, after reaching the 1971 highpoint of *Griggs v. Duke Power Co.*, is gradually being whittled away through a series of negative Supreme Court decisions in response to white backlash. "Progress peaked in the 1970s. In the 1990s, civil rights groups and their supporters are committing most of their resources simply to hold the line."[100]

Moreover, such progress as has been made can to a significant extent be given competing "materialist" explanations, thereby further undermining the case for a "contradiction"-driven moral dynamic being the hoped-for primary causal agent. Derrick Bell's "interest-convergence thesis" is the best-known contemporary exemplar of the view that major changes in blacks' racial status have come about largely through contingent convergence with white agendas.[101] The emancipation of the slaves eventuated out of sectional conflict over the future development of the country, and the need to assert Federal authority over the breakaway South, while global Cold War competition with the Soviet Union has been cited by some authors as a major factor in motivating Federal support for ending *de jure* segregation.[102] Undoubtedly many white Americans were morally disturbed by slavery, but as earlier pointed out, this by no means necessarily implied a commitment to black *equality*. If there had been a national change of heart on the status of blacks, a genuine radical moral transformation, why would the country have permitted the postbellum black codes, the Hayes-Tilden Compromise that essentially left blacks to the mercies of their former owners, the disappearance of the franchise, the institutionalization of Jim Crow, the thousands of unpunished lynchings? Or if *Brown* had genuinely signalled the desire, once and for all, to realize the supposed colorblind ideals, why should there have been "massive resistance" to desegregation, opposition to opening up the employment market, indifference to the fate of the black underclass once – with the postwar boom over – it became obvious that further black gains would mean white losses?

For the "anomaly" view of which Douglass's position is a variant, there is a constant problem in devising *ad hoc* explanations to account for this pattern of advance and retreat. At each crucial juncture, one has to cite contingent circumstances to explain the non-fulfillment of the constitutional ideal, the discrepancy between what is written down in paper and how it is interpreted, between what is said and what is enforced. Once one starts instead from the assumption that the US has historically been, and in some ways continues to be, a racial polity, a political system predicated on non-white subordination, then the pattern of promise and betrayal of black liberation can be explained with an explanatory elegance and simplicity impossible for the anomaly view. *The original and continuing intent has been to establish and maintain white privilege, giving up some manifestations, retaining the crucial ones, with progress coming largely through contingent convergence with white elite or majoritarian interests rather than independent white moral awakening.* The shifting meaning of the Constitution is then really determined by the white majority. Thus while constitutional reform is important, it is ultimately subject to a racialized interpretive logic, by which Federal action or inaction is determined by taking a status quo of historic white privilege as neutral, rather than as the legacy of the racial polity.[103] In Donald Lively's summary: "The jurisprudence of race over two centuries has consistently frustrated initiatives and theories that might animate the Constitution in a way that would significantly account for minority interests ... [E]qual protection [for blacks] over the course of its existence has not amounted to much more than cultural norms will allow."[104] Material changes may ultimately alter this – for example the impending demographic shift to a non-white majority, a possible labor shortage in the twenty-first century, or the increasing social costs of racism – but the role of detached moral enlightenment is unfortunately a limited one, unsurprising given how racially colored the original Enlightenment was. Douglass's faith in the official institutions was misplaced, because these institutions were not neutral to begin with. The John Locke he invokes to proclaim his self-ownership is, after all, the same John Locke who was an investor in the Atlantic slave trade, and author of the Carolina constitution that – in seeming contradiction to his own later prescriptions in the *Second Treatise* – enshrined hereditary slavery.[105] He would have been able to explain to Douglass the hard truth that in the eyes of a racial liberalism he was *not* self-owning.

VII Conclusion

This has been a lengthy essay, so let me summarize. I began by extracting what I suggested were four essential theses from Douglass's speech: that natural law is the appropriate framework for examining these moral and jurisprudential issues; that the original intent of the Framers is important, and that this intent was antislavery and anti-white supremacy; that there is an inconsistency between the actuality and the founding principles of the American polity which can be exploited by those agitating for change; and that grounds for optimism therefore exist that blacks will eventually be accepted as full citizens. The burden of my essay is that all of these claims are false, or at least need to be seriously qualified. A natural law framework hinders our understanding of the sociohistoric shaping of the law and of people's conceptions of the right. The original intent of the Framers is dubiously antislavery, is certainly not anti-white supremacy, should not be morally decisive for us, and is in any case less important as an independent causal factor than as a reflection of the white population's majoritarian racial intent. The notion of an internal inconsistency between the principles and the reality of the American polity evaporates once it is conceptualized, accurately, as historically a racial polity, though there is an *external* inconsistency between these principles and the reality of black personhood. But whether this inconsistency can be resolved will depend on largely "material" politico-economic factors, not an ideal juristic constitutional logic. So given the unfavorable political climate of the present, there is, at least for the near future, no reason for great optimism about the inclusion of the black population as a whole. Douglass was obviously mistaken about his own time and a century after his death his prognosis has yet to be fulfilled. In short, everything Douglass said is wrong.

Why then should we continue to value this speech a hundred and fifty years later? Because apart from being a dazzling piece of oratory, its courage, moral outrage, and political intransigence are still inspirational, and can be separated from the analysis itself. Douglass saw, correctly, that the Fourth of July belonged to white Americans rather than all Americans, and his anger at this continues to resound with us. What he did not see was how old and foundational this exclusionary ownership was, the white property of differential rights at the heart of the white property-owning polity that justifies its racial architecture and shapes the moral consciousness and sense of entitlement of its white citizens. What he did not see was that the very principles to which he was appealing had themselves been precoded by race. So one can reject his analysis and be more skeptical about the foundations of his optimism, while still applauding his conviction, and being awed by his resolution. His political illusions about white original intent are less important than his political affirmations of his own black will, the will he was not supposed to have. He stood up – this black slave who had become a black man, this piece of property who had stolen himself, this person who had repudiated his official sub-personhood – he stood up, defying white power's original and continuing intent to subordinate him, and asserted his *own* human intent to be free. He stood up for all of us, and in the end that is what counts and that is the example we need to follow.

Notes

1 "The Meaning of July Fourth for the Negro," in Philip S. Foner, ed, *Life and Writings of Frederick Douglass, vol. II* (New York: International Publishers, 1950), pp. 181–204. This volume will henceforth be cited as *Douglass*, II. (In William L. Andrews, ed, *The Oxford Frederick Douglass Reader* [New York and Oxford: Oxford University Press, 1996], the speech is anthologized under the different title "What To the Slave Is the Fourth of July?".) It was published later the same year in pamphlet form as *Oration, Delivered in Corinthian Hall, Rochester, July 5th, 1852.*
2 Andrews, *The Oxford Frederick Douglass Reader*, p. 108.
3 See, for example, Bernard R. Boxill, "Two Traditions in African-American Political Philosophy," in John P. Pittman, ed, *The Philosophical Forum*, special triple issue on "African-American Perspectives and Philosophical Traditions," vol. XXIV, nos 1–3 (Fall 1992–Spring 1993), pp. 119–35.
4 Andrew Hacker, *Two Nations: Black and White, Separate, Hostile, Unequal* (New York: Scribner's, 1992).
5 All quotations are from *Douglass, II*, pp. 181–204.
6 See Steven Butterfield, *Black Autobiography in America* (Amherst: University of Massachusetts Press, 1977), pp. 32, 47–64. Cited in Rafia Zahar, "Franklinian Douglass: The Afro-American as Representative Man," in Eric J. Sundquist, ed, *Frederick Douglass: New Literary and Historical Essays* (Cambridge: Cambridge University Press, 1990), p. 116, n. 14.
7 Shelley Fisher Fishkin and Carla L. Peterson, "'We Hold These Truths to Be Self-Evident': The Rhetoric of Frederick Douglass' Journalism," in Sundquist, ed, *Frederick Douglass*, pp. 189–204.
8 For this reason, John Hope Franklin gets Douglass completely wrong when he says that, in the July 4 speech, Douglass "found no consolation even in the words of the Declaration of Independence": John Hope Franklin, "Race and the Constitution in the Nineteenth Century," in John

Hope Franklin and Genna Rae McNeil, eds, *African Americans and the Living Constitution* (Washington and London: Smithsonian Institution Press, 1995), p. 26.
9 See Boxill, "Two Traditions."
10 Waldo E. Martin, Jr, "Images of Frederick Douglass in the Afro-American Mind: The Recent Black Freedom Struggle," in Sundquist, ed, *Frederick Douglass*, pp. 276–8.
11 Waldo E. Martin, Jr, *The Mind of Frederick Douglass* (Chapel Hill and London: University of North Carolina Press, 1984).
12 For an overview of different positions, see, for example, the readings collected in August Meier, Elliot Rudwick, and Francis L. Broderick, eds, *Black Protest Thought in the Twentieth Century*, 2nd ed. (New York: Macmillan, 1971).
13 Martin, "Images," pp. 280–3; Wilson J. Moses, "Writing Freely? Frederick Douglass and the Constraints of Racialized Writing," in Sundquist, ed, *Frederick Douglass*, pp. 78–81.
14 Thurgood Marshall, "Racial Justice and the Constitution: A View from the Bench," in Franklin and McNeil, eds, *African Americans*, p. 317.
15 Kenneth Clark, 1967 address to the convention of the Association for the Study of Negro Life and History, "Black Power is a Sour Grapes Phenomenon," in Meier et al., eds, *Black Protest Thought*, pp. 610–21.
16 Kenneth B. Clark, "Racial Progress and Retreat: A Personal Memoir," in Herbert Hill and James E. Jones, Jr, eds, *Race in America: The Struggle for Equality* (Madison, WI: The University of Wisconsin Press, 1993), p. 18.
17 See Elizabeth Mensch, "The History of Mainstream Legal Thought," in David Kairys, ed, *The Politics of Law: A Progressive Critique*, 2nd ed. (New York: Pantheon Books, 1990), pp. 13–37.
18 A. P. d'Entreves, *Natural Law: An Introduction to Legal Philosophy*, 2nd ed. (London: Hutchinson, 1970).
19 Ibid., pp. 79, 110.
20 Ibid., p. 79.
21 Cicero, *De Republica*, III, xxii, 33; cited in d'Entreves, *Natural Law*, p. 25.
22 d'Entreves, *Natural Law*, p. 26.
23 For an introductory discussion, see Jeffrie G. Murphy and Jules L. Coleman, *Philosophy of Law: An Introduction to Jurisprudence* (Boulder, CO: Westview Press, 1990), ch. 1.
24 d'Entreves, *Natural Law*, p. 79.
25 Allan C. Hutchinson, ed, *Critical Legal Studies* (Totowa, NJ: Rowman & Littlefield, 1989); Richard Delgado, ed, *Critical Race Theory: The Cutting Edge* (Philadelphia: Temple University Press, 1995); Kimberle Crenshaw, Neil Gotanda, Gary Peller, and Kendall Thomas, eds, *Critical Race Theory: The Key Writings That Formed the Movement* (New York: The New Press, 1995).
26 Meese called for a return to original intent as part of the Reagan Administration's rollback of civil rights progress in the 1980s; see Julius

L. Chambers, "Afterword: Racial Equality and Full Citizenship, the Unfinished Agenda," in Franklin and McNeil, eds, *African Americans*, pp. 319–35. He would also cite Douglass approvingly in a 1985 speech at Dickinson College; see Harry V. Jaffa, "Attorney General Meese, the Declaration, and the Constitution," in Harry V. Jaffa, ed, *Original Intent and the Framers of the Constitution: A Disputed Question* (Washington, D.C.: Regnery Gateway, 1994), pp. 55–73.

27 My account here and below follows Gregory Bassham, *Original Intent and the Constitution: A Philosophical Study* (Lanham, MD: Rowman & Littlefield, 1992).

28 Ibid., p. 2.

29 Bruce Ledewitz, "Judicial Conscience and Natural Rights: A Reply to Professor Jaffa," in Jaffa, ed, *Original Intent*, p. 110.

30 Bassham, *Original Intent*, pp. 29, 34–5. The quotes are not exact but my synopsis of his position.

31 Cass R. Sunstein, *The Partial Constitution* (Cambridge, MA and London, England: Harvard University Press, 1993), p. 93.

32 Cited in Bertell Ollman and Jonathan Birnbaum, eds, *The United States Constitution: 200 Years of Anti-Federalist, Abolitionist, Feminist, Muckraking, Progressive, and Especially Socialist Criticism* (New York and London: New York University Press, 1990), p. 96.

33 "Letter to Gerrit Smith," in *Douglass, II*, p. 150.

34 George W. Crockett, Jr, "Remembering Litigation, Protest, and Politics in Mississippi During the Civil Rights Movement," in Franklin and McNeil, eds, *African Americans*, p. 93.

35 Marshall, in Franklin and McNeil, eds, *African Americans*, p. 317.

36 "Change of Opinion Announced," in *Douglass, II*, p. 155.

37 "The Meaning of July Fourth for the Negro," in *Douglass, II*, p. 202.

38 "The Claims of our Common Cause," in *Douglass, II*, p. 261.

39 "The Kansas-Nebraska Bill," in *Douglass, II*, p. 317. Cf. "The Reproach and Shame of the American Government," in Philip S. Foner, ed, *Life and Writings of Frederick Douglass, vol. V* (New York: International Publishers, 1975), pp. 401–2.

40 "The True Ground upon which to meet Slavery," in *Douglass, II*, p. 368.

41 "The Dred Scott Decision," in *Douglass, II*, pp. 420–1.

42 "Essay #3 by Brutus," in Ollman and Birnbaum, eds, *The United States Constitution*, p. 85.

43 William M. Wiecek, *The Sources of Antislavery Constitutionalism in America, 1760–1848* (Ithaca and London: Cornell University Press, 1977), pp. 75–6.

44 Ibid., pp. 62–3.

45 A. Leon Higginbotham, Jr, *In the Matter of Color: Race and the American Legal Process: The Colonial Period* (Oxford: Oxford University Press, 1978).

46 Ian F. Haney Lopez, *White by Law: The Legal Construction of Race* (New York and London: New York University Press, 1996). Though it was

modified in various ways over the years, this act was not fully repealed until 1952.

47 "The Constitution and Slavery," in Philip S. Foner, ed, *Life and Writings of Frederick Douglass, vol. I* (New York: International Publishers, 1950), pp. 361–7. This volume will henceforth be cited as *Douglass, I*.

48 See, for example, Houston A. Baker, Jr, *Modernism and the Harlem Renaissance* (Chicago and London: The University of Chicago Press, 1987).

49 Paul Laurence Dunbar, "We Wear the Mask," cited in Baker, *Modernism and the Harlem Renaissance*, p. 39.

50 See chapter 2, "Abolitionism: The Travail of a 'Great Life's Work,'" in Martin, *Mind of Frederick Douglass*.

51 Jennifer L. Hochschild, *The New American Dilemma: Liberal Democracy and School Desegregation* (New Haven and London: Yale University Press, 1984), chapter 1.

52 Cited in Higginbotham, *In the Matter of Color*, pp. 377, 380.

53 Gunnar Myrdal, *An American Dilemma: The Negro Problem and Modern Democracy* (New York: Harper & Row, 1944), pp. lxix-lxxi.

54 For an excerpt of the crucial passages of the decision, see, for example, "Dred Scott v. Sanford, 1857," in Paula S. Rothenberg, ed, *Race, Class, and Gender in the United States: An Integrated Study*, 3rd ed (New York: St. Martin's Press, 1995), pp. 322–5, and for the definitive discussion, Don E. Fehrenbacher, *The Dred Scott Case: Its Significance in American Law and Politics*, (New York: Oxford University Press, 1978). The defendant, John Sanford, had his name misspelled as "Sandford" in the official report, so that there have been varying spellings ever since.

55 "Dred Scott," in Rothenberg, ed, *Race, Class and Gender*, pp. 323–4.

56 "The Dred Scott Decision," in *Douglass, II*, p. 411.

57 "Position of the Government Toward Slavery," in Philip S. Foner, ed, *Life and Writings of Frederick Douglass, vol. III* (New York: International Publishers, 1952), p. 105. This volume will henceforth be cited as *Douglass, III*.

58 Jaffa, ed, *Original Intent and the Framers of the Constitution*.

59 Jaffa, "Original Intent and Justice Rehnquist," in ibid., p. 103.

60 Jaffa, "Are These Truths Now, Or Have They Ever Been, Self-Evident?," in ibid., p. 78.

61 "[T]he idea that each person matters equally is at the heart of all plausible [modern] political theories." Will Kymlicka, *Contemporary Political Philosophy: An Introduction* (Oxford: Clarendon Press, 1990), p. 5.

62 See, for example: Susan Moller Okin, *Women in Western Political Thought* (Princeton, NJ: Princeton University Press, 1979); Ellen Kennedy and Susan Mendus, eds, *Women in Western Political Philosophy: Kant to Nietzsche* (New York: St. Martin's Press, 1987); Diana H. Coole, *Women in Political Theory: From Ancient Misogyny to Contemporary Feminism* (Boulder, CO: Lynne Rienner Publishers, 1988).

63 Aristotle, *The Politics*, trans. T. A. Sinclair, revised Trevor J. Saunders (Harmondsworth, Middlesex: Penguin, 1981); Anthony Pagden, *Lords of All the World: Ideologies of Empire in Spain, Britain and France c. 1500– c. 1800* (New Haven and London: Yale University Press, 1995), chapter 1.

64 Thomas Hobbes, *Leviathan*, ed Richard Tuck (Cambridge: Cambridge University Press, 1991), chapter XIII.

65 John Locke, *Two Treatises of Government*, ed Peter Laslett, Cambridge student edition (Cambridge: Cambridge University Press, 1988), *Second Treatise*, chapter V.

66 Emmanuel Eze, "The Color of Reason: The Idea of 'Race' in Kant's Anthropology," in Katherine M. Faull, ed, *Anthropology and the German Enlightenment* (Lewisburg and London: Bucknell University Press, 1994), pp. 196–237.

67 See, for example, "Emer de Vattel on the Occupation of Territory," in Philip D. Curtin, ed., *Imperialism* (New York: Walker and Company, 1971), pp. 42–5.

68 There is no space here to explore the interesting notion of Douglass as a politically divided "tragic mulatto," both resenting his rejection by his white father and seeking the consolatory embrace of the white Founding Fathers. But such an analysis would go some way to explaining Douglass's own ambivalence and conflicted divisions. As more than one commentator has pointed out, Douglass was a black leader who sometimes resented being classified as a black man, an opponent of racism who occasionally made disparaging remarks about Mexicans, Indians, and his fellow-blacks, a critic of white America's treatment of its native population who nevertheless accepted the legitimacy of the settler project, and insisted that blacks (more like Europeans than Native Americans, in his opinion) have equal rights within it. See Moses, "Writing Freely?,"in Sundquist, ed, *Frederick Douglass*, pp. 271–85 and Martin, *The Mind of Frederick Douglass*, chapter 8.

69 See, for example, Ronald Dworkin, *Taking Rights Seriously* (Cambridge, MA: Harvard University Press, 1977) and *Law's Empire* (Cambridge, MA: Harvard University Press, 1986).

70 Donald E. Lively, *The Constitution and Race* (New York: Praeger, 1992), pp. 34, 33.

71 Fehrenbacher, *The Dred Scott Case*, p. 5.

72 Unlike Douglass, contemporary black scholars have long perceived the underlying truth in the Taney decision. John Hope Franklin comments: "There is no evidence . . . to contradict his reading of the status of free blacks at the time of the Declaration of Independence and the framing of the Constitution." John Hope Franklin, "Race and the Constitution in the Nineteenth Century," in Franklin and McNeil, eds, *African Americans*, pp. 27–8. Derrick Bell observes that Taney's conclusion was "a view rather clearly reflecting the prevailing belief in his time as among the

Founding Fathers." Derrick Bell, "The Real Costs of Racial Discrimination," in ibid., p. 187.
73   George M. Fredrickson, *The Black Image in the White Mind: The Debate on Afro-American Character and Destiny, 1817–1914* (Hanover, NH: Wesleyan University Press, 1987), preface, chapters 1–2.
74   Ibid., pp. 1–4.
75   Ibid., p. 1.
76   Higginbotham, *In the Matter of Color*.
77   Reginald Horsman, *Race and Manifest Destiny: The Origins of American Racial Anglo-Saxonism* (Cambridge, MA: Harvard University Press, 1981).
78   Ronald Takaki, *Iron Cages: Race and Culture in 19th-Century America* (New York and Oxford: Oxford University Press, 1990), chapter 1.
79   George Fredrickson, *White Supremacy: A Comparative Study in American and South African History* (Oxford: Oxford University Press, 1981), p. 145.
80   Fredrickson, *The Black Image*, chapter 11.
81   Fredrickson, *The Black Image*, p. 320.
82   Alexander Saxton, *The Rise and Fall of the White Republic: Class Politics and Mass Culture in Nineteenth-Century America* (London and New York: Verso, 1990); Pierre Van den Berghe, *Race and Racism* (New York: Wiley, 1967); Myrdal *An American Dilemma*; Fredrickson, *White Supremacy*. I have included Myrdal's notion of a caste society despite the fact that Myrdal himself, as earlier pointed out, is *the* twentieth-century "anomaly" theorist. My justification is the useful point made by Stephen Steinberg: that Myrdal's framing of race primarily in dilemmatic, moral terms is flagrantly contradicted by the data in his own massive 1000+ page book, which make it abundantly clear that race is a matter of political economy. "Myrdal's conceptual framework placed a gloss over the raw facts . . . He took facts that were potentially explosive, and he defused them by cramming them into insulated conceptual boxes." Stephen Steinberg, *Turning Back: The Retreat From Racial Justice in American Thought and Policy* (Boston: Beacon Press, 1995), p. 40.
83   Hochschild, *The New American Dilemma*, pp. 5–8.
84   I do not, of course, mean by this that the definition of "America" cannot change – obviously it has changed considerably since the nation's founding – but that on the traditional understanding America *is* essentially a white nation.
85   Crenshaw et al., eds, *Critical Race Theory*, introduction, p. xxvi.
86   Gary Peller, "Race-Consciousness," in Crenshaw et al., eds, *Critical Race Theory*, pp. 127–58.
87   Similarly, one of the key ideas of Myrdal's *American Dilemma* is that once blacks begin to rise into the ranks of the middle class, racism will vanish, since what is keeping it alive is a naive empiricist extrapolation from the current racial division of labor. The fact that a century and a half after Douglass's speech, half a century after Myrdal's book, race is still so firmly embedded in the national white psyche that even middle-class and

professional blacks continue to receive differential treatment, shows the fundamental mistakenness of this analysis, and its rooting in the "anomaly" view of racism. See, for example, Ellis Cose, *The Rage of a Privileged Class* (New York: HarperCollins, 1993) and Joe R. Feagin and Melvin P. Sikes, *Living With Racism: The Black Middle-Class Experience* (Boston: Beacon Press, 1994).

88 George Fredrickson, *Black Liberation: A Comparative History of Black Ideologies in the United States and South Africa* (New York and Oxford: Oxford University Press, 1995), pp. 27–8.
89 "At Home Again," in *Douglass, II*, p. 126.
90 "Prejudice Against Color," in *Douglass, II*, pp. 128–9.
91 W. E. B. DuBois, *Black Reconstruction in America* (New York: Russell and Russell, 1963).
92 See my "White Supremacy," in John P. Pittman and Tommy L. Lott, eds, *A Companion to African-American Philosophy* (forthcoming, Blackwell Publishers).
93 Hacker, *Two Nations*, p. 32.
94 Reynolds Farley, "The Common Destiny of Blacks and Whites: Observations about the Social and Economic Status of the Races," in Hill and Jones, eds, *Race in America*, p. 228. In the passage quoted, Farley cites the following authors: Frances Fitzgerald, *Cities on a Hill: A Journey through Contemporary American Cultures* (New York: Simon and Schuster, 1986); James R. Kluegel, "If There Isn't a Problem, You Don't Need a Solution," *American Behavioral Scientist*, 28 (6), 1985, pp. 761–85; James R. Kluegel and Eliot R. Smith, "White Beliefs about Blacks' Opportunity," *American Sociological Review*, 47, 1982, pp. 518–32.
95 Thomas Ross, "Innocence and Affirmative Action," abridged in Delgado, ed., *Critical Race Theory*, pp. 551–63.
96 Benjamin DeMott, *The Trouble with Friendship: Why Americans Can't Think Straight About Race* (New York: Atlantic Monthly Press, 1995).
97 See, for example, Ernest Q. Campbell, "Moral Discomfort and Racial Segregation – An Examination of the Myrdal Hypothesis," *Social Forces*, 39 (2), 1960, pp. 228–34, and Frank R. Westie, "The American Dilemma: An Empirical Test," *American Sociological Review*, 30 (4), 1965, pp. 527–38. For a discussion, see Steinberg, *Turning Back*.
98 Stanford M. Lyman, "Race Relations as Social Process: Sociology's Resistance to a Civil Rights Orientation," in Hill and Jones, eds, *Race in America*, p. 390.
99 Cheryl I. Harris, "Whiteness as Property," *Harvard Law Review*, 106, 1993, pp. 1709–91; abridged in Crenshaw et al., eds, *Critical Race Theory*, pp. 276–91.
100 Chambers in Franklin and McNeil, eds, *African Americans*, p. 325.
101 Derrick A. Bell, Jr, "*Brown v. Board of Education* and the Interest Convergence Dilemma," abridged in Crenshaw et al., eds, *Race in America*, pp. 20–9.

102 Ibid., pp. 20–9; Mary L. Dudziak, "Desegregation as a Cold War Imperative," *Stanford Law Review*, 61, 1988; abridged in Delgado, ed, *Critical Race Theory*, pp. 110–21.
103 Sunstein, *The Partial Constitution*.
104 Lively, *The Constitution and Race*, p. 174.
105 See, for example, Jennifer Welchman, "Locke on Slavery and Inalienable Rights," *Canadian Journal of Philosophy*, 25, 1995, pp. 67–81.

Part III

Enlightenment and Enslavement

6

The Claims of Frederick Douglass Philosophically Considered

Roderick M. Stewart

"Give us the facts," said the [abolitionist] Collins, "we will take care of the philosophy . . . Better have a *little* plantation manner in your speech than not; 'tis not best that you seem too learned."[1]

Frederick Douglass, *My Bondage and Freedom*

If asked, most academic philosophers today would not recognize Frederick Douglass as a philosopher. Rather, if pressed, they would likely compare his historical importance to that of Pericles for Athens, Lincoln for nineteenth-century US history, or Martin Luther King, Jr, and Malcolm X for the twentieth century. Pressed further, they might invoke Aristotle's distinction between theoretical and practical wisdom: while Douglass (Pericles, Lincoln, or Martin Luther King, Jr, and Malcolm X) may be admired for their practical wisdom and political courage, none of these figures excelled in the theoretical domain (as Aristotle, Mill, or Rawls, and Nozick have). Finally, if pressed for criteria for theoretical virtue, philosophers would likely cite the production of sustained, treatise-style works involving subtle and careful argumentation. Pioneering philosophers might be further distinguished from derivative or amateur ones in terms of how groundbreaking, influential, and wide-ranging their works are. Such distinctions, then, are at the bottom of which writer shows up on our graduate seminar syllabi and hence in our Canon of Greats.[2] On this view, then, Douglass's speeches, writings, and political activism do not qualify him for inclusion in our lists of Greats; at best, he may only make it as an amateur philosopher.

This essay explores and challenges these implicit views about Douglass in the academic profession of philosophy. We shall do this by examining the argumentative context of his 1854 Commencement Address at Western Reserve College, "The Claims of the Negro Ethnologically Considered." Before we do this, though, let us reflect briefly on the problematic status of this theoretical/practical distinction within Western philosophical debates.

I

If we take at face value the theoretical/practical distinction, its evidential criteria, and its list of generated Greats, we would seem to have three options for evaluating and "rationally reconstructing" Douglass. First, on the basis of his extant, but ignored and repressed work, we may find him to be some degree of heavyweight/lightweight philosopher-theorist. Or, second, perhaps a scholar like Professor Blassingame will discover a hitherto unknown *magnum opus* by Douglass in proper treatise-style covering some wide range of topics. On either scope, we will adjust our syllabi and Canon accordingly. But, of course, no former Great will be removed from our lists.

Or, third, we may adopt a strategy offered by the feminist art historian, Linda Nochlin.[3] Here, after examining Douglass's and others' known work and papers, we might prepare ourselves to accept the conclusion that there likely have been in fact *no great African-American philosophers*, not because of some natural racial differences, but only because of lack of equal opportunity and access to appropriate institutional nurturing and support. Emancipatory scholarship, then, on this tack focuses on detailing, analyzing, and making public particular histories of oppression and denial of equal opportunity as an object lesson for later generations.[4] We then admire Douglass for what he was able to do given the circumstances, and perhaps console ourselves with some "what ifs." *De facto*, though, Douglass remains an amateur philosopher, or "man of letters" at best, and the Canon of Greats goes unchallenged.

But why should this theoretical versus practical virtue distinction be taken at face value? At the very least, we academic philosophers should recall that Aristotle directed this very distinction against the Platonic-Socratic view of the *unity* of the virtues and thus at the latter's views of the implications for *being* a philosopher: for starters, being politically engaged in gadfly/midwife conversations and therapy with one's fellow Athenians down in the *agora*. It is also important to recall that the effectiveness of such *therapeia* was not to be measured by the production of scholarly treatises, though the capacity for subtle and sustained, *conversational* argumentation and analysis was certainly important. At best, then, on this Platonic model, training in the *Academia* (discussing "dialogues" or seminar papers) constituted highly artificial simulations of real life conversations about life and death issues affecting the *polis*.

Or, from a more radical, quasi-Kuhnian perspective, we might view the Platonic Socrates as challenging an existing Athenian cultural paradigm in crisis and decline after the Peloponnesian Wars, with the Platonic Socrates offered up overagainst the traditional poets, sophists, and politicians as a new kind of founding hero in the tradition of Theseus. Aristotle, however, seems to be working from within a more stable cultural paradigm and does not have to compete against poets and sophists. Within a more "normalized" situation, it is easier to draw a distinction between those who have the *leisure* for theory and those who do not. Perhaps, then, in some sort of Socratic light we can begin to think about Douglass's status overagainst the academy of his day.

There are, of course, other ways to challenge the theoretical/practical distinction and its arguably overwrought valorization of systematic, argumentative treatise production: first, closer to Douglass's own time, we might recall Emerson's intuitive essays, poems, and religious sensibility directed to an American culture obsessed with commercialism; or, even Kierkegaard's call for a distinct kind of indirect, "edifying" discourse overagainst the all-too-enlightenment academy and its stultifying form of spirituality. With both Emerson and Kierkegaard in mind, we can imagine a Douglass who not only engages the officially "neutral," scholarly arguments of polygenist ethnologists as exercises in evidence-gathering, but does this from within a larger "speech act" of calling forth his audience to confront the "existential choices" this very scholarly debate served to cover over for the Union.

Or, perhaps it would also be helpful to see this existential-religious dimension of Douglass in terms of the "internal/external" prophets of the Old Testament.[5] Like the prophets of old and new, then, Douglass's speeches and journalism can be seen to constitute performances against a moral and political paradigm in crisis, performances themselves that seek to reshape, if not revolutionize, that very culture.[6] In this light, it would be no wonder that Douglass's status as a "scholar" or, more specifically, a philosopher, like that of Emerson and Kierkegaard, is difficult to pin down. Perhaps all three perform somewhere "between" paradigms.

Second, Douglass's status as at once political gadfly, orator, essayist, journalist, and social prophet, need not be seen as a "problem" at all if we press further our Kuhnian description of him as, say, prophet to a paradigm in crisis. If we take a "postmodern" perspective on his performative "texts" in their social and political situation, Douglass might be read as producing "anti-texts" that deliberately defy genre-classification by the dominant discursive practices of both his and our day, especially those preferred in a normalized academy. As many recent postmodernists have noted, such acts of defiance presuppose some sort of emancipatory project, even if only describable by some sort of counterpart in political theory to "negative theology."[7] Of course, more traditional intellectual historians will immediately object that Douglass's own "authorial intentions" are better described as contained in a progressive, natural law, liberal-religious tradition fighting against slavery. Many postmodernists would likely, then, reply by "deconstructing" the very idea of authorial intention (or any other single metaphysical construct) as determinative of the meaning of some text overagainst many other factors. I will not try to decide here the issues of objectivity and ideology in interpretation, even if I thought it was decidable by some list of formal rules of evidence (which I do not). I simply remind ourselves of its complexity and its tendency to elicit dismissive question begging on many sides, as we now proceed to see the heavily ideological argumentative context Douglass self-consciously seems to be working in and against.

II

Douglass delivered his Commencement Address, "The Claims of the Negro Ethnologically Considered," before the literary societies of Western Reserve College in Hudson, Ohio on July 12, 1854.[8] The topic is "a few thoughts on the subject of the Claims of the Negro, suggested by ethnological science, or the natural history of man" (499; 226). Douglass's own opening remarks indicate that his presence there was a rare and unexpected opportunity both for him and the college, if not for some there "an offense against good taste" (499; 226). Why was this?

Historical Context of the Address[9]

First, this speech was not only Douglass's First Commencement Address (and thus a "commencement" for him!), but apparently also the first time any major US university had invited a black person as its keynote speaker. However, second, Douglass was *not* invited by the trustees, administration, or alumni of Western Reserve College to give the main Commencement Address, but by its prestigious Philozetian and Phi Delta literary or debating societies to celebrate their four graduating students. Indeed, the trustees, administration, and alumni actively tried to discourage this invitation probably because they were themselves pro-colonizationist abolitionists in favor of settling freed slaves in Liberia and not near whites. So, even within the "progressive" academy, Douglass was not always welcome.

Third, Douglass finally accepted the offer upon advice of his close friends, Dr M. D. Anderson, president of the University of Rochester, and Dr Henry Wayland, a faculty member at Rochester. Both of these men also encouraged Douglass to spend several months working up a critical review of recent and influential work in ethnology. And Douglass knew full well that such a review would be tantamount to a moral indictment of much of the Academy.

Yet, fourth, Douglass personally came to regard this speech as a boring and "very defective production," even though every newspaper reporting on it extolled its ability to rivet the attention of nearly 3,000 people in the audience for two hours. Douglass later gave versions of the speech under various shortened titles and by delivering it by alternating reading extracts and speaking extemporaneously.[10] Why this fluctuation in styles of delivery?

It turns out, fifth, that in his early days on the antislavery circuit Douglass relied quite "naturally" on a more conversational style of humor, anecdote, and extemporaneous speaking, arguably derived from his roots in the call and response tradition of the A. M. E. Zionist church. However, Douglass became irritated about perceptions by Garrisonian abolitionists of his ability to contribute to public debate in more than just a "show and tell way." Blassingame cites the following passage from Douglass's autobiography *My Bondage and My Freedom*, where Douglass reflects on his early years as an antislavery lecturer:

> During the first three or four months, my speeches were almost exclusively made up of narrations of my own personal experience as a slave. "Let us have the facts," said the people. So also said Friend George Foster, who always wished to pin me down to my simple narrative. "Give us the facts," said Collins, "we will take care of *the philosophy*." [my emphasis] . . . "Tell your story, Frederick," would whisper my then reverend friend, William Lloyd Garrison, as I stepped upon the platform . . . "Be yourself," said Collins, "and tell your story." It was said to me, "Better have a little of plantation manner in your speech than not; 'tis not best that you seem too learned."[11]

Thus, to secure greater financial and intellectual independence from the Garrisonians, Douglass found it necessary to prepare more and more written speeches for more formal settings and for more lucrative fees. The price he paid, though, was losing much of the informal spontaneity and rhetorical power of his earlier style. Perhaps Douglass felt some loss of authenticity here, too. We can understand, then, how Douglass would attempt to mix styles when a later occasion presenting the address allowed it.

Moreover, far from his mixture of styles showing Douglass's *immaturity* as a serious academic thinker, we can just as well view him as shaping and participating in a unique form of edifying discourse over-against an academic audience he never really can belong to. Indeed, as we noted before, we should not be surprised if the complex speech acts of edifying and gadflying take place right alongside those of subtle argument analysis, claim-giving, and drawing of conclusions.

But suppose, as Blassingame notes,[12] Douglass likely exaggerated the restrictions placed on him by the Garrisonians, and that to some extent he was overly self-conscious of measuring up to educated white perceptions. Such white-intellect-envy would be both understandable and defensible given the degree of antipathy generally towards Africans by most eighteenth- and nineteenth-century Enlightenment thinkers. Indeed, many of us are now painfully aware of the dismissive contempt for Africans, other non-Europeans, and women by such luminaries as Hume, Kant, and Hegel.[13] However, whatever self-doubts Douglass may have had, we shall see that the address as a whole suggests that such feelings were temporary and unabiding.

His Opening, "Modest" Remarks

Thus, given that such attitudes were prevalent and hardly veiled even in most educated circles of his day, it is no wonder that Douglass seems to open this Commencement Address with a more than usual amount of gratitude, modesty, and deference to his audience of young (presumably, white-male) graduates. He says in the second paragraph:

> I engage today, for the first time, in the exercises of any College Commencement. It is a new chapter in my humble experience. The usual course . . . is to call to the platform men of age and distinction, eminent for eloquence, mental ability, and scholarly attainments – men whose high culture, severe training, great experience, large observation, and peculiar aptitude for teaching, qualify

them to instruct even the already well instructed, and to impart a glow, a lustre, to the acquirements of those who are passing from the Halls of learning, to the broad theatre of active life. To no such high endeavor as this, is your humble speaker fitted; and it was with much distrust and hesitation that he accepted the invitation, so kindly and perseveringly given.

Maybe this is just genuine modesty and gratitude on Douglass's part? After all, those who invited him surely undertook great risks. Or, is Douglass perhaps just "tommin'" for his new academic masters, showing proper servility, now that he has made it from the "field" to the "house"? There is, of course, another interpretive option: playing Sambo was often arguably a subtle form of masking behavior and self-defense.[14] While I think Douglass is expressing genuine gratitude to at least some in the audience here, the real possibility of his overly modest language functioning as masking behavior makes it possible for us to see a subtle irony at work in this address, but an irony in the Socratic sense designed to penetrate the overly complacent souls of his audience.[15] Can this interpretive possibility be further evidenced in the text?

Notice again how in the same paragraph Douglass describes the usual course of men called to this commencement platform: these "men of age and distinction . . . and scholarly attainments," etc. Could not such men very easily have been the eminent scholars, such as the much read, physician-ethnologist Samuel Morton, whom Douglass will criticize that very day and who at the time were producing an infamous instance of pseudo-science? That they very well could have been becomes clearer two paragraphs later, as we shall see. Remember also our second contextual point above about the colonizational politics of the trustees, alumni, and administration of Western Reserve College.

Along the same lines, consider Douglass's phrase for the usual commencement speaker as "men of . . . great experience, large observation" in this second paragraph: at the very least this phrase is ironic for us, for, according to Gould,[16] Morton's collection of skulls from North and South America was famous in its day for the *large amount of data* it provided for the much-discussed polygenic theory proposed by Professor Agassiz at Harvard. Polygenists, such as Agassiz and Morton, argued that (i) the "races" do not share a common ancestry and hence (ii) they are not biologically equal, especially in matters of intelligence.

Finally, there is also arguably a fine irony in referring to the traditional commencement speakers as qualified to instruct "even the already well instructed," the latter presumably being the new graduates before him and their local teachers. Such conventionally-chosen *illuminati* are to be contrasted with Douglass's own "humble experience" as a mere (!) slave and as a more or less self-taught man now before them as a speaker. I suggest that all this irony dawns on the audience as the Address proceeds and Douglass takes apart in detail Morton's and others' learned arguments.[17]

Consider now the fourth paragraph. Here Douglass cautions his young graduates that they are like a newly and fully fitted "gallant ship" that is about to leave the placid waters of the harbor of their College for the more "boisterous waves" and "measureless responsibilities incident to the great voyage of life." Indeed, Douglass says, in front of them lies "the ocean of the mind" with "theories, ideas, and systems, so various, and so opposite, and leading to such diverse results" that they must still worry about following a "false light, a defective chart, an imperfect compass," leading them to "drift in endless bewilderment" or "to be landed at last amid sharp, destructive rocks" (500; 227). The imagery here is on first glance the trite and hackneyed stuff one would expect at commencements, recalling perhaps Bacon's voyage of discovery imagery at the beginning of *Novuum Organum* or (more contemporary) Longfellow's "ship of state" imagery for the threatened Union.[18] In the larger context of the speech, though, it becomes clear that the young sailor-graduates can only get their false lights, defective charts, and imperfect compasses from the very Academy and teachers who produced and now celebrate Great Minds like Morton and Agassiz! Again, in light of the speech as a whole, I suggest that the result Douglass fears most for his young American graduates is the endless drift of cynicism and the running-aground of moral defeatism that an officially sanctioned, deterministic racial theory can produce in the debates over the justification of slavery and the nature and extent of humanity.

Consider next the fifth paragraph. Here Douglass modestly (ironically?) describes himself as a "preacher"[19] hoping to save from error and ruin at least one of these young minds on its graduate voyage. I suggest that we have Douglass here building upon his prior imagery as a man of "humble experience," but now as the plain-truth preacher overagainst the academic scribes and pharisees; or, in a different tradition, as the therapeutic Socrates of simpler narrative style overagainst the orators and sophists. What is really called for on this occasion, then, is a kind of sermonizing, even if on this almost "high church" occasion he is not at liberty to use the more improvisational, "call and response" style of his later performances of this same "text." In any event, perhaps Douglass is signaling that what is needed is a rhetorical strategy designed to combat the disengaged naiveté, or even cynical defeatism, of his otherwise educated audiences.

The sixth and final paragraph completes the foregoing points, but now with Douglass's least diplomatic and most direct challenge to his audience so far. His audience must understand the stakes involved in evaluating the "Claims of the Negro" raised by some practitioners of ethnological science. Both "thought" and "action" are required here. For a "man of letters" to claim to be a "neutral scholar" and not see that the "vital question of the age" (the abolition of slavery) stands behind the practice of some well-known ethnological science, would be to commit an "ignoble" act and ignore the "call" of both the Christian God (of justice) and of one's country.[20]

Indeed, Douglass is quite clear in this paragraph that on this issue "the scholars of America will have to take an important and *controlling* part" (my emphasis). Douglass's belief that scholars can make a difference here and "control in part" the country's moral debate may strike us academics today as overly optimistic and/or from a time when a Christian moral tradition dominated most colleges and a teacher/preacher was not a peculiarity. Perhaps. In context, though, perhaps we ought to read this as the claim that since certain well-placed intellectuals are openly lending the support of their "scholarly neutral" offices to the institution of slavery, there is no better place for the battle to be joined than in those very institutions and by some of their own practitioners.

Douglass then ends his opening call to arms in the sixth paragraph with a most curious claim: "I shall aim to discuss the claims of the Negro, general and special, in a manner, *though not scientific*, still sufficiently clear and definite to enable my hearer to form an intelligent judgment respecting them" (501; 227; my emphasis). How is Douglass conceiving of "science" here so that he can ignore it, on the one hand, but still proceed to form "intelligent judgments" in clear and definite discussions, on the other? I suggest that for Douglass rationality involves more than just the meticulous collection of evidence or data for some particular science. And Douglass himself is not about to embark on a summary of his own, new field observations! Rather, I suggest that he will focus his energies on assessing how conclusions have been drawn from the available evidence and whether all the available evidence has been considered. That is, Douglass will not generate *new* empirical findings, but limit his critical analysis to matters of logic and inference *per se* and to pointing out ignored, already existing counterevidence.

Douglass's Two Claims Defended

Thus, with his opening, tone-setting remarks made in the first six paragraphs, Douglass begins his actual assessment of the rational persuasiveness of various arguments used to justify slavery, some of which come from scientific ethnologists. (Question: "Is this, finally, the 'philosophy' part, where he starts writing like a Mill or a Hume, and sets aside mere oratorical matters?" Reply: "Do you ask the same question of a Socratic dialogue, separating its philosophy part from its *therapia* or preaching?")

For our purposes, the rest of the speech is structured around Douglass's defense of two "claims" about the Negro: (i) that the Negro is a man (human being), and (ii) that monogeny, not polygeny (a common origin and capacities, not distinct ones) is the most reasonable view about the relation between the various races. Of course, it should be obvious that both of these claims, if false, would mean that he cannot succeed in giving the very Commencement Address he in fact gives! Thus, as the Address progresses, Douglass's apparent opening humility shows interesting affinities with the irony and false modesty of Socrates to his interlocutors.

1 *The first claim*

The first argument Douglass considers against the first claim comes from "a respectable public journal" in Richmond, Virginia: (i) The slave system is unjustified only if its Negro slaves are deprived of inalienable human rights. But, (ii) Negroes are not human with inalienable rights (since they have no will and intellect). Thus, (iii) the slave system is not unjustified (as the abolitionists claim). Douglass's strategy is to attack the second premise and its "denial of the Negro's manhood."

Curiously, just before he challenges evidence for this premise, Douglass informs his audience in the eighth paragraph that of three apparently conventional ways to attack this premise (by ridicule, denunciation, or argument),[21] he may in fact use all three, and not just the argument mode. Douglass seems to justify this mixture of scholarly and unscholarly manners with a personal confession:

> I feel myself somewhat on trial; and that this is just the point where there is hesitation, if not serious doubt. I cannot, however, argue; I must assert. (501; 228)

As we have seen since the opening paragraphs of his address, the very fact that a self-taught, former slave of "humble experience" is lecturing to a group of privileged white scholars about their own lack of institutional self-knowledge and ignobility, has an uneasy, self-referential character to it. Douglass's own performance that day is thus "somewhat on trial"; its success or failure could just as easily count as evidence or counterevidence for the very topic he has chosen to debate. But why does Douglass's uneasy awareness of all this apparently prevent him from *arguing* his case and reduce him to the mere capacity to *assert*? Are we to take Douglass here as confessing to his own inability to justify certain claims or assertions he nevertheless cares very deeply about? (Thus, "We will take care of the philosophy/justification, Frederick"?)

Given that what follows these sentences in the rest of the paragraph and others are *many* instances of Douglass defending his two claims with a variety of arguments, I suggest we read him as drawing, not uncontroversially, some kind of "common sense" distinction between those beliefs that can readily be debated and those that are so "basic" (to common sense or our experience of ourselves and the world) that debate about them becomes unintelligible. For example, in the next paragraph Douglass appeals to our "instinctive" recognition of the difference between men and brutes, or to the "common sense" of the absence of human features of speech, reason, religiosity ("heaven-erected face"), and aspirations in monkeys and their presence in humans. While I think many of us would reject such intuitive appeals by Douglass as "question-begging" about the particular claims he is making, we might still be generally sympathetic with some form of "common sense" epistemology or even modest foundationalism.[22] In sum, then, the curious sentence in question about not arguing and only asserting need not be a rejection of argument *per se* by Douglass but only an indication of a familiar Aristotelian point about arguments requiring first principles. We can, of course, disagree with some of Douglass's first principles without rejecting his conclusions or claims.

Douglass then offers his first criticism of the second premise in question by showing that it too narrowly defines what can count as a man or human. Indeed, by citing only such distinguished white men as Clay, Webster, or Calhoun as evidence of superior white intellect and will over that of illiterate slaves, defenders of slavery set so high a standard that few whites could pass it. Moreover, though he does not make the point explicitly, again the very fact that Douglass is ably disputing this argument on this occasion celebrating a select few's intellect and will (or moral character) – this fact constitutes a living counterexample to the narrowness of the pro-slavery definition of human. (We will see Douglass offer similar kinds of counterexamples below when he defends the monogenist thesis against overly selective citation of skull specimens.)

Douglass's second criticism of the second premise and its denial of the Negro's humanity was just mentioned above. In the ninth paragraph he tries to argue that both instinct and common sense show a "palpable" and "eternal" difference between brute and man (having to do with being able to reason, use speech, acquire knowledge, to be religious, have aspirations) and that the same obvious distinction exists between Negro and brute.

We have already mentioned the problematic, question-begging character of Douglass's tack here. We may add that this second criticism is made even more problematic for most of us by what are its rather unsympathetic views about biological evolution "connecting men with monkeys" – what he labels "scientific moonshine." Douglass apparently assumed that if you advocate evolution of humans from non-humans, then you can draw no important distinctions between the two, given what he calls evolution's "sliding scale."[23] Perhaps Douglass feared that the more degrees of being non-human there were in nature, the more places there would be to consign Negroes away from their proper human home. Given our views on evolution today, of course, we see anything but support for the superiority of one "race" over another, since genetically speaking so-called "races" are no more biologically fundamental than grouping humans by height.[24] Moreover, there is interesting, but incomplete evidence for something like an African monogeny.[25] Nevertheless, however quaint we find Douglass's take on evolution, it behooves us to remember that Darwin's *Origin of the Species* officially does not appear for another five years (1859), though both he and others in England and America had been discussing similar ideas professionally for many years. In this light, given the controversial and revolutionary character of such a view, Douglass's "ridicule" and "denunciation" of it was probably not all that uncommon in educated quarters.[26] (We will see Douglass struggle again with science's cultural challenge to religion and morality below when we consider his second claim.)

Douglass' third defense to the claim that Negroes are human begins in the tenth paragraph. Here he cites approvingly "a very recondite author"[27] who draws the human/non-human distinction in terms of the capacity to adapt to new circumstances and work to improve one's lot. Douglass first cites the obvious evidence that Negroes all along have functioned as farmers creatively adapting their environments to survive. He concludes by finding it difficult to imagine how anyone could not

The Claims of Frederick Douglass

see that Negroes pass this test. With some "ridicule," he writes: "The horse bears him [the Negro] on his back – admits his mastery and dominion. The barnyard fowl knows his step." The sarcastic implication is, of course, if such non-human creatures can sense the Negro as adaptive problem-solver, should not intelligent human-scholars be able to also? Or, are they blinded by something? With this, Douglass considers the first claim "settled" and turns to the second one, the one most existentially challenging to his special commencement audience of academics.

2 The second claim

To defend his second claim that the races are unified (pre-Darwinian monogenism), in the rest of the speech Douglass adduces at least six kinds of considerations:

(1) a set of preliminary reminders to his largely Christian audience (a) that deciding this issue in no way involves just neutral scientific testimony, but a more complicated judgment necessarily presupposing larger moral, religious, and political considerations, and (b) by implication, that any pretensions to presuppositionless neutrality reveal a deep ideological bias infecting certain recent versions of ethnology;
(2) the problems with Samuel Morton's argument in *Crania Americana*; scholars who disagree with his findings;
(3) how to handle "superficial objections";
(4) an alternative, environmental hypothesis to explain racial differences;
(5) evidence from political history in favor of commonality;
(6) how even if polygeny is true, there still is no reason to conclude the superiority of one race over another.

Let us take each of these in turn.

Consideration (1): In paragraphs 12 through 14, Douglass once again expresses his concern that his audience of academics not fall into the moral trap of thinking that the debate over common *versus* diverse origins is merely an empirical question to be settled by "neutral" scholars using the latest scientific theory. Rather, in Nott, Gliddon, Agassiz, and Morton,[28] we have a "phalanx of learned men" – if you like, an armed squad of scholars linked arm in arm clearly defending the pro-slavery movement. Indeed, as Douglass will mention at the end of the next section of the Address, there is the Congressional Record of debate on the "Nebraska Bill" showing how "slavery propagating statesmen" have "availed themselves" of ethnological texts in support of their position.[29] More importantly, though, Douglass will show how these very scholars, in particular Morton, have ignored the available scholarly evidence against their view and for the monogenists. Such a scholarly "vice" from those who should know better is perhaps, then, the most powerful evidence of their ideological bias.

Second, given the moral or "existential" issues here for a nation deeply divided, Douglass then describes how best to proceed in rationally weighing both sides of a debate for which a definitive demonstration is not humanly possible:

> Which of these answers [yes or no to monogeny] is most in accordance with facts, with reason, with the welfare of the world, and reflects most glory upon the wisdom, power, and goodness of the Author of all existence, is the question for consideration with us? On which side is the weight of the argument, rather than which side is absolutely proved. It must be admitted . . . that, viewed apart from the authority of the Bible, neither the unity, nor diversity of origin of the human family, can be demonstrated. To use the terse expression of the Rev. Dr Anderson [President of the University of Rochester] . . . "It is impossible to get far enough back for that." This much, however, can be done. The evidence on both sides, can be accurately weighed, and the truth arrived at with almost absolute certainty. (504; 230)

What sense are we twentieth-century philosophers to make of his opening list of criteria that includes more than a look at the facts and how things were reasoned? What is it to answer an allegedly empirical question in accordance with "the welfare of the world" and whether that answer "reflects most glory upon . . . the Author of all existence"? Is Douglass confusing science with the metaphysics of morals?

In this context, recall his earlier reference in paragraph nine to humans (*versus* non-humans) as not only being capable of speech, reason, and knowledge acquisition, but also possessive of a "heaven-erected face," aspirations, and prophecies. Recall further that this sort of theological anthropology was then followed up by a (question-begging) "denunciation" of evolutionary ideas in biology as "scientific moonshine." While it would be tempting from our perspective today to read past these "quaint" remarks and seek out his (for us) more convincing counterarguments (i.e., see Douglass as anticipating us), let us dwell on what he says here with a bit more hermeneutic sensitivity.

First, we note Douglass's acknowledgment that for many academics the debate over polygeny can, of course, be imagined "apart from the authority of the Bible," but that without such an appeal no (scientific) "demonstration" is possible for either side. By "demonstration" Douglass presumably means an irrefutable scientific proof, perhaps like one in geometry or theoretical physics or, given his quotation from Dr Anderson, some appeal to directly evident, incorrigible observations of the very ancient origins themselves of the "races." Let us acknowledge, but leave aside, our view today that a confirmed scientific theory requires no such absolute "demonstrations," in particular the idea that positive evidence alone would be sufficient.[30] In doing this, let us not miss an important point Douglass is after.

For Douglass, any persuasive political and moral arguments against slavery will require some sort of account of our human dignity, our "heaven-erected" faces, as for example is appealed to in the Un-American document, *The Declaration of Independence*, and can be further appealed to in countering the distortions of the Constitution in the 3/5's Compromise clause and Justice Taney's *Dred Scott* decision.[31] Presumably, Douglass saw no viable secular, "natural law" option in this debate.[32] Nor, we may presume further, would Douglass's religious commitments allow him to opt for utilitarian, socialist/Marxist or postmodern efforts to account for valuing human dignity and freedom. But we should also not forget that some philosophers today would still argue for a similar, theologically based conclusion.[33] In this context, then, while we moderns and postmoderns may radically repackage, we cannot simply dismiss as "quaint" or *passé* Douglass's criteria of factoring in the "welfare of the world" or whether the glory of God is reflected in our debates about human differences. We today still want to make sense of our human dignity.

Let us now turn to Douglass's section titled, "The Bearings of the Question" (505–7; 230–2), and see the opening set of considerations against the polygenists further developed. First, Douglass picks up again on the ship and voyage of life imagery he opened the address with. For the likely majority in the audience who would profess to a Christian orientation in their voyage of life, what should their "compasses" and "charts" read? That is, what should their "bearings" be? With this in mind, Douglass reminds his listeners of the Apostle Paul's remarks[34] "that God had made of one blood all nations of men for to dwell upon all the face of the earth," and that this basic belief, what Douglass calls here a "sheet anchor"[35] of hopes, will either have to "get a new interpretation or be overthrown altogether, if a diversity of human origin can be maintained" (505; 231). While we moderns and postmoderns might like to hear more from Douglass on getting "a new interpretation" of these texts (ones less metaphysically entangled), we can at least admire his sensitivity to what is at stake in changing the web of beliefs and concerns when confronted by something like slavery or *apartheid*.

Second, Douglass reminds his listeners of the "learned and pious Godwin," an important abolitionist and missionary to the West Indies, who wrote a book arguing against the view that it was sinful to baptize Negroes and Indians and bury them as Christians. For Douglass, the situation has not changed for Christians two hundred years after Godwin: the debates over abolishing slavery are at bottom once again a basic choice between the "selfish" and "philanthropic" part of mankind. Indeed, for Christians, however situated, there is apparently no other defining choice or either/or.

Finally, Douglass finishes this section by considering the possible objection that "views and opinions, favoring the unity of the human family, coming from one of lowly condition [such as himself!], are open to the suspicion, that 'the wish is father to the thought'" (506; 232). That is, what is motivating at least Negro abolitionists like Douglass is simple wishful thinking and thus a refusal to accept the verdicts of neutral empirical science. Douglass replies that "indeed, it may be so." Yet, his use of "may" here indicates that this need not be the only motivation, particularly if he can adduce weighty considerations against the polygenist thesis, which he attempts to do in the remainder of the speech. At this point, though, Douglass points out "that this deduction from the weight of the argument on the one side, is more than counterbalanced by the pride of race and position arrayed on the other." *Tu quoque*, then! He begs no more questions than they do. Indeed, he continues, "if the origin and motives of most works, opposing the doctrine of the unity of the human race, could be ascertained, it may be doubted whether *one* such work could boast an honest parentage." Then, with a sharp understanding of how ideology can blind those in questionable positions of power, he continues: "Pride and selfishness, combined with mental power, never want for a theory to justify them – and when men oppress their fellow-men, the oppressor ever finds, in the character of the oppressed, a full justification for his oppression . . . The evils most fostered by slavery and oppression, are precisely those which slaveholders and oppressors would transfer from their system to the inherent character of their victims" (507; 232). In any event, at least Douglass does not *pretend* to think he can argue the larger questions here with "scholarly neutrality."

Having shown, then, the inevitable moral, religious, and political presuppositions surrounding the polygeny debate, as well as the disingenuousness of those academics (even in the audience?) who would make it a neutral scholarly matter, Douglass moves on to the evidence that weighs *against* polygeny. Philosophers familiar with Plato's Socratic dialogue *Meno*, I propose, can hear a familiar opening numbing of the pretensions of the interlocutor (trained in the latest intellectual fashions by some Gorgias) so that a more open discussion can take place.

Consideration (2): Douglass's second set of considerations, as I am dividing it here, is found in the third and fourth sections of the speech entitled, respectively, "Ethnological Unfairness towards the Negro," (507–15; 233–6) and "Authorities as to the Resemblance of the Egyptians to Negroes" (515–18; 236–8). Both sections constitute a lengthy rebuttal of specific claims in Samuel Morton's well-known, *Crania Americana* of 1839. For our purposes, I will group these into three subsets of considerations: from the third section, (i) whether Morton can handle the embarrassing case of Egypt, and (ii) why Morton "leans" toward polygeny (his unacknowledged biases); from the fourth section, (iii) other evidence Morton overlooks.

The case of Egypt is embarrassing or problematic for Morton because, on the one hand, he accepts Egypt as one of the "earliest abodes of civilization," one that through Greece and Rome came to influence European and Euro-American culture greatly. On the other hand, he must square this view with his belief in polygeny (and the superiority of lighter races). Morton tries to show that while the Egyptians were not white people, they and their "degenerate" descendants, the Copts and Fellahs, have more of a brown complexion, straighter noses, and only rather thick lips and curly hair. To this reasoning, Douglass simply points out what his audience clearly knew in those times, that anyone with such features in the States then would clearly be treated as a Negro.[36]

Douglass also considers Morton's conclusion about an ancient historian (presumably in the Bible) who does not note the color of the Pharaoh's daughter that Solomon married, reasoning that if a European monarch married a Negro surely this would not have gone unnoticed. Douglass replies insightfully, if not definitively: "This is a sample of the reasoning of men who reason from *prejudice* rather than from *facts*. It assumes that a *black skin* in the *East* excites the same prejudice which we see here in the West" (509; 234).

The "leanings" that would produce such tortured reasoning by otherwise learned men beg, then, for explanation. Douglass points his audience to a similar prejudice common in England and the States, "that an educated man in Ireland ceases to be an Irishman, and an intelligent black man is always supposed to have derived his intelligence from his connection with the white race" (510; 235). To the latter prejudice he reminds the audience that it contradicts the existence of mulattos (by white fathers) and what for Douglass is apparently the reasonable hypothesis that intelligence is "uniformly derived from the maternal side." Douglass's use of "uniformly" seems to indicate a hereditarian view here, though it does not totally rule out certain forms of environmental determinism.[37] In any event, for us it, of course, makes little sense to attribute intelligence in general to either parent's biology exclusively.

In a related vein, next Douglass points out how not just Morton, but many naturalists and phrenologists distort their catalogues of the types of faces and skulls that "give an idea of the mental endowments of the Negro" by conveniently forgetting those of such distinguished African Americans as Alexander Crummell, M. R. Delaney, and others. Douglass writes powerfully: "If the very best type of the European is always presented, I insist that *justice*, in all such works, demands that the very best type of the Negro should also be taken. The importance of this criticism may not be apparent to all; – to the *black* man it is very apparent. He sees the injustice, and writhes under its sting" (514; 235). We, of course, saw a similar point above in paragraph 8 when Douglass defended his first claim against the assertion that no slave can match the intellectual powers and eloquence of Webster or Clay.

Douglass then ends the third section of the address with an exercise in "parity of reasoning" that shows a further inconsistency in Morton and others' reasoning:

> It seems to me that a man might as well deny the affinity of the American to the Englishman, as to deny such affinity between the Negro and the Egyptian. He might make out as many points of difference, in the case of the one as in that of the other. Especially could this be done, if, like ethnologists, in given cases, only typical specimens were resorted to. The lean, slender American, pale and swarthy, if exposed to the sun, wears a very different appearance to the full, round Englishman, of clear, *blonde* complexion. (514–15; 235–6)

Douglass follows this point up by suggesting that one revisit the common portraits of the American presidents, allegedly showing a progression from a more wiry appearance to those with more "serene amplitude." I read Douglass here to be saying ironically that given the kind of superficial evidence both the catalogues in question and these portraits amount to about attributions of mind, one conclusion is as good (or bad!) as another. In fact, both the catalogues and the paintings are consistent with the view he will address in more detail in the last section of his speech, that differences between and within races can just as well be explained by reference to varying environmental factors as by biological ones.

Douglass now begins his fourth section, "Authorities as to the Resemblance of the Egyptians to Negroes." First, he cites among others Denon's *Travels in Egypt*, Prichard on the Colchians, Volney on the Copts, all of whom attest that while the Egyptians "differ very strongly from the Negro, debased and enslaved, that difference is not greater than may be observed in other quarters of the globe, among people notoriously belonging to the same variety, the original stock" (515; 236). Second, Douglass adduces the work of philologists or historical linguists at that point who argue that just as there are linguistic similarities between Egyptians and the more northern, semitic language groups, so too are there similarities if one goes south and west into Africa. Leaving aside the problems with any such historical linguistic theory then or now,[38] we may at the very least credit Douglass with pointing out then available, plausible counterevidence to polygenesis.

We come now to Douglass's third set of considerations against polygenesis, the fifth section of his paper entitled, "Superficial Objections" (518–19; 238–9). Here Douglass gives shorter treatment to what in his mind are less important assertions about the differences between the races. First, he responds to three claims in Charles H. Smith's 1851 *Natural History of the Human Species*: (1) that the structure of the Negro head is better fit for carrying burdens; (2) the "hard pushed" or pressed claim that the male Negro voice is feeble and hoarse, indicating servility and inferiority; and (3) that no "woolly haired races" have ever discovered an alphabet. Contrary to (1), Douglass points to the examples of such burden-carrying in German and Irish immigrants to the United States, and to the long practice of it by oriental societies, adding that what is arguably a "custom" is no clear proof of an "original difference." To (2), Douglass again opposes a reasonable counterhypothesis that such vocal effects are the result of oppression and not nature. Indeed, Douglass's own powerful speaking voice surely also struck his audience as ironic in citing this objection. Then, to (3) he cites work by philologists on the Mandingoe's alphabet and even holds up to his audience a grammar of the Mpongwe language given to him by President Anderson. Finally, he notes in passing a topic for another series of lectures, Nott's and Gliddon's 1854 *Types of Mankind*, to which we have referred earlier.

With these "superficial objections" behind him, Douglass moves to the last two sections of his address. The sixth section is short and seems to function as a transition to the seventh.

Douglass now turns to a different strategy, one that does not require him or anyone to "attend to the anatomical and physiological argument connected with this part of the subject" (520; 240). The point now is to emphasize how conditions in the work environment can more easily explain differences in groups of people. Douglass begins by relating the story of how a bootmaker could not believe that Douglass had been a slave since his instep, unlike that of hard laborers in the bootmaker's experience, was too high. Clearly here the discrepancies were best explained by who was exposed to what circumstances. Douglass follows this story up with references to the common people he had seen in Ireland or other workers in the United States. About the Irish particularly, Douglass says: "The open, uneducated mouth – the long, gaunt arm – the badly formed foot and ankle – the shuffling gait – the retreating forehead and vacant expression . . . all reminded me of the plantation . . . The Irishman educated, is a model gentleman; the Irishman ignorant and degraded, compares in form and feature, with the Negro." For Douglass, such everyday "facts" are more readily explained by "the vicissitudes of barbarism" than a more controversial theory about hereditary differences: "Need we look higher than a vertical sun, or lower than the damp, black soil of the Niger, the Gambia . . . rising ever from the rank growing and decaying vegetation, for an explanation of the Negro's color? If a cause, full and adequate, can be found here, *why seek further?*" (521; 241).

Yet, mindful of the limited character of all such arguments by polygenists and monogenists alike, Douglass cautions his audience: "Again, what does it all prove? Nothing, absolutely; nothing which places the question beyond dispute; but it *does* justify the conjecture before referred to, that outward circumstances *may* have something to do with modifying the various phases of humanity" (522; 242). Once again Douglass shows his sensitivity to the degrees of justification, if not absolute proof, possible in so-called inductive arguments. Finally, before leaving this point, Douglass notes that everything he has said about the effects of "outward circumstances" is still consistent with the existence of a God who endowed its creatures with broad capacities capable of "countless variations in form, feature and color, without having it necessary to begin a new creation for every new variety." His, then, is the *simpler* and less revolutionary explanation (particularly relative to those polygenists who are theists).

Douglass comes next to what I am calling his fifth kind of consideration. Here he cites the "facts" from political history that dissimilar nations can be united in one social state to their mutual advancement. Such facts would at least be explained by monogenism. Douglass cites the case of England after all its invasions, the Medes and Persians, and the Russians over the Tartars and Poles. We can, of course, see this sort of evidence as a version of the "change the outward circumstances, change the behavioral traits" argument just reviewed.

Finally, Douglass senses time slipping and brings to bear his last argument. Suppose it turns out that his reasoning so far is unsound and that there is a greater preponderance of evidence for polygenesis than monogenesis, say, in particular that Egyptians and Nubians, etc. are not related to Negroes (e.g., evidence from a science that uses less "manifest images" of the groups). So what? "Does it follow, that the Negro should be held in contempt? . . . that to enslave and imbrue him is either *just* or *wise*? I think not," replies Douglass (523; 243). For, even if there are diverse origins, why does it follow that at bottom a common nature is not shared? Or, at least enough of a shared nature to share a "common destiny"? (Think of parallel "what ifs" that imagine rational and caring extraterrestrials we would want to admit to our moral community.)

Douglass then follows up the previous hypothetical reasoning with a pragmatic point about a "common destiny" between Negroes and the white man. Consider three ways Negroes might disappear as a problem for whites: (1) separation and emigration/colonization elsewhere, (2) extermination, or (3) dying out. The first option, though often proposed (e.g., by the trustees of Case Western!), is too unrealistic now that Negroes have a two-hundred-year attachment to the soil. The second option, extermination, Douglass urges, is unlikely because of the abiding influence of Christianity (if you are not a Native American) and the self-interest of an expanding country that needs pioneers and laborers now.[39] The third option of dying out is also simply statistically improbable given how well blacks have survived slavery in North America. So, short of the second option acted upon by whites (shades of Derrick Bell), Negroes are here to stay. *Ergo,* the most probable conjecture is that whites and blacks share a "common destiny," whether they like it or not, whether they have common origins or not.

We come then to Douglass's final paragraph where he reverts to the ironical tone he opened with. He writes:

> The subject is before you. I shall not undertake to make the application. I speak as unto wise men. I stand in the presence of Scholars. We have met here to day from vastly different points in the world's condition. I have reached here . . . by little short of a miracle; . . . by dint of some application and perseverance. Born,

as I was, in obscurity, a stranger to the halls of learning, environed by ignorance, degradation, and their concomitants, from birth to manhood, I do not feel at liberty to mark out ... what is the precise vocation of the Scholar. (525; 244)

Rather, in the final analysis, he can close only by speaking as a "denizen of the world" and a "citizen of a country rolling in the sin and shame of Slavery." The irony here, I think, consists in the way in which Douglass, by miracle or (good) "moral luck"[40] and "by dint of some application and perseverance," has mastered many of the theoretical (argumentative) skills of the Scholar and Commencement Speaker, but still is a "stranger to the halls of learning." For, *only* as a slave-denizen of the world outside the ivory towers, "environed by ignorance, degradation," and now as an engaged abolitionist-citizen of his threatened Union, has he been able to speak with any moral authority about the false charts and compasses all too easily overlooked by the comfortable Scholar and philosopher.

We are left, then, with the question we opened this essay with: what sort of evidence, and according to what criteria, do we find in this Commencement Address that Frederick Douglass is a Philosopher (a kind of scholar)? If we take the traditional criteria for measuring theoretical wisdom (analytical rigor, subtlety of argument – preeminently found in sustained, treatise-style texts; breadth of major issues covered; originality of ideas and theories), Douglass probably surprises many first-time readers with his refined sense of argument and debate and with the fact of his autodidactism. Does he, however, cover issues outside of the social and political realm (say, the way Mill did)? Apparently not. But, then, neither did Socrates, Emerson, nor Kierkegaard, with their turn to "the human things" and the issue of "subjective truth."

What about the *influence* of his ideas? Can they be called groundbreaking? If we look at Douglass's own religious liberalism, its concomitant anthropology and appeals to Divine natural law, his ideas clearly seem derivative and not terribly well worked out. So, what we seem to have is a good candidate for the earlier-mentioned Nochlin-strategy: "Hey, he's pretty darn good, given his late start and lack of opportunity."

But, again, this sort of reply does not consider any interpretive possibilities where the performative texts of Douglass (or of a Socrates, Emerson, or Kierkegaard) function like the admonitions of Old Testament prophets, perhaps even as "anti-texts," making both internal and external criticisms of a cultural practice or paradigm in crisis, and calling it forth to its ownmost "Either/Or." Viewed as such a provocative gadfly-performance, then, Douglass's Commencement Address attempts to edify the "halls of learning" he is an invited "stranger" to. In this light, then, argument and rigorous analysis have their place, but only as sub-acts within a larger, edifying (perlocutionary?) act of confronting his audience with the Choice before them in the seemingly "neutral" scientific arguments of ethnology. Of course, whether this larger, edifying act is, in John Austin's words, a "felicitous" one, is hard to tell, both for audiences then and now. Finally, as for whether his performance constituted "doing philosophy," we have seen in this essay the makings of an affirmative case from within the complex of metaphilosophical positions already available in the tradition.[41] It is in this sense, then, that Douglass's texts continue to make a claim on us, philosophically considered.

Notes

1 Frederick Douglass, *My Bondage and Freedom*, pp. 361–2; as quoted by John Blassingame, ed, *The Frederick Douglass Papers* Series I/vol. I, p. xlviii.
2 See Frank M. Kirkland, "'Loose Canons' and Canons of Justification," paper read at March 1993 Pacific Division Meeting of the *APA*, San Francisco, CA.
3 Linda Nochlin, "Why There are no Great Women Artists," in *Women, Art, and Power and other Essays* (New York: Harper & Row, 1988), 145–78.
4 The particular social theory used here to analyze why "equal opportunity" has not been there can, of course, vary somewhat. Presumably, natural law theory, libertarianism, and Millean liberalism would not alter who is already in the Canon of Greats, just argue for greater inclusivity (at least in the future).
5 See Michael Walzer, *Interpretation and Social Criticism* (Cambridge: Harvard University Press, 1987). Walzer distinguishes between an external social critic (like Jonah to Ninevah) and an internal critic (like Amos to the Hebrews). I suggest that Douglass's status as a former slave and self-taught preacher-orator gives him qualities of both kinds of prophetic critics. Especially with respect to the Academy, without an official pedigree Douglass was more of an outsider than, say, Cornel West, Henry Gates, or Houston Baker are. For all these scholars, though, "insider/outsider" is a matter of degree.
6 Whether in this Kuhnian vocabulary Douglass is a "revolutionary" or in Gadamer's term a "rehabilitator" of US moral and political ideals, is not a simple matter. Herbert Storing has argued that Douglass moved from a more radical, Garrisonian position condemning the US constitution as irreparable and requiring emigration for blacks, to a more "statesman-like"

position re-emphasizing the *Declaration of Independence* as a more foundational document that can be used to reconstruct ("deconstruct"?) the Constitution and its offending clauses. See his essay, "Frederick Douglass," in Joseph M. Bessette, ed, *Toward a More Perfect Union: Writings of Herbert J. Storing* (Washington, D.C.: American Enterprise Institute, 1995), pp. 151–75.

7 See Barbara Johnson, ed, *Freedom and Interpretation: The Oxford Amnesty Lectures 1993* (New York: Basic Books, 1993).

8 In what follows, all page references to this address will be given in parentheses, with the Blassingame edition (*The Frederick Douglas Papers*) first, then the page number in Howard Brotz's popular anthology, *Negro Social and Political Thought: 1850–1920* (Basic Books: New York, 1966).

9 I derive the following remarks primarily from two sources: Blassingame's introductory notes to the speech, vol. II, pp. 498–9; and from A. and J. McCluskey, "Frederick Douglass on Ethnology: A Commencement Address at Western Reserve College 1854," *Negro History Bulletin*, 40, Sept.–Oct. 1977, pp. 747–9.

10 Blassingame, ed, *The Frederick Douglass Papers*, vol. I, pp. lxv, lxviii.

11 Ibid., p. xlviii.

12 Ibid., p. xlviii.

13 See Hume's essay, "Of National Characters"; Kant's *Observations on the Feeling of the Beautiful and the Sublime*, and Hegel's Introduction to his *Lectures on the Philosophy of History*. For Thomas Jefferson's refusal to countenance the work of the black mathematician, Benjamin Banneker, or both Jefferson's and Lincoln's ambivalence toward the equality of the races, see Ronald Takaki, *A Different Mirror* (Boston: Little and Brown, 1993), chapters 3 and 5. Or, for the "reception" of Phyllis Weatley's poetry, chapter 3 of Henry Louis Gates, Jr, *Loose Canons: Notes on the Culture Wars* (New York: Oxford University Press, 1992).

14 See Howard McGary and Bill E. Lawson, *Between Slavery and Freedom: Philosophy and American Slavery* (Bloomington: Indiana University Press, 1992), chapter 3 especially.

15 Of course, it is also possible to attribute a more complex intentionality to Douglass here: he may simultaneously be feeling somewhat overwhelmed, grateful, and yet full of Socratic gadfly purpose, thereby harboring all these intentional states in a seemingly Samboish choice of words. That is precisely the *ambiguity* attributed to such behavior.

16 Stephen Jay Gould, *The Mismeasure of Man* (New York: Norton, 1981), p. 51. I am greatly indebted to Gould's critical review of Morton's data gathering and skull collecting in chapter 2.

17 Think of what arguably happens to the readers of Plato's *Euthyphro* as they soon discover that they are not much better able to answer Socrates's questions than the comically pious Euthyphro himself.

18 Note one: the title page to the 1620 edition of *Novuum Organum* displayed a ship sailing through the Pillars of Hercules at the Western end of the

Mediterranean (the limits of Ancient Wisdom) out into the new knowledge of Nature by empirical science, declaring at the foot of the waves, "Multi pertransibunt, et augebitur scientia" ("Many will pass through and knowledge will be increased.")

Note two: I am indebted to Dr Jim Gray for pointing out the striking similarity of this ship metaphor with that in Longfellow's well-known 1849 poem, "The Building of the Ship," especially with its famous last stanza where the ship the yard-master has built is paralleled to the "ship of state," the "Union, strong and great!." Indeed, the sixth to the last line warns of "false lights on the shore." Whether Douglass was aware of this poem in writing his Commencement Address, I have not been able to ascertain. The parallels are uncanny, though.

19 In the early 1840s Douglass in fact worked sometimes in Bedford, Massachusetts as a preacher for the A. M. E. Zionist church, inspired by the Reverends William Serrington and Thomas James. Garrison was to hear Douglass here for the first time. See William S. McFeely, *Frederick Douglass* (Norton: New York, 1991), pp. 81–3.

20 Two notes here. First, that Douglass's appeals to "country" are not just clichés is evidenced by many of his other speeches. In particular, one should note the shift that takes place from his famous Garrisonian, Fourth of July speech to his post-Garrisonian speeches: i.e., from rejector of the Constitution as irredeemably corrupt and defender of black expatriation *to* rejector of such expatriation/separation and defender of the Constitution and the *Declaration of Independence* as requiring the abolition of slavery. For more on Douglass as a candidate for "statesman," see Herbert Storing's interesting article, "The Case Against Civil Disobedience," in Robert Goldwin, ed, *On Civil Disobedience* (Chicago: Rand McNally, 1969), pp. 106–20.

Second, Douglass's many appeals to God are also genuine, even though Douglass was known, and criticized, in his own day for his attacks on organized religion and his own move to a more "liberal" model where less emphasis was put on God's will controlling events and more was put on the power (given by God) to transform human social and political institutions on the basis of Christian love. For a helpful discussion of Douglass's shift to religious liberalism, see Waldo E. Martin, *The Mind of Frederick Douglass* (Chapel Hill: University of North Carolina Press, 1984), esp. chapter 7, pp. 175ff.

21 I am assuming here that Douglass is referring to recommendations that might have been found in some handbook of oratory at that time, but I have no evidence of this.

22 E.g., Thomas Reid or G. E. Moore or Wittgenstein in *On Certainty*, or related "transcendental arguments," attempting to establish a class of indispensable truths. If there is such a class of truths, then they may be labeled as "basic" or "foundational." For more subtlety on the various possibilities for foundationalism, see William P. Alston, *Epistemic Justifica-*

tion (Ithaca: Cornell University Press, 1989), especially the essay, "Two Types of Foundationalism," pp. 19–38.

23 See, however, Jonathan Bennett's 1987 APA Presidential Address, "Thoughtful Brutes," *Proceedings and Addresses of the APA*, supplement to 62 (1), Sept. 1988, pp. 197–210. Bennett gives a thoroughgoing materialist argument that, given what we know about terrestrial beings at least, humans seem to have very unique linguistic capacities not readily attributable to non-humans with only more rudimentary ones.

24 See Sharon Begley's brief and helpful overview, "Three is not Enough", *Newsweek*, February 13, 1995, pp. 67–9. Also, Kwame Anthony Appiah, "Illusions of Race," in his *In My Father's House* (New York: Oxford University Press, 1992), pp. 28–46.

25 See the debate, "Where did Modern Humans Originate?," in *Scientific American*, April 1992, pp. 66–83. The paleontologists, Alan Wilson and Rebecca Cann, present a case for a common African woman ancestor of some 200,000 years ago whose line outlived the lines of "her" counterpart mothers: "The Recent African Genesis of Humans," pp. 68–73. The paleoanthropologists, Alan Thorne and Milford Wolpoff, argue that there is better evidence for no common "mother" (lineage traced through mothers) and that various human groups arose where they are found today: "The Multiregional Evolution of Humans," pp. 76–83.

26 Martin, *The Mind of Frederick Douglass*, pp. 248–9, indicates that Douglass adjusted his views with the rise of Darwinism, moving from a Lamarckian environmentalism with elements of evolutionism to, if not a Darwinian evolutionism, a form of social Darwinism. According to Martin, he was never comfortable with biological links to non-humans.

27 Blassingame speculates that this passage refers to Samuel Smith whose ethnological views dominated in the US before the emergence of the American School of Agassiz and Morton in the 1840s.

28 Blassingame, *The Frederick Douglass Papers*, p. 503, n. 5 explains that Nott, Gliddon, Agassiz, and Morton formed the American polygenist school of ethnology, which questioned the monogenist thesis advocated by the British physician/ethnologist James Prichard and the American naturalist Samuel Stanhope. Douglass is, then, clearly weighing in on the side of the older theories of the monogenists, Prichard and Stanhope.

29 Douglass refers (p. 232) to "the Nebraska Bill," which I take as the famous Kansas-Nebraska Act debated over the winter of 1853 and passed in the spring of 1854 just before this Commencement Address in July. In this bill, proposed by Illinois Democratic Senator Stephen A. Douglas (!), "popular sovereignty" was passed as a way of determining which new territories and states would admit slavery, thereby overturning the Missouri Compromise of 1820. I am indebted to Dr Light Cummins for help in interpreting this reference.

30 For more on how scientific theories and hypotheses are confirmed and accepted, see John Earman and Wesley Salmon, "The Confirmation of

Scientific Hypotheses," in Wesley Salmon, John Earman et al. eds, *Introduction to the Philosophy of Science* (Englewood Cliffs, NJ: Prentice Hall, 1992), pp. 42–103.

31 Again, see Storing's article, "The Case Against Civil Disobedience," cited above.

32 See David E. Schrader's essay, "Natural Law in the Constitutional Thought of Frederick Douglass" in this volume.

33 See Alistair MacIntrye, *After Virtue*, 2nd ed (Notre Dame: Notre Dame University Press, 1984), and West, *Keeping Faith* (New York: Routledge, 1994). While MacIntrye and West would be sympathetic with Douglass's conclusion, their respective positions arguably result from a more detailed treatment of the fragmentation of modern culture and attempts at secular ethics.

34 In his sermon to the Athenians on Mars Hill in *Acts* 17:26.

35 Following out the nautical imagery here, we may note that sheet anchors are those lines on sailing ships used to regulate the angle at which a sail is set in relation to the wind. Presumably, then, they are very important to one's "bearings."

36 Martin, *The Mind of Frederick Douglass*, p. 226, notes that in his later, 1844 *Crania Aegyptica* Morton acknowledges that ancient Egyptians were a mix of Negroid, Caucasoid, and Semitic influences, but insists that all greatness of the Egyptians was derived from the Caucasian admixture.

37 Ibid., p. 325, points out quite helpfully that Douglass, himself a mulatto with strong affection for his slave mother, was deeply offended by the theory of mulatto degenerationism also espoused by many polygenists.

38 I have not been able to track down what particular studies Douglass is referring to here. However, given the current state of historical linguistics, I would guess part of what he says would be accepted now and part not: current theories (more or less the same since the 1950s) propose 4 macro-groupings of language for Africa as opposed to an earlier 3-group model: Afro-Asiatic (the older Hamitic-Semitic), Niger-Kordofanian, Nilo-Sahara, and Khosian. The groups Douglass refers to all seem to fall in the first group, which includes not only Coptic (descendant of old Egyptian), but Cushitic (Ethiopia, Sudan, Somalia, Kenya), Berber, Chadic (Lake Chad area), Omotic (maybe a branch of Semitic), and Semitic. I have not been able to tell what sorts of (weak) connections all the 4 groups may have in common, if any. The biggest problem for such research is, of course, having access to the earliest possible root connections, if any, there may have been. My research has been limited by lack of expertise to a cursory study of Kirsten Malmkjaer, ed, *The Linguistic Encyclopedia* (Routledge: London, 1991), pp. 189–216; and to William Bright, ed, *International Encyclopedia of Linguistics* (Oxford: New York, 1992), vol. 1, pp. 31–6.

39 The second option sounds curiously similar to Derrick Bell's "Space Traders" thought-experiment. See his *Faces at the Bottom of the Well* (New York: Basic Books, 1992), chapter 9.

40 See Bernard Williams, "Moral Luck," in his *Moral Luck* (Cambridge: Cambridge University Press, 1981), for an analysis of how fortunate and unfortunate events outside of the agent nevertheless call forth virtuous deliberation and action, often at the cost of some happiness.

41 Note that even if we read Douglass as a postmodernist constructing anti-texts/performances over against the dominant "discursive practice" (here identified with Aristotle's theoretical/practical distinction), such postmodernism is not obviously totally outside the tradition it is criticizing; it may only be appealing to possibly forgotten, "revolutionary" remnants in that very tradition. See Heidegger's attempts to evoke forgotten "gods" in his later essays overagainst the dominant age of technology. Or, see Derrida's invocation of the thrust of negative theology in reflecting on his own attempts to "deconstruct" a dominant metaphysics of presence. (We may note that neither Heidegger nor Derrida need be taken as "discovering" latent or "deep meanings" objectively there in Western discourse when they speak of their continued connection to that very tradition of discourse.)

7

The Grammar of Civilization: Douglass and Crummell on Doing Things with Words

Stephen L. Thompson

Just as Kant heralded an epoch defined by universalistic moral reason before them, black thinkers in the nineteenth century optimistically anticipated a modern era of practical reason based on universal rather than contingent concerns. By Alexander Crummell's estimation, for instance, a "new era" awaited blacks in which concepts germane to practical discourses about freedom, justice, and the like were cognitively accessible to newly emancipated black persons. A modern age of universalistic moral thought and talk was to be the birthright of modern African Americans.

Maria Stewart's estimations are perhaps the earliest extant articulation of black modernity. She understood that slaves desired:

> to rise above the conditions of servants and drudges. I have learnt, by bitter experience, that continual hard labor deadens the energies of the soul, and benumbs the faculties of the mind; the ideas become confined, the mind barren, and, like the scorching sands of Arabia, produces nothing; or, like the uncultivated soil, brings forth thorns and thistles.[1]

Like every significant black thinker in that century, Stewart (1803–79) took the threat to the integrity of black minds posed by their oppressive circumstances to be the chief obstacle (besides racism itself) to modernity. Underscoring this in another address she argued that:

> it is not the color of the skin that makes the man or the woman, but the principle formed in the soul. Brilliant wit will shine, come from

whence it will; and genius and talent will not hide the brightness of its lustre . . . The dark clouds of ignorance are dispersing. The light of science is bursting forth. Knowledge is beginning to flow, nor will its moral influence be extinguished till its refulgent rays have spread over us from East to West, and from North to South.[2]

Her sense of urgency and optimism about minds and modernity is only intelligible against a deeper view about minds and morals. Knowledge and science have the "moral influence" needed for moral uplift.

This view sharpens in Crummell (1819–98) and Frederick Douglass (1818–95); indeed, no serious challenge to the view unfolds in that century. On it one's *moral* biography is only as robust as one's *mental* biography. A rich cognitive and – as becomes increasingly obvious – linguistic repertoire underwrites the life of the genuinely modern mind. The view's broad appeal reached educators, for instance, who took it as their mandate, while political reformers saw it as the moral center of their respective causes.[3] Any smoldering controversies among intellectuals – and there were plenty – erupted around claims derived from the view rather than the view itself.

Two such derivative positions arm-wrestled in the middle of that century. Douglass championed one. The terribly fragile life of the slave's mind required knowledge his or her peers likely had – knowing paths to freedom, say, or else arguments for abolition. But communicating knowledge requires mastering language skills. And if knowledge needs protecting those skills must be that much more subtle, conveying meanings indirectly if necessary, using context and implication rather than bald assertion. Slaves could thus propagate ideas using a nuanced linguistic repertoire to increase both their hatred of slavery and love of freedom. Literacy, by awakening faculties of mind, gave ideas power.

However, Crummell doubted that even subtle communicative resources as such were sufficient to render the powers of mind and the ideas minds entertain emancipatory. A black nationalist who took a degree in philosophy at Cambridge in the 1840s, he argued that if black people dwell on such past horrors as slavery, they forgo the benefits of a civilization built on the guiding ideals of an intellectually rich future. For Crummell, such ideals engineer progress in history. No hindrance is too sacred to sacrifice in their pursuit. Actively recalling ideas like the horrors of slavery (rather than merely remembering them) compromises fragile civilizing tendencies. He thus emphasized the scholarly dimensions of the language of the Anglo-Saxon more than the communicative language of the Negro, his black nationalism notwithstanding, to nurture intellectually rich ideals. Standard English, for instance, can better sustain fine differentiation of meaning and reference and, since it can be faithfully written and read, better express formal, complex argument. Language thus civilizes the community of its users.

Freedom and race have been commented on extensively by others. I will not explore those topics here. Instead, I will reconstruct the views Douglass and Crummell defended about language and the mind. It turns out that there are several remarkable turns of argument in their respective work. And although most philosophy of language since the end of the nineteenth century has rejected the view of grammar undergirding many of these arguments, there remain a number of important insights to be gained. This is all the more so given the prominence of speech act theory in recent decades, as well as generative theories of grammar. Reconciling deep features of a universal grammar with the robust communicative dimensions of language use remains at the top of the research agenda of the philosophy of language. Douglass and Crummell shared that agenda.

To get at this, I will argue from behind the thinkers a bit. First, there is the broad mind-language-morals (I will refer to it as the MLM) thesis in black thought; I distinguish three moments in it. What *states of mind* are necessary for a robust moral life? What sort of *grammar* does this states-of-mind view presuppose? And how ought *communication* to proceed in a community where the right states-of-mind command the right grammars? These three themes – and hence the MLM thesis they constitute – appear in various stages in Stewart, Douglass, and Crummell. This is so despite the fact that Stewart addressed states of mind though never language as such. It is thus only with respect to mind and morals that the MLM thesis occurs in her thinking. I begin there.

I   States of Mind

The "daughters and sons" of Africa of and to whom she often spoke were to "improve your talents" and "show forth your powers of mind." As in my opening, "the principle formed in the soul" – specifically those of "piety, morality and virtues" – determine one's readiness for modernity.[4] The power to navigate moral reasoning, that is, mind, thus comes to dominate her views.

Several striking features give her thinking its logical contour. Generations transmit knowledge from older to younger, for instance, and so bear a civilizing duty. A building metaphor of hers suggests that this is in fact the mechanism of progress. By setting examples for younger generations, the "minds of tender babes" may be prepared to observe pure moral principles. Notice the appeal to purity of mind to establish purity of character:

> Did the daughters of our land possess a delicacy of manners, combined with gentleness and dignity; did their pure minds hold vice in abhorrence and contempt, did they frown when their ears were polluted with its vile accents, would not their influence become powerful? Would not our brethren fall in love with their virtues? Their souls would become ambitious to distinguish themselves. They would become proud to display their talents. Able advocates would arise in our defense. Knowledge would begin to flow, and the chains of slavery and ignorance would melt like wax before the flames.[5]

Knowledge, by eradicating ignorance, diminishes the damage slavery inflicted. In her thought, purity of one's state of mind and moral character is necessary for the progressive development of black people. Stewart put mind and morals (complete with their transgenerational reach) on distinctively modern footing.

While blacks have the raw materials required for self-improvement, the "*'I can't,'* is a great barrier in the way. I hope it will soon be removed, and *'I will,'* resume its place."[6] The dimensions of mind operative here are not merely its powers to *represent what is known*, but also its powers to *exercise will*. Practical reason, on which representation and volition converge, command the pursuit of better black futures in modernity. Note that she does not shun theoretical reason. Instead, she merely orients reason toward practice to provide an entry point into black forms of life. Every subsequent African-American thinker during the nineteenth century embarks from that point.

The Kantian character of the argument is obvious. His moral maxims were pure by definition, not to mention the will, which wills them to be universal laws in an idealized moral community. His "kingdom of ends," like Stewart's modern black future, took pure moral principles to have regulative sway. And purity on both accounts is moral. One's contingent interests do not generate the duties one has.

This is nonetheless ambiguous. Stewart sometimes spoke of the purity of moral principles as if that were due to their foundational role in modern reasoning. But is purity a cognitive category? Do the principles of morality possess pure *logical* features that thus befit them for modern *moral* reasoning? Does the logical drive the moral? Is that what makes an ideal black future modern? For Kant moral reasoning turns not only on suspending interest, but on the logical character of maxims of action as well – that is, whether they may be coherently universalized. A logical property of a rule for action thus puts it into moral play. Should we read Stewart along these lines?

If she took the purity of moral principles to be definitive in this way, which she seemed to do, then her "state-of-mind" argument takes on central importance. Abstract reasoning, as in one's adopting a universal perspective, depends on a suitably adept state of mind.

However, a competing reading might take her to claim that for a principle to be moral, it must pass some morally specifiable test, say one of fairness or sensitivity to duty. This alternative reading puts the moral story at the center of practical reasoning, on which the *moral* drives the *logical*. Modern blacks are to discern their duties – that which is good for racial uplift – and propagate knowledge to younger generations accordingly. Knowledge follows duty.

The problem with this latter version is twofold. How do persons discern their duties? Those who reason morally have to follow some lights, whether intuitive or inferred. Otherwise – if morality is instinctive – there is no moral issue. Doing what comes naturally is simply doing what comes naturally. But this is clearly not what Stewart is talking about. Moral character has been corrupted by slavery, and a guiding light, a corrective ideal, is necessary for a viable black future. On a view like Stewart's, based solely on principle, there is no recourse other than raw analytical effort applied to foundational precepts. And that implies adopting a standpoint one does not normally occupy. Practical reasoning for Stewart must be abstract and universalistic. And black minds must be up to the challenge that presents. Besides (and this is the other problem) if morals drive logic the state-of-mind issue is not simply placed at a different priority. It becomes irrelevant. If all there is is specifying duties or articulating fairness, then one need not develop a state of mind ripe for cognitive flourishing. All one needs is an appropriate directive from a trusted authority. And nothing threatens modernity more than tutelage, as Kant understood.[7]

Stewart's transgenerational ethic falls in place against the preferred reading I suggest. Mothers (especially) have a responsibility to children, namely to "create in the minds of your little girls and boys a thirst for knowledge, the love of virtue, the abhorrence of vice, and the cultivation of a pure heart." This work is progressive. Parents lay the foundation, teaching the "first rudiments of useful knowledge," on which higher and more formalized education builds:

> I am of a strong opinion, that the day on which we unite, heart and soul, and turn our affection to knowledge and improvement, that

day the hissing and reproach among the nations of the earth against us will cease ... Let us make a mighty effort, and arise; and if no one will promote or respect us, let us promote and respect ourselves.[8]

The cognitive, oriented toward the practical, drives the moral. Hence Stewart's challenge to her audience to turn ideas and thoughts into effective moral practice. "Let us not say, we know this, or, we know that, and practice nothing; but let us practice what we do know."[9] Continuing: "[o]h, then, turn your attention to knowledge and improvement; for knowledge is power."[10] Note that sheer "moral capability," though adequate, is considerably less than ideal:

[T]here are no chains so galling as the chains of ignorance – no fetters so binding as those that bind the soul, and exclude it from the vast field of useful and scientific knowledge. O, had I received the advantage of early education, my ideas would, ere now, have expanded far and wide; but, alas! I possess nothing but moral capability – no teachings but the teachings of the Holy Spirit.[11]

It followed for Stewart that barren minds led to moral deficiency. In what turns out to be an opening salvo in the debates between Douglass and Crummell, Stewart claimed that anticipating a life of unending servitude brings to the mind a "horrible idea," that of possessing a noble soul capable of high achievement and development, and yet confined by ignorance and poverty to servitude. This is profoundly debilitating and (literally, on her account) demoralizing. Premodern ignorance renders the mind (as in one of the passages I opened with) "barren." Hence the meager literary accomplishments (in her view) of blacks. "Had we the opportunity you [that is, Stewart's audience of white women] have had, to improve our moral and mental faculties, what would have hindered our intellects from being as bright, and our manners from being as dignified as yours?"[12]

It is via the purity of principles, and an appropriately rich set of cognitive resources, that modern blacks will enter their better futures. Stewart, in line with the Kantian thrust of earlier enlightenment thought, endorses a nascent MLM thesis. Robust states of mind provide the essential condition for moral reasoning, for their ability to entertain certain categories of ideas, their powers of processing those ideas within a logical framework consisting of pure (practical) principles, and their level of volitional integrity, on which character can be built and knowledge can be transmitted.

The Grammar of Civilization 179

What is so interesting is, although she was quite clear here, we actually have some wiggle room as to whether we call Crummell or Douglass the rightful heir to her view. As I shall discuss below, Douglass appealed (negatively) to ignorance as the essential condition of the slave's state of mind. That turns out to imply (on one spin) that blacks ought to keep its horrors fresh in their minds. Crummell likewise saw ignorance as undermining black progress. But (on a different spin) that implies embracing high civilizing ideals. First Douglass.

Like Stewart before him, Douglass thought slavery subverts morality.[13] And neither slave nor slaveholder was exempt from moral defect. He noted, for example, that had his former master "been brought up in a free state, surrounded by the just restraints of free society . . . [Captain] Anthony might have been as humane . . . and respectable as are members of society generally. The slaveholder, as well as the slave, is the victim of the slave system."[14] And nothing less than the power and integrity of reason itself is at stake:

> Reason is imprisoned here, and passions run wild. Like the fires of the prairie, once lighted, they are at the mercy of every wind, and must burn, till they have consumed all that is combustible within their remorseless grasp. Capt. Anthony could be kind, and, at times, he even showed an affectionate disposition . . . But the pleasant moods of a slaveholder are remarkably brittle; they are easily snapped; they neither come often, nor remain long. His temper is subjected to perpetual trials.[15]

(This could easily be confused with a clinical description of bipolar disorder.) Anthony's corrupt state of mind led to abuses of language, as Douglass saw it. Note his MLM-style gloss:

> [Anthony] seldom walked alone without muttering to himself; and he occasionally stormed about, as if defying an army of invisible foes. "He would do this, that, and the other; he'd be d....d if he did not," – was the usual form of his threats. Most of his leisure was spent in walking, cursing and gesticulating, like one possessed by a demon. Most evidently, he was a wretched man, at war with his own soul, and with all the world around him.[16]

His own language conspired in the corruption of his morals, all evidencing a corrupt mind. And, unlike the rest of civilized society, he knew little of what sort of talk was appropriate, and when:

> To be overheard by the children, disturbed him very little. He made no more of our presence, than of that of the ducks and geese which he met on the green. He little thought that the little black urchins around him, could see, through those vocal crevices, the very secrets of his heart. Slaveholders ever underrate the intelligence with which they have to grapple. I really understood the old man's mutterings, attitudes and gestures, about as well as he did himself. But slaveholders never encourage that kind of communication, with the slaves, by which they might learn to measure the depths of his knowledge. Ignorance is a high virtue in a human chattel; and as the master studies to keep the slave ignorant, the slave is cunning enough to make the master think he succeeds. The slave fully appreciates the saying, "where ignorance is bliss, 'tis folly to be wise."[17]

This is a cornerstone of the MLM thesis. Slavery as a system violated one's state of mind. That corrupt state of mind had moral consequences, though it itself was subject to moral corruption. The entire syndrome further undermined how speakers communicated, removing all sense of the proper conditions of talk. Douglass here walked Stewart's views about mind and morals into the domain of language use, extending the usefulness of the analysis.

The impact all this has on knowledge is striking. Slaveholders violated norms of talk without believing themselves to be letting on anything to anyone, precisely because they did not believe anyone to be listening when only slaves were present. But slaves covertly developed a strategy for accruing knowledge nevertheless. They eavesdropped, collected, sorted, analyzed, all the while feigning ignorance and indifference. The bite, of course, is that what was being spewed was nonsense. The mechanics of cognition were in place, though its content was problematic.

In one of the most poignant passages in nineteenth-century writing, Douglass recalled a childhood query that went straight to resolving the relation between cognitive content and mechanics. "Why am I a slave?," he asked himself. Once he realized that neither nature nor God could be responsible for his condition, he inferred that slavery must have a human cause. He coupled this with the more general principle that "what man can make, man can unmake." Cruelly and ironically this bit of logical inference explained his condition even as it dampened his hopes. While an "appalling darkness faded away," the knowledge that many slaves could say that "their fathers and mothers were stolen from Africa – forced from their homes, and compelled to serve as slaves . . .

was [a kind of] knowledge which filled me with a burning hatred of slavery, increased my suffering, and left me without the means of breaking away from my bondage."[18]

An important epistemological pathway had thus been established which Anthony's incoherent ramblings had nearly jeopardized. A slave could gain knowledge in the form of external information – the plight of other slaves and their ancestry, for instance – and introduce that information into a chain of inferences pursued reflectively. In a setting where content and mechanics were problematic, this is a profound move.

This led (of course) to anxiety. No one capable of sophisticated inference and generalization, of grasping cause, responsibility, and the like, could fail to see how grim the prospects were for changing an American slave's condition:

> Yet it was knowledge quite worth possessing. I could not have been more than seven or eight years old, when I began to make this subject my study. It was with me in the woods and the fields; along the shore of the river, and wherever my boyish wanderings led me; and though I was, at that time, quite ignorant of the existence of the free states, I distinctly remember being, *even then*, most strongly impressed with the idea of being a freeman some day. This cheering assurance was an inborn dream of my human nature – a constant menace to slavery – and one which all the powers of slavery were unable to silence or extinguish.[19]

This gloss shows clearly that Douglass had no problem with entertaining morally uncomfortable – even degrading – thoughts to achieve moral uplift. States of mind, albeit it some negative sense, are nonetheless pivotal to moral progress.

This view underwrites the argument Douglass advocated for many decades hence. He recognized that even after emancipation, knowledge remained a key to racial uplift, especially since it helped motivate protest against persistent racism. So to actively recall how slavery had brutalized black life was crucial to motivating the moral and political action needed to bring about social justice. The knowledge of what was done, what was lost, along with the epistemic mechanics to process it, would move modern blacks to pursue an emancipatory future, to crave the full life of freedom. Douglass thereby emphasized shared knowledge replete with robust communicative dimensions for its ability to be readily coded and cued by its users, accommodating meaning shifts as needed. (Surely blacks had motivation under Jim Crow to protect emancipatory knowledge.) Moreover, communicative language's force and directness make it that much more effective for prompting protests. (Reread his first *Narrative*[20] to see what I mean; every key turn in the plot is preceded by some vital communication, or else a moment of lettered clarity, or the like.) His advocacy of protest against injustice, his very claim to fame, rests on this view. The active recall of slavery's evils, he argued, serves to transmit knowledge about past wrongs which is sufficient to motivate protest. One could view his entire career as an abolitionist speaker as literally fulfilling this mandate.

Perhaps the most profound argument he offered about states of mind in slavery goes to the mental bankruptcy slavery demanded (echoing Stewart's claims about mental barrenness), which Douglass-the-character-in-the-story had himself clearly violated:

> To make a contented slave, you must make him a thoughtless one. It is necessary to darken his moral and mental vision, and, as far as possible, to annihilate his power of reason. He must be able to detect no inconsistencies in slavery. The man that takes his earnings, must be able to convince him that he has a perfect right to do so. It must not depend upon mere force; the slave must know no Higher Law than his master's will.[21]

Volition and reason travel together:

> The whole relationship must not only demonstrate, to his mind, its necessity, but its absolute rightfulness. If there be one crevice through which a single drop can fall, it will certainly rust off the slave's chain.[22]

If powers of mind together with ideas of bondage and freedom illuminated slaves about their condition, closing down both powers and ideas is necessary to making a slave fit for unquestioning service. What seems so obviously a moral matter turns out on Douglass's gloss to be an epistemological problem at bottom. Like Stewart, to understand the (more superficial) moral character of modernity in Douglass we need to uncover its (deeper) logical and epistemological structure.

The texts of Stewart and Douglass I have been commenting on appeared before emancipation. However, Crummell wrote the arguments I now turn to nearly four decades later, in the thick of black modernity, where many of the same problems of mind and language continued to present themselves.

To be modern is to be directed toward the future. Crummell therefore lamented what he read as the "irresistible tendency in the Negro mind in this land to dwell morbidly and absorbingly upon the servile past" to the detriment of the needs of the future. Talk of slavery, he argued, jeopardized black advancement:

> Now I know, my brethren, that all this is natural to man. God gave us judgment, fancy and memory, and we cannot free ourselves from the inheritance of these or of any other faculty of our being ... There is a capacity in human nature for prescience. We were made to live in the future as well as in the past. The qualities both of hope and imagination carry us to the regions that lie beyond us.[23]

But this habit is harmful, tending to "morbidity and degeneracy":

> Accustom this race to constant reminiscence of its degradation and its sorrow, bring before your own minds or the minds of the rising generation, as a perpetual study and contemplation, the facts of servitude and inferiority, and its mind will, of necessity, be ever "sickled o'er with the pale caste of thought"; and there will be a constant tendency to "nurse the dreadful appetite of death!"[24]

Although both he and Douglass shared a deep concern with states of mind – including powers and ideas – and hence took the MLM thesis to be fundamental, Crummell clashed publicly with Douglass on exactly this point about black preoccupation with the horrors of slavery.[25] Crummell took modernity's future-directedness to imply a sharp break with the past. That break was not simply moral, but epistemic. Sorting out the epistemology will thus help settle the moral issues.

Crummell's view dovetails with one he endorsed earlier (1862) in Liberia as a colonialist seeking to civilize Africa via the settlement there of freed American blacks. It is useful to consider that view in detail. The English language, he argued, represents a quantum leap to a modern black future, since its cognitive richness could most effectively mitigate an oppressive and degrading past. After all, robust states of mind require language that does not bring to the mind the scars of the past, but the proper duty of the future. "If men *will* put themselves in narrow and straightened grooves," argued Crummell, "if they will morbidly divorce themselves from large ideas and noble convictions, they are sure to bring distress, pettiness, and misery into their being; for the mind of man was made for things grand, exalted, and majestic."[26] The intellectual focus of a people, if focused on past wrongs, will lead to deprived mental, linguistic, and thus moral resources for fulfilling the duties of the future. Modernity thus presumes the cogency of the MLM thesis:

> For 200 years the misfortune of the black race has been the confinement of its mind in the pent-up prison of human bondage. The morbid, absorbing and abiding recollection of that condition – what is it but the continuance of that same condition, in memory and dark imagination? Dwell upon, reproduce, hold on to it with all its incidents, make its history the sum and acme of thought, and then, of a surety, you put up a bar to progress, and eventually produce that unique and fossilated state which is called "arrested development." For it is impossible for a people to progress in the conditions of civilization whose thought and interest are swallowed up in morbid memories, or narrowed to the groove of a single idea or purpose.[27]

Although (as he himself conceded) remembering so epochal an event as slavery is a natural thing to do, Crummell claimed that it "is not the memory of slavery" to be guarded against "but the constant *recollection* of it, as the commanding thought of a new people, who should be marching on to the broadest freedom of thought in a new and glorious present, and a still more magnificent future."[28] Distinguishing memory from recollection turns on the sorts of inferences in which each kind of state of mind plays a role. Memory is passive. It is "the necessary and unavoidable entrance, storage and recurrence of facts and ideas to the understanding and the consciousness." Recollection, however, implies active retrieval, "the actual seeking of the facts, . . . the painstaking endeavor of the mind to bring them back again to consciousness." Crummell continued that "[a]s slavery was a degrading thing, the contant recalling of it to the mind serves, by the law of association, to degradation."[29]

He here invoked an interesting empiricist account of thought, on which ideas have associative and habitual character in a passive mind. The law of the association of ideas to which Crummell alluded is a staple of empiricist philosophy of language. (It would certainly have been a significant component of his philosophical training at Cambridge.) But the mental life plays a role in ethical life beyond simply willing rational acts. On the MLM thesis, the ethical life of the mind includes habits of character as well, wherein self-respect and dignity have a cherished central place. Degrading thought, then, degrades the character of the thinker. This latter move is more characteristic of continental European views of language, say that of Herder (1767) or

Humboldt (1836/1988). (Again, his Cambridge training is consistent with this, since that institution has long served as a conduit for continental philosophy into British thought.) Like his American contemporaries Peirce and Royce, Crummell's thought is ecumenical in that it bridges German and British traditions without conflict. And like Stewart, his notion of modernity shuns thoughts of oppression.

Association and habit, however glossed, require suitable language to get out of the head and into the community. "Words are vital things," argued Crummell. "They are always generative of life or death. They cannot enter the soul as passive and inoperative things."[30] Words are the vehicles of thought in that they mediate how ideas (the objects of thought, the contents of states of mind) liaise with the ethical life of the mind. They are thus central to the mind as it fulfills its modern duties. States of mind, along with their linguistic properties, were fundamental to Crummell's account of the degrading character of slavery.

Part of what makes it difficult for twentieth-century readers to fairly evaluate Crummell's arguments are their dated and, to our sensibilities, offensive aspects. Unfortunately, the same century that gave us pragmatism and quantification theory also gave us "scientific" racism and colonialism. This is not a special problem about Crummell, though. For better or worse, such views were widespread. History is messy, morally ambiguous, even harsh, and hence not for the faint of heart. So when Crummell argued that the language of the "savage" fails to successfully underwrite modern structures of thought, we should evaluate the epistemology as we suspend the bad social taxonomy. I think the payoff makes this worthwhile. Modern ideas thus require appropriate words, a point on which Douglass and Crummell agreed.

To be limited in word and thought is to uncouple the epistemological mechanics of modern life, thereby rendering association and habit merely private issues. That is the condition of the "savage," which no people can survive:

> My desire is that we should escape "the limit and restraint" of both the *word* and the *thought* of slavery. As a people, we have had an exodus from it. We have been permitted by a gracious Providence to enter the new and exalted pathways of freedom. The thought, the routine, the usages, and calculations of that old system are dead things . . . These changed circumstances bring to us an immense budget of new thoughts, new ideas, new projects, new purposes, new ambitions, of which our fathers never thought.[31]

States of mind form the cornerstone of the MLM thesis, but that common emphasis informed varying analyses of modernity. To understand these cognitive images requires probing the theory of language which makes its epistemic features obvious. Hence, grammar.

II Grammar

Grammar captured much for nineteenth-century thinkers. Like its contemporary lean sense, it included language's systematic skeleton. But unlike our sense, it also reflected the character of the ideas it conveys. To those thinkers this meant that a people could be elevated or degraded by the richness of the grammar of the language they mastered. (Hence the debates during that time about whether blacks could learn Greek and Latin grammar.) Douglass's stress on literacy appropriated this wide sense of grammar. It is telling that hearing Sophia Auld (one of his slaveholders) read the Bible aloud awakened his curiosity to the "mystery of reading."[32] It aroused in him the desire to learn, a positive character trait. Her husband, though, prevented her from teaching Douglass, since not only was it unlawful, it would lead to mischief.

> [I]f you give a nigger an inch, he will take an ell; "he should know nothing but the will of his master, and learn to obey it." Learning will spoil the best nigger in the world; "if you teach that nigger["] – speaking of myself – ["]how to read the bible, there will be no keeping him"; "it would forever unfit him for the duties of a slave"; and "as to himself, learning would do him no good, but probably, a great deal of harm – making him disconsolate and unhappy." If you learn him how to read, he'll want to know how to write; and, this accomplished, he'll be running away with himself.[33]

In an ironic twist which only distant hindsight permits, Douglass regarded this tirade as "the first decidedly antislavery lecture to which it had been my lot to listen." Here is his gloss:

> The effect of his words, *on me*, was neither slight nor transitory. His iron sentences – cold and harsh – sunk deep into my heart, and stirred up not only my feelings into a sort of rebellion, but awakened within me a slumbering train of vital thought. It was a new and special revelation, dispelling a painful mystery, against which my youthful understanding had struggled, and struggled in vain, to wit: the *white* man's power to perpetuate the enslavement of the

black man. "Very well," thought I; "knowledge unfits a child to be a slave." I instinctively assented to the proposition; and from that moment I understood the direct pathway from slavery to freedom. This was just what I needed; ... the information, so instantly derived, to some extent compensated me for the loss I had sustained in this direction ... That which [Mr Auld] most loved I most hated; and the very determination which he expressed to keep me in ignorance, only rendered me the more resolute in seeking intelligence.[34]

The rest of the story is familiar. Douglass stole opportunities to read. Once he learned the alphabet, he began navigating books, finding his way to abolitionist literature. He thus began to "gain in intelligence ... adding much to my limited stock of language, [which] enabled me to give tongue to many interesting thoughts, which had frequently flashed through my soul, and died away for want of utterance."[35] The power of the mastery of grammar – learning to read – led directly to the mind of a free person.[36] This, in fact, gives the state-of-mind argument its teeth, since mental powers were a direct consequence of the linguistic powers honed by grammar.

Words animated Douglass's imagination. Three in particular – *slave*, *slavery*, and *abolitionist* – provoked him, though he had no idea what an abolitionist was. The term was always raised with contempt by slaveholders, and often came up when slavery was discussed. But its meaning remained unclear. And dictionaries were notoriously unhelpful. (*Abolition* was there defined as *the act of abolishing*.) What solved this semantic puzzle for him were the contextual cues he gleaned from slaveholders' conversation, as well as newspaper accounts which provided additional disambiguating context. The term *abolitionist* occurred there not only as a simple expression but also in phrases – such as *abolition of slavery*.

This is a fascinating point. There is no way the young Douglass, passionate as he had become about freedom, could have divined the meaning of the term which designated what was to become his path to freedom. But upon mastering the *grammar* of English he possessed the very tool he needed to decode the term. He had to understand what systematic contribution to meaning constituents of phrases make. This problem about terms, which stands between every slave and freedom in some way or other, can be solved only by grammar. The point is simple, yet its impact remains sharp.

The term *abolitionist*, after careful grammatical decoding, came to embody "hope" since it implied that someone besides himself was concerned about ending slavery. Moreover, the "rage and fear" it prompted in the slaveholders who used it implied that abolitionists had power worth fearing.

On the face of it, Douglass's view of grammar is pegged to a broad humanism. To be human is to be free, and to be free is to have the full cognitive powers characteristic of human inner life. Grammar is the skeleton over which those powers drape, hence it is essential for full, modern humanity.

An appeal to civilization lurks in the account though. True, that appeal is explicit to the extent that modernity in the nineteenth century entails civilizing tendencies. But Douglass seemed also to appeal to a *qualitative* change mastery of grammar introduces. Certainly illiterate persons are persons. And certainly upon emancipation the issue is no longer humanity as such. It must be that literacy is a goal not simply for its strategic benefits during slavery (smuggling guns to slaves would have been more effective) nor for its powers to render enslaved "non-humans" human. Learning to read makes a person better than they were, and that because of the intrinsic character of grammar itself.

If there is question about whether to read Douglass this way (as there may be) there is little question how to read Crummell on grammar. Some background is helpful, though.

Humboldt's grammar theory took the deep structure of a natural language – its "inner form" – to express the "psyche" of the nation in which it develops, which it in turn binds together. The form of all languages is the same, an ideal universal grammar, though each language's means for expressing that common core vary. The root words of that language as well as its characteristic patterns of word combinations contribute to its inner form, giving it both syntactic and etymological – and hence content-sensitive – dimensions. Languages thus accommodate different nuances of meaning, reflecting the different worldviews of their users.

In a subtle and difficult move, Humboldt sees the expression of grammatical form (the emergence of language, so to speak) to be like a work of art, an articulation. Art works, of course, may be good or bad, depending on the genius they express, a point he thought language use shared. A "true inner fixity"[37] due to a correct intuition of language reflects how well this articulation captures the laws of thought and reason, the very bedrock of universal grammar. Crummell's emphasis on grammar and civilization is easy to understand against Humboldt. As Humboldt himself puts it, the "intellectual merits of language therefore rest exclusively upon the well-ordered, firm and clear mental organization of peoples in the epoch of making and remaking language, and are the image, indeed the direct copy, of this."[38] In a helpful recent commentary Hans Aarsleff put it this way. "Hearing is as much an act of imagination as speaking; the greater the fixing of the sentence, the better the synthesis that the hearer can achieve by the imaginative re-creation of the synthesis that was in the speaker's mind."[39]

This approach implies that to know that verbs occur at the ends of German sentences, for instance, is to know something about how German speakers relate actions to those who perform them. That Spanish adjectives follow rather than precede the nouns they qualify is to understand a little set theory vis-à-vis Spanish speakers. Though no contemporary philosopher of language would accept theorizing logic towards psychology and anthropology, it was a widely held view then.

Though syntax is tricky, etymology is not. It is obvious – and Crummell made much of this – that some relationships among root words are historical and social, having much to do with worldviews. Humboldt thought that the lexicon of a language revealed whatever intellectual sophistication a nation possessed. As mind and language respond to the demands of life and reality, concepts get expressed which amount to an analysis of some state of mind – namely, the one prevailing among that nation's members. Lexicon thus serves as the accumulation of ideas and concepts needed for conduct. In short, a people's lexicon reveals their highest state of mind.

A mundane example helps show this. We call short cups of brewed coffee *espresso* drinks after the Italian for at least three reasons. They are made quickly. Americans have no equivalent drinks, so we have no term to substitute. And cafes can charge more for coffee that sounds European. To know a bit of etymology is to know a bit about American life and habits. Aarsleff gives the right spin:

> Thus at any given moment in history, a nation's speakers will inherit a mass of forms that contain the work already done, the *ergon*, and since these forms record the analysis already performed they also express the nation's worldview ... The evolution of language is like a stream that keeps flowing past us toward greater degrees of analyticity and prose.[40]

Language forms thus suggest something about national character, an important premise in Crummell's arguments.

But besides his emphasis on association and habit in thought and language use, Crummell also followed an empiricist line in the language and thought relation at the heart of the Humboldt-style inner-form theory. Locke's[41] view that words stand for ideas in a speaker's mind is well known. That is, the content which a word expresses is an idea in the mind of a speaker. To paraphrase Bentham[42], the immediate subject of a communication is the state of a speaker's mind. Not only did Crummell suppose grammar to influence character, but he supposed words to reflect character as well.

Complementing the universal-grammar program of the continental thinkers is a story about language's abstract features. Propositions, the abstract entities at the heart of language and logic, were emphasized by Bentham to give language its shape, its logical topography. They are not identical to thoughts, but instead form the contents of thoughts. I can think *there is water at the bottom of the ocean* but so can you. Certainly we each have our own thoughts, but just as certainly do we each think *of* the same thing. The same goes for statements we could each make about water at the bottom of the ocean, especially if we speak different languages. Words and ideas are ontologically distinct, even if they are semantically identical. Universal grammar, coupled with a theory of propositions, promises to become a viable approach.

It is useful to see Crummell's endorsement of English for blacks as implementing this approach. Grammar, complete with syntax and etymology, is content- and hence user-sensitive. But content sensitivity is not simply anthropologically interesting, but goes to something universal, namely, propositions. These aspects of his arguments resonate philosophically with recent grammar theory, even as it anticipates the basic tenets of speech act theory, that such acts may be expressed in terms of propositions and performative verbs. (But this goes beyond this essays's scope.)

His observation about the bittersweet history of English thus becomes both intelligible and poignant:

> [T]his English, which we [Negroes] are speaking, and teaching the heathen to speak, is not our native tongue. This Anglo-Saxon language, which is the only language ninety-nine hundredths of us emigrants have ever known, is not the speech of our ancestors . . . [We] all speak in a foreign tongue, in accents alien from the utterance of [our] fathers. Our very speech is indicative of sorrowful history; the language we use tells of subjection and of conquest. No people lose entirely their native tongue without the bitter trial of hopeless struggles, bloody strife, heart-breaking despair, agony, and death! Even so we.[43]

"Providence," though, ordains that "this fact of humiliation" can usher "new ideas into the language of a people; or . . . serve, as the transitional step from low degradation to a higher and nobler civilization."⁴⁴

The mechanics of civilization, to paraphrase Crummell, are at once cognitive and linguistic. Providing the "transitional step from low degradation to a higher and nobler civilization" to its speech communities, English has "unusual force and power." It is thus a "fit channel" for the thoughts of common sense, honest minds, and upstanding character. Grammar transmits uplifting moral character throughout a nation. This is not to say that native African dialects, languages, and acquired tongues were without their respective value. But it was very clear for Crummell that English was superior, not just in its "genius" – its national character – but in its actual morphology. African languages fail – for Crummell – to meet those exacting cognitive and linguistic demands. It followed rather easily that "definite marks of inferiority" of these languages – their harshness, abruptness, few grammatical forms and meager lexicons, all his terms – underscored how inadequate they were for Crummell's civilized vision.

He was taken not only by English's structural features, but also its possessors. It is, he observed, "characteristically the language of freedom."⁴⁵ This is not incidental or accidental, but essential to its very character as the language of the freedom-loving English:

> I know that there is a sense in which this love of liberty is inwrought in the very fibre and substance of the body and blood of all people; but the flame burns dimly in some races; it is a fitful fire in some others; and in many inferior people it is the flickering light of a dying candle. But in the English races it is an ardent, healthy, vital, irrepressible flame; and withal normal and orderly in its development.⁴⁶

The facility with which English serves to enshrine moral precepts – especially biblical ones – underscores this link. English, thought Crummell, is adept for constructing "Tracts, and Tales, and Allegories; . . . Catechisms, and Homilies, and Sermons; . . . heavenly Songs, sacred Lyrics, and divine Epics; . . . Liturgies and Treatises, and glowing Apologies for the Faith."⁴⁷ For the grammarian, this is a crucial premise supporting the advocacy of learned, standard English.

Setting aside large difficulties with nineteenth-century grammar, it is clear that few theorists of Crummell's day recognized the difference between how words *mean* – and thus how they should be interpreted – and how words *are used* in such linguistic acts as referring. This gets in

Crummell's way. On the empiricist view of grammar, where hearers interpret utterances by decoding the semantic content of ideas conveyed, the utterance (1) "I served her more glasses of wine than her doctor advised" is (partially) interpreted by determining the content of "glasses," "served," and "doctor advised." But while "glasses" may express something like an abstract idea in the speaker's mind – that is, its *meaning* – its reference, given the utterance, is several concrete objects which the speaker served someone. This becomes more obvious if you compare (1) to the utterance (2) "Yesterday I broke my glasses." "Glasses" in (2) can *express* the same thing that it does in (1), namely the idea *objects made of glass*, but its reference given the two ways it is *used* diverges. If interpreting utterances requires determining the content of words, then something more complex must be going on. (Of course, Frege recognized this,[48] though my point (unlike his) is not simply semantic but pragmatic. Referring can be understood as a speech act with semantic consequences.)

There is a corollary to this point for specifically moral communication. If part of the point of language mastery for Crummell is to make intelligible the moral exhortations which form the basis of modern forms of life, then interpretation has to both determine the meanings of words – their general, abstract content – as well as their reference – how they are used and what they pick out in a particular situation. Teaching a young person what it is to follow medical advice and to respect the needs of others to do so, depends on his or her understanding the difference between idea and referent. How else can s/he tell what is going on?

Another difficulty is that empiricist "ideas" were developed by Locke to account for the perception of objective phenomena. However, they are often recruited – by Locke and Hume, no less than Crummell to do work in communicative interaction which, especially in light of the normative content of much communication, gives perceptual ideas a job they are scarcely equipped to do. It is not at all obvious that the semantic analysis of the objective language of perceptual ideas, as in reporting empirical observations, is the correct analysis for morally inflected communicative language. Words in an objective description of the world need not relate to their meanings the same way that words in a normative exhortation to a member of one's social group relate to theirs. If a mother tells a child "the garbage is full," we can interpret her to mean "you should take it out," an interpretation diverging from that of a mere objective report that the garbage is full. And while speaker intentions and implications may also attend objective reports, the facts relevant to those implications will presumably be empirical, not socially regulative. Different off-stage stuff – facts and intentions – will bear on words, and may do so in different ways.

Since he wrote long before speech acts were understood, Crummell could not systematically distinguish regulative performative utterances from mere constative utterances.[49] That is, he maintained no systematic distinction between utterances which *do* work – "promise" in the utterance "I promise to pay you back," or, "I do," following, "do you take this man . . .?" – and those which do not – "rained?" in "it rained last weekend."

As such, Crummell cannot appreciate the extent to which knowledge and use in vernacular communication is both cognitively sophisticated and linguistically subtle. He was deeply suspicious that black communicative language was cognitively shallow, and hence inadequate for modernity. Were he to see speech acts as richly structured his might have been a different assessment.

A crucial consequence of this difficulty is that Crummell cannot, without the tools of speech act theory, give an account of interpretation which recognizes how discerning meaning puts into play conditions *independent* of grammar as such, as Douglass so readily saw. Crummell did not understand that language users decode meaning by relying on performance conditions in speech situations (perhaps) as much as grammatical features.

These difficulties notwithstanding, Crummell took black mastery of English to imply a derivative duty. Since languages may be corrupted by uncivilized influences, English-speaking blacks should try to preserve it. The proximity of English to native African language groups posed a particular threat. This may be mitigated by training non-English speakers "to the spirit, moral sentiments, and practical genius" of English even as they learn its grammar. This is an important point, as Crummell supposed that not all who speak English are automatically Anglicized (civilized) by that fact. One must be acquainted with its genius: "Is our influence upon [Africans] to touch only the brain, and not life, manners, the family, society? or rather should we not as a Nation, take upon us the duty of so training these people, that as they receive the language, so they may likewise the civilization, the order, the industry, and the mild, but transforming influences of a regulated Christian state?"[50]

He took this very seriously, arguing in a way which has impact on black American speakers who spoke (what was then called) plantation English, the forerunner of (what is now called) African-American Vernacular English. If the spirit and genius of the English language is not imparted to Liberians (and Negroes generally) then, just as the body without the spirit is dead, so the English language without its genius is dead. To support this point he referred to an edition of the Bible then published in the style of English spoken by Caribbean speakers. He derided the project as enshrining "broken English," a "miserable caricature of their noble tongue." This was a momentous issue for Crummell, since "a language acts in divers ways, upon the spirit of a people; even as the spirit of a people acts with a creative and spiritualizing force upon a language."[51] Anthony Appiah has seen this issue as one of a struggle between nativism and positivism.[52] For Appiah, nativism about language and race turns on the claim (echoing Herder's nationalism) that languages and traditions are "expressive of the collective essence of a pristine traditional community" defined, of course, in racial and national terms. Positivism, however, turns on a view of languages as "mere tools" which are detachable, so to speak, from the ideas and "essences" they convey. There is much to be said about this sort of conception of the controversy. It explains, for instance, why a variety of writers, such as Jefferson,[53] embraced the Anglo-Saxon "dialect." The pull of the *Sprachgeist* which the English language expresses, it would follow, recommends its diligent study and mastery.

There remains, however, a nuance which Appiah's approach risks overlooking. A figure like Crummell can only in some qualified sense be said to be nativist about language. His argument from civilization which I have been giving relies on a move from Negro language (understood racially) to Anglo-Saxon language (also understood racially), not simply because the Anglo-Saxon tongue expresses that race's essence, but – perhaps more importantly – it facilitates the elevation of the Negro race itself, qua Negro. Consider, for example, Crummell's[54] essay on the "destined superiority" of the Negro race. There he argued that Africans need to recognize the hand of providence in the particular dealings they have faced historically, toward the end that they would see how, in all, they as a race would flourish. Crummell was not arguing for English to be spoken by African Americans so that they may *cease* to be Negro, but so that they may be more *fully* Negro.

Crummell is confusing because he does not consistently distinguish African Americans from continental Africans. Instead, in articulating the condition of Africans, he made use of racial categories – Negro – advocating its adoption of English institutions. Sometimes this sounds as if he dispensed with nativism and embraced the positivist conception of language: *English is a tool for the Negro race*. Other times it sounds as if he embraced nativism: *the Negro race, in developing cultural resources, is acquiring language which can express its essence*. Neither reading, though, can consistently be maintained in Crummell, and so an important nuance slips between the cracks of Appiah's distinction.

Seeing the issue instead in terms of pragmatic resources explains more. Crummell certainly took seriously the claim that language expresses racial essence. However, he understood that some of language's character is due to how it is used. These claims can be reconciled on the terms I have used in discussing him. Language reflects an ontological property – call it "race" if you like, or whatever – supporting how a group of speakers develops its social character. Adopting English thus resolves both a social and an ontological problem. It enables access to cognitive resources which elevates the race. And the entire process only becomes workable to the extent that language is seen pragmatically, that is, from the perspective of use. In all, though Crummell's arguments suffer for their lack of pragmatic sophistication, they actually hold up well on their own terms, since they anticipate later conflicts in philosophy over meaning and use.

Grammar mattered to both thinkers for intrinsic reasons, as I have been saying. A significant part of its point though, especially given the MLM thesis, is communication. Douglass registers a surprising endorsement of standard-English use, given an emphasis on communication, but it is more intelligible given the grammar of the MLM thesis. I turn to that now.

III   Communication

The strength and reach of the MLM thesis consists in its ability to explain cognitive elements in play in a community of speakers. Douglass offered this account of grammar and communication, making striking points about grammar and communicated ideas along the way:

> There is not, probably, in the whole south, a plantation where the English language is more imperfectly spoken than on Col. Lloyd's. It is a mixture of Guinea and everything else you please. At the time of which I am now writing, there were slaves there who had been brought from the coast of Africa. They never used the "*s*" in indication of the possessive case. "Cap'n Ant'nay Tom," "Lloyd Bill," "Aunt Rose Harry," means "Captain Anthony's Tom," "Lloyd's Bill," &c. "*Oo you dem long to?*" means, "Whom do you belong to?" "*Oo dem got any peachy?*" means, "Have you got any peaches?" I could scarcely understand them when I first went among them, so broken was their speech; and I am persuaded that I could not have been dropped anywhere on the globe, where I could reap less, in the way of knowledge, from my immediate

> associates, than on this plantation. Even MAS' DANIEL, by his association with his father's slaves, had measurably adopted their dialect and their ideas, so far as they had ideas to be adopted.[55]

The deficient grammar, as he saw it, limited the powers of ideas conveyed significantly. But it was not simply grammar and cognition which suffered, but communication:

> Mas' Daniel could not associate with ignorance without sharing its shade; and he could not give his black playmates his company, without giving them his intelligence, as well. Without knowing this, or caring about it, at the time, I, for some cause or other, spent much of my time with Mas' Daniel, in preference to spending it with most of the other boys.[56]

This problem did not shake Douglass's emphasis on communicative language though. It was merely a part of his analysis of what was needed to make black communication – indeed, communication generally – sound. The importance of trust to communication is a case in point.[57] One slave unwittingly told his master that he was treated cruelly. That he was subsequently sold into the deep South without a moment's notice makes Douglass's point, that slaves spoke only well of their masters when asked. That fear established:

> among the slaves the maxim, that a still tongue makes a wise head. They suppress the truth rather than take the consequence of telling it, and, in so doing, they prove themselves a part of the human family. If they have anything to say of their master, it is, generally, something in his favor, especially when speaking to strangers. I was frequently asked, while a slave, if I had a kind master, and I do not remember ever to have given a negative reply.[58]

A profound lack of trust made genuine communication problematic. For Douglass this did not suggest the inadequacy of communication but its richness, as double meanings were increasingly employed.

The Great House Farm was eagerly anticipated by slaves who were allowed to go to it, since it signaled confidence and favor in them by their slaveholder, but also for the break in routine it presented. En route, with no overseer present, "the slave was comparatively free; and, if thoughtful, he had time to think."[59] Irony and double meaning were scarcely more evident to Douglass than here. His comments on it are worth quoting at length:

Slaves are generally expected to sing as well as to work. A silent slave is not liked by masters or overseers. *"Make a noise,"* *"make a noise,"* and *"bear a hand,"* are the words usually addressed to the slaves when there is silence among them. This may account for the almost constant singing heard in the southern states.⁶⁰

Singing was not a sign of joy, but of grief, especially in the "wild notes" of the songs sung on the way to the Great House Farm – they "told a tale of grief and sorrow"⁶¹:

> In the most boisterous outbursts of rapturous sentiment, there was ever a tinge of deep melancholy. I have never heard any songs like those anywhere since I left slavery, except when in Ireland. There I heard the same *wailing notes*, and was much affected by them. It was during the famine of 1845–6.⁶²

A typical verse sung:

> "I am going away to the great house farm,/ O yea! O yea!/ O yea! My old master is a good old master,/ O yea! O yea! . . ." This they would sing, with other words of their own improvising – jargon to others, but full of meaning to themselves. I have sometimes thought, that the mere hearing of those songs would do more to impress truly spiritual-minded men and women with the soul-crushing and death-dealing character of slavery, than the reading of whole volumes of its mere physical cruelties. They speak to the heart and to the soul of the thoughtful.⁶³

Quoting his 1845 *Narrative:*

> I did not, when a slave, understand the deep meaning of these rude, and apparently incoherent songs. I was myself within the circle, so that I neither saw nor heard as those without might see and hear. They told a tale which was then altogether beyond my feeble comprehension; they were tones, loud, long and deep, breathing the prayer and complaint of souls boiling over with the bitterest anguish. Every tone was a testimony against slavery, and a prayer to God for deliverance from chains. The hearing of those wild notes always depressed my spirits, and filled my heart with ineffable sadness. The mere recurrence, even now, afflicts my spirit, and while I am writing these lines, my tears are falling. To those songs I trace my first glimmering conceptions of the dehumanizing

character of slavery. I can never get rid of that conception. Those songs still follow me, to deepen my hatred of slavery, and quicken my sympathies for my brethren in bonds. If any one wishes to be impressed with a sense of the soul-killing power of slavery, let him go to Col. Lloyd's plantation, and, on allowance day, place himself in the deep, pine woods, and there let him, in silence, thoughtfully analyze the sounds that shall pass through the chambers of his soul, and if he is not thus impressed, it will only be because "there is no flesh in his obdurate heart."[64]

This passage has been much commented on by literary theorists. Henry Louis Gates, Jr,[65] for instance, has argued that double meanings in slave songs ought to be understood as deeply ironic. Hearers of such songs – say, Douglass himself – understand covertly what is meant and they do so despite the features of language employed and how they are used.

But this cannot be correct. Hearers cannot divine meanings of deeply ironic language without already having established some conventional patterns of meaning of use. Even Wittgenstein[66] who argued that meaning just is use in a language game, deferred to language rules governing use. True, his rules were a posteriori and malleable, but they were rules nonetheless. *Some* normative background for language use must be operational in order for nonsense to be sorted from sense, unironic singing distinguished from ironic. Irony and double meaning remain anomalous and opaque if no normative dimension exists.[67] Of course, there is no reason to think there must be some access to it by those outside the circle. How else to distinguish those on different sides of the circle? That is precisely Douglass's point. To miss that is to obscure what he clarified.

I think my point is confirmed elsewhere. As an escape plan was being formed, Douglass and others sang. As he states:

> A keen observer might have detected in our repeated singing of
> "O Canaan, sweet Canaan,/ I am bound for the land of Canaan"
> something more than a hope of reaching heaven. We meant to reach the *north* – and the north was our Canaan.
> "I thought I heard them say,/ There were lions in the way,/ I don't expect to stay/ Much longer here./ Run to Jesus – shun the danger – / I don't expect to stay/ Much longer here,"
> was a favorite air, and had a double meaning. In the lips of some, it meant the expectation of a speedy summons to a world of spirits; but, in the lips of *our* company, it simply meant, a speedy pilgrim-

age toward a free state, and deliverance from all the evils and dangers of slavery.⁶⁸

The need for trust, the value of double meaning, and the usefulness of singing converge on this point. A bit later:

> We had several words, expressive of things, important to us, which we understood, but which, even if distinctly heard by an outsider, convey no certain meaning. I have reasons for suppressing these *pass-words*, which the reader will easily divine. I hated the secrecy; but where slavery is powerful, and liberty is weak, the latter is driven to concealment or to destruction.⁶⁹

This is not deep deconstructive irony, but plain-old irony, made possible by an appropriate linguistic practice slaves knew. And if one learned it, they entered the circle. Hence the need to revise and protect knowledge in communication vigilantly. Anomalous, deconstructive codes cannot be broken, since they are not codes in the first place.

Like Crummell, Douglass wrote off "broken" black dialects, but his double-meaning account captures the nuances of use, and the inventiveness of communication. To be fair to Crummell, though, Douglass's account of language is in large part a theory of communicative language. Crummell's is much more intended as a theory of language as a system for representing knowledge which is used only secondarily to communicate as such. No wonder Douglass is more sophisticated about double meaning in communication.

The striking thing about much of this is that Crummell turns out to provide a much more compelling account (if its racial component is dropped out) of the epistemology of language than does Douglass. It needs, however, a new mechanism for hitching it to the mind – a mechanism largely undiscovered in philosophy prior to Peirce and Frege. Language's representational features do not consist simply in ideas (as the empiricists urged), and certainly not in ideas associated with some racial ontological stuff. Rather, those features consist in propositions which enjoy systematic liaisons with one another. Moreover, sentences and phrases which express those propositions inherit their representational features, preserving in their grammar the relevant epistemic liaisons. The clue Bentham began to articulate needs much systematic development to plausibly complete Crummell's account.

Crummell is thus clearly wrong in thinking that ideas could enjoy an independent relationship to anything which is both ontological and cultural at once. But he is just as clearly correct in thinking that a robust linguistic endowment is necessary for a robust cognitive endowment, his ignorance about whether African languages satisfy this requirement notwithstanding.

Douglass and Crummell thus jointly contribute to a nascent philosophical account of knowledge and communication in black American thought. Although it is limited in its direct usefulness in the ways I have been saying, several lines of questioning open up. How secular should knowledge, meaning, and language be? Should we tie them to community and forms of life (non-secular accounts)? Need we suppose any wide basis for understanding languages and thought? Much needs to be done here.

Notes

Thanks to Frank Kirkland and Elliot Weininger for helpful comments on earlier drafts of this essay. Thanks also to students in my seminars at Howard University on American and African-American Philosophy for fruitful discussions on these topics, especially Patrick Troup and Rachel Zellars.

1. Maria Stewart, Lecture in Boston, Mass., September 21, 1832, reprinted in Marilyn Richardson, ed, *Maria W. Stewart, America's First Black Political Writer: Essays and Speeches* (Bloomington, Ind.: Indiana University Press, 1987), pp. 45–9, esp. p. 47.
2. Maria Stewart, *Productions of Mrs Maria W. Stewart* (Boston: Published By Friends of Freedom and Virtue, 1835), p. 70.
3. See also the editorial introduction to Bert James Loewenberg and Ruth Bogin, eds, *Black Women in Nineteenth-Century American Life: Their Words, Their Thoughts, Their Feelings* (University Park, Penn.: The Pennsylvania State University Press, 1976) for a helpful sketch of some of these influences.
4. Maria Stewart, "Religion and the Pure Principles of Morality, the Sure Foundation on Which We Must Build," reprinted in Richardson, ed, *Maria W. Stewart*, pp. 28–42, esp. p. 30.
5. Ibid., p. 31.
6. Ibid., p. 35.
7. Immanuel Kant, 'What is Enlightenment?', reprinted in *Kant on History*, ed and trans. by Lewis White Beck (Indianapolis, Ind.: Bobbs-Merrill, 1963), pp. 3–10; see also Kant, *Foundations of the Metaphysics of Morals*, reprinted in *Kant's Critique of Practical Reason and Other Writings in Moral Philosophy*, ed and trans. Lewis White Beck (Chicago, Ill: University of Chicago Press, 1949).
8. Stewart, "Religion and the Pure Principles of Morality," p. 37.
9. Ibid., pp. 38–9.
10. Ibid., p. 41.

11 Stewart, Lecture in Boston, 1832, p. 45.
12 Ibid., p. 48.
13 Although I focus on his published autobiographies, a lot of nuance appears in his speeches on these topics. See especially Frederick Douglass, "colonizationists Measures," Address in New York, N.Y., April 24, 1849, reprinted in J. Blassingame, ed, *The Frederick Douglass Papers* (New Haven, Conn.: Yale University Press, 1979), vol. 2, pp. 158–67; "America Before the Global Tribunal," Address in Rochester, N.Y., June 30, 1861, reprinted in ibid., vol. 3, pp. 445–51; and "The American Apocalypse," Address in Rochester, N.Y., June 16, 1861, reprinted in ibid., vol. 3, pp. 435–45. For treatments more closely related to states of mind and language, see Douglass, "Celebrating the Past, Anticipating the Future," Address in Philadelphia, Penn., April 14, 1875, reprinted in ibid., vol. 4, pp. 407–14; "'It Moves,' or the Philosophy of Reform," Address in Washington, D.C., November 20, 1883, reprinted in ibid., vol. 5, pp. 124–45; "The Negro Problem," Address in Washington, D.C., October 21, 1890, reprinted in ibid., vol. 5, pp. 436–56; "Great is the Miracle of Human Speech," Address in Washington, D.C., August 31, 1891, reprinted in ibid., vol. 5, pp. 474–7; and "The Blessings of Liberty and Education," Address in Manassas, Va., September 3, 1894, reprinted in ibid., vol. 5, pp. 616–29.
14 Frederick Douglass, *My Bondage and My Freedom* (New York, N.Y.: Dover, 1969), p. 79.
15 Ibid., p. 80.
16 Ibid., pp. 80–1.
17 Ibid., p. 81.
18 Ibid., pp. 90–1.
19 Ibid., p. 91.
20 Frederick Douglass, *Narrative of the Life of Frederick Douglass, a Slave*, reprinted in Henry Louis Gates, Jr, ed, *The Classic Slave Narratives* (New York, N.Y.: Penguin, 1987), pp. 243–331.
21 Douglass, *My Bondage and My Freedom*, p. 320.
22 Ibid., p. 320.
23 Alexander Crummell, "The Need of New Ideas and New Aims for a New Era," *Africa and America* (Miami, Fla.: Mnemosyne, 1862), pp. 11–36, esp. p. 14.
24 Ibid., p. 15.
25 This clash becomes more interesting considering that Douglass and Crummell had early common goals concerning colonization (see Douglass, 'colonizationists Measures').
26 Crummell, "The Need of New Ideas," p. 17.
27 Ibid., pp. 17–18.
28 Ibid., p. 18.
29 Ibid., p. 19.
30 Ibid., p. 19.

31 Ibid., pp. 19–20.
32 Douglass, *My Bondage and My Freedom*, p. 145.
33 Ibid., pp. 146–147.
34 Ibid., pp. 147–148.
35 Ibid., p. 158.
36 Houston Baker, "Autobiographical Acts and the Voice of the Southern Slave," in William Andrews, ed, *Critical Essays on Frederick Douglass* (Boston, Mass.: G. K. Hall, 1991), pp. 94–107, provides an informative discussion; Baker draws existential implications from this point.
37 Hans Aarsleff, "Introduction," in W. Humboldt, *On Language: The Diversity of Human Language-Structure and its Influence on the Mental Development of Mankind*, ed By H. Aarsleff and trans. by Peter Heath (New York, N.Y.: Cambridge University Press, 1988), pp. vii-lxv.
38 W. Humboldt, *On Language*, p. 81.
39 Aarsleff, "Introduction," pp. xxvi, xxvii.
40 Ibid., p. xxx.
41 John Locke, *An Essay Concerning Human Understanding*, ed by P. H. Nidditch (New York, N.Y.: Clarendon, 1975), esp. book III.
42 C. K. Ogden, *Bentham's Theory of Fictions* (London: K. Paul, Trench, Trubner, 1932).
43 Alexander Crummell, "The English Language in Liberia," in *The Future of Africa* (New York, N.Y.: Scribner, 1862), pp. 9–54, esp. pp. 17–18.
44 Ibid., p. 18.
45 Ibid., p. 23.
46 Ibid., p. 23.
47 Ibid., p. 29.
48 Gottlob Frege, "On Sense and Nominatum," trans. by Herbert Feigl, reprinted in A. P. Martinich, ed, *The Philosophy of Language*, 3rd ed (New York, N.Y.: Oxford University Press, 1996), pp. 186–98.
49 Note that the status of constatives is controversial within speech act theory. For example, see J. L. Austin, "Other Minds," in *Philosophical Papers* (Oxford: Oxford University Press, 1961), pp. 76–116; and John Searle, *Speech Acts* (Cambridge: Cambridge University Press, 1969), p. 68, on the distinction between saying and promising. However, I mean to beg no questions here. The distinction I here invoke can simply be read as that between utterances recruited to do regulative work and those that do not.
50 Crummell, "The English Language in Liberia," p. 48.
51 Ibid., pp. 50, 52.
52 Kwame Anthony Appiah, *In My Father's House: Africa in the Philosophy of Culture* (New York, N.Y.: Oxford University Press, 1992), pp. 47–56.
53 Thomas Jefferson, *Notes on the State of Virginia* (Boston, Mass.: Lilly and Wait, 1832).
54 Alexander Crummell, "The Destined Superiority of the Negro," reprinted in W. J. Moses, ed, *Destiny and Race: Selected Writings, 1840–1898* (Amherst, Mass.: University of Massachusetts Press, 1992), pp. 194–205.

55 Douglass, *My Bondage and My Freedom*, pp. 76–7.
56 Ibid., p. 77.
57 Douglass makes a related point in his "Trust: The Basis of Charity," Address in Rochester, N.Y., January 5, 1854, reprinted in Blassingame, ed. *The Frederick Douglass Papers*, vol. 2, pp. 451–3.
58 Ibid., pp. 117–18.
59 Ibid., p. 97.
60 Ibid., pp. 97–9.
61 Ibid., p. 99.
62 Ibid., p. 98.
63 Ibid., p. 98.
64 Ibid., p. 99.
65 Henry Louis Gates, Jr, *Figures in Black: Signs and the Racial Self* (Oxford: Oxford University Press, 1987), esp. pp. 80–124.
66 Ludwig Wittgenstein, *Philosophical Investigations*, trans. by Elizabeth Anscombe (New York, N.Y.: Macmillan, 1953).
67 The issue between Thad Ziolkowski ("Antitheses: The Dialectic of Violence and Literacy in Frederick Douglass" *Narrative* of 1845,' in Andrews, ed, *Critical Essays on Frederick Douglass*, pp. 148–65) and Gates on the aesthetic dimensions of communication is interesting in this light, though beyond the scope of my discussion, concerning (as it does) the more formal and literary aspects of Douglass's thought.
68 Douglass, *My Bondage and My Freedom*, pp. 278–9.
69 Ibid., pp. 279–80.

Part IV

Moral Suasion and Rebellion

8
Douglass as an Existentialist

Lewis R. Gordon

> The first phase of liberation must thus involve a rejection of the material conditions and ideological images contrived in the interests of the slaveholder class. The slave must reject his/her existence as a slave. In the words of Frederick Douglass, "Nature never intended that men and women should be either slaves or slaveholders, and nothing but rigid training long persisted in, can perfect the character of the one or the other."
>
> *Philosophy Born of Struggle*, Angela Y. Davis[1]

In 1994, I found myself collecting responses to a call for papers on black existential philosophy. Responses ranged from discussions of the African roots of black existential philosophy to the liberating struggles of blacks in a racially hostile world. There were, however, a few mysterious abstracts. There is no black existential philosophy, these argued, since existentialism is a European phenomenon addressing European experience. Look for thought from Søren Kierkegaard to Simone de Beauvoir, and one would find more bourgeois *Angst* than material conditions of black misery. To this criticism, I wrote letters with the following response: the body of literature that constitutes European existentialism is but one continent's response to a set of problems that date from the moment human beings faced problems of anguish and despair. Conflicts over responsibility and anxiety, over life-affirmation and suicidal nihilism preceded Kierkegaardian formulations of fear and trembling and raised questions beyond Eurocentric attachment to a narrow body of literature. Existential philosophy addresses problems of freedom, anguish, responsibility, embodied agency, sociality, and liberation. It addresses these problems through a focus on the human condition. At the heart of existential thought are two questions: "What are we?" and "What shall we do?" These questions can be translated into questions of identity and moral action. They are questions, further, of ontological and teleological significance, for the former addresses being and the latter addresses what to be, in a word, "purpose." Such questions can be further radicalized through reflection on their preconditions: how are such questions, in a word, possible?

In my replies to the skeptical, I asked them, "Did slaves not wonder about freedom, suffer anguish, paradoxes of responsibility, concerns of agency, tremors of broken sociality, and burning desire for liberation?" "Do we not find struggles with these matters in traditional West African proverbs and folktales?" And more, even if we do not turn to the historical experiences of slaves of African descent and the body of cultural resources indigenous to the African continent, there are also the various dialogical encounters between twentieth-century Africana theorists and European and Euro-American theorists. Not only were there Richard Wright's, Léopold Senghor's, and Frantz Fanon's engagements with existential philosophy to consider, but also the engagements of black academic philosophers as well, such as William R. Jones, Thomas Slaughter, Lucius T. Outlaw, Cornel West, and more.[2] In the end, when chapters were evaluated and edited and the work was finally complete, I stared at a text with many surprises.

One surprise emerged from composing the index of proper names. There was a clear list of influential figures in black existential philosophy. I have already mentioned some of these figures. But particularly surprising were the many references to Frederick Douglass and W. E. B. DuBois. Upon reflection, however, the surprise wanes when we think of the obvious, at least in the case of DuBois. For his contributing motif of double consciousness holds many fruits for inquiry not only on the *identity* dimension of existential thought but also on its focus on lived experience; double consciousness raises interesting considerations, after all, for our understanding of *consciousness*. Being simultaneously one identity and its outsider raises problems of anguish that permeate the writings of New World blacks from Wheatley through Wright as well as Ellison and Morrison. In black writing is the question of black consciousness, that black people have perspectives on the world. The familiar acknowledgment at the beginning of some slaves narratives – "as written by him [or her] self" – is but an instance of this reminder. Appeal to black consciousness' manifesting itself in black writing is not sufficient, however, for the substantiation of black existential thought; for then all black writing would be black existential thought (and the same would apply to all writing from other peoples). To show that a text is a contribution to black existential thought one needs to show that the work raises theoretical questions of an existential variety on the situation of black people. That Douglass is a major contributor to African-American philosophy is indubitable.[3] Unlike DuBois, whose analyses focus explicitly on consciousness as regionally situated (in the United States) and globally situated (in relation to Africa), Douglass's references require different intratextual resources. To situate Douglass in existential thought requires an articulation that addresses both slavery and struggle. For in Douglass's lifetime, a transition from slavery *de jure* and *de facto* to slavery *de facto* but not *de jure* was the underlying contradiction. (In DuBois, there is the added transition from colonialism to neocolonialism, from Jim Crow to the contradictions of bourgeois democracy.) In Douglass, one is pushed to perhaps the most concrete challenge to existential thought. Slavery and its legacy must be answered by black existentialists if their thought is to be of any relevance to African-American philosophy. Douglass's life and thought would have *to be* the historical exemplification of my reply letters to the skeptics.

In her "Unfinished Lecture on Liberation – II," Angela Y. Davis focuses on the impact of slavery and the significance of struggle in Douglass's thought. Albeit critical of Sartrean existentialism, Davis's discussion of Douglass utilizes many existential motifs.[4] Observe her formulations of Douglass's situation: "One of the striking paradoxes of the bourgeois ideological tradition resides in an enduring philosophical emphasis on the idea of freedom alongside an equally pervasive failure to acknowledge the denial of freedom to entire categories of real, social human beings" (p. 130). There is not only here the centering of the question of freedom, but also a critique of the practice of using abstract humanity to conceal what existential phenomenologists call "human being in the flesh."[5] Davis's reading of Douglass focuses on the existential problematizing of philosophical anthropology, where the human being's "essence" of freedom militates against *essentialism* – the doctrine of necessary preclusion of possibilities. Freedom, like existence, is not a property and therefore resists essentialism. As Sartre argued, existence is transphenomenal; it exceeds predications we ascribe to it.[6] For Davis, the concrete implication of freedom is that it must be achieved. Her own words are instructive:

> The slave who grasps the real significance of freedom understands that it does not ultimately entail the ability to choose death over life as a slave, but rather the ability to strive toward the abolition of the master–slave relationship ... The slave is a human being whom another has absolutely denied the right to express his or her

> freedom. But is not freedom a property that belongs to the very essence of the human being? Either the slave is not a human being or else the very existence of the slave is itself a contradiction. Of course, the prevailing racist ideology, which defined people of African descent as subhuman, was simply a distortion within the realm of ideas based on real and systematic efforts to deny Black people their rightful status as human beings . . . The most extreme form of human alienation is the reduction of a productive and thinking human being to the status of property. (pp. 131–2)

Broadus Butler makes a similar assessment, but he adds a thesis on humanism. African-American thought, he argues, is human-centric, as opposed to the system-centrism that marks much of the thought of Europe.[7] Douglass, he adds, focuses constantly on the relevance of ideas for *human* welfare. The onus of human existence is thus borne by the human being. The "unfinished" dimensions of Davis's assessments carry a similar appeal: no lecture on liberation is ever a *finished* lecture since the human struggle for humanity ends only when there are no longer any human beings. Douglass as a liberation text, then, emerges from his efforts to understand human possibilities in the midst of dehumanizing realities. We find ourselves on familiar terrain.

"Man is born free," wrote Jean-Jacques Rousseau in the eighteenth century in *Du contrat social*, "and everywhere he is in chains . . . How can this be made legitimate?"[8] For African slaves in that century and Frederick Douglass in the nineteenth, however, the man who is born free is one to whom they are only related in Rousseau's formulation in the abstract. They face a different question, which might be formulated thus: "The slave is born in chains, but she has freedom within her bosom. How is this possible?" The chains that Rousseau wanted to make legitimate were different from those faced by Douglass. Douglass's chains can never be legitimated except through some form of false consciousness and the most crass form of legal positivism, where the laws simply are "right" by virtue of being laws of the state.[9]

In his three autobiographies, Frederick Douglass had occasion to recount the significance of his conflict with the slave-breaker Edward Covey.[10] In what follows, I am less interested in the historical matter of his shaking loose from the ideological grip of the Garrisonians, where his role as interpreter of his experiences was first denied and subsequently asserted. What is important here is the portrait that emerges from the interpretations, how Douglass reads this important event in his life. Douglass could have chosen many interpretations (for example, that *his* "nature" "compelled" him to resist his condition or that his resistance constituted no more than an individual success). Yet we find what is in the annals of existential thought a portrait that foreshadows some of the best of Richard Wright and Frantz Fanon. The fight with Covey raises as many questions as it addresses. Although a moral tale, it challenges many of our assumptions, much of what we take for granted – which, in the end, is a lesson that a slave's condition reminds all of us who simply assume our freedoms. In teaching us about ourselves, Douglass's discussion raises questions on what it means to be human, and in that regard carries the leitmotif of philosophical anthropology.

The anthropological question is a normative one here. For although we are biologically identified as members of the human species, the normative, existential credo is that one *becomes* human. Alone, alienated, a thing amid nature, the individual lacks the social resources through which and by which even individuality can be realized. Thus, "first steps," as they were, are moments of existential awakening. The Hebrew analogy is well known, if we consider the story of Adam and Eve that emerged in Genesis 2. There Yahweh has created a species high on the chain of being, but a species whose realization of self is absent.[11] An injunction is added: Don't eat from the fruit of the tree of knowledge. In philosophies of sin from St Augustine to Frederick Douglass to Jean-Paul Sartre and William R. Jones, injunctions serve a unique, identity-forming role.[12] The world that existed for Adam and Eve before the injunction is a boundless world, a world without distinction of self from the rest of the universe, a world without reason to fold inward toward self-realization, a world without negativity. When Yahweh admonished Adam and Eve, however, a new form of consciousness emerged (at least in this Eden). Now there was the question of disobeying Yahweh, a question through which the question of *obeying* Yahweh emerged. Both possibilities ironically constituted a consciousness *beyond* Yahweh, for it was not – could not – be Yahweh's place to make the decision for them here. The decision in such a case would be Yahweh's. Thus, "The Fall," if we will, preceded the actual consumption of forbidden fruit.

But what is *The Fall*? The problem faced by Adam and Eve is that it is *their* responsibility what they shall do. In Kierkegaardian language, they are in anguish. Anguish is a struggle against making decisions that are constitutive of responsibility for the self.[13] In anguish, we fear decision; we attempt to decide not to decide. The performative contradictions of an undecided decision or a decided indecision are familiar in philosophies of existence. The "Catch-22" is that in either case responsibility is borne, for the struggle itself makes the denied more apparent. I am a slave. I know my options are limited. I am told that my existence is deserved because I am by nature a slave; I am by nature someone whose existence is so lowly, so inferior that I am without courage even to resist my identity as a slave. But I feel in my bones that I "am" without courage so long as I do not try to escape. There are those who have taken the risk. Some are caught by dogs, brought back, whipped, castrated, lynched, or burned. Others never return. Then there are those who help. They return to help others escape, and they provide stories of those who made it. To take that risk would "be" an act of courage, and ironically so even where throughout I may be frightened to the bone. However afraid, I would not "be" by nature one who performatively accepts the existence of slavery. Even though failure to act against slavery does not *logically* entail acceptance of slavery, it is a feature of all oppressive credos that one's actions proverbially speak louder than one's words, and one's words speak louder than one's thoughts. The anguish folds upon the self. A familiar scene in all cases of oppression and vicitimization – the rape victim who "wants it" if she does not resist sufficiently, yet whose rape is intense, exemplified more and more, over and over, each time she constitutes dissent by resisting. (It is progress when verbal resistance has standing in courts of law.) Returning to Genesis and to the existence of slavery, the power of the injunction is the absolute relation, sedimented in anguish, that it establishes between Adam's and Eve's selves. It is the negative instantiation of their freedom, which here is, ironically, their humanity. Their humanity is the moment of maturation in which they realize, out of their lived-experience, the responsibility of constituting, at least morally, who they are. For the slave, this moment is manifested in the distinction between the institution of slavery and the lived-reality of being a slave.

The slave from his or her *inside* is a rupture of an overdetermined exteriority the moment the slave simultaneously imagines his or her experience from the outside as having an inside, of seeing an Other. Slavery denies the slave any status as an Other or a self. The slave is property, which means that the (unjust) legal system of slavery regards him or her as no more than a system of relations: a "life estate," a "fee simple absolute estate," a "fee simple absolute subject to conditions subsequent."[14] These are terms in the English law of property. They mean, roughly, that non-slaves can have access to slaves in forms of use but without rights of sale as long as the non-slaves are alive, use with rights of sale, or inheritance of slaves upon meeting certain conditions after which rights of sale are also acquired. In none of these relations is there a slave's point of view. To state a slave's point of view is to initiate a rupture in such a system. A correlate is Frantz Fanon's effort, in *Peau noire, masques blancs*, to articulate *l'expérience vécue du Noir*, "the Lived-

Experience of the Black," which has been erroneously translated as "the Fact of Blackness." Fanon explored this point of subjectivity in response to the overdetermined reality of "epidermal" schematization. The black, he argued, lives in conscious realization of denied insides, a reductionism premised upon surfaces. The rub of racialized property reductionism is that at times even property has more standing than slaves. Frederick Douglass tried to assert his lived-experience, and consequently his humanity, through his early *Narrative* with the addendum "as written by himself." His written text made its way through the Library of Congress and was protected by the laws of the land, but he had no standing before those laws. Legally inferior even to his text, Douglass was what Fanon accurately described in his introduction to *Peau noire* as "a zone of nonbeing."

For African-American slaves, there are obvious similarities between the biblical injunction against knowledge and US slave-owners' injunction against literacy among their slaves. (In antiquated times, slaves were often teachers; in the Roman Empire, for instance, one learned from a teacher who was also a Greek slave, of whom Aesop was the most popular.) The uniquely dehumanizing project of US slavery was such that the significance of literacy marked a peculiarly humanizing possibility. To pose an analogy between Yahweh and slave-owners would, however, be remiss. The historical reality was that slave-owners imposed their relation to slaves with a hubristic analogy of being on a par with Yahweh made flesh in the form of a white Christ. The obvious difference, however, is the interpretation of Genesis 2 as a loving act of indirection on Yahweh's part by his pointing to knowledge in the negative in order to achieve the positive consequence of human consciousness and freedom. However loving an identity ventured on the part of Amercian slave-owners and in the light of their ideology, the bottom line was that the injunction against literacy was for another purpose. To believe that Yahweh loves humanity and poses an injunction that initiates the humanizing process is one thing.[15] The slave-owner's relation to the slaves is misanthropic. He attempts, at all cost, to deny their humanity. It is perhaps this realization that enabled slaves to develop a syncretic adoption of Christian faith with great emphasis on the Hebrew Bible. The *re-*Africanization of Christianity was underscored by the poignant realization that the god of the Hebrew Bible, Yahweh, was not misanthropic, and the white slave-owners' appeals to curses on children of Ham or Jesus's supposed white skin began to wear thin in the face of Noah's having been a *human being* and Jesus having been Hebrew, colonized, and poor. The terrain is familiar, so I will not here rehearse the tenets of Black Theology.[16] Of importance is that literacy, knowledge, is an initial humanizing moment. And in each of Douglass's narratives, he speaks of his entry into the world of learning by Sophia Auld, whose realization of what that literacy represented later led to her dehumanization into a *slave mistress de facto* instead of merely *de jure*.[17] Douglass's description of her "fall" in *My Bondage, My Freedom* is full of biblical existential motifs:

> I was *more* than that [chattel], and she felt me to be more than that. I could talk and sin; I could laugh and weep; I could reason and remember; I could love and hate. I was human, and she, dear lady, knew and felt me to be so. How could she, then, treat me as a brute, without a might struggle with all the noble powers of her own soul. That struggle came, and the will and power of the husband was victorious. Her noble soul was overthrown; but he that overthrew it did not, himself, escape the consequences. He, not less than the other parties, was injured in his domestic peace by the fall . . . In ceasing to instruct me, she must begin to justify herself *to* herself; and, once consenting to take sides in such a debate, she was riveted to her position. One needs very little knowledge of moral philosophy, to see *where* my mistress now landed. She finally became even more violent in her opposition to my learning to read, than was her husband himself. She was not satisfied with simply doing as *well* as her husband had commanded her, but seemed resolved to better his instruction. Nothing appeared to make my poor mistress – after her turning toward the downward path – more angry, than seeing me, seated in some nook or corner, quietly reading a book or a newspaper.[18]

Radically understood, however, we can also argue that Douglass began his humanizing path at the moment he could imagine an act that exceeded his masters' will. Punishment, however ineluctable, only intensifies that realization: "being" a literate slave was an act of disobedience. This was surely the position of the masters of the household, who "unfolded to [Sophia Auld] the true philosophy of slavery, and the peculiar rules necessary to be observed by masters and mistresses, in the management of their human chattels."[19] He continues:

> Mr Auld promptly forbade the continuance of her instruction; telling her, in the first place, that the thing itself was unlawful; that it was also unsafe, and could only lead to mischief. To use his own words, further he said, "if you give a nigger an inch, he will take an ell"; "he should know nothing but the will of his master, and learn

to obey it." "Learning would spoil the best nigger in the world"; "if you teach that nigger – speaking of myself – how to read the bible, there will be no keeping him"; "it would forever unfit him for the duties of a slave"; and "as to himself, learning would do him no good, but probably, a great deal of harm – making him disconsolate and unhappy." "If you learn him how to read, he'll want to know how to write; and, this accomplished, he'll be running away with himself."[20]

The act of reading exemplified a transgression; it exemplified being able to do what was both denied and forbidden. But the moment the *possibility* that it could be achieved was raised, Douglass was thrown into a process of imagining himself beyond his condition. He became aware that there was nothing *inside him* that occluded the possibility of reaching beyond his circumstance. His self became, as Sartre would put it, a project. He faced himself in existential anguish. But this realization, that disobedience raised an anguish-riddled relation to the system of oppression, also raised the question of how far *should* he go. Being secretly disobedient draws the weight of existence onto the self. Public disobedience needs to be waged at some point as absolute disobedience. Later on, exemplification of this disobedience on a group level took the form of black Union soldiers. But, for Douglass, this absolute disobedience took existential, situational form, which we shall discuss below.

We have here, then, the basis of all existential theses. The human being emerges but must paradoxically be presumed if but for the sake of that emergence. Kierkegaard pleaded in *The Present Age* to break down systemic dehumanization so authentic individuals could emerge. But he was aware that such emergence depended upon contexts of universal and then absolute preconditions. In the same century, Douglass explored these issues through the developmental reality of human life: from birth through childhood into adulthood. His biographies provide details of the struggle of slave children and their grandmothers (since their fathers, mothers, older sisters, and brothers were put to toil as soon as they were able), struggles in which there was effort to nurture the human spirit in an inhumane world.

At this point, we find Douglass's thought bearing many similarities to one of his successors, Frantz Fanon, who has perhaps written the most influential body of black existential texts. In an illuminating passage of *Peau noire*, Fanon observes that "a black who quotes Montesquieu had better be watched. Please understand me: watched in the sense that he is starting something."[21] Starting something is of course here an assertion of his humanity. The similarities between Douglass and Fanon lead to a question on the liberating project itself in both writers. For both start with autobiographical reflections that lead to reflections on violence. For Fanon, the latter is addressed in the discussion of violence in *Les Damnés de la terre*;[22] for Douglass, it is the fight with Covey. Fanon's discussion of violence has its early formulation, however, in *Peau noire*.[23] There, Fanon brings to the surface the limitations of the sparks of freedom as struggle for humanity that Douglass was experiencing in his initial encounters with written literacy. The clue is in chapter one of *Peau noire*, where Fanon discusses language. Fanon's argument is a provocative performance of indirection. For he explores what appear to be solutions only to point out their folly: that if they succeed, they have failed. What do I mean? Fanon points out that the location of the human being in a colonial, racist world has been displaced. Thus, *human* has collapsed into whites. Thus, most of the structural resources by which the term *human* is designated have been infected by whiteness. The black then faces the problem of trying to overcome negative blackness when the linguistic and semiotic resources available for positive identity are white. Semiotically, to resignify oneself out of blackness leads to signifying oneself in terms of whiteness. "Nothing is more astonishing," observes Fanon, "than to hear a black express himself properly, for then in truth he is putting on the white world."[24] The semiotic project must be waged. Something is achieved through achieving what is deemed an impossibility, a feat against nature. All liberation struggles are to an extent that: a defiance of "nature" as ontological closure. Something *ontological* is achieved when black people read and write, when they do, that is, what supposedly cannot be done. But the underlying limitation of this view is that it lacks a *creative* moment. It carries the sense of *taking-from* instead of *being-entitled-to*. In Euromythological terms, the black's immediate satisfaction is Promethean. Prometheus has stolen fire. (His other transgression is an attempt to trick the gods into eating fat and bone.) He is punished: forever chained to a mountain where an eagle flies down and plucks out his liver, which grows back each day for the eagle to repeat the cycle. Nature as repetition emerges here.

Fanon's claim, however, is that the contradiction of a black speaking the language *as a contradiction* plays against the hopes of a semiotic reconfiguring of racial reality. For example, the celebrated former host of the Today Show, Bryant Gumbel, had been the brunt of criticism, because he speaks *simply as a news anchorman* ("Is he white?"). This is so precisely because his blackness brings out the contradictions of semiotic assimilation. However much he tries to suppress black embodiment through white linguistic signification, he becomes just that: *a black who speaks like a white*. Fanon argues that the frustration of this realization first pushes the black inward to personal life, where he or she may try to escape racism through romantic, interracial liaisons. But even there, it is the white beloved who is the source of the liaison's value, making the liaison self-defeating for the black. (Fanon does not, by the way, claim that it is impossible to have interracial liaisons not based on legitimating whiteness. He claims only that those pursuing such liaisons for the sake of escaping blackness find themselves in such a self-defeating circumstance.)

Turn, then, to the lived-experience of the black, where there is a struggle to instantiate a self as mundane self, as ordinary self – concerned with everyday things, in the face of constant impositions of semiotic, gestural, political-economic, carceral limitations. The black attempts to live as a "yes," but emerges, almost always, as a "don't!" I say *almost always* since Fanon points out elsewhere that it is the black, after all, who creates negritude, a conception of blackness that, in spite of its limitations that Fanon uncovers in *Peau noire* and *Les Damnés*, is nevertheless a creative assertion of positive blackness. The semiotic limitations recur with a vengeance here, since even the negritude writers' conception of black positively found its substantive elements from overdetermined, white interpretations of blackness.[25] A dialectical resolve takes over here, a resolve that Fanon reluctantly conceded to Sartre, that the semiotic upsurge prepares one for struggle; it is a humanizing moment, but not achieved humanization. The Sartrean model, in "Orphée Noir," appeals to a non-racial working class, which cannot work for Fanon since the semiotic reality in the historic antiblack world is that a "non-racial working class" remains white.[26] The struggle must be waged, Fanon concludes, on two levels: the ontogenic level of individual struggle and the phylogenic level of structural and biological imposition. The mediating factor here bridges the gap between the two as *sociogeny*. Without the addition of sociohistoric considerations, the black does not appear and cannot consequently be understood through theoretical appeals to value/racial neutrality. At the end of *Les Damnés de la terre*, the restructuring of this conclusion is an appeal to new concepts and a new humanity. This is because Fanon recognized that purely physical levels of struggle, although necessary, require what Sylvia Wynter has identified as the liminal struggle to restructure epistemic categories into new semiobiogenesis, into new forms of life.[27] Freedom, that is, always calls for a new humanity to emerge out of unfreedom, a new humanity that is paradoxically the guiding telos underneath a humanity denied. Returning to Douglass's world of the slave, it is the underlying realization that, when all is said and done, slaves are in the end human beings.

My Bondage, My Freedom signals an early, biographical portrait of a similar existential journey. Douglass tells a tale from unfreedom to a qualified freedom. The irony of "my freedom" is that Douglass was in the end free in the sense of self-recognition of the important humanizing activity of his life's mission. Two wars need to be waged. The effort to persuade slave-owners of the moral turpitude of slavery focuses too much on *their* moral welfare instead of the ongoing misery of the slaves. Liberation of slaves had to be waged through force, and similarly the *text* of post-slavery (Douglass's "freedom") laid foundations for future texts of post-slavery, autobiographical texts that led to a conflict in African-American and Africana thought to the present: Booker T. Washington, Anna Julia Cooper, W. E. B. DuBois, Richard Wright, Malcolm X, Lorraine Hansberry, Angela Y. Davis, and more. Identity, in other words, emerges from struggle, but a subsequent struggle emerges over identity itself. This is the hallmark of existential struggles: existence preceding essence; praxis preceding concepts. The limitations of the early initiation of a struggle for freedom through discourse, reading, and writing are that they do not in themselves translate into freedom. They create an epistemic rupture, but without a material/ historical rupture, there is a gap that must be closed. Douglass recognized at a certain level his situation by learning to read and write. But what is more telling is the crucial moment when he fights for his self-respect in his encounter with the slavebreaker Edward Covey.

The circumstances are classic. His owner Thomas Auld deems Douglass unruly. He is sent to Edward Covey, a former overseer turned tenant farmer, who was lent unruly slaves for the purpose of "breaking" their spirit as would a tamer of wild horses. Covey's methods were simple. He would subject the slave to prolonged misery in an environment of seeming order and regularity. Unachievable tasks would be commanded, the purposes of which were to make the slave fail at them. Failure would be addressed by severe corporal punishment. Moreover, Covey would use techniques of manipulation and camouflage to create a sense of his seeming omnipotence. As Douglass relates:

> He had the faculty of making us feel that he was always present. By a series of adroitly managed surprises, which he practiced, I was prepared to expect him at any moment. His plan was, never to approach the spot where his hands were at work, in an open, manly and direct manner. No thief was ever more artful in his devices than this man Covey. He would creep and crawl, in ditches and

gullies; hide behind stumps and bushes, and practice so much of the cunning of the serpent, that Bill Smith and I – between ourselves – never called him by any other name than "*the snake.*" We fancied that in his eyes and his gait we could see a snakish resemblance. One half of his proficiency to the art of negro breaking, consisted, I should think, in this species of cunning. We were never secure. He could see or hear us nearly all the time. He was, to us, behind every stump, tree, bush and fence on the plantation. He carried this kind of trickery so far, that he would some times mount his horse, and make believe he was going to St Michael's, and, in thirty minutes afterward, you might find his horse tied in the woods, and the snakelike Covey lying flat in the ditch, with his head lifted above its edge, or in a fence corner, watching every movement of the slaves![28]

We see here Fanon's and Douglass's credo of liberation turned on its head. Covey starts with a brutal, material introduction to reality, but a reality designed to push the slave one step short of despair. Despair would mean giving up to the point of indifference to life itself, which would mean that the slave would cease to be productive.[29] Covey's strategy is to break the slave's spirit, but break it enough for the slave *to remain* productive. Douglass interestingly makes a classic existential distinction between remaining and living – "I remained with Mr. Covey one year (I cannot say I *lived* with him)"[30] – the former being analogous to being-in-itself, a form of being suited for "things," and the latter being-for-itself, a form of being with open possibilities, with self-reflection – in other words, human being. Covey's goal is to convince the slaves of their inferiority, to convince them that they *are* equivalent to animals on the farm, to make them identify with that existence. "Find your equality," he seems to urge, "below humanity."

Perhaps most telling are the events that led to the moments of anguish that the four-chapter account on Covey in *My Bondage, My Freedom* is meant to signify. Covey orders Douglass to gather wood in the forest and transport them back by wagon with some supposedly tamed oxen. The perversity of the command – Douglass is expected both to identify with the oxen and see Covey's position of having to tame him! The oxen took flight, however, and Douglass found himself in a situation of having to retrieve them and negotiate his way back home with untamed oxen. He declares, "I now saw, in my situation, several points of similarity with that of the oxen. They were property, so was I; they were to be broken, so was I. Covey was to break me, I was to break them; break and be broken – such is life."[31] Douglass managed to retrieve the oxen and make his way back to Covey's farm, but upon arriving, the oxen broke loose again and damaged the entranceway. The result was Douglass receiving a severe flogging.

As time went on, and many floggings later, Douglass took ill one day and attempted to rest, despite Covey's kicking him and ordering him to continue laboring. Douglass resolved to appeal to Thomas Auld, his legal owner, by issuing a complaint against Covey's cruelty. That Douglass did this at all is a sign of his unusual naiveté with regards to matters of justice, morality, and pity in his youth (he was approximately sixteen at the time). His appeal indicates a guiding motif of pacifist reasoning – always give the oppressor, violator, or colonizer the opportunity of doing the right thing; give him, that is, the benefit of the doubt. Auld's response, however, was to accuse Douglass of trickery and laziness and to order him to return to Covey.

Returning to Covey's farm, Douglass made some important resolutions. I won't here relate them all since they have been amply discussed elsewhere.[32] Instead, I shall focus on his decision to defend himself if Covey were to attack him again. We should note that this "defense" at first took symbolic form. He speaks of a charm handed to him by Smith, a fellow slave. The charm was to protect him from flogging. In addition, there was the expectation of Christian prayer – although Douglass mentions, throughout, the limitations of Christianity as a means of moral suasion: Covey was, after all, a devout Christian. In the charms and Christianity, we see a restatement of the theme of semiotic limitations. They represented moments of resolve, but the concrete reality of contention is Covey in the flesh.

After a period's calm, typical of Covey's penchant for surprise, Covey charged Douglass from behind and attempted to tie him up. Douglass's account warrants a lengthy quotation:

> Whence came the daring spirit necessary to grapple with a man who, eight-and-forty hours before, could, with his slightest order have made me tremble like a leaf in a storm, I do not know; at any rate, *I was resolved to fight*, and, what was better still, I was actually hard at it. The fighting madness had come upon me, and I found my strong fingers firmly attached to the throat of my cowardly tormentor; as heedless of consequences, at the moment, as though we stood as equals before the law. The very color of the man was forgotten. I felt as supple as a cat, and was ready for the snakish creature at every turn. Every blow of his was parried, though I dealt no blows in turn. I was strictly on the *defensive*, preventing him from injuring me, rather than trying to injure him. I flung him on

the ground several times, when he meant to have hurled me there. I held him so firmly by the throat, that his blood followed my nails. He held me, and I held him.[33]

Notice Douglass's observation that *"The very color of the man was forgotten."* The existential dimension of the situation was such that it collapsed reflective, conceptual reality. It broke through the saturated composition of skewed, racist reality. Covey called for help; first from his cousin Hugh; then from his hired hand Bill. Douglass fought each off, leaving only Covey to contend with him. "Covey at length (two hours had elapsed) gave up the contest. Letting me go, he said – puffing and blowing at a great rate – 'now, you scoundrel, go to your work; I would not have whipped you half so much as I have had you not resisted.' The fact was, *he had not whipped me at all.*"[34] For the remaining six months, Covey never struck Douglass again, and Douglass even gained a reputation as a slave who would have to be killed if any one attempted to strike him. For philosophers of existence, however, Douglass's reflections on the incident are of great value:

> Well, my dear reader, this battle with Mr Covey . . . was the turning point in my *"life as a slave."* It rekindled in my breast the smouldering embers of liberty; it brought up my Baltimore dreams, and revived a sense of my own manhood. I was a changed being after that fight. I was *nothing* before; I WAS A MAN NOW. It recalled to life my crushed self-respect and my self-confidence, and inspired me with a renewed determination to be A FREEMAN. A man, without force, is without the essential dignity of humanity. Human nature is so constituted, that it cannot *honor* a helpless man, although it can *pity* him; and even this it cannot do long, if the signs of power do not arise . . . After resisting [Covey], I felt as I had never felt before. It was a resurrection from the dark and pestiferous tomb of slavery, to the heaven of comparative freedom. I was no longer a servile coward trembling under the frown of a brother worn of the dust, but, my long-cowed spirit was roused to an attitude of manly independence. I had reached the point, at which I was *not afraid to die*. This spirit made me a freeman in *fact*, while I remained a slave in *form*. When a slave cannot be flogged he is more than half free. He has a domain as broad as his own manly heart to defend, and he is really *"a power on earth."*[35]

It should be borne in mind that Douglass does not take the position that a slave who does not defend himself deserves to be a slave.[36] For

Douglass, slavery is a categorical evil. What Douglass is focusing on here is the normative dimension of freedom, of its coextensive manifestation in the human spirit of responsibility and self-respect. His conclusions are not naive. He speaks of "comparative freedom." This is because he is aware, always, like Rousseau, Marx, (C. L. R.) James, Cabral, and Fanon, of the need for structural change. He speaks of "force," but force here is ambiguous since he also contrasts it with helplessness. Force here refers to will, agency, of the human being as active. At the heart of the tale, then, is a statement on agency, and what is the point of any liberation project, as Sartre observed in the *Critique de la raison dialectique* and Fanon observed throughout his corpus, without oppressed people's agency?[37]

There is much in this tale, which warrants perhaps a full-scale study in the form of a treatise. Douglass speaks of his experience as a rite of passage, and he speaks of two traditions – Africa (the charm) and Christianity (the prayers). Extraneous to the context of oppression and violence is a leitmotif of West African and Christian rituals of spiritual maturation through physical trial. The possibilities may well be endless. For our purposes, the importance of the existential reading is that it accommodates all of those since they *succeed* the act itself. In his discussion of Douglass's account, Bernard Boxill articulates this dimension through pointing out that none of the consequences of the act could have been foreseen in the act itself.[38] Boxill is correct. I should like to add, however, that an added dimension of the account is precisely the explorations that Boxill and many others have pondered. Douglass's account draws us not simply into a contemplation of the moral wrongness of slavery, but also into the meta-ethical level of morality's *relevance* in exigent situations. It is the hallmark of all philosophies of existence that the meta-ethical level is their terrain. The source of anguish here is the human capacity not only to judge morality, but also to go beyond it.

The account concerned Douglass throughout his life. It returns in his final biography, *The Life and Times of Frederick Douglass* (1893), in pretty much the same form as *My Bondage, My Freedom*.[39] In both accounts, he stands firm with regards to its emancipatory significance, but he is unsure about its significance for Covey himself. Douglass was here thinking in classical Christian terms about the moral welfare of his tormentor. To close, however, I would like to offer another consideration. Throughout our discussion, we have seen analogies between Douglass's expected existence and those of farm animals. American slavery was a concerted dehumanizing project. It is this dimension that garnered its peculiarly *antiblack racist* characteristic. The tale itself reveals much about racism. Racism, properly understood, is a denial of the humanity of another human being by virtue of his or her racial membership. This denial, properly executed, requires denying the presence of another human being in such relations. It makes the Other a form of presence that is an absence, an absence of human presence. That being so, the Other falls below the category of otherness, for an Other is another human being. Forced into the realm of property, even linguistic appeals – cries for recognition – are muffled, unheard; waving hands, gestures for acknowledgment are invisible. It is not that they do not trigger impulses between the eye and the brain. It is that there has been a carefully crafted discipline of unseeing. The black slave is thus a paradoxically seen invisibility in this regard; seeing him or her *as a black slave* triggers not seeing him or her as a human being. The fight with Covey, then, is a moment of scratching through this veil of non-seeing and raising the question of Otherness. Whatever Covey may have said, he *knew* that Douglass was a human being, and Douglass *knew* that Covey knew it. The *physical* struggle dragged Covey into a moment of equilibrium; it was a point at which the only way for any of them to survive, both would have to move "upward." For Covey, whether through fear, rational self-interest of preserving his reputation, or limited respect, it meant leaving Douglass alone. For Douglass, however, it meant, as he suggested, reaching for the heavens. His autobiographies are important *ethical* documents in this regard. They signify a testament that the voice from below is also a SOS from an Other.

The twentieth century has been marked by the continued struggle of that Other against projects of denigration. At the century's end, a message we can learn from the existential Douglass is perhaps best exemplified by a Haitian proverb, a proverb from a place fitting for closing this discussion, since Douglass later became a US Ambassador there: "Beyond the mountains, there are more mountains." So it has been, and so it continues to be.

Notes

1 "Unfinished Lecture on Liberation – II," in *Philosophy Born of Struggle: Anthology of Afro-American Philosophy from 1917*, ed with an intro. and select bibliography of Afro-American works in philosophy by Leonard Harris (Dubuque, Iowa: Kendall/Hunt, 1983), p. 132.
2 See Lewis R. Gordon, ed, *Existence in Black: An Anthology of Black Existential Philosophy* (New York and London: Routledge, 1997) for a collection on all these themes and thinkers.
3 His thought has influenced nearly every text in African-American philos-

ophy. For explicitly philosophical collections with many references to Douglass, see not only Gordon, ed, *Existence in Black* but also Harris, ed, *Philosophy Born of Struggle*.

4   The popular versions of Sartrean existential phenomenology have been contested recently in my two books, *Bad Faith and Antiblack Racism* (Atlantic Highlands, NJ: Humanities Press, 1995) and *Fanon and the Crisis of European Man: An Essay on Philosophy and the Human Sciences* (New York and London: Routledge, 1995) and Linda Bell's *Ethics in the Midst of Violence* (Lanham, MD: Rowman & Littlefield, 1993). In my work, I point out the distinction between existentialism and philosophy of existence. Sartre rejected existentialism (see "Question de method," in *Critique de la raison dialectique*, vol. 1 [Paris: Gallimard, 1960]) but not philosophical discussions of existence. Compare, for instance, the *systematic* nature of Sartre's thought versus the *anti*systematic thought of Martin Buber and Albert Camus. For collective discussions of these issues, see the discussions of Sartre in Gordon, ed, *Existence in Black* and in Lewis R. Gordon, T. Denean Sharpley-Whiting, and Renée T. White, eds, *Fanon: A Critical Reader* (Oxford: Blackwell Publishers, 1996).

5   For discussion see my treatments of the body in *Bad Faith* and *Fanon and the Crisis of European Man*. In those works, I point not only to the works of Merleau-Ponty, Sartre, Husserl, and Bergson on the body, but also to Alain Locke's (the lived-body) and Fanon's (the epidermal schema).

6   See Jean-Paul Sartre's *L'être et le néant: essai d'ontologie phénoménologique* (Paris: Gallimard, 1943), "Introduction."

7   Broadus Butler, "Frederick Douglass: The Black Philosopher in the United States: A Commentary," in Harris, ed, *Philosophy Born of Struggle*.

8   Jean-Jacques Rousseau, *Du contrat social*, chronologie et intro. par Pierre Burgelin (Paris: GF Flammarion, 1966), p. 41 (my trans.).

9   Greg Moses discusses Douglass's various struggles with problems of legal positivism on the problem of obeying the US Constitution. Douglass's position, argues Moses, is that laws can be changed and interpreted and hence made more just. The Constitution is thus an interpretable document; that is why the democratic process is a struggle. Competing interpretations vie for public authority. See Moses's essay, "Frederick Douglass and the Republican Heritage on Affirmative Action" in Andrew Light, ed, *Globalization from Below: Proceedings of the 2nd National Radical Philosophy Association Conference* (Atlantic Highlands, NJ: Humanities Press, forthcoming).

10 The three autobiographies, from the earliest (1845) to the latest (1893) are: *Narrative of the Life of Frederick Douglass, An American Slave, Written by Himself* (New York: New American Library, 1968); *My Bondage, My Freedom*, ed with an intro. by William L. Andrews (Urbana and Chicago: University of Illinois Press, 1987); *The Life and Times of Frederick Douglass: The Complete Autobiography*, intro. by R. W. Logan (NY: Crowell-Collier, 1962).

11 Yahweh is the name used in the *J* version of Genesis. My interpretation is philosophical and far from orthodox. It is my goal here to raise the

identification that a slave like Douglass would have with certain stages of the myth. For a popular discussion of the history of the various versions of Genesis, including the various Canaanite and Midianite deities that converge as the God of Abraham, see Karen Armstrong, *A History of God: The 4,000-Year Quest of Judaism, Christianity, and Islam* (New York: Ballantine, 1993).

12 See St Augustine's *City of God*, trans. Marcus Dods with an intro. by Thomas Merton (New York: The Modern Library, 1950); Jean-Paul Sartre's *L'être et le néant*; and William R. Jones, *Is God a White Racist?: A Preamble to Black Theology* (New York: Anchor Press, 1973; forthcoming reprint by Beacon Press).

13 See Søren Kierkegaard, *The Concept of Anxiety: A Simply Psychologically Orienting Deliberation on the Dogmatic Issue of Hereditary Sin*, trans. and ed with an intro. and notes by Reidar Thompte in collaboration with Albet Anderson (Princeton, NJ: Princeton University Press, 1962) and my discussion of the phenomenon in Part I of *Bad Faith and Antiblack Racism*, especially chapter 3.

14 These are the terms of property studied in Anglo legal systems to the present day. See Roger A. Cunningham, William B. Stoebuck, and Dale A. Whitman, *The Law of Property* (St. Paul, Minn.: West Publishing Co., 1984). Among the best critical portrayals of the reduction of human beings to property are C. L. R. James's *The Black Jacobins: Toussaint L'Ouverture and the San Domingo Revolution*, 2nd ed revised (New York: Vintage, 1989), chapters 1–3, and Herbert Gutman, *The Black Family in Slavery and Freedom: 1750–1925* (New York: Vintage, 1976).

15 Again, this is but one interpretation, a uniquely existential one, meant to be heuristic. Yahweh's possible history as a warrior god with highly partisan politics and military predilections toward obedience suggests also an interpretation in which he loves a select or elect group, given particularly the interpretations that emerge in Deuteronomy. The issue has been debated in many Judaic, Christian, and Muslim theologies. Armstrong's *A History of God* provides an introductory analysis of the debate, but for discussion in a context relevant here – namely, Black Theology – see Gayraud S. Wilmore, ed, *African American Religious Studies* (Durham NC: Duke University Press, 1989), especially the section on theology. The most forceful challenge to this theology is Jones's *Is God a White Racist?* See Cone's discussion of the impact of Jones's work in "Black Theology as Liberation Theology," in the Wilmore volume.

16 For a collection of studies on these facets of Black Theology, see Wilmore, ed, *African American Religious Studies*.

17 Douglass, *My Bondage, My Freedom*, chapter 10.

18 Ibid., p. 97.

19 Ibid., p. 97.

20 Ibid., p. 97.

21 Frantz Fanon, *Peau noire, masques blancs* (Paris: Editions de Seuil, 1952),

p. 27 and *Black Skin, White Masks*, the Markmann translation (New York: Grove Press, 1967) p. 35.

22 Frantz Fanon, *Les Damnés de la terre*, préface par Jean-Paul Sartre (Paris: Gallimard, 1991).

23 See my discussion of Fanon's theory of violence in *Fanon and the Crisis of European Man*, chapter 4.

24 Fanon, *Peau noire*, p. 28, and *Black Skin*, p. 36.

25 For a powerful, recent criticism of negritude, especially as expressed by Léopold Senghor, see Tsenay Serequeberhan, *The Hermeneutics of African Philosophy* (New York and London: Routledge, 1994), pp. 42–53. Serequeberhan takes Senghor to task for making the semantic features of his interpretations Eurocentric.

26 See Jean-Paul Sartre's *Situations*, III (Paris: Gallimard, 1949).

27 See her essay, "Is 'Development' a Purely Empirical Concept or also Teleological?: A Perspective from 'We the Underdeveloped,'" in Aguibou Yansane, ed, *Prospects for Recovery and Sustainable Development in Africa* (Westport, CT: Greenwood Press, 1996).

28 Douglass, *My Bondage, My Freedom*, pp. 133–4.

29 For perhaps the best statement on despair, see Søren Kierkegaard's *The Sickness unto Death: A Christian Psychological Exposition for Upbuilding and Awakening*, trans. and ed by Howard V. Hong and Edna H. Hong (Princeton: Princeton University Press, 1980). Compare also Richard Wright's treatment of the subject in Book Four of his misunderstood classic, *The Outsider*, with an intro. by Maryemma Graham (New York: Harper Perennial, 1993).

30 Douglass, *My Bondage, My Freedom*, p. 133.

31 Ibid., p. 132.

32 For two excellent examples, see Bernard R. Boxill's highly subtle reading of the tale in "The Fight with Covey," in Gordon, ed, *Existence in Black* and Cynthia Willett's discussion, "Frederick Douglass," in Lewis R. Gordon, ed, *Key Figures in African-American Thought* (Oxford: Blackwell Publishers, forthcoming).

33 Douglass, *My Bondage, My Freedom*, p. 149.

34 Ibid., p. 151.

35 Ibid., pp. 151–2.

36 For discussion, see Boxill, "The Fight with Covey," in Gordon, ed, *Existence in Black*, p. 288.

37 For discussion of agency and liberation, see also my *Fanon and the Crisis of European Man*, chapters 2, 3, and 4, and my "Identity and Liberation: A Phenomenological Approach," in Kevin Thompson and Lester Embree, eds, *Phenomenology of the Political* (Dordrecht: Kluwer Academic Publishers, forthcoming).

38 "The Fight with Covey," in Gordon, ed, *Existence in Black*, pp. 276–84.

39 For discussion on the similarities between this account and *My Bondage, My Freedom*, see Boxill, "The Fight with Covey." in Gordon, ed, *Existence in Black*.

9

Honor and Insurrection
or
A Short Story about why John Brown (with David Walker's Spirit) was Right and Frederick Douglass (with Benjamin Banneker's Spirit) was Wrong

Leonard Harris

I argue for honoring the character traits that enlivened David Walker's *Appeal to the Coloured Citizens of the World, But in Particular, and Very Expressly, to Those of the United States of America* (1829).[1] Walker's pamphlet influenced insurrectionists in Virginia, South Carolina, North Carolina, and Maryland. He eloquently appealed for slaves to defend themselves, escape from slavery, and initiate insurrection. Supporting insurrection against race-based slavery was for Walker a Christian, and especially Protestant, morally compelling responsibility. The character traits exhibited by David Walker, such as tenacity, irreverence, passion, enmity – and the associated actions of insurrection – are due esteem. Insurrectionists, with their absolute belligerence and disdain for slavery's authorities, were magnanimous in ways different from abolitionists that relied on moral suasion to change civil and government behavior.

It is David Walker's spirit that, according to legend, inhabited John Brown, the famous insurrectionist that commandeered Harpers Ferry, W. Virginia, in 1859.[2] That spirit, it is said, was inherited by Walker from slave insurrections in 1521 Hispaniola; from 1526 insurrectionists in the Spanish colony of South Carolina, under the explorer Ayllon; from the insurrectionists of Gloucester County, Virginia, in 1663; from the 1712 Coromantee Indians, Paw Paw Negroes, Africans, whites, mestizos, Spanish, and Portuguese insurrections in New York – from stalwart souls engaged in killing the entrepreneurs of the vicious trade, sacking neighborhoods of slave supporters, and destroying ill-gotten assets. Imagine that! Blacks, marooning, just like slaves, serfs, and indentured servants leaving Europe for America; killing overseers and soldiers much like patriots breaking British law and killing supporters and soldiers of the British crown, then burying their bodies head down, their anuses pointing toward heaven so that their souls would go quickly to hell. But I am getting ahead of the story. Back to the dramaturgical potential of moral suasion.

Douglass was a moral suasion abolitionist. Moral suasionists believed that the power of moral argument, particularly arguments that emphasized Christian moral requirements, could persuade persons to radically change their behavior. Either directly, or through general social pressure, it was often believed that the profit, personal power over others, and privileges gained by whites from slavery might be relinquished with the aid of moral persuasion. In addition, suasionists believed that if they, or members of the enslaved racial/ethnic type, demonstrated enviable character traits the demonstration would help convince government and civil authorities of the humanity or potential humanity of the slave community. The demonstration would have such persuasive influence because it would be irrefutable evidence that there were esteemable contributions of which the slave type was capable. The demonstration would presumably then be useful in motivating authorities to end slavery. African-American suasionists practiced a politics of "representation" by which they saw themselves as representing what slaves could become. The virtues of benevolence, piety, temperance, restraint, serenity, and compassion were usually considered commanded by Christianity, nature, or reason. Suasionists, if they were not absolute pacifists, often encouraged the use of government and direct military or economic force to end slavery. Neither the theology nor moral psychology of suasionists included a stringent responsibility to engage in highly risky insurrection against racial slavery. The evaluation of what strategies would be instrumentally successful to either end, or help end, slavery usually did not include insurrection as a wise or prudential option. Thus, suasionists did not believe that there were compelling moral grounds for insurrection and/or that insurrection as an instrumental or practical tool was likely to be successful or sufficiently valuable for ending slavery.

In an early version of the suasionist tradition, Francis Hutcheson's *A System of Moral Philosophy* argued against the idea that slavery was justified as the right of conquest, a reflection of unavoidable conquests resulting from the state of war between competing groups, or an entitlement held by owners from just transactions.[3] Rational human beings should never, for Hutcheson, be made to suffer. Rather, for Hutcheson, we should be motivated by a natural sense of benevolence and pity to eradicate suffering. Moreover, "All men have strong desires of liberty and property, have notions of right, and strong natural impulses to marriage, families, and offspring, and earnest desires for their safety ... We must therefore conclude, that no endowments, natural or acquired, can give a perfect right to assume powers over others, without their consent."[4] Slavery denies the inherent humanity of slaves and was therefore always unjust. There is presumably a vital, if hidden, "calm impulse of the soul to desire the gravest happiness and perfection."[5] In some versions of suasionism, a vitalist impulse is replaced by appeals to reason or nature as the font of such desires. In later versions of benevolent ethics, evolution is treated as inherently inclined to create or make manifest such desires. The character traits most often associated with suasionists were considered best instilled by abolitionists through mental discipline, moral education, and industrial training. Moral suasionists envisioned future communities as having a fair degree of equanimity of opinion, congenial associations, pastoral surroundings, and industrial cooperation. Morally suasive abolitionists, for example, William Lloyd Garrison and Frederick Douglass, greatly respected Walker, but considered his works dangerous and incendiary.[6]

Walker was born in 1785 in North Carolina of a slave father and a free mother. He inherited the status of his mother. However, by the time he was a man, racial slavery was the norm. Free blacks were considered inferior and as a class themselves always under danger of being enslaved. Walker, an owner of a second-hand clothing business, became a pamphleteer, distributing his *Appeal* throughout America beginning in September 1829 from Boston with the help of seamen and stewards. Walker published the third and last edition of the *Appeal* in June 1830; on June 28th of that year Walker was found dead near his clothing shop.

Walker provided a Christian-inspired justification and legitimization for insurrection. He eloquently advocated slave insurrection and the rights of slaves to revolt, escape, and kill overseers, masters, and those that stood in the way of a slaves freedom. The character traits he considered admirable were not at all like the traits associated with Hegel's slaves – subservience, docility or vicarious living through the will of the other. Nor were they the traits moral suasionists considered intrinsically admirable *and* instrumental for the purposes of ending slavery, e.g., restraint, compassion or "representing" an acceptable kind.

The actual death of Jim and Jane Crow were not losses to be lamented for Walker; rather, the emphasis was on the entitlement of those seeking to end slavery and slaves seeking manumission. One of those entitlements included the use of deadly force to defend themselves and seminal principles of human worth, e.g., that persons, regardless of race, creed, or color, are full human beings. The virtues of tenacity, irreverence, passion, and enmity were features of full human persons *and* they could be instrumental in ending slavery. These virtues were best instilled by independent entrepreneurship, moral living, and competition. The insurrectionist tradition envisioned future communities as primarily identical to the communities within which they lived – excluding slavery. There were very few slave insurrectionists that envision structural changes in future communities, even if they did envision special religious communities. Walker envisioned communities with a fair degree of contending beliefs, conflicting associations, chaotic intertwining, cross-fertilizing cultures, and competition over resources. That is, he envisioned a future world like the one he inhabited, but without the degrading reality of slavery. Enviable traits such as frugality or self-confidence and hierarchically arranged social statuses such as farmer or wheelwright, for example, would be due deference in future communities envisioned by Walker.

Walker described the character of the slaves as degraded, wretched, servile, ignorant, deceitful, and abject. Blacks, according to Walker, were forced into a mean, low, and abject condition. The condition of forced servitude made the character traits of willed servility possible. Overseers, drivers, and slave-owners were considered by Walker as avaricious, greedy, usurpers, sordid, wicked, tyrannical, unmerciful wretches, and murderous. They practiced hellish cruelties, butcheries, debaucheries, and degradations. Walker argued that the system of racial slavery practiced in America was the worse form of slavery in human history. Barbarian, heathen, and uncivilized nations according to Walker were never so cruel as the white American Christians. Two reasons Walker provides for describing American race-based slavery in this way are particularly striking: first, no other nation of so vast, advanced, and importance made a whole class of people irredeemably, collectively, and individually condemned across generations to servitude. Secondly, race, as a criterion for the complete exclusion from any role of divine grace, spiritual embodiment, and membership in the human family, was if not completely unique to American race-based slavery, certainly historically a form involving more persons than any other. American slavery was thus preeminently sinful. It was sinful, on my reading of Walker, not because America practiced slavery. Walker seems to think that other slave systems were benevolent. As Walker puts it, "I call upon the professing Christians, I call upon the philanthropist, I call upon the very tyrant himself, to show me a page of history, either sacred or profane, on which a verse can be found, which maintains that the Egyptians heaped the *insupportable insult* upon the children of Israel, by telling them that they were not of the *human family*."[7] It is, for Walker, heaping insult upon injury "having reduced us to the deplorable condition of slaves under their feet" to then insult by exclusion.[8] It was sinful because it made slaves, their progeny, and every one of their kind spiritually irredeemable. They could never be full Christians and they could never be free. Individuals of the kind and the kind itself were condemned. American slavery was sinful also because it used race as a criterion of distinction:

> I ask you then, in the name of the Lord, of what kind can your religion be? Can it be that which was preached by our Lord Jesus Christ from Heaven? I believe you cannot be so wicked as to tell him that his Gospel was that of *distinction*. What can the American preachers and people take God to be? Did not God make us all, as it seemed best to himself? What right, then, has one of us, to despise another, and to treat him cruel, on account of his colour, which none, but the God who made it can alter? Can there be a greater absurdity in nature, and particularly in a free republican country? . . . O Americans! Americans!!! I call God – I call angels – I call men, to witness, that your DESTRUCTION *is at hand*, and will be speedily consummated unless you REPENT.[9]

Destruction would be imminent, for Walker, if there were no general repentance, either through the hand of God or the agency of the enslaved. Walker was not so romantic as to believe that Americans would change peaceably. Moreover, he entitled the slave to the same sort of worth as the free; thus, self-defense and pursuit of freedom were well worth the effort.

Even Henry D. Thoreau, in 1859, arguing against the romantic idea that humanitarian sentiments would soon be diffused in the Americas, thus leading to the rapid end of slavery through moral indignation, recognized that:

> The slave ship is on her way crowded with its dying victims; new cargoes are being added in mid ocean; a small crew of slaveholders, countenanced by a large body of passengers, is smothering four millions under the hatches, and yet the politician asserts that the only proper way by which deliverance is to be obtained is by "the quickest diffusion of the sentiments of humanity without any outbreak." As if the sentiments of humanity were ever found unaccompanied by its deeds, and you could disperse them all finished to order, the pure article, as easily as water with a watering pot, and so lay the dust. What is that I hear cast overboard? The bodies of the dead that have found deliverance. This is the way we are "diffusing" humanity and its sentiments with it.[10]

It would take a civil war before slavery in America came to a progressive end.

Characteristic of most persons of his time, Walker understood the world in terms of collective entities. Walker's representative heuristics – the way individuals define themselves as representing collective entities – are the representative heuristics of complex identities. Walker argues against the plans of colonization societies – societies designed to encourage blacks, particularly free blacks, to return to Africa. Colonization societies tended to believe that blacks and whites could never live together in America and free Christian blacks were needed in Africa to "uplift" the heathens and create a worthy civilization. Especially for blacks in favor of colonization plans, however, a civilized and empowered Africa would stand as material evidence of black equality.

It was perceptive of Walker to see that the variables of national identity and rootedness in material culture (i.e., how blacks produced, what property they worked to own, what physical neighborhoods they felt a sense of historical continuity with, where their loved one's lived and died, etc.) were far more salient than ethnic and racial bonds. Explanations and programs dependent on Negroes or Africans bonding with one another by virtue of common racial oppression were explanations and programs with little hope of predicting the future or achieving civilization missions. Moreover, the African American for Walker had as much entitlement to America as any other ethnic group and as much entitlement to have an American identity. Blacks, as individuals and as racialized Africans, created America in cooperation with other individuals of various backgrounds – all, ultimately, subordinating their original ethnic identities to a broader American identity and republican governance. There is thus no expectation in Walker that each black person represents, stands for, or functions as an individual leader for the creation of a civilization for all Africans when this meant rejecting their American entitlements. Moreover, the collective entity or social categories of "Negro" or "African" are not stable racial or ethnic essences. Rather, they are variegated, multiple, and transforming categories through which representative heuristics operate. This view of Walker's perception of identity, I believe, helps us understand why his commitments are for republican principles, equality, individual liberty, and religion.

Walker believed in providential determinism. Providence, for Walker, worked ultimately on behalf of the oppressed; oppression was motivated by wicked, vile, and immoral free-willed persons. God, for Walker, was on the side of the enslaved and thereby redemption and salvation from servitude for enslaved groups were assured. Slavery for Walker was a humanly created institution. In time, cruel, mean, wicked, and brutal persons would be punished in this life or the next; the abject, beaten, and innocent would be redeemed in this life or the next. For Walker, cruel nations would be punished, bad preachers condemned, and good Christians eventually rewarded. Responsibility for deviations from the Gospel rest with men and women, and the enslaved are required to take responsibility for their own redemption. For Walker ancient civilizations consisted of the Greeks, Romans, Egyptians; the ethnic geography consisted of Europeans, Africans, Jews, Indians, and numerous subgroups of the period. Walker, however, does not envision entitlements as group-based goods, nor the future as a world of alienated group identities. Walker does not envision persons as representatives of racial, national, or religious inalienable or natural kinds. Yet, he is deeply committed to representative heuristics; he sees himself as representative of Christianity, of humanity, and of the Negro. Moreover, these were for Walker ontological entities and categories, yet variegated, diffracted, and beset with internally conflicting subgroups.

The idea that injustice does not pay, i.e., that the rewards of injustice are not forthcoming to its agents, was a myth deeply held by Walker. The emotionally comfortable romantic belief that those who are avaricious and greedy are, in this life, likely to face due hardships was also held by Walker. He was, in addition, committed to the myth that those who suffer will, at least in the afterlife, be especially accommodated.

Bernard Boxill is right and Socrates is most definitely wrong – injustice pays.[11] Similarly, Sissela Bok in *Lying* is right in arguing that lying, or at least withholding vital information in order to gain an advantage, can be very profitable.[12] Martha C. Nussbaum argues successfully in *The fagility of godness* that accident and luck make goodness fundamentally a fragile goal even if it is earnestly sought, regardless of whether one believes that goodness exists.

There is abundant empirical evidence that injustice often pays. It is beneficial to quite a few individuals and many nation-states with long histories of slavery, indentured servitude, and serfdom. We also know that those who practiced well-directed butchery in the service of primitive or corporate capital accumulation in America's history of slavery more often than not lived longer, healthier, and happier lives than those they enslaved. Moreover, they died having received the services of modern medical care and with the good companionship of their thriving families, more often than those they oppressed did. In addition, persons that remained agnostic about slavery, or at least were not often engaged in contestation to end slavery, lived far more comfortably than those in the eye of the storm.

Walker's noble, but completely romantic notions of the instrumentality and wily ways of justice, avarice, and greed may not be neatly separated from his more realistic notions of honor and respect. Moreover, it is arguable that Walker did not have a defensible theory of oppression, because he was so deeply dependent on romantic notions of God's authority in the world on the behalf of good. Walker did have, however, a clear idea of what was unacceptable. As Walker put it:

> Yet those men tell us that we are the seed of Cain, and that God put a dark stain upon us, that we might be known as their slaves!!!! Now, I ask those avaricious and ignorant wretches, who act more like the seed of Cain, by murdering the whites or the blacks? How many vessel loads of human beings, have the blacks thrown into the seas? How many thousand souls have the blacks murdered in cold blood, to make them work in wretchedness and ignorance, to support them and their families? [How many millions souls of the human family have the blacks beat nearly to death, to keep them from learning to read the Word of God, and from writing. And telling lies about them, by holding them up to the world as a tribe of TALKING APES, void of INTELLECT!!!!!! *incapable* of LEARNING, &] However, let us be the seed of *Cain, Harry, Dick*, or *Tom !!!* God will show the whites what we are, yet.[13]

Representative heuristics are never, for Walker, of greater weight than entitlements a person has by being a member of the human family and therefore a member of a properly formed moral community. By a "moral community" I mean membership in a society in which persons grant, *primie facie*, trust, empathy, admiration, and obedience to persons that are otherwise strangers. Persons can imagine themselves as interchanged with others, feel a sense of sameness, and feel as if they can reasonably predict the behavior of others. Race-based slavery completely excluded a population from being understood as having the embedded character traits and moral psychology necessary for membership in vast spheres of social existence, for example, banking, trade in precious metals and jewels, production and sale of weapons, authors of medical technologies and regard as physicians.

One way to see the importance of Walkerian character traits is to see why Walkerian traits are essential to honor and self-respect. Honor is a social good.[14] That is, the possibility of an individual or group being honored is always dependent on the "whole" social entity understood as worthy. Slaves, eunuchs, and the poor, for example, are never considered honorific social entities. Aristocrats, soldiers, or elected officials can be considered bearers of honor. "Honorableness – in the sense of being worthy of honor – *is* a true personal quality; what I have suggested is that you may have honor without being honorable, and that you may be honorable without having honor."[15] My examples of these seemingly paradoxical features of honor are: slave-owners had honor as a function of their status, but any given slave-owner need not be honorable. A slave could be honorable, and recognized as such, but could never, by virtue of her status, attain honor, i.e., attain the position of being understood as a representative and embodiment of honor. My concern is not with whether honor is a consequence of social relations, conscience, precedence, or power. What is crucial here is that honor is contingent on individuals having the possibility of representing a social entity considered worthy of being exalted. Put another way, honor for individuals is contingent on the subtle and nuance ways that men, women, daughter, soldier, scholar, worker, African, and European are necessarily perceived as embodiments of kinds due regard.

Far more than many of his contemporaries, Walker was clear on his disdain for the exclusion of slaves from the possibility of honor as a category of persons because they were considered inferior beings. This exclusion, as well as others, was among racial slavery's most damaging – it made redemption impossible and thereby made the possibility of honor, for individuals and for the group, impossible. *This is the insult that justifies enmity*, if not vengeance, as a natural response. It is natural responses that racial slavery systematically denies to slaves. The obviousness of the humanity of slaves is irrelevant in such systems. Slavery tries to hide, destroy, and prevent natural responses. It must, like any system that hopes to exclude whole categories, demean, insult, and exclude the group from membership in the moral community. *Prima facie* trust, empathy, admiration, and obedience are never granted to persons outside of a moral community.

Torture, burning, and starvation were some of the practices used in the process of creating and reinforcing the exclusion of slaves. The denial of agnate bonds of family, for example, were some of the most common. Slaves were denied control of their children and denied the authority to make decisions about the lives of themselves or their mates. Such forms of authority were always considered, not rights or entitlements by virtue of their sentiments and commitments, but goods granted by those to whom allegiance was due.

Possibly overstated, but nonetheless important, it has been argued that "It was threat of honor lost, no less than slavery that led them [southern American states] to secession and war."[16] A noted description of lynching, a practice customized in slavery and carried on long after its ending, is described in the Vicksburg, Mississippi, *Evening Post*, 1904:

> When the two Negroes were captured, they were tied to trees and while the funeral pyres were being prepared they were forced to suffer the most fiendish tortures. The blacks were forced to hold out their hands while one finger at a time was chopped off. The fingers were distributed as souvenirs. The ears of the murderers were cut off. Holbert was beaten severely, his skull was fractured, and one of his eyes, knocked out with a stick, hung by a shred from the socket . . . The most excruciating form of punishment consisted in the use of a large corkscrew in the hands of some of the mob. This instrument was bored into the flesh of the man and woman, in the arms, legs and body, and then pulled out, the spirals tearing out big pieces of raw, quivering flesh every time it was withdrawn.[17]

The most reasonable and emotionally coherent response to insult is a tenacious, irreverent, passionate response of enmity. Such responses are one way that slaves, or agents understanding themselves as advocates for slaves, see themselves as authorial voices. Such responses take the slave to be full persons due membership in a moral community of persons. It is a response due praise and exalted regard, i.e., honor.

At the National Hall in Philadelphia, Douglass lectured on "Self-Made Men," the same day that John Brown raided Harpers Ferry – October 17, 1859.

Douglass used Benjamin Banneker, the stalwart architect and almanac author praised by Thomas Jefferson as an example of a self-made man. Moreover, Banneker was seen as exemplar of the Negro race and

Jefferson's opinion of him as a goal to be achieved, because Jefferson took Banneker's work as indicative of why doubts about the humanity of Negroes were misguided. "This was the impression upon the father of American Democracy, in the earlier and better years of the Republic. I wish that it were possible to make a similar impression upon the children of the American Democracy of this generation. Jefferson was not ashamed to call the black man his brother and to address him as a gentleman."[18]

Douglass, as we know, was wrong in his opinion of the slave-owning Jefferson. Jefferson was a paternalist toward blacks, including his slave mistress and his interracial children that he maintained as slaves until they reached adulthood. Moreover, Jefferson never supported or engaged in warfare to end slavery, but he was most active as a commander-in-chief to protect whites and government institutions, all of which were supportive of the innocuous institution of brutal force.

Douglass discussed Brown's plans on more than one occasion. As early as 1847, Brown and Douglass discussed the feasibility of an insurrectionary force to maintain itself in the Allegheny Mountains at Douglass's home in Rochester, New York. Douglass rejected the plan because slave-owners might sell their slaves farther south rather than risk any contact with insurrectionists in the Allegheny Mountains of Virginia. In addition, it would be difficult to maintain supplies in the mountains and generate public sympathy for insurrectionists in such a remote area. On February 1, 1858, Brown visited Douglass's home again in Rochester, New York and Brown explained in detail his plans for a stronghold in the Allegheny Mountains. Shields Green, an escaped slave residing at the Douglass home, was recruited by Brown as a co-conspirator. Douglass remained informed, although not directly involved in, Brown's continued efforts to establish an insurrectionary force.[19]

On the night of August 20, 1859, in Chambersburg, Pennsylvania, in an old quarry, Douglass learned from Brown of his plan to seize Harpers Ferry. Brown tried to recruit Douglass, but to no avail. Brown promised to defend Douglass with his life. After three days of discussions, Douglass declined to join Brown. Turning to Shields Green, Douglass asked Green about his intentions, and Green's famous reply was that he would go with the "old man."

Douglass believed that Brown's plan would not succeed. He thus did not feel warranted to risk his life and die in Virginia. Brown's plans were considered gallant, but not wise. They were not wise for Douglass, I believe, given his important and well-deserved position as a moral suasionist leader. But was it wise from the standpoint of what counts as the most important form of action to free slaves, i.e., end slavery and warrant respect and the possibility of honor?

Insurrection is never instrumentally wise. It is never certain that the insurrectionists will survive or that they will effect any substantive consequences. Neither uncertainty, however, is sufficient reason to refrain from insurrection. The women of the second Seminole War, for example, had every reason to support and fight against the colonizing and enslaving whites – nothing awaited them but rape, torture, loss of land, starvation, subordination of their agnates, and further erosion of their ability to increase their assets. They could not know for certain, any more than the women that supported the law-breaking militia of the American Revolution, that they would win or lose. If high probability of success were a precondition for insurrectionist actions, one would find it very difficult to justify the American revolution, non-violent direct action protests, anti-lynching pamphlets by black and white women, or membership in any of the insurrectionary forces that fought against colonialism, apartheid, or the Third Reich.

Walker's Christian theology, like Martin L. King's, held a stringent requirement for moral action against obvious evil.[20] Assured success for any given action, or type of action, was hardly sufficient reason to reject a type of action. Theologically defined responsibilities and conceptions of meritorious character traits justify radical risks. Unlike a phenomenologist, existentialist, nominalist, rationalist, empiricist or utilitarian, a condition of being a person as well as a Christian for Walker was that persons necessarily had responsibilities to act in certain ways. That is, personal experiences, reasoned judgments or instrumental calculations of how best to secure one's self-interest do not provide the rationale for compelling responsibilities. There is an *a priori*, apodictically knowable, structure of personhood that should be mirrored in each person's life. Self-ownership of one's labor, family bonds, and the ability to transfer assets across generations, for example, are definitive of full personhood for Walker whether a person is a Muslim or Christian. *Walker's ridged ahistorical standards of self-respect is what makes submissive slaves wretched and the conditions that maintain self-loathing persons, abject.* A Christian inspired insurrectionist method, not a hermeneutic method, is foundational and offers timeless truth claims about the nature of persons. Actual revolutionaries and insurrectionists, rather than status-seeking pundits, academicians, popular intellectuals, or ministers without callings to radically liberate the poor, are driven by a sense of deep-seated responsibility to take unfathomable and unrewarded risks. Thus Douglass in "The Heroic Slave" and Harriet B. Stowe's *Dred: A Tale of the Great Dismal Swamp* could support maroons and insurrectionists as literary gestures, but neither had any beliefs that required a responsibility to be a maroon or insurrectionist. The difference between observers and activists, like the difference between Douglass and Brown, is unbridgeable.

Douglass was fraternal with Brown and highly regarded his desire for slave insurrections. He placed himself in great peril by being associated with Brown. He allowed Brown to visit and reside at his home and supported Brown in small but important ways. Douglass did not lack in courage. After Brown's failed raid, Douglass was immediately suspected and was forced to flee the country. Nonetheless, Douglass applauded Brown. He recognized that Brown and his co-conspirators demonstrated more courage (or more properly, a form of courage due high esteem), that he did not demonstrate. "To have been acquainted with John Brown, shared his counsels, enjoyed his confidence, and sympathized with the great objects of his life and death, I esteem as among the highest privileges of my life. We do but honor to ourselves in doing honor to him, for it implies the possession of qualities akin to his."[21] The difference between Douglass and Brown, however, does not turn on their different forms of magnanimous courage, but on different conceptions of honorable character traits and warranted forms of representation.

Brown's plan to attack Harpers Ferry was not supported by Douglass for a reason of particular note not mentioned above – Harpers Ferry was a federal government installation. An attack on such an installation would occasion a response by the federal government. Moreover, the attack would be directed at the national government, not at an organ of civil society, i.e., individual entrepreneurs or their agents involved in slavery, religious groups, auction houses that sold slaves, pro-slavery apologists such as scholars or newspapers. The attack would directly seek destruction and usurpation of a storage facility and production site. The basic materials needed to sustain slavery were located at Harpers Ferry – weapons, a system of production, a system for the distribution of weapons, and a community of persons in which normal life meant sustaining the means to support cargo in persons. Harpers Ferry was such a community.

Douglass was right in his perception that an attack on Harpers Ferry would occasion a response by the federal government and right about the unlikelihood of its success. He was wrong if he thought that Brown should not attack the fundamental agent of slavery, its principal supporter, and a primary institution profiting from the taxes and largess of slavery; he was wrong if he thought that strategically Brown's raid, or raids of Brown's type, were any less capable of successfully hastening slavery's end than attacks on strictly civil or state-managed targets. Because there is no record that Douglass ever participated in, or supported, an insurrection any more directly than Brown's, there is no reason to suppose that Douglass would have participated in, or directly supported, insurrection as a normal feature of his protests.

But, again, I have moved far too afield of one of my objectives – to tell David Walker's story and consider the dramaturgical potential of insurrection. As Alice in *Alice in Wonderland* came to understand, it is the story that matters, especially so if the central character of the story is to be reincarnated, metaphorically or actually.

Once upon a time, not so long ago, not so very long ago at all, David Walker's spirit migrated, or so the story of this legendary figure goes. It is not known whether Walker's spirit ever migrated into the body of a moral suasionist. His soul, so they say, avoids bodies and webs of belief that would not be agents of insurrection, incendiary pamphlets, and persons who kill their masters and mistresses to get free.

Walker was himself the beneficiary of spirits from earlier generations: "In 1754, C. Croft, Esq., of Charleston, South Carolina, had his buildings burned by his female slaves, for which crime two of them were burned alive." Or again, "In 1755, Charleston, a Mr John Cadman had made provision for the liberation of his slaves, Mark and Phillis, at his death. The slaves learned of this and murdered their master hoping to hasten matters along. Mark was hanged and Phillis was burned alive."[22] Unsung heroes and sheroes.

Walker was in Richmond, Virginia, in January of 1830 to meet with other insurrectionists and distribute his pamphlet; shortly thereafter, but not personally organized by Walker, Nat Turner's insurrection occurred. Journalists were writing in North Carolina in 1831 about the need to control distribution of the notorious "Walker Pamphlet." In Washington City, North Carolina, the incendiary pamphlet was freely distributed. By 1859, John Brown caught the fever. Shields Green's liberation, and his goal of liberating his wife, was the ideal goal and persona for emulation.

This is why legend has it that David Walker's spirit migrated into the body of John Brown. We know he directly influenced Maria W. Stewart, the first major black woman political essayist for women's rights. Some say he lived in Pauli Murray, an insurrectionist.

There should be plaques, awards, statues, monuments, honoraria, schools, churches, and children named after insurrectionists.

Maroons in Florida, South Carolina, New Mexico, and Canada were successful insurrectionists, either in the sense of having achieved freedom through attacking civil supports of slavery or through organized resistance and escape. This is how Walker's spirit, inherited or not, lives.

Possibly modern insurrectionists and maroons will not hold the misguided belief that the virtues of benevolence, piety, temperance, restraint, serenity, and compassion are inimical to sustaining oppression or that tenacity, irreverence, passion, and enmity are inimical to the cause of authoritarianism and oppression. Possibly they will pursue assets and take control of their lives, using the same means as every individual or group in human history, including subterfuge, guile, disdain, and belligerence toward maniacal and malicious authorities.

Maybe, with a few conjuring tricks, the insurrectionist spirit will more frequently find its way into the lives of those viciously abused by modern Christians, rapacious entrepreneurs, sex exploiters, and racists amassing ill-gotten wealth.

Notes

I am indebted to students Daphne Thompson and Daryl Scriven for interesting discussions in Independent Study courses that I taught which included works on David Walker; to J. Everet Green for critical comments; and to discussions at my lecture "Revolutionary Pragmatism," Dotter Lecturer, Pennsylvania State University, March 1996.

1   I use here the original tittle of Walker's book. However, all quotes from the book will be taken from David Walker, *Appeal to the Coloured Citizens of the World*, ed, Charles M. Wiltse (New York: Hill and Wang, 1969).

    See, for the history of David Walker and early insurrectionists, Peter P. Hicks, *Awaken My Afflicted Brethren* (Pennsylvania: The Pennsylvania State University Press, 1997).

2   See Joseph C. Carroll, *Slave Insurrections in the United States, 1800–1865* (New York: Negro Universities Press, 1938).

3   Francis Hutcheson, *A System of Moral Philosophy* (reprint of 1755 edition, New York: A. M. Kelley, 1968). Also see Wylie Sypher, "Hutcheson and the 'Classical' Theory of Slavery," *Journal of Negro History*, 24 (3), July 1939, pp. 263–80.

    See, for interesting discussions of the traits of patience, sympathy, sentiment, temperance, and belief in God the redeemer – despite the obvious fact that slaves lived miserable lives, were raped, beaten, worked without due compensation, robbed of their inheritance, stripped of assets, and died while their oppressors lived longer and happier lives – Robert S. Levine, *Martin Delany and Frederick Douglass* (Chapel Hill: University of North Carolina Press, 1997).

4   Hutcheson, *System of Moral Philosophy*, p. 299.

5   Ibid. p. 10.

6 See Howard H. Bell, "National Negro Conventions of the Middle 1840s: Moral Suasion vs Political Action," *The Journal of Negro History*, 42 (4), October 1957, pp. 247–60.
7 Walker, *Appeal*, p. 10.
8 Ibid., p. 10.
9 Ibid., pp. 42–3.
10 Henry D. Thoreau, "A Plea for Captain John Brown (1859)," in *Civil Disobedience and Other Essays*, (New York: Dover Pub. Co., 1993), p. 39.
11 See Bernard R. Boxill, "How Injustice Pays," *Philosophy & Public Affairs*, 9, (4), summer 1980, pp. 359–71.

Also see my arguments in "Honor, Eunuchs, and the Postcolonial Subject," Emmanuel C. Eze, ed, *Postcolonial African Philosophy* (New York: Blackwell Pub. Co., 1997), pp. 252–9; "Honor: Empowerment and Emasculation," eds Larry May, Robert A. Strinkwerda, *Rethinking Masculinity* (New York: Rowman and Littlefield, 1992), pp. 191–208; republished: second edition, pp. 275–88; "Autonomy Under Duress," *African American Perspectives on Biomedical Ethics*, eds, Harley E. Flack, Edmund D. Pelligrino (Washington, DC: Georgetown University Press, 1992), pp. 133–49.
12 See Martha Nussbaum, *The fragility of goodness* (Cambridge: Cambridge University Press, 1986); Sissela Bok, *Lying* (New York: Pantheon Books, 1978).
13 Walker, *Appeal*, pp. 60–1.
14 I argue for this view in my "The Horror of Tradition or How to Burn Babylon and Build Benin While Reading '*A Preface to a Twenty Volume Suicide Note*'," *Philosophical Forum*, 24 (1–3), Fall–Spring 1992–3, pp. 94–119.
15 Frank H. Stewart, *Honor* (Chicago: The University of Chicago Press, 1994), pp. 20–1.
16 Ibid., p. 10.
17 See Trudier Harris, *Exorcising Blackness* (Indiana: Indiana University Press, 1984).
18 Thomas Jefferson's Letter to Benjamin Banneker, August 30, 1790, cited in Philip S. Foner's "Introduction," in Philip S. Foner, ed, *Life and Writings of Frederick Douglass*, vol. 2 (New York: Inernational Publishers, 1950), p. 86.
19 Ibid., pp. 88–92.
20 See Greg Moses, *Revolution of Conscience* (New York: Guilford Press, 1987). The tenacity and stringent requirement of action exemplified by King's philosophy occasions the same sort of honor due insurrectionists.
21 Douglass to James Redpath, June 29, 1860, *Liberator*, July 27, 1860.
22 Carroll, *Slave Insurrections*, pp. 30–1.

10
Enslavement, Moral Suasion, and Struggles for Recognition: Frederick Douglass's Answer to the Question – "What is Enlightenment?"

Frank M. Kirkland

> Douglass . . . was destined, by natural disposition, for a different field of action. He was by temperament a politician and, like all politicians, more or less of an opportunist. He was less interested in the theory upon which slavery should be abolished than he was in the means by which freedom could be achieved.[1]
>
> Booker T. Washington, *Frederick Douglass*

> Douglass personified intellectual activism: a sincere concern for the uses and consequences of ideas . . . The guiding assumption unifying Douglass' thought was an inveterate belief in a universal and egalitarian brand of humanism . . . As a child of the Enlightenment, he inherited critical ideological support for his rational sensibility.[2]
>
> Waldo E. Martin, Jr, *The Mind of Frederick Douglass*

I Introduction

Moral suasion has been widely recognized as a significant feature in the intellectual and political life of Frederick Douglass. Employed by William Lloyd Garrison and his abolitionist movement, of which a young Douglass became a leading advocate and later came to be one of its leading detractors, moral suasion is *prima facie* the use of rhetoric to persuade others about the moral wrongness of slavery and the moral rightness of abolition. What is here operative in moral suasion, however, is the presupposition that the language of morality directly influences conduct. That is to say, moral suasion requires the belief that it can awaken through rhetoric moral sensibility and, as a consequence, motivate us to do what is good. Moreover, as Waldo Martin notes, moral suasion is buttressed by Douglass's affirmation of Enlightenment ideas concerning a universal humanism, i.e., a singular human nature, and the sanctity of life, liberty, and happiness.[3]

Nonetheless Douglass-scholars have given varied representations of it. Historians such as Philip Foner and Waldo Martin regard moral suasion as a strategy or tactic peculiar only to the Garrisonian wing of the abolitionist movement. In their eyes, moral suasion is a particular strategy or an "instrument" the success of which is measured by the effectiveness of influencing or swaying people toward the conscientious, rather than the political, abolition of slavery.[4] In contrast, the historian John Blassingame and the literary critic Peter Walker look at moral suasion as part of a broader "rhetorical theory," the use of which reflects Douglass's brilliance and efficacy as either an orator and lecturer of the first order or an autobiographer of enormous complexity and subtlety.[5]

However, in both accounts, little attention is paid to the moral dimension of the rhetorical or communicative settings in which Douglass is engaged. On this point, the philosopher Bernard Boxill appears to provide a more considered evaluation. Before anything further is said, allow me then to focus briefly on Boxill's reflections on Douglass and moral suasion in order to do a bit of "scene setting" for what will be addressed thereafter.[6]

According to Boxill, moral suasion involves Douglass's promulgation of the basic elements of a Lockean-inspired moral theory, viz., the self-evidence of human nature and human rights. These ideas are employed by Douglass to exhort the moral fact of the humanity of black people and to reprove slavery's violation of their self-evident humanity.[7] Boxill is right not to call Douglass a "pedestrian Lockean,"[8] because Douglass's political views were more egalitarian and were favorable to a more inclusive sense of democracy than Locke's. Yet Locke's influence on American political thought,[9] particularly on the "Founding Fathers," makes it possible for Douglass to extend the inalienability of rights to enslaved Africans and to insist on the plain and self-evident character of those rights to reason. So, if Douglass were asked in the light of this scheme "what is enlightenment?" he would probably say the intuitively plain and evident insight of the moral fact of humanity and the inalienability of human rights (now inclusive of blacks, Native Americans, and women).

However, Boxill locates the moral or normative dimension of Douglass's rhetoric in what is clairvoyant to the mind's eye rather than to what is agreed upon in communication. He has to argue that Douglass, like Locke, regards individuals as capable of treating the moral validity of an idea, say, the inalienable rights of human beings, as something *intuitively* plain and evident, clear and distinct, to one's own, yet providentially designed, reason.[10] But if that is the case, what need for moral *suasion*, what need for moral testing and questioning in communicative settings? Douglass entertains something to this effect, when at a women's rights convention in 1853, he claims that he "considered all this argument about woman's right to speak an almost waste of time in view of the fact that it was so self-evident . . ."[11] So it appears that the importance of moral suasion for Douglass diminishes when he is made to rely on the Lockean-inspired thesis of the self-evidence of human nature and human rights.

Boxill himself is not unaware of this dilemma and he believes that Locke provides an opening for a way out. Locke concedes that human beings can turn a morally blind eye to the humanity and rights of others as well as make others morally ignorant of both, despite the self-evident character of both to *all* human beings. Boxill finds confirmation of similar claims in Douglass's texts. In *My Bondage and My Freedom*, Douglass discusses the effects of what enslaved Africans called "juba," i.e., the holidays given to them by their slaveholders. "These holidays," he states, "serve the purpose of keeping the minds of slaves occupied with prospective pleasure within the limits of slavery."[12] "To enslave men, successfully and safely," he adds, "it is necessary to have their minds occupied with thoughts and aspirations short of liberty."[13] Moreover, the submission of enslaved Africans to their fetters becomes for Douglass another source of the slaveholders' moral blindness toward them. In short, as Boxill frames it, the institution of slavery for Douglass engenders in slaveholders a moral blindness to the humanity and rights of enslaved Africans and instills in enslaved Africans a moral ignorance of the humanity and rights of which they are deprived and a passive submission to their condition.

At this point, the reason for moral suasion seems to come into view. Moral suasion would be used to *counteract* the moral ignorance of and blindness to the self-evident character of human nature and rights. But when examined more closely, the role of moral suasion becomes ambiguous, even when, like Boxill, we consult Locke or Douglass. Locke himself does not have a conception of moral suasion, because the self-evident truth of one's humanity is to be had only through one's intuitive insight of its intelligibility to oneself *without the aid of others*. Furthermore, he does not make governments or social institutions the cause of the moral ignorance of those confined to the drudgery of labor and life because, in his mind, moral ignorance is their natural lot.

Douglass, however, represents a picture of ambivalence. Early in his career as a Garrisonian abolitionist, Douglass engages in moral suasion to appeal to others' sense of the good in the abolition of enslavement and to remedy the moral blindness that was at the source of enslavement. However, as his thought matures, he speaks of the wisdom and justice in the violent resistance of or in behalf of enslaved Africans against enslavement and the entrenched moral blindness and ignorance supporting it.[14] Such resistance, Douglass believes, thwarts the use of a slave's submission to his condition as *evidence* of his moral ignorance and of his natural fittingness to be enslaved. As Boxill claims, struggle or resistance "denies [slaveholders] the semblance of a rational justification of slavery"[15] and provides them little or no defense to turn a morally blind eye to the moral fact of the humanity and rights of those enslaved.

In the light of Douglass's endorsement of struggle or resistance, again the question can be raised "what need for moral suasion?" If we follow Foner, moral suasion is surrendered in favor of resistance, because the latter is a more effective strategy in slavery's abolition. If we follow, for example, Blassingame or Gates, Douglass's *promulgations* of moral suasion and of resistance are simply reflective of his rhetorical excellence. And repeating earlier remarks, if the human nature and rights of black people are intuitively evident, then moral suasion appears moot. Moreover, if an act of struggle is that which eliminates the moral ignorance and blindness that clouds and distorts the intuitively plain character of black people's human nature and rights, then moral suasion seems unnecessary.

But Boxill provides a more engaging interpretation. Douglass, he claims, sees resistance as a *continuation* of moral suasion, as a "form of moral suasion,"[16] because acts of struggle touch or "communicate with" the sentiments of slaveholders concerning the injury to others and violation of rights engendered by their conduct. Resistance "refutes" the "argument in the mouths of the [slaveholding] community that Negroes are, by Nature, only fit for slavery; that slavery is their normal condition."[17] As Douglass asserts, "something must be done to make the slaveholders feel the injustice of their course . . . [W]e must, as John Brown, Jr., has taught us this evening, reach the slaveholders' conscience through his fear of personal danger."[18] Struggle, then, is an extension of moral suasion by offering "proof" of the slave's desire for freedom and, hence, unfittingness to be enslaved. Under Boxill's interpretation, moral suasion neither diminishes nor disappears when Douglass takes the turn toward struggle or resistance. Indeed it abides and proceeds in acts of struggle. So, if Douglass were to be asked in the light of Boxill's interpretation "what is enlightenment?" he would probably say morally informed struggle as moral suasion.

Yet what does Boxill mean by claiming that resistance is a form of moral suasion? How is violent resistance or struggle moral *argumentation*? Boxill rightly wants to claim that, for Douglass, acts of struggle or resistance are not just strategic, but have an ethical or moral significance that ought not be overlooked. But, then, should this mean that acts of struggle are equivalent to the *discursive* aspects and, even for that matter, have the same moral ends as moral suasion? If Blassingame's Douglass pays too much attention to the linguistic qua rhetorical bearings at the expense of the moral features of moral suasion, Boxill's does something of the converse paying too much attention to its moral aspects at the expense of its discursive dimension. If Blassingame's Douglass emphasizes his promulgations of resistance at the expense of the acts of resistance, Boxill's emphasizes the continuity of acts of resistance with moral suasion at the expense of their difference.

However, since I agree with Boxill that Douglass does not drop moral suasion from his philosophical arsenal, but supplements or complements it with acts of, not just promulgations of, struggle, a number of things has to be shown. *First*, the rational acceptability of Douglass's claim that human nature and rights of black people are self-evident would have to rely less on intuitive insight, despite his Lockean predilections. Rather the rational acceptability of his claim would have to be linked *at the outset* to discursive deliberations seeking general agreement. Moral suasion, then, would be the discursive articulation about the validity and violation of norms concerning, in Douglass's case, the immorality of enslavement, the humanity of enslaved Africans, and the extension of rights to them, with the aim of seeking general agreement for their validity and against their violation. Nevertheless, as we shall eventually see, Douglass's thought will have to undergo a reconstruction, making room for the *moral relevance of political abolitionism*, (something very few Douglass-scholars, including Boxill, concedes), in order to generate an interpretation of moral suasion along wholly discursive lines mentioned above. *Second*, the notion of struggle or resistance for Douglass would have to be rethought in order to show that even *violent* acts of struggle against the denial of recognition, respect, and individual identity are morally deserving of encouragement. *Third*, in Douglass's reflections, acts of struggle, despite their moral significance, serve as *a constraint on, and not as a continuation of*, moral suasion (as Boxill believes).

Since my prime concern is to flesh out these three distinct points, my discussion will be of necessity somewhat diffuse. So it is divided into six sections. In section II, I shall argue that Douglass's conception of moral suasion has to be connected to a conception of enlightenment reflective of an attitude and a communicative practice, instead of an intuitive insight. Kant's essay, "An Answer to the Question: What is Enlightenment?" will serve as a heuristic device in this regard, because it will enable me to link Douglass's conception of moral suasion directly to Kant's dicta regarding enlightenment – having courage to use one's own understanding and making public use of one's own reason.

In section III, I shall show that moral suasion normally relies on moral sentimentalism, and that this reliance creates two problems: (1) it obscures the relation between obligation and motivation; (2) it leaves the impression that moral suasion alone can serve as the *exclusive* antidote to enslavement. What this set of problems entails can be expressed in the following questions. When moral suasionists argue for the abolition of slavery, are they claiming either that human beings have a moral obligation to abolish slavery, an obligation which itself motivates us to carry out, or that all human beings have moral sentiments to do good, sentiments once rhetorically affected motivate us to abolish slavery? When Douglass calls for the abolition of slavery, is he appealing to human beings' moral sense of goodness or is he appealing to their obligation to do what is right? Although moral sentimentalists do not dismiss the notion of obligation, they do not have the conceptual wherewithal to explain its role or how it comes into force. Moreover, is there a place for morally guided *political* action?

Given the problems of moral suasion addressed in section III, I shall contend in section IV that there are two modalities of moral suasion, one inspired by moral sentimentalism and represented by Garrison and his followers (including the "young" Douglass), the other complemented by the idea of natural law and political abolitionism and represented by the "mature" Douglass. We can thus speak about a shift in Douglass's thought in terms of a reconstruction in moral suasion. Whereas the former, as a form of argumentation, is unable to justify our obligation toward the abolition of slavery, the latter, I shall argue, as a form of argumentation, can. I shall call the former "moral suasion$_1$," and the latter "moral suasion$_2$." Only in the latter, I believe, would political abolitionism carry ethical or moral relevance without succumbing to political romanticism.

In section V, I shall address some ambiguities and problems surrounding the relation between Douglass's use of moral suasion$_2$ and (1) the self-evident status of natural law, (2) the "original intent" of the "Framers" and "Founders" of the Declaration and the Constitution, and (3) political abolitionism.

In section VI, I shall argue that, for Douglass, violent struggle or resistance has moral relevance, but is not a form of either moral suasion$_1$ or moral suasion$_2$. But, nonetheless, it has a strong relation to moral suasion$_2$ such that Douglass can endorse both of them without paradox or contradiction and can *conditionally* rebut the moral presumption against violence. The moral import of violent resistance is due, in part, to his understanding of the slave's physical struggle against the slaveholders not as one necessary for survival and self-preservation, but as one necessary for moral recognition. Douglass can construe acts of violent struggle as a struggle for moral recognition, because their aim is to "repair" the normative violations to the integrity of a slave's life. Moral suasion$_1$ and moral suasion$_2$ are in fact incapable of "repairing" it, because the former does not seek to persuade anyone of the moral necessity to act against slaveholders and the latter is a mode of argumentation whose approach engenders binding convictions and not repair of one's worthiness to be recognized and respected. Any relation between moral suasion$_2$ and violent struggles for recognition must exemplify that division of labor.

Finally, in section VII, I shall offer some concluding remarks on why the above-mentioned relation establishes a novel sense of enlightenment.

II Douglass, Kant, and Enlightenment

As John Blassingame has correctly affirmed, Douglass's skills as an orator first developed while he was enslaved. His apprenticeship, so to speak, as an orator began within the institution of slavery where he paid attention to the tones, styles, and inflections of enslaved griots or raconteurs, where he studied the rhetorical deliveries of preachers in black churches or at camp meetings, where he pronounced words distinctly when he conducted school on Sundays for other enslaved Africans, and where he both received his knowledge of literacy (from Sophia Auld) and stole it (and other knowledge) reading surreptitiously books such as *The Columbian Orator*, a collection of famous pieces of oratory compiled by Caleb Bingham.[19]

As a fugitive slave, Douglass not only followed Bingham's oratorical rules, but also found, Blassingame asserts, new sources for his rhetorical ideas and theories, analyzing those he found worthwhile and employing those he found appropriate and effective. He claimed that speech should be logical, clear, and comprehensive, revealing originality and organization of ideas, "quickness and carefulness of observation," "extensive research, combined with admirable taste and judgment."[20] Speakers should possess "strong nerve, determined will, moral courage, strong powers of analysis, depth and breadth of concentration, and correct judgment."[21] Douglass brought all these characteristics to the task of moral suasion, the characteristics of a man of learning.

I mention this brief history of the genesis and this litany of the elements of Douglass's oratory, because they exemplify for the most part the practice and attitude of what the philosopher Immanuel Kant calls "enlightenment." One of the most philosophically significant enlightenment enterprises was proclaimed by Kant in his famous 1784 essay "An Answer to the Question: What is Enlightenment?" with its enjoinments "to emerge from one's self-incurred tutelage or immaturity" and "to have the courage to use your *own* understanding!"[22] These injunctions have often been connected with his conception of rational autonomy and registered in terms of the practical reasoning of an individual person. In that essay, however, Kant soon claims that practical reasoning is not just simply an activity exercised by oneself alone, but an activity exercised in concert with others. Kant, then, can characterize enlightenment as the interrelationship between the courage to employ one's own reason and the "freedom to make *public use* of one's reason"[23] to which all claims to authority are submitted. As Kant puts it, "by the public use of one's own reason I mean that use which anyone may make of it *as a man of learning* addressing the entire *reading public*."[24]

This proposal concerning the public dimension of practical reasoning is not peculiar to the 1784 essay. It also resonates strongly in the *Critique of Judgement* (1790) where Kant develops the reciprocal relationship between the independent employment of one's own reason and the open employment of reasoning in concert with others through the maxims of "think for oneself" and "think from the standpoint of everyone else."[25] Generally throughout Kant's work, the public use of reason is typically described as critical and widespread, bound by rules of consistency and coherence, and free of undue constraint. Although Kant states that the public use of reason involves debate and critique in front of "the entire *reading* public," something akin, say, to *The Federalist Papers*, which were opinion pieces of Hamilton, Jay, and Madison originally published in newspapers over a period of time, we would not be off the mark in ascribing to Kant's project of enlightenment the expansion and advancement of the public use of reason in all areas and forums of intellectual, cultural, and political life.[26]

Kant's depiction of the enlightenment enterprise, then, does not simply refer to the vocations of scientists or politicians engaged in public discourse promoting and criticizing ideas. Rather it refers to a widespread critical attitude in the examination of our fidelity to beliefs and motivations to action. The interrelationship between the independent employment of one's own reason and the open employment of reasoning in concert with others are, for Kant, reflective of the "test upon the understanding of others whether [the] grounds of the judgment, which are valid for us, have the same effect on the reason of others as on our own." It is indicative of a "touchstone" for securing whether a judgment has objective grounds by "communicating it and finding it to be valid for all human reason."[27]

What relevance does Kant's depiction of enlightenment have on Douglass? It should be made clear, first of all, that I am *not* trying to assert that Kant had a direct theoretical influence on Douglass or that Douglass had some familiarity with Kant's views or that Douglass was self-consciously Kantian. Rather I am simply stating the weaker case that Douglass is already engaged with a critical attitude in the communicative or social practice of justification, which Kant described as criterial for answering the question "what is Enlightenment?" Douglass does not come to this practice through an explicit acknowledgment on his part of a Kantian discovery, methodology, or set of beliefs. He comes to it rather through an orientation consisting of *his* own refusal of dependence and "self-incurred tutelage," on the one hand, and *his* own search for bona fide independence and maturity, on the other, an orientation Kant counts as enlightenment.[28] In short, Douglass's relation to Kant, if I may so speak, is not based on a fidelity to Kant's textual doctrine, but based on an ongoing renewal of an orientation to a communicative practice of justification, described by Kant as enlightenment and directed by Douglass at the abolition of enslavement, the moral affirmation of human freedom and equality, and the elevation and improvement of Negro people and of women of the United States.

There are numerous occasions in the life of Douglass, in which he acts in accord with Kant's dictum "freedom to make public use of one's reason." In the Preface to *My Bondage and My Freedom*, Douglass expresses his commitment to this enjoinment in the following way:

> [This autobiography is] . . . to vindicate a just and beneficent principle, in its application to the whole human family, by letting

in the light of truth upon a system [of slavery], esteemed by some to be a blessing, and by others as a curse and a crime ... [T]his system is now at the bar of public opinion – not only of this country, but of the whole civilized world – for judgment. Its friends have made for it the usual plea "not guilty;" the case must, therefore, proceed. Any facts, either from slaves, slaveholders, or bystanders, *calculated to enlighten the public mind*, by revealing the true nature, character, and tendency of the slave system, are in order, and can scarcely be innocently withheld.[29]

Moreover, Douglass claims to have "felt a degree of freedom"[30] as soon as he started to speak at his first public forum to a predominantly white audience of Garrisonian abolitionists in Nantucket. Indeed it is not a political freedom coupled with rights, but simply a freedom to express his views in public which will last till his death. Throughout his speaking and writing career, Douglass freely makes public use of his reason; he experiences freedom of thought and speech in the public sphere where the autonomous voluntary association and reasoned communication of free and equal individuals occur.

At the same time, he acts in accord with Kant's other dictum "have courage to use your own understanding." As a fugitive slave, he risks recapture and, possibly, death when he becomes an advocate of abolitionism, denouncing in his speeches slavery on the basis of moral sentimentalism or natural law philosophy. The risks become even greater when he subsequently condemns slavery in narrations of his own personal experience as a slave, because he now identifies the verifiable particulars about himself that would make it easier for his owner legally to reclaim him.

Kant also refers to enlightenment as *"man's emergence from his self-incurred tutelage."* "Self-incurred tutelage" means "the lack of resolution and courage to use one's own understanding without the guidance of another."[31] Douglass's emergence from "self-incurred tutelage" is best seen in his relation with the Garrisonians. As a rule, he refrains from being cast as a mouthpiece for other abolitionists, and especially resents, and ultimately refuses, being on exhibit as the staged "chattel object" for the speeches of other American Garrisonians. As Douglass tells it, Garrisonian abolitionists, even Garrison himself, would dictate to him that his speeches were only to convey the facts about the horrors of his life as a slave and that they themselves would advance the antislavery and pro-abolitionist philosophy.[32] This appears contrary to the "freedom felt" by Douglass in speaking his mind in public. Indeed, at the height of his association with and exuberance for the Garrisonians,

Douglass believes that the freedom he feels exercising his reason publicly in front of predominantly white audiences leads him "to forget that [his] skin [is] dark and [his] hair [is] crisped."[33]

As stated previously, Douglass is constantly directed by the Garrisonians to narrate only the facts about his life, despite the new views and ideas he acquires on the subject of slavery and its abolitionism through his own reading and thinking. So his break with them is not just due to his increasing divergence on issues with them, such as whether there should be a dissolution of the Union (Douglass, ultimately no; Garrison, yes), whether political action is necessary for the abolition of slavery (Douglass, ultimately yes; Garrison, no) and whether the Constitution is a pro-slavery or antislavery document (Douglass, ultimately antislavery; Garrison, pro-slavery). Rather it is eventually due to what Douglass perceives in the American Garrisonians as a kind of racist paternalism, demanding a tutelage to which Douglass himself is supposed to surrender, acquiesce, and incur. Douglass gives credence to this view in a letter to Charles Sumner referring to the Garrisonian position as a "school through which I have passed, a school which has many good qualities, but a school *too* narrow in its philosophy and too bigoted in spirit to do justice to any who venture to differ from it."[34] In short, then, Douglass maintains the independence of mind in his denunciations of slavery. He is neither intimidated by the impending terror of slaveholders nor welcoming of the looming tutelage that emerges from the paternalism of the American Garrisonians.

But despite these similarities of Kant's claims with Douglass's, we must pay heed to the significant differences in their respective approaches to enlightenment. And, as I can see, there are three of them. First, although both Kant and Douglass subscribe to the promotion of independence and self-reliance enlightenment has wrought, Kant's *main* intention is *not* simply to describe the communicative practice of justification, i.e., not to show that the expression of enlightenment in our theoretical and practical claims presupposes a model of reasoned communication or a freedom of thought and speech. Rather it is to show that the expression of enlightenment presupposes a kind of self-determining freedom as a necessary *non-empirical (yet non-metaphysical) condition*. It is an *a priori* condition not for the essence of things or for the analytic consistency of our thoughts, but, regarding human knowledge, for objectively representing things in our judgments *and*, regarding human agency, for objectively representing obligation as the primary motive in our freely chosen maxims. Fulfilling this intention, however, leads Kant to defend the features of the enlightenment under a robustly *a priori* idealist framework within his three *Critiques*.[35]

As a consequence for Kant, those features – having the courage to use one's own reason, seeking agreement through communication, and making public use of one's own reason – *need not entail real communication or argumentation*. But they can remain within the idealist perspective of Kant's *a priori* point of view, which is the same for all human beings. This means they are developed in ways that respectively, (1) do *not* take into account the preconceptions, prior understandings, or what a person already takes for granted even in making use of one's own reason; (2) do *not* take into account the constant and continual disagreement even in rationally informed discourse seeking agreement; and (3) do *not* take into account the importance of the variety of audiences and situations while considering the persuasiveness of our arguments and the power of our justifications even in the public use of reason. In short, those features are not cultivated in ways to account for the communicative dimension Kant's depiction of enlightenment reveals. The *a priori* idealist framework, according to which Kant ultimately considers enlightenment, moots this dimension.

Douglass, however, supports the features of the enlightenment along the lines of a model of communication according to which the preconceptions involved in the use of one's own reason, the continual disagreements involved in communication seeking agreement, and the impact of diverse audiences and situations on the cogency and strength of arguments are given serious consideration. They are attached for Douglass to communicative practices of justification which are viewed not in an idealist framework, but in their sociocultural context if they are to be evaluated and understood.

Secondly, Kant claims that the freedom involved in making public use of one's reason is the "most innocuous"[36] one of all. Douglass, too, appears to give credence to this view when he speaks about the "degree of freedom felt" at the above-mentioned speaking engagement in Nantucket. But it would be very naive to think that Douglass regarded his freedom to make public use of his reason solely as innocuous. As mentioned earlier, Douglass risks both recapture and death by exercising that freedom. Rather than "innocuous," "dangerous" probably best describes the freedom Douglass exercises in making public use of his reason. Kant too makes claims for the importance of persons of learning exercising their freedom to argue and to engage their reason freely and openly about the appropriateness and utility of authority. Hence, there could be "danger" in doing so. But he also requires those persons, as their moral duty, to obey authority while publicly arguing against it. In contrast, Douglass promotes the wholehearted disobedience to the laws sanctioning the "peculiar institution of slavery." He even advocates the killing of persons, authorized as federal marshals to bring back fugitive slaves, while freely and openly arguing for slavery's abolition.[37] So, with regard to the legal authority backing slavery, the maxim "argue, but obey" would not be part of Douglass's enlightenment enterprise. It more likely would be the maxim: argue and "agitate, agitate, agitate." Indeed Douglass just about says as much in an 1846 letter responding to that of Samuel H. Cox, who thinks he insults Douglass by calling him an "abolition agitator and altruist." In his response, Douglass redefines an "abolition agitator and altruist" as "simply . . . one who dares to think for himself – who goes beyond the mass of mankind in promoting the cause of righteousness – who honestly speaks out his soul's conviction."[38]

Finally, unlike Douglass, Kant is ensnared in the Enlightenment views on race. That is to say, Kant believes that race is grounded in (allegedly real) biological natures, which differentiate groups from one another, which are (supposedly) inherited and shared by members of a group, and which are used to define and explain the intellectual, moral, and aesthetic qualities and the cultural and social status of a group. So Kant believes that the character of individuals is wholly defined by their membership in a race. With skin color as the mark, race catalogues the kind of qualities and registers the caste naturally pertinent to the individual's group. Moreover, it becomes criterial for justifying why certain groups, say, blacks, and not others (1) cannot be in a political association with other groups, (2) can be subject to unequal treatment, and (3) can be enslaved, colonized, or exploited. Indeed it has been argued that Kant attributed the features of enlightenment to those whose race favorably assigned them in nature.[39]

Clearly Douglass fights against the use of race which fixes, if I may use the cliché, the "Negro's place in nature" as a disparaged and inferior one. It is Douglass's own embodiment of the above-mentioned features of enlightenment, his own competence to engage in communicative practices of justification thereby making those features his own, that throws into question for many the place in nature race supposedly assigned blacks. Indeed, as Douglass notes, it is not the mark of race, skin color, that is the cause of their persecution. According to Douglass, it is rather, say, the communicative competence of black people to make the features of the enlightenment their own, because it disrupts and challenges the moral and intellectual qualities race allegedly prescribes for them. For Douglass, then, this said competence is both the cause of *and* solution to the persecution of black people. Allow me to cite a very lengthy passage of a Douglass editorial:

color is not the cause of [colored people's] persecution; that is, it *is not our color* which makes our proximity to white men disagreeable. The evil lies deeper than prejudice against color. It is . . . an intense hatred of the colored person when [s/he] is distinguished for any ennobling qualities of head or heart. If the feeling which persecutes us were prejudice against color, the colored servant would be as obnoxious as the colored [cultivated person], for the color is the same in both cases; and being the *same* in both cases, it would produce the *same* result in both cases. We are then a persecuted people; not because we are *colored*, but simply because that color has for a series of years been coupled in the public mind with the degradation of slavery and servitude. In these conditions, we are thought to be in our place; and to aspire to anything above them, is to contradict the established views of the community to get out of our sphere, and commit the provoking sin of *impudence*. Just here is our sin: we have been a slave; we have passed through all the grades of servitude, and have, under God, secured our freedom; and if we have become the special object of attack, it is because we speak and act among our fellow-[persons] without the slightest regard to their or our own complexion; and further, because we claim and exercise the right to associate with just such persons as are willing to associate with us, and who are agreeable to our tastes, and suited to our moral and intellectual tendencies, without reference to the color of their skin, and without giving ourselves the slightest trouble to inquire whether the world [is] pleased or displeased by our conduct.[40]

Something paradoxical rings here. Under the auspice of race, impudence is the vice attributed to black people, who take on the features of enlightenment. Douglass, however, transforms this vice into a virtue for black people, who embody enlightenment features, because it signals their resolve of will *not* to acquiesce to the tutelage arising from white people, be they pro- or antislavery. Indeed, it could be argued that Douglass himself succumbed for a while to this tutelage after his speech in Nantucket where his association with American Garrisonians first solidified. As he puts it, for a time, "I [Douglass] was made to forget that my skin was dark and my hair crisped." This state of affairs changes rather quickly when the Garrisonians demand that his speeches consist *only* of "narrations of [his] personal experiences as a slave," i.e., just a litany of the facts without any argumentation, and that his speeches contain "a little of the plantation manner of speaking than not; 'tis not best that you [Douglass] seem too learned."[41] Notice that at Nantucket just as he had felt freedom in speaking his mind in the company of Garrisonians and could ignore his racial identity in so doing, so too does he soon thereafter recognize the use of race in the very trifling and disparaging vernacular forms of the antislavery speeches they want him to deliver.[42] Hence, the paradox. Although Douglass desires to speak in ways consistent with enlightenment that would enable him and his audience to ignore his racial identity, he still affirms that identity by speaking just in those ways and therewith commit impudence to those insistent on black people remaining in some form of tutelage *wittingly and willingly*.

Nevertheless, these differences between Douglass and Kant should not lead us to regard Douglass as an anti-enlightenment figure. (Nor should the differences between Douglass and Garrison lead us to rate Garrison as an anti-enlightenment character.)[43] If anything, they should be understood as Douglass's variant on Kant's depiction of what counts as enlightenment themes rather than his rejection of the themes themselves. As a consequence, they neither challenge nor undermine the idea of moral suasion as an enlightenment-inspired and Kantian-framed communicative practice of justification. So let's turn our attention to the notion of moral suasion and Douglass's philosophical stake in it.

III Moral Suasion and the Theory of Moral Sentiment

As we have stated, Douglass engages in the public use of reason by entering the political and literary spheres of public expression amongst free and equal persons. He discusses and debates the injustice and ultimate rejection of slavery, speaking against the slaveholding community, its allies, and its state-supported and Christian-sponsored institutions. In exercising his public use of reason, Douglass engages in moral suasion. What provokes this claim of mine is as much due to John Blassingame's and Ronald Burke's guidance as it is due to Kant's. As noted above, it is Blassingame who proclaims Douglass a "rhetorical theorist," one who masters and even extends the rules of rhetoric. This suggests that Douglass's use of moral suasion is governed by his public use of reason *and* his rhetorical theory, and this has significant consequences for how moral suasion is to be construed in Douglass's thought.

Moral suasion, in general, is a form of argumentation in which the *appellative* qualities of the process of speech or rhetoric, highlighting the requisites of morality, are used to persuade those of opprobrious behavior to change their conduct. In the context of American slavery, it is the abolitionist's use of rhetoric to influence slaveholders and their allies towards a "change of heart," whereby they surrender the personal and material advantages and acquire the moral benefits that come with slavery's abolition. Furthermore, black individuals, who engaged, like Douglass, in moral suasion, were regarded to be of such an exemplary nature that their conduct alone would be supposedly taken as proof positive for persuading others of the intellectual and moral endowments of black people in general.

However, most are unaware that moral suasion, even in the abolitionist's context, has roots in the eighteenth-century theory of moral sentiments.[44] Two of the theory's leading proponents, Francis Hutcheson and Adam Smith, were themselves against slavery, because slavery forced persons to disavow the intrinsic well-being and humanity of those enslaved and, therefore, could not be approved for any benevolence of motive or for any tendency toward beneficent consequences. Nevertheless their antislavery stance should not be the basis on which moral suasion stands with respect to the theory of moral sentiments, because, as it is well known, another leading proponent of the theory, David Hume, denied the humanity of people of African descent and supported their enslavement. The significance of the theory of moral sentiments for our discussion of moral suasion lies in its account of the manner in which we act from the motive of duty, i.e., how the relation between obligation and motivation is established. We shall first provide a preliminary discussion of moral sentimentalism[45] to examine its relation to moral suasion within the viewpoint of philosophical ethics.

Ordinarily ethically competent laypersons believe that an action's rightness is a reason for doing it. The reason why an action is morally right is the reason or motive for doing it. This would make moral action intrinsically obligatory. Moral sentimentalists do not believe that the rightness or obligatory character of an action can be extrinsic to the action. Yet, although they support the notion that moral action is obligatory and is supposed to embrace both aspects of the normative character of morality, viz., its capacity to motivate and to obligate, difficulties abound in their explanation of obligation and of how motivation and obligation are combined. Moral sentimentalists tend to address these points by way of motivation, but at the expense of obligation.

According to Hutcheson, for example, God has given human beings a moral sense which prompts them to approve benevolence and regard it as a virtue. Benevolence is a disinterested affection which leads us, separate from any regard for our own individual interests, to be attentive to the well-being of others. "All the actions which are counted as amiable any where always appear as Benevolent, or flowing from the Love of others, and Study of their happiness."[46] However, despite that the rightness of an action ought to be intrinsically obligatory, the benevolence of an action cannot be so, because God's omnipotence overrides His benevolence. (Indeed God could have provided us with a moral sense which could have prompted us to approve malevolence.) Furthermore our acceptance and appreciation of benevolence are good for us, because our God-given moral sense has prompted us to accept and appreciate it. Our moral sense enables us to have an awareness, which *prima facie* seems to apprehend rightness inherent in an action, but which instead actually appreciates being moved by the benevolence of an action.

This is why moral sentimentalists turn toward an analysis of motivation. To know which actions are right, human beings must know which motives are good. But if the only good motive is the motive of duty, it seems that, for Hutcheson, we are engaged in a vicious circle. Say, for example, someone desires to do what is right, and seeks from another advice on what that is. The other person says to the first – right actions are those performed simply because they are right. For a moral sentimentalist, such a response appears to be question-begging. The imperatives "do the right thing!," (because it is the right thing), or "perform your duty from the motive of duty!" appear to be vacuous. This emptiness reflects the importance of a moral sense, which enables human beings to detect the virtuous motives which make actions right. Moreover, the moral sense must approve motives different from the motive of duty in order to introduce content into moral norms. Yet this too yields something of a paradox. On the one hand, if we hold onto the belief that motives fundamentally make actions right, then they must be motives different from a concern for rightness itself. On the other hand, if we hold onto the belief that the primary motive of virtuous action is the motive of duty, then there must be a way of defining the rightness of actions which does not rely on the motive of duty.

In short, then, Hutcheson is of the view that our approval of natural motivating affections renders actions virtuous, and such motivating affections are the primary motives to morally right action. But this yields two complementary problems for moral sentimentalism, one involving obligation, the other involving motivation.

Regarding the problem with obligation, an action is considered to be right, because we approve its motive. But since we could have been provided with a differently constituted moral sense, we could have approved another motive and, hence another action. So the action is *not necessarily* right, and as such it would be difficult to grasp how it could be obligatory, since an obligatory action is that which is necessary to perform. Yet if the action is *not necessarily* right, how can it be necessary to perform? Put another way, if the moral motive were just a natural, disinterested affection like benevolence, we would not have obligations, because we would need an obligation to have the motive which provides us obligations. How could we be obligated to act, unless we were obligated to have the motive that furnished them?

Regarding the problem with motivation, if the primary motives are splendid natural motives, then the motive of obligation must needs play merely an ancillary role. For moral sentimentalists, this is due to their belief that a good action is *not necessarily* motivated by a person's approval of it. To say that someone is morally obligated to an action only means that the moral sense just approves the action. As Hutcheson states, "the prospect of the pleasure of self-approbation is indeed often a motive to choose one action rather than another; but this supposes the moral sense, or determination to approve, prior to the election."[47] Here the motive of obligation would be no greater than a desire for self-approval or a secondary moral motive. Action from a moral sense approving of benevolence would be a far greater virtuous motive.[48]

What significance do these issues about obligation and motivation under the purview of moral sentimentalism have for the call of moral suasionists for slavery's abolition? Moral suasion appeals to our motivation for abolishing slavery at the expense of our obligation to abolish it. Moral suasion's appellative qualities are important, because they are used to reach "all who have hearts to feel to come forward in the work of banishing slavery from our land and to be a light unto the world."[49] It appeals to the benevolence in one's nature, trying to convince that one's self-love is not at odds with benefiting others. Citing the fourth annual report of the Parent Society, an antislavery organization, Garrison states that the goal of moral suasion is "to subvert the relation of master and slave *not by machinery, POLITICAL OR ECCLESIASTICAL,* but by establishing in the hearts of men a deep and wide-spreading conviction of *the brotherhood of the human race.*"[50]

Clearly this is neither to state nor to imply that moral suasionists dismiss the notion of obligation or duty. For example, Garrison believes that the moral obligation to abolish slavery "belongs to our nature" and that the recognition of the slave as a human being is a "duty too plain to be mistaken."[51] He recognizes that if the obligation to abolish slavery morally belongs to our nature, then we are morally charged to do so by God.[52] God as the source of the obligation enables the abolition of slavery to get a grip on us, to be prescribed for us, to bind us. But, once again, this would make the obligation *extrinsic* to the act of (or even claim for) abolition, and the obligation's source (God's benevolence), reflected in our moral sense to do good, (not in the rightness intrinsic to the act or claim itself), would be what motivates us, not obligates us, to abolish slavery. Hence moral suasion could not persuade us of the claim that the abolition of slavery is morally right *necessarily*; it could only convince us of the moral benevolence that would be both the source of and the incentive for abolishing slavery.

Moreover, if the recognition of enslaved Africans as human beings is an obligation much too evident to be false, then this obligation would have to be *intrinsic* to the act of recognition in order to be grasped as a rational truth. However, inspired by the theory of moral sentiments, moral suasion would not lead to the intuitive discernment of our obligation to recognize enslaved Africans as human beings; rather it would lead to influencing other people's moral sense to be benevolent, which would then have to motivate, not obligate, them to recognize enslaved Africans as human beings.

When we turn to Douglass's early speeches and drafts, his use of moral suasion also bears the moral sentimentalist mark. In a speech entitled "Emancipation Is An Individual, A National, and An International Responsibility," delivered in London on May 18, 1846, Douglass states that "[d]uring the last fifteen years, the abolitionists have been arduously labouring, amidst all kinds of odium, to establish the conviction, that holding human beings in the condition of slaves is a sin against God, and ought so to be regarded by the Churches. They have laboured to create such a moral and religious sentiment as would purify the Churches of America from all connexion with the slave system."[53] Douglass knows that American clergy and worshipers abet or remain silent about slavery in the light of placing religion (Christianity) in the service of enslavement. This is done, for example, by marshaling biblical verses such as those from *Ephesians* 6:5: "Slaves be obedient to your masters . . . with fear and trembling, in sincerity of heart, as to Christ." Both the cause and the price for such a strained interpretation of biblical verse are the dampening of their spirituality or, less religiously, their moral sense.

In this context, Douglass claims that moral suasionists (Garrisonians) have had partial success in appealing to American clergy and worshipers of various faiths to acknowledge their moral inclinations to cultivate their benevolent propensity toward the abolition of slavery. Although Douglass recognizes slavery as a moral evil and regards the American clergy and worshipers in complicity with it, he does not utter a word persuading them of their moral obligation to act/speak against it. Rather he speaks of their "failure to raise a whisper against it" as a matter for moral suasionists to pursue and alter, because of the belief of moral suasionists that American clergy and worshipers still have a very clear and strong idea of goodness that can still be tapped to establish the conviction in them "that holding human beings in the condition of slaves is a sin against God."[54] In short, Douglass is engaged in a morally suasive speech to both clergy and worshipers as auditors to convince them of their natural goodness which both prompts and encourages them to abolish slavery. Thus Douglass seems to be left holding the position that the virtue of abolition is conferred by or dependent on the natural benevolence of his auditors.

In a speech similar to the one in London, delivered in New York City on May 9, 1849 when Douglass extrapolates that the "blinded moral sense of the American people" is due to their having "substituted religion for humanity," having "turned off [their] attention from humanity altogether."[55] Although he has a number of things in mind when making this claim, such as the conferment of honor to warmongers and slaveholders (Zachary Taylor) rather than to peacemakers or the bestowal of honor to those whose aim is to abolish slavery, but *languorously*, and emancipate enslaved Africans, but *imperceptibly*, by means of *prolonging* slavery and *expatriating* free blacks (Henry Clay), he is referring mostly to the tendency of many American clergy and worshipers to be more interested in glorifying the Lord than in eliminating slavery, to be more interested in giving Bibles rather than freedom to enslaved Africans. But Douglass calls for his auditors to "put [themselves] in the place of the slave" in order to "feel that [the slave would be their] brother and sister and slavery would soon be at an end."[56] Moral suasion would then lead auditors to empathize with the plight of enslaved Africans, and if such empathy were to flourish, say, on a grand scale, then enslavement's abolition would be imminent. But this would suggest auditors who are themselves led to call for slavery's abolition by impartially inspecting their moral sense and empathizing with the slaves' predicament, and not auditors who are so led by deliberating on the wrongness of the slaves' predicament and acting accordingly.

That Douglass here holds this as a real possibility, indeed as the only possibility, for slavery's abolition amounts to a trust on Douglass's part that the benevolence of auditors/readers will move them to overcome slavery in the end, will lead them to a concern with the well-being of enslaved Africans, once auditors are prompted by moral suasionists to inspect their moral sense independently of any attention paid to their own interests. It expresses unconditional trust in the ultimate victory of good in the world. Although this trust would not be problematic in a purely moral sense, it would entail the rejection of any justification of benevolent moral action in terms of its foreseeable political consequences. It also would entail that politically Douglass would have to follow this trust unequivocally *and* would have to accept negative consequences as either an expression of the irrationality of the "peculiar institution" or a test of the resoluteness of his convictions.

Indeed Douglass is known to stand the test of the firmness of his moral beliefs regarding the wrongness of American slavery. He is also known to speak eloquently about the stability of the "peculiar institution" as a paradoxical expression of that institution's irrationality. But do these two features require that his call for slavery's abolition and for the extension of liberty and rights to enslaved Africans rests on the benevolence of auditors or, say, "the kindness of strangers?" If his use of moral suasion is marked by moral sentimentalism, the answer would have to be – yes. And if so, his use of moral suasion could not at the same time persuade auditors of the moral necessity of the abolition of slavery as a course of action taken *independently* of their natural benevolence. Hence Douglass would accept the very problematic view that the presence of moral sense and its natural benevolence serves as the basis for the morally necessary obligation to abolish slavery.

IV From Moral Suasion$_1$ to Moral Suasion$_2$: Moral Suasion$_2$ and its Discursive Amplification

Repeating earlier remarks, moral suasion is a form of argumentation in which the appellative qualities of the process of speech, emphasizing the requisites of morality, are used to convince those of either immoral or amoral beliefs to change them in the light of their natural benevolence. As a form of argumentation, then, moral suasion is concerned with communication that persuades, but more so than with communication's content (truth or "rightness") or lack thereof. The "young" Douglass appears to affirm this point when he claims in an 1845 speech that "truth needs but little argument, and no long drawn metaphysical detail to establish a position. There is something in the heart which instantly responds to its voice."[57]

Nonetheless, like *all* forms of argumentation, moral suasion communicatively engages complex issues (at the least) and tries to settle them by advancing reasons yielding binding convictions. This is consistent with moral suasion's relation to the public use of reason. But moral suasionists conceive of reasons exclusively as *inducements* to change belief and behavior. On that note, however, they then have less ground to conceive of them as *warrants*, which (1) would make what is said in communication justifiable and rationally acceptable, and which (2) would serve simultaneously as motives that allow people to be persuaded of what is said in communication by the "force" or discursive cogency of the argument. In contrast, moral suasionists would draw upon a manifold of rhetorical patterns and techniques to be effectively persuasive for the appropriate audience at the appropriate occasion, but, in so doing, more often than not, they would foreshorten the role of reasons as warrants in argumentation.

This is a problem unforeseen and, hence, unresolved by Douglass-scholars, who place emphasis on the rhetorical dimension of Douglass's intellectual life. Although Blassingame and Burke trenchantly deal with this dimension, they curtail consideration of Douglass's use of argumentation beyond the scope of rhetoric. Despite Burke's assertion, for example, that Douglass had sense to know that "stylistic devices alone did not influence hearers" and that "both speech content and style working together were essential to deliver the significance of the message,"[58] neither Burke nor, for that matter, Blassingame offer full-scale analyses of the cogency of Douglass's arguments, because to do so would require them to disregard or, better said, de-emphasize the argument's rhetorical effectiveness as well as the importance of the speaker (Douglass) making the argument. For the most part, then, the rhetorical effectiveness of Douglass's use of moral suasion would come at the expense of its discursive cogency in Burke's and Blassingame's inquiries, because they simply would presume that discursive cogency is already operative in Douglass's use of moral suasion. The issue for them simply would be whether Douglass's morally suasive arguments are, say, rhetorically saturated.

But *how* is the discursive cogency, i.e., the advancing of reasons as warrants, operative in Douglass's use of moral suasion, especially when he engages in moral suasion wherein reasons generally are advanced as inducements, not as warrants, due to their dependence on moral sentimentalism? Is it possible to show how moral suasion is discursively amplified, i.e., defined by its discursive cogency? To do so would be to present moral suasion in a light that at least makes it less reliant, if not non-reliant, on moral sentimentalism. This requires a conception of moral suasion in which moral sentimentalism plays little or no role at all.

Douglass, I believe, takes moral suasion in this direction, but he himself never makes this transformation explicit. Hence I shall flesh out and argue for *two* different modes of moral suasion, *one that rests on moral sentimentalism and whose advancement of reasons is rhetorically saturated*, the other that hinges on natural law and whose advancement of reasons is discursively amplified. The former we shall call *moral suasion*$_1$, the latter *moral suasion*$_2$. Moral suasion$_1$ appeals exclusively to an auditor's benevolent *motivation* to abolish slavery. It puts forward reasons only as incentives to change people's attitudes and behaviors toward enslavement in the face of auditors' natural benevolence. Moral suasion$_2$, however, appeals to an auditor's morally necessary *obligation* to abolish slavery by putting forward reasons as warrants for both criticizing enslavement and motivating auditors to change their attitudes and behavior towards enslavement in the face of those warrants.

This transformation in moral suasion can be *prima facie* marked chronologically by the movement from the "young" Douglass (pre-1851) to the "mature" one (post-1850). Along this line, Douglass eventually engages in moral suasion$_2$, becomes morally suasive in a discursively amplified way. In order to make this point, let us begin by looking at a speech by Douglass, entitled "Love of God, Love of Man, Love of Country," delivered to an audience in Syracuse, New York in 1847. Here the "young" Douglass expresses his commitment to moral suasion$_1$ when he states the following. "Friends, Slavery must be abolished, and that can only be done by enforcing the great principles of justice. Vainly you talk about voting it down. When you have cast your millions of ballots, you have not reached the evil. It has fastened its roots deep into the heart of the nation, and nothing but God's truth and love can cleanse the land. We must change the moral sentiment."[59] What Douglass lays out in this passage is the claim that the necessity of enslavement's abolition is possible through the enforcement of the principles of justice. He seems to be affirming lawful political action to abolish slavery. But this is misleading, because he speaks of the debility of that kind of action (e.g., voting) to tackle the evil of slavery. So how is slavery *necessarily* to be abolished by the enforcement of the principles of justice? Only if the principles of justice are exclusively "God's truth and love," and only if their enforcement is executed by influencing moral sentiment.

Engaging in moral suasion$_1$, Douglass believes that, despite attitudes and behaviors supportive of unjust actions such as slavery, people share a "God-given" moral sentiment and that this sentiment is naturally benevolent and the source of our motivations. The fact that people promote, support, and engage in slavery simply means, Douglass thinks, that they are oblivious to their sentiment and, hence, oblivious to the benevolent motives that would induce them away from slavery if only they were persuaded to heed or consult that sentiment.

But Douglass invites a number of problems with his acquiescence to moral suasion$_1$, one of which we addressed earlier. First, due to moral suasion$_1$'s reliance on moral sentimentalism, Douglass falls victim in similar fashion as Garrison to the conundrums of explaining how we are morally and, hence, necessarily obligated to abolish slavery in conjunction with our motivating natural benevolence. He thereby overlooks the other *philosophical* view that the abolition of slavery is morally right, because it is morally right necessarily and because the desire to abolish slavery is a rationally motivated response to abolition's moral and necessary rightness. Secondly, moral suasion$_1$ tends to assume that, despite the communicative dimension, morality is established from the viewpoint of an individual inspecting one's natural benevolence as the source of one's moral conceptions. There is no opportunity to treat individuals as deliberative agents engaged in forming opinions about enslavement with the right kind of reasons in moral suasion. Finally, moral suasion$_1$ engenders political romanticism, if political action has an unequivocal fidelity to the natural benevolence of humankind as its guide. Otherwise political action is independent of moral sentiment. Under moral suasion$_1$, Douglass closes himself off from any political action not motivated by moral sentiment, because to promote, say, political abolitionism outside of that sentiment would be to call for the end of enslavement without affecting the moral sentiment of others and, hence, without persuading them of the benevolence in abolition. For the "young" Douglass, political action cannot be insulated from moral sentiment.

These problems in moral suasion$_1$ would continue to haunt Douglass, if he did not make the shift to moral suasion$_2$. Yet Douglass does not make this shift as the result of a single line of reasoning drawn from moral suasion$_1$. Moreover, he does not come to adopt moral suasion$_2$ in order to make it a moral principle and develop a proceduralist ethics and legal theory under a discursive model.[60] Rather the shift is the result of a family of considerations comprising of Douglass' acceptance of natural law, political abolitionism, and struggle. Clarity here is imperative, because I want to argue, nonetheless, that the realm of ideas, not just the realm of events (his break with those raised up by Garrison's banner, the 1851 Fugitive Slave Law, the 1854 Kansas-Nebraska Bill, and the 1857 Dred Scott Decision), leads Douglass toward moral suasion$_2$. This is important, because it provides another relevant way in which the turn in Douglass's thought should be characterized.

For example, Douglass never characterizes his break from Garrison as one from moral suasion$_1$ to moral suasion$_2$. But it should be clear by now that the "young" Douglass's embrace of moral suasion$_1$ emerges from his association with Garrison. Although there are personal differences between them, some historians and biographers of Douglass locate the cause of their break in Douglass's expressed turn to political abolitionism in May 1851 which, they say, led the "mature" Douglass away from moral suasion altogether.[61] Others see the break with the Garrisonian form of abolition as a four- to six-year gradual process (beginning some time between 1845–7) in which moral suasion imminently recedes into the background and political abolitionism eventually comes into the foreground.[62] Nonetheless, in both interpretations, political abolitionism is not guided by moral suasion$_1$, but by a non-moral orientation toward adjustment, prudence, and success.[63] In short, the shift is from morality to political action, from political romanticism to *realpolitik*.

Philosophically, however, there is another tack that can be taken – treat the shift as a move from one moral orientation to another moral orientation, from moral suasion$_1$ to moral suasion$_2$. As a consequence, political abolitionism for the "mature" Douglass would still have a moral orientation, but no longer tied to moral sentimentalism. This would be sufficient to describe the break between the "mature" Douglass and Garrison. Indeed there are personal and political reasons for the break between Douglass and Garrison, which could lead one to presume that moral suasion and political abolitionism are themselves mutually indifferent to or exclusive of each other. Yet, despite those reasons, there is nothing to prevent us from considering political abolitionism and moral suasion$_2$ as practices which may traverse the other instead of being adverse to the other. Political abolitionism, then, would not eclipse moral suasion$_2$, but would complement and supplement it. In this vein, however, any reliance of moral suasion$_2$ on moral sentimentalism would be mitigated, if not eliminated, because the idea of natural law, which the "mature" Douglass employs with political abolitionism, would now provide the moral dimension to moral suasion$_2$. So the shift from moral suasion$_1$ to moral suasion$_2$ turns on the replacement of moral sentimentalism with natural law when moral suasion is bridged with political abolitionism. As we shall see, moral suasion, then, can continue, even uncoupled from moral sentimentalism, because it still remains a form of argumentation whose employment to persuade morally is now combined with natural law doctrine *and* the success of the political action amenable to it.

Now Douglass's turn to moral suasion$_2$ commences when he proclaims that the Constitution of the United States is an antislavery document based on natural law and not, as he previously thought, a pro-slavery document based on positive law. Briefly stated, modern natural law is the doctrine that, usually with religious or metaphysical underpinnings, law and morality are identical. Its jurisdiction is the moral realm, which is ubiquitous and without boundary in social space and historical time; its extension encompasses all past, present, and future generations of natural persons, all of whom "inhabit" this realm; and its purpose is to morally protect the integrity of such persons as fully free, equal, and individuated. Given its jurisdiction, extension, and purpose, modern natural law, in principle, lays out the moral framework for any and all positive legislation and, hence, could never back the legality of slavery, since the morality of law, i.e., the freedom, equality, and individuation of natural persons would be violated. Any law or action that violated the three elements of natural law doctrine would not only be illegal, but would be a violation of morality itself, a threat to the moral realm altogether. In the light of this doctrine, then, law-making would have moral argumentation as its paradigm, because moral considerations would always have to be entertained in legislative activity. Moral law-making would be expressed in juridical law-making, so that the legal order would both emulate and embody the moral one.

By virtue of this persistent "Platonism," modern natural law would always comprise the gist of positive law and would always have a superordinate relation to it. The legal order's legitimacy would be established by not contravening the moral order. All natural persons as morally accountable subjects of this moral realm would enter into the domain of social space and historical time and obtain the determinate shape of a legal community, in which moral norms govern intersubjective relationships and conflicts between natural persons acknowledging one another as members of a legal community and as inviolable individuals.

Outside of the natural law context, law is always positive law whose positivism is established by the disassociation of legality from morality. Its jurisdiction is a legally circumscribed geographical region or locale; its extension covers a socially spatial and historically temporal legal order; and its purpose is to legally safeguard the integrity, not of natural persons, but of agents with the status of individual holders of legal entitlements and legal duties. Positive law governs intersubjective relationships and conflicts between agents recognized not as morally accountable subjects, but as bearers of rights individually oriented to their own inclinations within a legal order. In the light of positive law, then, law-making is not relegated to moral argumentation, because empirical, pragmatic, and historically contingent issues come into play necessarily without moral considerations in establishing any piece of legislation as legally valid.

So the affinity of the advocates of moral suasion$_2$ to political abolitionism can be had once the view that the Declaration of Independence and the Constitution are construed as documents fashioned in accord with modern natural law, not positive law, is established. Modern natural law provides the moral orientation for political abolitionism and gives to moral suasion$_2$ a moral framework beyond sentiment, a set of "moral facts" from which moral argumentation could proceed. This is evident in those speeches, wherein the "mature" Douglass stresses the importance of either political action or the Constitution (and the Declaration of Independence) to the antislavery cause. For Douglass, both those documents and antislavery political action would be shaped and would be guided respectively by the moral orientation of modern natural law.

Moral suasion$_2$ is implicitly at work in Douglass's first public announcements of his change of opinion about the Constitution delivered from the 9th through May 23, 1851.[64] It is expressly at work in his most renowned and celebrated speech of July 5, 1852, "What to the Slave is the Fourth of July?"[65] But we obtain a good characterization of moral suasion$_2$ in a speech delivered on May 10, 1854 entitled "We Are in the Midst of a Moral Revolution,"[66] to which we now attend.

The moral revolution, about which Douglass speaks here, does not refer to anything theoretically complex. It is not, for example, a ready parallel with the Kantian shift from heteronomously based moral theories to those based on autonomy, although there may be a family resemblance between this Kantian turn and the turn in moral suasion. Rather what Douglass has in mind is the nadir in American history, the decade preceding the Civil War, wherein the "complete suppression of all antislavery discussion, the extension of Slavery over all the territories of the US, the legal nationalization of Slavery, and finally the extension of Slavery over the entire continent and the absolute destruction of all liberty"[67] abound. These states of affairs, prevailing in Douglass's America, is what he claims to be the moral "revolution," which "involves [us] in moral darkness" and "threatens to extinguish the moral light ... bestowed upon us to enable us to go through our earthly pilgrimage in the peace and beauty of a common brotherhood."[68] And the response to this moral revolution does involve the turn from moral suasion$_1$ to moral suasion$_2$.

Douglass's *rhetorical* use of "light" and "darkness," representing morally unblemished (antislavery) and morally tainted (pro-slavery) sentiments respectively, emerges also in an earlier 1849 speech entitled "Of Morals and Men."[69] However, whereas the evidence of the "moral darkness" of the American nation in the earlier speech is reflected in the *morally challenged character* of America's most honored men (Clay and Taylor) and their inability to extend their natural sense of benevolence to works of benevolence, works that "sacredly and continually engage in shedding the blessings of freedom upon mankind,"[70] the evidence of "moral darkness" in the 1854 speech is revealed in the *arguments* of American statesmen attacking America's founding political documents, the Declaration of Independence and the Constitution of the US, arguments in which the doctrine of human equality and freedom, morally and legally endorsed by those documents, is denied for the sake of defending enslavement and racial inegalitarianism. As we shall see below, despite the rhetorical use of the same metaphor of "light" and "darkness" in both speeches, each speech emphasizes *different* moral orientations, reflective of moral suasion$_1$ and moral suasion$_2$, posed to offset what Douglass distinctly counts as evidence of the "moral darkness" of American slavery.[71]

In the speech "Of Morals and Men," pro-slavery sentiment is due to people being oblivious to their moral sentiment, failing to heed and consult it and, as a consequence, not being motivated to take the antislavery stance. "Moral darkness" is, therefore, a result of what Douglass once called the "blinded moral sense of the American people." Yet, in the speech "We Are in the Midst of a Moral Revolution," pro-slavery sentiment is fueled by arguments declaring the doctrine of human freedom and equality, expressed in the American founding documents and framed under the auspice of natural law, a "false doctrine," a "rhetorical flourish," only "hypothetically true," words "inserted [in the founding documents] without any necessity," "not true in fact," "not true in law," "not true morally," and ultimately a "self-evident lie,"[72] all with respect to enslaved Africans. These characterizations show that the pro-slavery sentiment is no longer about the morally blinded sense of the American people and their inability to inspect and consult their natural benevolence to counteract that sentiment. Rather they show that the pro-slavery sentiment is the outcome of denying both the moral credentials of natural law and the founding documents expressing them.

This change should not be surprising because of the shift from moral suasion$_1$ to moral suasion$_2$. Douglass no longer attaches in moral suasion the nature of the wrong of enslavement to the harm or degradation inflicted directly or indirectly on the enslaved African by those oblivious to their moral sentiment. His morally suasionist defense of human equality based on natural law now leads him to argue that those who would support slavery and inequality blunder in not recognizing what follows from the *fact* that the life that is enslaved is the life of a person. For Douglass, defenders of inegalitarianism fail to count the natural personhood of African-descended people as intrinsically providing a reason not to enslave – a reason that trumps those reasons for enslaving gleaned from the defenders' or slaveholders' pursuit of private ends or acceptance of social convention – because, under natural law, it is necessarily impermissible to discount the personhood of human life in favor of the currency of our conventions or purposes. In short, then, what makes enslavement wrong for Douglass in moral suasion$_2$ is not some harm or degradation inflicted on others by people oblivious to their own natural benevolence. Rather what makes it wrong is the erroneous yet, at the same time, deceptive evaluation which bespeaks a lack of respect for African-descended people as human beings.

V Moral Suasion$_2$: Ambiguities and Problems

Admittedly Douglass's approach to the moral fact expressed in natural law is both ambiguous and problematic. Let us begin with the ambiguity. There are times when he approaches it according to the self-evident status it possesses. This generates the issue raised earlier about the need for moral suasion at all, regardless of modality, since natural law's self-evident status would preclude any requirement for discursive deliberation.[73] However, there are instances when, in regard to those who appear to challenge constantly the natural law doctrine and its self-evident status expressed in America's founding documents, Douglass tells those abolitionists engaged in moral suasion to do the following: "Continue to do precisely as you have done; continue to write, speak, and publish; continue to enforce, by precept and by example, the great principles of liberty, justice and human brotherhood, as individuals, as church members, as citizens at home, in the church, and at the ballot box, yes ... at the ballot box."[74] Here Douglass recommends to abolitionists that their enlightenment-inspired public use of reason should still proceed. In other words, moral suasion$_2$ must still be employed to provide warrant to others of the importance of natural law doctrine, expressed in Americas's founding documents, for justifying the antislavery cause, despite that doctrine's self-evident status. So, in terms of the ambiguity, is moral suasion$_2$ required or not required to justify the antislavery cause through natural law?

Douglass himself is far from satisfactory in addressing this question. But there is a way to remove the ambiguity. I would suggest that his use of moral suasion$_2$ is not directed to giving warrant to others that natural law is a fact reflected in the Constitution and the Declaration. Moral suasion$_2$ is not set to prove that the proposition – all natural persons are self-evidently free, equal, and individuated – is revealed in America's founding political documents. *Rather it is focused on giving others warrant on what the fact of natural law shows as expressed in those documents, viz., that the doctrine's jurisdiction, extension, and purpose morally comprise a ground of obligation and, hence, legally reaches African-descended people and makes their enslavement morally, hence, legally wrong.* This is what moral suasion$_2$, for Douglass, is called upon to continually do, because the bone of contention, for which moral suasion$_2$ is required, is not whether the doctrine of natural law is plain and evident, but whether the doctrine, as a moral fact, evinces a ground of obligation. When Douglass is engaged in moral suasion$_2$ against *political* defenders of enslavement, he takes them to be arguing not against the doctrine's self-evidence, but against the doctrine as a ground of obligation.[75]

At first sight, it does appear, contrary to what I have stated, that political defenders of enslavement, such as Calhoun and Pettit, are denying the self-evidence of natural law as a moral fact by claiming that the doctrine is a "self-evident falsehood" and a "self-evident lie" respectively. In other words, that the proposition, "all men are created equal," expressed in the Declaration is either a falsehood or a lie plain and clairvoyant to intuitive insight. But such a denial is not repudiating that everyone has a distinct and explicit intuitive awareness of the validity of that proposition. It is rather disavowing that the validity of that proposition serves as a ground of obligation which morally constrains what human beings can freely establish and recognize as necessarily permissible and legitimate.

Since a ground of obligation refers to an indispensable attribute of ourselves that sets the limits of what we freely and rationally can determine, a political apologist for enslavement would have to pose to himself the following question: is he as an apologist for slavery able to certify that others not regard the natural personhood of his life as a reason not to enslave him without performatively contradicting himself? Answering this question in the affirmative means that the apologist could guarantee that his indifference to the natural personhood of black life could not conflict with what else he freely establishes and recognizes for himself. But the rub with this state of affairs is that it is impossible to certify, because even the apologist must freely establish that others take his natural personhood as a limiting condition or constraint on what others can permissibly do to him.

Such an argument concerning the performative contradiction of apologists or slaveholders is suggested by Douglass when he asserts, "It was against the universal instincts and habits of freemen, at least white men, when their lives and property are in danger, to weigh every tittle of language to condemn him, if condemned at all. Why, then, are we so ready to infer the rights away from the black man? We are in the habit of construing the Constitution, the laws, and everything against the Negro."[76] Or when he sarcastically yet pointedly claims in his famous "Fourth of July" speech, "Must I undertake to prove that the slave is a man? That point is conceded already. Nobody doubts it. The slaveholders themselves acknowledge it in the enactment of laws for their government. They acknowledge it when they punish disobedience on the part of the slave. There are seventy-two crimes in the State of Virginia, which, if committed by a black man (no matter how ignorant he be), subject him to the punishment of death; while only two of the same crimes will subject a white man to the like punishment. What is this but the acknowledgement that the slave is a moral, intellectual and responsible being?"[77] What these statements point to is Douglass's understanding of the performative contradiction that emerges once the fittingness and saliency of natural law as a ground of obligation are rejected as justifying reasons in moral matters. So moral suasion$_2$ amounts to acknowledging that one cannot be indifferent to or reject natural law as such a ground.

Douglass also has available to him another avenue to drive home his morally suasive critique of the apologists for slavery, although he never takes advantage of it, because he is unaware of it. Nonetheless, it rests on certain assumptions inherent in argumentation, which moral suasion is. Assuming every claim staked that is rationally acceptable involves the belief that those to whom the claim is made can be convinced that this is so. A claim that is rationally acceptable consists of the possibility of uncoerced assent or dissent. And any assent/dissent rendered under coercive circumstances could not itself be considered rationally acceptable. These points would hold too for apologists of inequality and enslavement. Their claims in favor of slavery and for "white supremacy" over non-white others would entail the belief that they could be shown to be rationally acceptable even to those designated for enslavement or unequal treatment. On this note, non-whites ought to accept wittingly and willingly the rationality of "white supremacy." But herein lies the dilemma. If defenders of inequality and slavery were to stake rational claims about racial inequality and slavery, they would have to acquire the *uncoerced* assent of non-whites who were to be enslaved or treated unequally. But this would mean conceding the rationality of non-whites to assent or dissent freely. So claims supporting racial inequality and slavery would be irrational, because they could not acquire the uncoerced assent of those non-whites they would address, or they would be unjust, because they would deny the prospect that those non-whites about whom and to whom they would address would rebuff it.

Nevertheless, as I stated previously, besides ambiguity, Douglass succumbs to certain problems in his use of moral suasion$_2$, problems that are associated with (1) his interpretive strategy regarding the founding documents and (2) his political abolitionism. Let me start with the interpretive strategy. In using moral suasion$_2$, Douglass tries to persuade others by providing justification on what the moral fact of natural law shows as expressed in America's founding documents. According to Douglass, those documents are expressive of the morality of natural law doctrine by virtue of the *"original intent"* (or what we now call *"originalism"*) of the "Founding Fathers" and "Framers of the Constitution." Put another way, the commonly shared intention of the authors or Framers of America's founding documents is Douglass's interpretive criterion for understanding those documents as the embodiment of natural law doctrine. Natural law provides the objective moral framework, the set of "moral facts," for moral suasion$_2$ through the founding documents, *only if* the Framers originally intended for those documents to carry the meaning or sense of natural law *as a ground of obligation against slavery* on which moral suasion$_2$ relies.

It is important to see that the plurality of Framers be characterized in terms of the "common shareability" or "singleness" of intention, rather than the miscellany of intentions because, as an interpretive criterion, singleness of intention, reflecting an integral (set of) author(s), reveals coherency and singularity of meaning of the documents or texts. Singularity of intent is "original," because an interpretation ought not include anything other than or extend beyond the meaning intended by the author. On the basis of originalism, an interpretation cannot circumvent the exclusivity of the author's intention as the source of interpretation. Originalism as a hermeneutically criterial standpoint steers plurality of intentions toward ambiguity and incoherence of meaning. Douglass must represent the Founders and Framers as being of one mind, so to speak, on the antislavery meaning of the founding documents. Furthermore, outside of the "original intent" of the Framers, there appears to be no way for Douglass to determine whether the founding documents embody modern natural law and, hence, whether they serve as the medium in and through which natural law guides moral suasion$_2$. Indeed, for Douglass, outside of the "original intent" of the Framers, the founding documents can only be interpreted as the expressions of positive law, carrying no moral orientation beyond which they are framed and bearing the empirical, pragmatic, and historical imprimatur of the social context in which they are established.[78]

However, there are strong reasons for thinking that Douglass is wrong in believing that the founding documents must be interpreted in accordance with "originalism" in order to reveal their natural law imprint which serves as the guide of moral suasion$_2$. Prior to 1851, the "young" Douglass regarded the originalism of the Framers to be of a *pro-slavery* sentiment which pervaded the meaning of America's founding documents.[79] Clearly the Framers' originalism as a pro-slavery sentiment would not (and did not) inform moral suasion$_1$, because it would be construed as the expression of their own ignorance to their moral sense or benevolence, an ignorance moral suasion$_1$ would supposedly counteract. (It would also serve as a reason why Douglass [till 1851 and Garrison always] did not recognize the legitimacy of America's founding documents.) So "originalism" of the Framers can take on either pro- or antislavery sentiments, and hence may not be the unproblematic interpretive criterion previously suggested. Furthermore, it would seem that the shift from moral suasion$_1$ to moral suasion$_2$ is concomitant with a shift in what is construed as the original intent of the "Framers" or vice versa. However, by imputing one or the other meaning to the documents that the Framers adduced in the initial circumstance, Douglass has to resort to some kind of *empathy theory of interpretation*, which aims at *nothing more than* the explication of the "true" (originary) meaning of a document intended by the author(s). Should moral suasion$_2$ be guided by documents whose meaning can only be interpreted by virtue of a theoretical assumption that we can crawl into an author's mind to ascertain his meaning?

To a large extent, Douglass appears to have believed so. Admittedly, however, Douglass hints at another theory of interpretation in an 1860 speech that goes well beyond originalism and, indeed, is somewhat more reflective of contemporary theories of interpretation, wherein the intention of the author is of minor or zero, not of major, significance in an interpretation and only has an oblique rather than a direct role in it.[80] In this context of contemporary theories, ranging from deconstruction to reconstructive hermeneutics, this would entail, however, that natural law loses its prominent and superordinate place in regard to positive law in moral suasion$_2$. It would be either supplanted for or supplemented with positive law. But there is no evidence that Douglass, after 1851, ever surrendered natural law's priority status, since political abolitionism or political action were never in his mind to cede the "higher" moral ground natural law offered.

Let us now turn to the matter of political abolitionism. Natural law as a ground of obligation does not by itself give reasons for political action. It does, however, through the founding documents, set the terms for moral suasion$_2$ to fuel political abolitionism with moral relevance. So through moral suasion$_2$, Douglass attempts to give the best means of abolishing slavery by bridging the requirements of morality (justice based on moral accountability) with the requirements of politics (obedience based on legal stability). Since America's founding documents do not sanction slavery, given the mature Douglass's take on the original intent of the Framers, political abolitionism could legitimately and legally be discharged to bring about immediate emancipation. The naivete of such a position is enormous and has led many, as I have already indicated, to treat moral suasion and political abolitionism as totally separate and disparate matters in Douglass's thought. Since I believe, on the contrary, that Douglass regards them as related, it is important to flesh out their relationship.

Unlike moral suasion$_1$, which has, in a certain way mentioned above, an intimate or immediate connection to political abolitionism,[81] the connection between moral suasion$_2$ and political abolitionism is mediated by the founding documents and their natural law endorsement as given in the originalism of the Framers. Political abolitionism, then, can be subject to two different moral orientations: either it is sustained by the unequivocal trust in the ultimate victory of good in the world (moral suasion$_1$) or it is sustained by the legal order saturated by natural law interpretation (moral suasion$_2$). However, we know the former would render political abolitionism pan-moralistic or politically quixotic, but so too, it could be argued, would the latter. In both cases, political abolitionism's worthiness, many Douglass-scholars could say, would be measured solely by the moral conviction attached to it and not by the assessment of its outcome. As we know, most Douglass-scholars, especially those who believe that moral suasion and political abolitionism are antithetical to each other, do not make the distinction between the two modes of moral suasion. But it appears that would not matter, because they could still claim that neither mode compromises their representation of Douglass as the non-moral political realist or "opportunist."[82] So even moral suasion$_2$, bridging the moral and the political and issuing a different moral direction to political action than moral suasion$_1$, seems to give political abolitionism a politically romantic identification.

To avoid this quixotic characterization of Douglass's political abolitionism, moral suasion$_2$ would have to bridge something else about which Douglass is aware, yet not altogether explicit. Moral suasion$_2$ does not just entail bridging the moral and the political, but it also entails bridging the morality of political abolitionism with the demands for and consequences of political abolitionism's success. If political abolitionism is not to be politically romantic, its moral import cannot solely rest on its connection with the founding documents. Rather its normative relevance would also have to be favored by the success of its outcome which involves taking seriously its foreseeable consequences in moral deliberation. In brief, the *success* of political abolitionism too would have moral import.

Douglass is well aware that political abolitionism would be operating in the main without the support of an accommodating political culture, without the basic attitudes of a population accustomed to the emancipation and independence of black people. But addressing this matter in the light of the possibility of successful political action never arises for Douglass while he is engaged in moral suasion$_1$. For example, in 1841, a young Douglass claims, slaveholders "care nothing about your political action, they don't dread the political movement; it is the *moral* movement, the appeal to men's sense of right, which makes them and all our opponents tremble."[83] Yet, in his "We Are In The Midst of a Moral Revolution," he claims that "political anti-slavery – that anti-slavery which does not hesitate to make its words *deeds* – has not proved a failure. Indeed, political abolition is now the most powerful agency at work for the overthrow of Slavery."[84] Notwithstanding his aspirations for political abolitionism to have moral status, Douglass's concern with the success of antislavery "deeds" appears to affirm that political abolitionism has been successful despite being ensnared in the meshes of a morally irrational world. And this means that political abolitionism carries not only normative relevance, but also that *the demands for it to be successful in a morally irrational world, where the politics of slavery has prevailed, must bear normative relevance*. If moral suasion$_2$ renders political abolitionism normatively relevant, giving to political action the strongest conviction of moral obligation, it must do so in a way that also accounts for the foreseeable consequences of the action's success according to the best available knowledge. That is to say, not just political abolitionism, but its success as well, is morally relevant, because the demands arising from moral suasion$_2$ for that success are to be acknowledged.

The normative relevance of political abolitionism's success can be proven in the political culture of slavery, that is, only in a situation of action comprised of other values, elements, and actions favorable to slavery's expansion. Moral argument must be coordinated with successful yet morally informed political action. It is important to be clear on this point. For Douglass, even moral suasion$_2$ can be too anemic to become effective in action, so that leaving human beings alone to engage in moral suasion$_2$'s argument for the abolition of slavery places too great a burden on them in that political culture.[85] Since it really can lack the strength to prevail politically on its own, many believe Douglass jettisoned moral suasion altogether in favor of an amoral political abolitionism. But they miss something quite significant. Douglass is also well aware that a political culture, *even one that is antislavery*, let alone an intractable pro-slavery one, does not in and of itself set a standard for moral justification, as evidenced by the role of natural law in his thought. Political culture does not determine the content of moral suasion$_2$; it can either enhance or, as this case dictates, inhibit the capacity of individuals to believe slavery is morally wrong and to eliminate it immediately. Given these states of affairs, what Douglass seeks "is an antislavery Government in harmony with our antislavery speech, one which will give effect to our words, and translate them into acts."[86] The success of political abolitionism carries normative relevance when a pro-slavery political culture is rendered conducive to the development of the capacity of its members to believe slavery is morally wrong, to reject it immediately, and to enlarge the realm of rights-bearers to include formerly enslaved Africans.

Although this reorientation is the result of a successful political abolitionism, it is the demand of moral suasion$_2$, which leads political abolitionism to eliminate the burdens and risks of people falling victim to exploitation or enslavement when following their antislavery beliefs in practice. Nonetheless, without the success of political abolitionism, moral suasion$_2$ alone is feeble politically. ("If speech alone could have abolished slavery, the work would have been done long ago."[87]) Hence the reason why it is important that, unlike moral suasion$_1$, moral suasion$_2$ involves the assessment of the outcomes of actions with respect to their success of reaching the goal of abolishing slavery. Through moral suasion$_2$, Douglass argues for and demands a political culture conducive to making individuals capable of recognizing the wrongness of slavery as well as assess the kinds of action capable of bringing about such a culture without fail. As Douglass puts it, "far be it from us to undervalue the power of truth when honestly addressed to the hearts and consciences of men; but truth to be efficient must be uttered in action as well as in speech."[88] In this coordination of moral suasion$_2$ and political abolitionism, Douglass would no longer rely *solely* on how compelling his warrants and arguments were. Instead he could also rely on an extant political culture whose tendencies, shaped by a morally oriented political abolitionism, either bears or strives toward the results he morally demands.

Moral suasion$_2$ must survive the effects of political abolitionism in order to overcome the romantic and quixotic edge and destroy the illusions to which one generally falls prey, viz., that the rightness of one's moral convictions alone is sufficient for the direction of political action. Morally oriented political abolitionism that fails at redirecting the political culture not only fails gaining at least a foothold, but threatens the viability of moral suasion$_2$, if moral suasion$_2$ does not continue to evaluate actions in terms of the moral orientation it holds and to assess the probability of their success. Does this concern for the success of political abolitionism compromise or nullify its moral orientation? I do not believe so, because there is no successful action ending slavery whose consequence would force Douglass to surrender moral suasion$_2$. At the same time, repeating earlier remarks, a political action to end slavery, which does not have successful consequences, renders moral suasion$_2$ less viable in the political culture. Nevertheless, by placing moral convictions in conjunction with the assessment of the foreseeable consequences of actions in moral suasion$_2$, Douglass exposes his convictions to strategies that are either productive or counterproductive, but for the sake of bringing his convictions to realization. The key is to understand that, for Douglass, at least, this exposure does not subvert the practice of moral suasion$_2$, but only expands and enhances it.

VI Violent Resistance[89] as a Moral Struggle for Recognition

I have tried to make a case for the viable connection of moral suasion$_2$ to political abolitionism. Rather than treat them as disparate and unrelated, if not antithetical, activities, I have argued for their correlation in Douglass's thought. But what place or role do their correlation have in Douglass's reflections on violent resistance? How much impact does the moral presumption against violence have on Douglass? To address these issues, allow me to begin with two lengthy citations from Douglass. The first, call it "Citation A," is from "The Do-Nothing Policy," published in the *Frederick Douglass' Paper* on September 12, 1856:

> When will colored men learn to discard the do-nothing tactics, the "masterly activity," for which their course in the past has been distinguished? . . . the cry is we must be quiet, we must not make ourselves be heard or felt in this contest, lest we injure the cause for which we pray. And we fold our hands and indolently gaze at the tremendous struggle going on in the nation, by which our rights will be determined. This is a false position. Who of all the people in this country have the deepest stake in the contest for supremacy

between slavery and freedom? The colored people. Who ought then to be the most active, the most vigilant and self-sacrificing? The colored people. It is vain for us to expect any degree of liberty and respect in our country, unless we are willing to bear our share in the struggle . . . Happily the strife we are called upon to enter is not, in the northern States, a war-like one. The republicans of France and of Italy can achieve their freedom only by bloodshed, by the overthrow of their governments, and slaughter of their enemies. With us the only hardship is the industry and persistence with which our efforts must be made. The right of petition, the right of the press, and free speech are left to us, and the use of these *is all that is required for the acquisition of our rights* in the northern States. Will we use them? . . . If [we] are united, if [we] are resolved to use with unwavering energy the press, the orator, and the petition, [we] will gain all [we] desire . . . The open sesame for the colored man is action! action!! action!![90]

The second citation, call it "Citation B," comes from a quotation by Douglass published in a book in January 1857 by William Chambers entitled *American Slavery and Colour*:

> While we feel bound to use all our powers of persuasion and argument; to welcome every instrumentality that promises to peacefully destroy that perpetual condemner of God's laws, and disturber of a nation's peace – Slavery; *we yet feel that its peaceful annihilation is almost hopeless . . . and contend that the slave's right to revolt is perfect, and only wants the occurrence of favourable circumstances to become a duty* . . . [S]hall the millions forever submit to robbery, to murder, to ignorance, and every unnamed evil which an irresponsible tyranny can devise, because the overthrow of that tyranny would be productive of horrors? We say not . . . The slaveholder has been tried and sentenced, his execution only waits the finish to the training of his executioners. He is training his own executioners.[91]

Both citations are representative, not occasional, positions which the "mature" Douglass has staked throughout his entire career, the former underscoring moral suasion, the latter violent resistance. Clearly ambiguity and complexity emerge when Douglass is presented as endorsing *both* of these positions. So the question is how can Douglass embrace both positions without falling into contradiction or discrepancy? How can an advocate of moral suasion be at the same time an advocate of violent resistance? One could take Boxill's view and claim that violent resistance is a form of moral suasion. But usually the response is that Douglass can endorse only one or the other, *either* the pacifism of moral suasion *or* the violence of physical resistance. Certainly if we were to take Douglass as an advocate of moral suasion$_1$, it would be extremely difficult for him to defend violent resistance, because violence would fly against the moral suasionist's (or Garrisonian) aim of prompting the moral sense even of slaveholders to follow their natural benevolence and rid themselves of their association with slavery. This would be a reason why a number of Douglass-scholars believe that the "mature" Douglass eventually jettisons moral suasion altogether for violent resistance.[92] I have not found scholars claiming that Douglass ultimately gives priority to moral suasion over violent resistance, but they would claim that Douglass's emphasis is on social reform and social upward mobility of blacks over violent resistance.[93] Regardless of that fact, however, it is not surprising then that no ambiguity whatsoever would be attached to Douglass's stance on violent struggle. The ambiguity and complexity surrounding Douglass's endorsement of both moral suasion and violent resistance would, therefore, be rescinded. There would be no ambiguity to be resolved from either viewpoint.

Yet that belief rests only on the presumption that the moral suasion, about which Douglass speaks, is moral suasion$_1$. If, however, we rightly take "Citation A" as representative of moral suasion$_2$, especially of moral suasion$_2$ as bridging not only the moral and the political but, more importantly, the morality of political abolitionism and the demands for and consequences of political abolitionism's success, then the complexity of Douglass's advocacy of both moral suasion and violent resistance can be addressed and, possibly, settled rather than simply annulled.

As I stated previously, moral suasion$_2$ is a form of argumentation demonstrating that the moral wrongness of slavery can be decided on the basis of reasons and resulting in the generation of binding convictions against slavery. In this regard, contra Boxill, an act of violent resistance could not be a form of argumentation, because it would be more so an action taken when argumentation or moral suasion$_2$ were to fail, to cease, or simply be non-existent. But moral suasion$_2$, merely understood as a form of argumentation, does not enable enslaved people to become rights-bearing, morally accountable, and thereby free individuals. Political abolitionism would be required to make a political culture open and accommodating to such a result by vigorously protesting enslavement, discursively championing that result, and non-violently using the most effective way of bringing it about. And, as I have already argued, for Douglass, its success would carry moral relevance once justifiably promoted in moral suasion$_2$. This speaks to what I called the bridging function of moral suasion$_2$.

But can the violent resistance of enslaved Africans be a political act carrying moral relevance, through moral suasion$_2$, and aiming to make the political culture supportive of an institutional arrangement abolishing slavery and guaranteeing blacks their rights-bearing, morally accountable freedom? In its bridging function, can moral suasion$_2$ provide moral relevance to a political abolitionism combined with violent resistance? Answering that question in the negative would mean that Douglass ought not be read as endorsing both moral suasion$_2$ and violent resistance, but read supporting one or the other, in which case his stance on the moral presumption against violence would be clearly either affirmative or negative. Answering that question in the affirmative, however, means, I believe, that Douglass's endorsement of both comes at the cost of a paradox and makes his stance on the moral presumption against violence ambiguous. Since I believe Douglass embraces both, allow me to work through the paradox and the ambiguity respectively in order to reconstruct the manner Douglass *ought* to endorse both moral suasion$_2$ and violent resistance.

First and foremost, if we take the affirmative posture on Douglass's double endorsement, then the issue is not explicitly about his advocacy for both moral suasion$_2$ and violent resistance. Rather it is about his *endorsement of both a morally informed political abolitionism wedded to nonviolence and a morally informed political abolitionism wedded to violence*. Indeed, in "Citation A," Douglass eschews political action that embarks on violence, stating that what "colored people" need to do is to exercise their "right of free speech, of petition, and of the press" in order to make the political culture supportive of their rights-bearing capacity. Colored people's political action for the sake of the abolition of slavery does not require violence, i.e., overthrowing the government or slaughtering enemies, as the "republicans of France and Italy" have done, because the struggle in the northern States does not require a "war-like one." Whether such violent insurgency is morally informed, morally neutral, or immoral is never raised. On the other hand, in "Citation B," the moral dimension of violent resistance is raised when Douglass speaks of the "slave's right to revolt," the right to overthrow violently that political culture which supports an "irresponsible tyranny," rebukes God's laws, and violates the nation's peace, viz., the political culture of slavery. Without delving into the question of such a right's existence or validity, it seems that Douglass regards the right to engage in violent revolt as morally "perfect" for the political abolition of slavery in the southern States. Indeed it could be inferred that Douglass is able to endorse both a non-violent mode and a violent mode of morally informed political action against slavery, because the former mode is pertinent to one geographical region and the latter to another.

Although there is historical accuracy to the strategic relevance of sectionalism attached to these modes of political abolitionism, a bit of absurdity resonates from this inference, however, because Douglass is of the mind that the slave's violent resistance is a right governed by natural law and sustaining natural freedom. Such a right would be morally exercised, according to Douglass, not by virtue of its pertinence to geographical region, but by virtue of any suppression of that freedom. Douglass does not offer a strong argument for this claim, but a clue to his acceptance of it is his comparison of violent slave insurrections or mutinies with the violence of patriots of the American Revolution in the name of independence and liberty. For example, the following statement from *My Bondage and My Freedom* is a typical one: "if [the slave] kills his master, he imitates only the heroes of the [American] revolution."[94]

A literary theorist, like, say, Eric J. Sundquist, perceives Douglass's affirmation of the slave's violent resistance for freedom as his attempt to make it a paradigm of black political achievement on par with the acquisition of American independence from the British Empire through violent resistance based on an appeal to natural law.[95] Acknowledging that the "mature" Douglass is trying to conceive the slaves' right to revolt in the light of an emancipation connected to the popular interpretation of the American Revolution, Sundquist also recognizes rightly that Douglass is well aware about drawing too much of a parallel between the two, since the acquisition of American independence was made agreeable with the enslavement of Africans. And as we know, Douglass's ambivalence about drawing too close of a connection is best exemplified in his famous speech "What To the Slave is the Fourth of July?"

Nonetheless, despite Sundquist's awareness of Douglass's ambivalence, he still misses a significant problem in Douglass's reflections on the parallelism between the slaves' and the American rebellion. *The difficulty in Douglass's comparison is that whereas the right to violent resistance in the American Revolution served to defend emancipation in an extant political culture from a distant mother country, the slaves' right to violent resistance would serve to overthrow an extant regime for emancipation in a new political culture.* In the former, the right to revolt serves to establish independence only as a consequence of which a new constitution becomes indispensable for the extant political culture; in the latter, however, it would serve to lay the foundation for an emancipation based fundamentally on a new constitution, a new system of rights, for a new political culture.

Different conceptions of revolution are at work here, despite Douglass's attempt to make them comparable and despite his feelings of ambivalence to their correlation. Although both are construed as morally defensible under the right to revolt, the slaves' violent resistance yields a different political end from the violent insurgency operative in the American Revolution.[96] By linking the violent resistance of enslaved Africans to the natural right to revolt and thereby compare it with that of the American Revolution, Douglass does not see the opposing ends to which each is put in the name of emancipation.

Furthermore, the violent mode of morally informed political abolitionism (made morally defensible, in Douglass's mind, by the natural right to revolt) stands at odds with Douglass's affirmation of a non-violent mode of morally informed political abolitionism, not because the former is violent or really non-moral and the latter non-violent or really moral, but because, in bringing an end to slavery, the latter mode would support the US Constitution and would reject dissolving or overthrowing the Union, while the former mode would subvert the extant system of rights and would engage in dissolving the Union in favor of a new system of rights supportive of a wholly new political culture. Hence, the paradox: how can Douglass, in short and in principle, support, on the one hand, a morally informed political action, which abolishes slavery while *preserving* the Union and its system of rights to accommodate the freedom of blacks as rights-bearing and morally accountable individuals in the *extant* political culture, and support, on the other hand, a morally informed political action, which abolishes slavery while *dissolving* the Union and its system of rights to accommodate the freedom of blacks as rights-bearing and morally accountable individuals in a *wholly new* political culture with a *totally new* system of rights?

Historically events were such that the United States was never seriously imperiled by slave insurrections[97] and that ultimately slavery was abolished and the Union preserved through a lengthy violent conflict, the Civil War. Under these historical circumstances, it would appear, in the words of Sundquist, that "Douglass' appeal to the right of revolution was left hanging in the balance, neither affirmed nor denied."[98] If Sundquist is right, we are still left in the dark, especially in the face of textual evidence, on how Douglass advocates for both moral suasion$_2$ and violent resistance or the non-violent and violent modes of morally informed political abolitionism. Perhaps Boxill's answer of reducing violent resistance to moral suasion might be correct.

Nevertheless, Boxill can still offer light to the problem of Douglass's double endorsement, because he makes the enslaved African's restoration of *self-respect* the end toward which resistance, especially violent resistance, is directed.[99] Minimally self-respect is a person's awareness of her unassailable worthiness as a person and her moral expectation that such worthiness is to be recognized. Now this matter of the slave's restoration of self-respect is not lost on Douglass-scholars who, for example, make Douglass's fight with Covey a focal point of their discussions. However, for the most part, in their discussions, either that matter takes a back seat to that of the slave's acquisition of emancipation through violent resistance or it gets eclipsed by that of the slave's acquisition of freedom because, in addressing both, Douglass himself appears generally to give greater emphasis to violent resistance in behalf of the slave's freedom than to violent resistance in behalf of the slave's self-respect. Douglass's emphasis on violent resistance in behalf of the slave's freedom is reflected in his linkage of that resistance to the natural right to revolt and in his comparison of it to that of the American Revolution. And that linkage and comparison, as we have seen, put him in the position of (1) being blind to the opposing ends to which each revolution is pitched in the name of freedom and of (2) succumbing to the paradox of endorsing two modes of political abolitionism (or moral suasion$_2$ and violent resistance) that are at odds with each other. Indeed (2) gives a further and, perhaps, stronger reason to those who claim that Douglass can endorse only one or the other, not both.

Since Douglass's contentions for violent resistance in behalf of the slave's self-respect are, for the most part, tightly woven with those in behalf of the slave's freedom, it would indeed be important, I believe, to extricate them and thereafter shift the emphasis to Douglass's argument for the former. There would not be a need for reconstructing Douglass's case for violent resistance in the slave's restoration of self-respect, because it normally is cloaked by his views on violent resistance in behalf of the slave's acquisition of freedom. With that separation and shift, I believe, there is an approach for Douglass to escape the paradoxical result in his endorsement of both moral suasion$_2$ and violent resistance (or the two modes of political abolitionism). Violent resistance in behalf of the slave's restoration of self-respect, I shall contend, will have to turn on a connection not with the natural right to revolt, but rather with casuistical elements supported by *struggles for recognition*[100], in order for Douglass's double endorsement to be unencumbered by the above mentioned paradox.

As a struggle for recognition, violent resistance for the sake of restoring self-respect is morally tenable, because it is exercised as a response to both the denigration of the integrity of an enslaved African's sense of self and the manipulation of the slave's life into an object of aggression and assault.[101] In a word, it is a kind of self-defense, a self-defense not for the sake of survival or self-preservation, but for self-respect, a self-defense in which a slave acquires the awarenesss of her worthiness of being a person as something unassailable and gains, if not the approval, at least the assumption, of that worthiness from aggressors who violently discredit it. As Douglass puts it in his remarks about his fight with Covey, "I . . . remembered my pledge to *stand up in my own defense*." "I was strictly on the *defensive*." "I was . . . *defensive* toward Covey, but *aggressive* toward Hughes." As Douglass states further, allow me to quote his comments at length:

> this battle with Covey . . . was the turning point in my "life as a slave" . . . I was a changed being after that fight. I was *nothing* before; *I WAS A MAN NOW*. It recalled to life my crushed self-respect and my self-confidence, and inspired me with a renewed determination to be *A FREEMAN*. A man, without force, is without the essential dignity of humanity . . . After resisting him, I felt as I had never felt before. It was a resurrection from the dark and pestiferous tomb of slavery, to the heaven of comparative freedom . . . I had reached the point, at which I was *not afraid to die*. This spirit made me a freeman in *fact*, while I remained a slave in *form* . . . [A]fter I had so grievously offended Mr Covey, he did not have me taken in hand by the authorities . . . The story that he had undertaken to whip a lad, and had been resisted, was, of itself sufficient to damage him; for his bearing should, in the estimation of slaveholders, be of that imperial order that should make such an occurrence *impossible*. I judge from these circumstances, that Covey deemed it best to give me the go-by.[102]

In the struggle with Covey, the fact that Douglass's life could be terminated does not compromise the moral worthiness he is aware of possessing, because his violent resistance is to show that he is morally entitled to counteract Covey's violent use or misuse of his life for Covey's own purposes and to dissent from being a victim of assault. Douglass is seeking to enjoin more than moral permissibility to resist self-defensively for the sake of one's self-respect. Such resistance, for Douglass, takes on a kind of moral necessity, clearly not of a kind the violation of which would circumvent morality itself, but of a kind that would demand and deserve to be advanced and encouraged in the case of aggression. Douglass believes "doing nothing" when facing aggression severely diminishes one's self-respect, but he further contends that even if one is unable to engage in self-defense, one is still called upon not to be compliant with the violent misuse of one's life by another.[103] Hence he would appear to suggest that non-compliance does not entail self-defense. Nevertheless, this shows that *what provides moral entitlement to self-defense and non-compliance is not self-preservation in the face of death itself, but rather the restoration of self-respect in the face of the denigrating aims of an aggressor who uses violence even to the point of death as a vehicle for his aims.* It is the sense of being vulnerable to moral injury, not the fear of mortality, that provokes Douglass's resistance and gives that resistance or struggle for recognition its moral force. Douglass's motivational impetus for such a struggle is Covey's violation of normative expectations constitutive of Covey's disparagement of his self-respect. It is not the gaining of the upper-hand or advantage over Covey.

Since Douglass's fight with Covey is not motivated by the fear of his life being threatened, but by the sentiment of his self-regard being denigrated and his will being deprived of any and all occasion to dispose over his own body, the fight yields from Covey a *withdrawal* of his denial of recognition extended toward Douglass's assumptions of his own worthiness. This needs to be laid out carefully. Indeed, after the struggle, Covey clearly does not regard Douglass as a person endowed with rights because, even in Douglass's own self-conception, he is still a "slave in form." Covey still *cannot* recognize Douglass as a person with morally obligating qualities. However, reinforced by a struggle which takes as its point of departure a sense of moral indignation, what Douglass thinks of himself is a self-conception he can expect to be met without disrespect and violation in Covey's considerations and plans regarding him. From that fight, then, Covey *can* recognize Douglass's self-conception because of Douglass's possession of certain personal qualities whose *social significance* has an impact on how the worth of Covey's talents as a slavebreaker is measured. This is why Douglass can refer to himself as a "freeman in fact"; Douglass's self-conception as a "freeman in fact" is thus tied to the socially evaluative framework in which he recognizes his relevance for himself and also on Covey's worth.

This is an example of what Moody-Adams has rightly called the "social construction of self-respect," which "sets the parameters within which we initially learn to evaluate our own worth."[104] But she does not see that such "parameters" are always subject to shifts and revisions over time due to struggles of recognition which expand (or narrow) the boundaries and extend (or restrict) the conditions of self-respect's social construction. That Douglass sees struggles of recognition as broadening those parameters is implied in his own characterizations of himself as a "slave in form" and a "freeman in fact." Each characterization indicates a level of recognition, one which involves no recognition as a person with morally obligating qualities, the other which involves, at least, minimal recognition as an individual whose self-conception has a social effect on the relevance of others. This suggests that struggles for recognition do not yield full-fledged mutual recognition all at once, but partial, overlapping layers of social recognition.

Although the details for defending such a position cannot be presented here, that the achievements of such struggles are complex and overlapping is somewhat evident even from Douglass's self-characterizations. As the results of such struggles, I believe, Douglass moves over time from both "slave in form" *and* "slave in fact" to "slave in form" *and* "freeman in fact" and, by implication, to freeman in form (a person with morally obligating attributes) to both freeman in form *and*, in a more enriched way than previously had, freeman in fact. The prospect of broadening the social parameters of recognition to the fullest extent through morally guided struggles is the goal Douglass sets for enslaved Africans, because involvement in such struggles serves not only to gain for enslaved Africans from others an attention to and regard for their morally obligating traits, but serves also to disinhibit those enslaved Africans whose actions have been stifled by their diminished self-conceptions that accompany their compliant acquiescence to slavery's denigrating endeavors. Such struggles can force "from below," so to speak, a removal of that which impedes the expansion of the boundaries of those levels of social recognition for the sake of including those excluded through enslavement. Douglass makes this point in remarks from "Is It Right and Wise To Kill a Kidnapper?":

> Such submission, instead of being set to the credit of the poor sable ones, only creates contempt for them in the public mind, and becomes an argument in the mouths of the community, that Negroes are, by nature, only fit for slavery; that slavery is their normal condition. Their patient and unresisting disposition, their unwillingness to peril their own lives, by shooting down their pursuers, is already quoted against them, as marking them as an inferior race. This reproach must be wiped out, and nothing short of resistance on the part of colored men, can wipe it out. Every slavehunter who meets a bloody death in his infernal business, is an argument in favor of the manhood of our race. Resistance is, therefore, wise as well as just.[105]

There are significant issues that are raised here however. They touch on the wisdom and justice claimed in that essay for violent resistance involving homicide supposedly for the sake of the slave's self-respect. When the "Kidnapper" essay is examined in full, it is not difficult to see that Douglass assumes a different posture from that of the Covey episode regarding the exercise of violence. Whereas Douglass's battle with Covey is a struggle for the sake of restoring self-respect and carried out in a *self-defensive* posture, his position in the "Kidnapper" essay involves a struggle carried out in an *aggressive* mien. Moreover, in the former, where violent resistance against aggression appears to be an action of last resort, in the latter, the violent resistance involving the homicide of a kidnapper is claimed to be morally salient on first resort. Thus there appears to be a discrepancy between Douglass's stance on violence in the Covey episode and in the Batchelder (the slave kidnapper) incident. But this discrepancy is due to the fact that, perhaps more so than the narrative of the Covey fight, the "Kidnapper" essay reflects the problem I alluded to earlier regarding Douglass's tendency to entangle his arguments supporting violent resistance, on the one hand, for the acquisition of freedom and, on the other, for the restoration of self-respect. Arguments for the first eclipse those for the second and are emphasized over the latter. So this comparison between the Covey episode and the Batchelder incident shows the need for keeping both arguments separate.

However, the comparison raises another issue which may also establish doubt about the wisdom and justice Douglass attaches to violent resistance involving Batchelder's homicide in the "Kidnapper" essay. Douglass presents his self-defense against Covey as a case for employing a norm of casuistry for the use of violence when one's self-respect is at risk. In contrast, he appeals to the natural "right to kill in defense of one's liberty"[106] in the Batchelder incident, whereby the slave kidnapper *forfeits at once his moral entitlement to live* when he puts a slave's freedom at stake. Unlike Martin Luther King, to whom he is so often compared, Douglass apparently is not one to accept the moral presumption against violence. But, in the Covey episode, his non-acceptance is *qualified*. It is Douglass's belief, as shown by that event, that *only* the slave's self-defensive posture, *exercised as a last resort* in his struggle for recognition or the restoration of his self-respect, governs the claim why the slave ought *not* be burdened by the terms of that presumption. Yet, in the Batchelder incident, Douglass is compelled to claim that, in any and all cases where the natural freedom of the slave is aggressively threatened, the slave is *unconditionally* released from that moral presumption because of the natural right to kill in behalf of one's freedom. Moreover, the slave would not be burdened by that presumption in his use of violence *even when committed as a first resort*.

That is rather a strong contention with serious implications. In the "Kidnapper" essay, we find the absence of casuistical elements and the affirmation for the immediate forfeiture of Batchelder's moral entitlement to life. Speaking charitably, it appears quite unclear how the justice-question is met, in the exercise of violence, under these circumstances. Moreover, there also appears the absence of proportionality of response which seems to render the wisdom of such violence questionable to say the least. So it would not be out of step to claim that violent resistance supported by the natural right to kill in behalf of one's freedom casts deep suspicion over whether wisdom and justice have been satisfied in it. This becomes an important reason for placing greater emphasis on violent resistance in behalf of the slave's self-respect and establishing it as the other component (with moral suasion$_2$) in Douglass's double endorsement.

Given the greater plausibility and viability for justice and wisdom in violent resistance in behalf of the slave's self-respect than in the other, how, then, can it be shown that Douglass's advocacy for both moral suasion$_2$ and this kind of violent resistance can be had without paradox or discrepancy? In order to address this question finally, I will refer to a remark by Douglass which is so often cited that it has reached the point of cliché. "Power concedes nothing without a demand. It never did and it never will."[107] When a remark is often cited and becomes a cliché, it has achieved for readers and auditors its force, its significance, and its capacity for reiteration without relying on the context or the occasion to which it belongs. So, too, with Douglass's remark. And the force and significance, to which readers and auditors are constantly and repeatedly attaching it, indifferent to its context, express the following point, viz., that individuals or groups must prudently or violently seize or obtain control, or expand their control, over the material and symbolic resources necessary for their survival given the state of antagonism among different individuals or groups over power. At no time is Douglass's remark construed as even hinting an association with the moral dimension of social struggles for recognition.

Yet that remark's oft-cited force and significance change dramatically when we simply look at the remark immediately preceding it. "This struggle," Douglass states, "may be a *moral* one, or it *may be a physical* one, and it may be *both moral and physical*, but it must be a struggle."[108] And when we examine the context of both remarks, a major part of that context addresses, again, as stated previously, his objections against colored people doing nothing in the face of enslavement and his belief that their "doing nothing" is an impediment to both the restoration of their self-respect and their achievement of social recognition. Quoting Douglass at length, he asserts:

> It is said that we, the colored people, should do something of ourselves worthy of celebration, and not be everlastingly celebrating the deeds of a race by which we are despised . . . I am free to say, that nothing is more humiliating than the insignificant part we, the colored people, are taking in the great contest now going on with the powers of oppression in this land . . . [T]he stolid contentment, the listless indifference, *the moral death* which reigns over many of our people, we who should be all on fire, beats down my little flame of enthusiasm and leaves me to labor, half robbed of my natural force. This indifference, in us, is outrageous. It is giving aid and comfort to the men who are warring against our very manhood. The highest satisfaction of our oppressors is to see the Negro degraded, divested of public spirit, insensible to patriotism, and to all concern for the freedom, elevation, and respectability of the race . . . The general sentiment of mankind is that a man who will not fight for himself, when he has the means of doing so, is not worth being fought for by others, and this sentiment is just. *For a man who does not value freedom for himself will never value it for others, nor put himself to any inconvenience to gain it for others* . . . A man of this type will never lay the world under any obligation to him, but will be a *moral pauper*, a drag on the wheels of society, and if he, too, be identified with a peculiar variety of the race he will entail disgrace upon his race as well as upon himself. The world in which we live is very accommodating to all sorts of people . . . Its favors to individuals are measured by an unerring principle in this: viz. *respect those who respect themselves, and despise those who despise themselves.*[109]

So if "power concedes nothing without a demand," it does so within a social context where, *minimally*, the demand/struggle for recognition of one's self-conception complements the demand/struggle for control of resources for one's self-preservation, if not supplants it. On this interpretation, we have a way of showing how Douglass's endorsement of both moral suasion$_2$ and violent resistance can be held without paradox.

In the speech, Douglass pays homage to two kinds of abolitionism, the abolitionism based on moral suasion ("moral struggle") and the abolitionism based on violent resistance ("physical struggle"). Officially, historically, that is, the former is that of the Garrisonians and the latter that of John Brown and, perhaps, Henry Highland Garnet. But the official account is of narrow explanatory significance, because, as we have argued, the former represents moral suasion$_1$ and the latter represents a mode of violent resistance posed as a natural right for the sake of the slave's acquisition of freedom. Under these characterizations, when Douglass embraces both, he would be then endorsing a form of moral suasion whose only acceptable form of action is an inspection of one's moral sense with an absolute acquiescence to the moral presumption against violence. Furthermore, that mode of violent resistance is not only at odds with moral suasion$_1$ but, more importantly, with moral suasion$_2$ because, as previously argued, the political action, to which moral suasion$_2$ would be connected, would be guided by political ends in significant ways contradictory with that mode of violent resistance.

So when Douglass embraces both, he would have to endorse moral suasion$_2$ in behalf of the immediate abolition of slavery and the slave's acquisition of freedom and violent resistance in behalf of the slave's restoration of his self-respect and his worthiness to be recognized. It is this combination that Douglass can endorse without incongruity. *The task of moral suasion$_2$ is to produce, through discursive deliberation, rationally binding moral convictions concerning the wrongness of slavery and thereby give moral import to the demands for the success of political action against slavery.* This latter point signifies that the foreseeable consequences of antislavery political action must be seriously taken into account in morally discursive deliberation, otherwise the pro-slavery social context or political culture, upon which that political action works, could become too hardened for moral suasion$_2$ to penetrate. Political abolitionism, informed by moral suasion$_2$, non-violently works on a pro-slavery political culture to render it favorable to the development of its members to regard slavery as morally wrong, to abrogate it immediately, and to extend rights-bearing qualities to formerly enslaved Africans. This counts as the outcome by which moral suasion$_2$ holds antislavery political action accountable and measures its success.

But Douglass is keenly aware of the tension between, on the one hand, the moral insight moral suasion$_2$ yields and the political action it demands and measures and, on the other hand, the self-conception of enslaved and slaveholders a pro-slavery culture yields. Moral suasion$_2$ demands a morally informed political action which cannot be enacted by enslaved Africans and slaveholders without ceasing to be who they respectively are or want to be in a pro-slavery context. And as we have argued, besides enslavement abounding, that context spawns and sustains, more violently than not, the denigration of the slave's integrity and self-conception and the depreciation of freedom's value in the eyes of the slave. This speaks to Douglass's belief in *de facto* constraints on moral suasion$_2$, viz., the belief that the actual chances for reaching agreement through moral suasion$_2$ are limited and, since for both sides the integrity, the basic priorities, and the meaning of their lives are at stake, the disagreements will be partly fought out by weapons other than moral suasion$_2$.

On this matter, Douglass has called upon the use of "physical struggle" as a kind of antislavery political action. But "physical struggle" would not be geared toward the immediate elimination of the "peculiar institution." Nor would it be directed toward expanding the domain of rights-bearers. *It would rather be aimed at the renewal of the slave's self-conception, the repair of the slave's sense of integrity, and the appreciation of freedom's value through non-compliant resistance inclusive of the self-defensive use of violence against the denigrating aims of the slaveholder's aggression.* It is this aim that makes "physical struggle" moral, not by moral suasion$_2$, but as a struggle for recognition. To engage in "physical struggle" involving violent resistance along these lines is to engage in a struggle for recognition, i.e., to act for a morally necessary end, whereby the act is (1) not aggressive, (2) not a means to another end, and (3) not supportive of allegations regarding the slave's moral preeminence over the slaveholder. Although "physical struggle," within this view, does not engender the immediate abolition of slavery, it can be still construed as antislavery political action wedded to a mode of violence "from below," because its constant recalcitrance, enacted for the sake of the slave's self-respect, can encumber the brandishing of a pro-slavery political culture by diminishing both the slave's compliant acceptance of it and the slaveholder's denial of any recognition to the slave within it.

Only under the auspice of this "moral division of labor," so to speak, can Douglass embrace, without paradox, moral suasion and violent resistance. "Moral struggle," guided by moral suasion$_2$, and "physical struggle," guided by a moral struggle for recognition, refer to two modes of antislavery political action respectively tied to the abrogation of slavery and the acquisition of freedom, on the one hand, and the restoration of self-respect, on the other. Under this scenario, antislavery struggle or political action is morally permeated, such that it would not be far fetched to claim, as Douglass insinuates, that moral suasion$_2$ is a form of resistance. Although Douglass himself never explicitly endorsed this version, it still is in keeping with his advocacy for both and, furthermore, with what I take to be his core project – to formulate and make serious use of ideas and actions and comprehend their consequences in promoting the moral dimension of slavery's abolition, of freedom and equality, and of the elevation of enslaved and formerly enslaved Africans. Admittedly this mode of violent resistance appears to be a weaker version of what people usually have in mind when thinking about Douglass's advocacy of "physical struggle." Violent resistance involving some form of strategic action for the sake of the overthrow of the slave system and the consequent acquisition of the slave's freedom is usually assumed. Indeed Douglass himself subscribes to this much stronger version. Nonetheless, if Douglass's advocacy of both moral suasion and violent resistance is to escape paradox, then, given his "sincere concern for the uses and consequences of ideas," as Waldo Martin puts it, this weaker version of violent resistance would have to be maintained in conjunction with moral suasion$_2$.

VII Postscripts and Dead Certainties

We have tried to show that Douglass's use of moral suasion is reflective of a moral orientation and a communicative practice consistent, to a large extent, with Kantian characterizations of "enlightenment." Moreover we have attempted to sustain the claim that a certain kind of moral suasion, i.e., moral suasion$_2$, is a significant element in Douglass's intellectual and political life. In moral suasion$_2$, that Douglass *independently and openly* employs his own reason in concert with others is affirmation of his enlightenment commitment to critical argument. At the same time, Douglass believes that morally suasive argumentation is *de facto* not enough to bring about the immediate abolition of slavery and the institutional establishment of freedom and equality of those formerly enslaved. This is why Douglass extends his enlightenment commitment to include agitation, struggle, resistance. If *"argue as much as you like and about whatever you like, but obey!"*[110] is Kant's enlightenment-motto, then Douglass's would be *"argue as much as you can about the injustice of slavery and its concomitant violation of normative expectations, but agitate, agitate, agitate!"* Indeed this motto, consistent with Douglass's position, it could be argued, reflects his double endorsement of moral suasion$_2$ and violent resistance. Yet there are five issues with which Douglass's double endorsement ought to be confronted: (1) the stronger version of that endorsement, (2) the Covey incident, (3) the role of history in that endorsement, (4) Bernard Boxill's continuation thesis, and (5) Robert Levine's temperance thesis.

(1) Douglass's double endorsement has two versions, a stronger and a weaker one. The stronger version, to which Douglass subscribes, holds that the natural right to revolt or kill warrants violent resistance against the suppression of and for the acquisition of freedom. But why does Douglass go this route? Since moral suasion$_2$, bridged with political

abolitionism, rests on natural law, Douglass believes, I contend, that violent resistance turns on it also. Natural law doctrine, then, would provide the seamless moral dimension to both moral suasion$_2$ and violent resistance or, more generally, to both "moral" and "physical" struggle, although Douglass nowhere expresses this thesis. It would make violent resistance on behalf of the acquisition of freedom *categorically* moral and would provide the grounds, in this situation, for *unconditionally* putting into abeyance the moral presumption against violence. As we stated previously, however, subscription to this version yields paradoxical results for Douglass's conceptions of antislavery political action.

(2) and (3) Yet another problem arises when that thesis and another are extended to Douglass's narration of his fight with Covey. In his three autobiographies, Douglass makes that fight stand as a powerful symbol of his struggle for freedom and his mastery of self-assertion in the face of racist attempts at denigration. So it is not surprising that Douglass-scholars follow suit in emphasizing that the fight is on par with other emancipatory struggles, receiving moral backing from natural law (the right to revolt) or *history*. The fight with Covey would be, then, categorically moral through either natural law or history as "the court of the world" and, hence, would reflect too the unqualified nullification of the moral presumption against violence in behalf of the slave's acquisition of freedom.

There is a problem with such a reading however. It does not discern that Douglass's narration of the fight is not entwined with justificatory claims about the natural right to revolt or the fight's place in history. In that narration, Douglass does not seek grounds from either natural law or history to warrant morally his violent resistance. Rather he uses *casuistical* elements for justifying his exercise of violence in behalf of restoring his self-respect. Douglass's use of violence in the Covey incident is, then, *casuistically* moral, so those elements would supply grounds, in that situation, only for *conditionally* suspending the moral presumption against violence. On this note, Douglass could kill Covey to resist his aggression, not on the grounds that he has a (natural) right to do so or that history vindicates him, but on the grounds that he acts self-defensively as a last resort for the sake of refusing to be a victim of aggression. If the Covey incident is to serve as a paradigm for morally informed violent resistance against aggression *within* a larger context of antislavery political action (moral *and* physical struggles), it would have to be featured along these lines, giving credence to the weaker version of the endorsement.

Moreover, since history is not to be viewed as the court of the world, moral suasion$_2$, although connected to historical struggles, cannot proceed from them. Rather it must always be at the ready of arguing for the ever wider extension and continuous practice of full reciprocal recognition. Its purpose would be to demystify, through argumentation, pro-slavery power relations and the public dialogue, which makes them inviolable. It would also entail identifying enslaved Africans as those who have not had access to means of public discourse and advocating their inclusion as well as stating what would be in the nation's interest as against the universalization of what would be only the interests of slaveholders.

(4) As stated previously, Douglass's violent resistance against Covey is morally informed as a struggle for recognition. And to be sure, such struggles can be found throughout history. Furthermore, they can be either violent or non-violent. As Douglass states:

> Find out just what any people will quietly submit to and you have found out the exact measure of injustice and wrong which will be imposed upon them, and these will continue till they are resisted with either words or blows, or both. The limits of tyrants are prescribed by the endurance of those whom they oppress. In the light of these ideas, Negroes will be hunted at the North, and held and flogged in the South so long as they submit to these devilish outrages, and make no resistance, either moral or physical ... If we ever get free from the oppressions and wrongs heaped upon us, we must pay for their removal. We must do this by labor, by suffering, by sacrifice, and if needs be, by our lives and the lives of others.[111]

Although Douglass has linked moral suasion$_2$ ("words") to non-violent antislavery political struggle, it can be strongly argued that, for Douglass, morally informed political abolitionism wedded to non-violence is part of or coordinated with social struggles for recognition and freedom, struggles inclusive of violence which have made throughout history full reciprocal recognition of free and equal mutual respect of and among persons a principle to be held. In this vein, moral suasion$_2$ would be less construed as arguments against slavery and for the freedom and equality of the formerly enslaved than battles and struggles thereof waged with words. As Douglass appears to suggest, it would be a form or a component of struggle or resistance, in short, *a continuation of resistance* rather than resistance as a form or continuation of moral suasion as Boxill has maintained.

If it were claimed that Douglass's double endorsement is simply an expression of the continuation thesis, I think that it could not take the shape Boxill has stated it to be. Under Boxill's conception, moral suasion is marked by moral sentimentalism, so it could neither serve as a form of resistance nor make resistance an embodiment of it. There could be no double endorsement here, because morally we would be *either* at each other's mercy *or* at each other's throats. And although Boxill rightly characterizes the Covey incident as an act of violent resistance in behalf of Douglass's self-respect, that incident is not a form of moral suasion because of the experience of shame Covey undergoes as Boxill claims.[112] The shame Covey suffers is not due to his change of heart through an inspection of his moral sense, but to having his actions physically and unexpectedly rebuffed by Douglass because of his denial of recognition toward Douglass's self-conception.

(5) Besides Boxill's, Robert Levine's recent and excellent work, *Martin Delany, Frederick Douglass and The Politics of Representative Identity*, represents the most intriguing interpretation on Douglass's double endorsement.[113] Levine, too, claims that Douglass "yokes together" or embraces both violent resistance and some kind of non-violent moral orientation, viz., revolutionary social change and the virtue of temperance. He, too, is critical of those who fail to see that Douglass's quest for revolutionary social change, i.e., violent resistance for the sake of the slave's acquisition of freedom, has a moral link. But, for Levine, revolutionary social change is not informed by moral suasion or natural law, but by temperate self-control. He has a good deal of textual and historical evidence for rejecting moral suasion in favor of temperance. As argued earlier, it is not uncommon to read the transition from the "early" to the "mature" Douglass as involving his total rejection of moral suasion, rather than his modification of it. Moreover, a good number of abolitionist movements were directly associated with temperance movements. Furthermore, there are a wealth of essays and speeches by the "early" and "mature" Douglass himself addressing the value of temperance.

From this evidence, Levine claims that Douglass's double endorsement takes the form of what he calls "temperate revolutionism." Temperate revolutionism expresses the thesis that Douglass adopts a "measured self-defensive violence" to show that blacks, both free and enslaved, should be under self-control when engaged in violence on behalf of the slave's acquisition of freedom. Measured self-defensive violence reflects a person under control, evincing a self-mastery of one's mind and body and an ability never to be a "slave" to one's appetites and passions. In so doing, blacks would stand in stark contrast to the brutish and "intemperate violence" of slaveholders. Levine, too, points to the Covey fight in which Douglass places his measured self-defensive violence alongside Covey's intemperate violence. So the Covey fight, for Levine, ultimately reflects not only Douglass's mastery over Covey, but his mastery of himself.

However, there are a number of problems with Levine's thesis. First, temperate revolutionism would make sense if Douglass believed that blacks, free and enslaved, were "doing something" against slavery's tyranny and denigrating effects. Douglass could claim that they ought to exercise self-control in their resistance. But, as I have shown, Douglass is critical of them, because they have been "doing nothing" in the face of slavery's tyranny and denigrating effects. "Doing nothing" threatens their self-respect. This state of affairs makes self-respect, not self-mastery, the issue about which Douglass is concerned.

Secondly, by shifting the issue to self-mastery, Levine must focus on the self-formative processes that enable Douglass to escape enslavement to his appetites and passions to achieve a desired mode of being as a "self-made man," capable of governing himself even in the use of violence. But the freedom reflected in undergoing temperate self-control is antithetical to the one operative in social interaction. For example, any action of Covey on Douglass is conceived to be an exercise of power in which Covey governs Douglass's conduct, gets Douglass to do what he wants, through intemperate violence. Under Levine's purview, Douglass's freedom, then, can consist only in actions carried out by Douglass *on himself* in which he governs his actions (violence) against Covey temperately. *The action Douglass takes on himself takes precedent over the action he takes against Covey*. Douglass's freedom is thus placed *outside* the interaction-context or the struggle with Covey, because it shows Douglass's self-mastery at the expense of his dissent from being a victim of assault.

Finally, measured self-defensive violence for Douglass does not settle "temperance" issues, but "justice" ones. If temperance were to be the matter settled, then the goal of a measured self-defensive violence would be to show the agent in self-control, not losing herself to her passions. But since justice is the matter, for Douglass, to be settled by measured self-defensive violence, then the goal of such violence, as I have already argued, would have to be the restoration of the agent's self-respect, to heighten the agent's self-conception. For a diminished self-conception, under self-mastery, would be one in which a person could not take control of herself; whereas a dimished self-conception, under self-respect, would be one in which a person is subject to and tolerant of others' disrespect. In this context, then, the question to ask Levine is the following: is the motivational impetus for Douglass's "measured self-defensive violence" against Covey to show that Douglass is not "nasty, brutish, and short" or to show that Douglass will not suffer Covey's violation of normative expectations constitutive of Covey's denigration of Douglass's self-respect?

Only the weaker version of Douglass's double endorsement avoids the above-mentioned problems whereby moral suasion$_2$ and violent resistance in behalf of the slave's self-respect, as exemplified by Douglass's struggle with Covey for recognition, morally complement the ends of the other. Under the weaker version, the two modes of antipolitical action, representing a kind of "moral division of labor," would contribute to bringing about the existence of a self-reflexive political culture in which the immediate abolition of slavery, the slave's acquisition of freedom, and the slave's restoration of self-respect are morally warranted and they are understood by all as what the political culture demands. And if a gap were to emerge between these demands and the actual state of affairs of the culture, it would not be due to the paradoxical results of the stronger version. It would be due to acts of injustice within a political culture requiring more of the kind of enlightenment Douglass embraces – argue and agitate, agitate, agitate.[114]

Notes

1 Booker T. Washington, *Frederick Douglass* (New York: New York University Press, 1968), p. 131.
2 Waldo E. Martin, Jr, *The Mind of Frederick Douglass* (Chapel Hill: The University of North Carolina Press, 1984), pp. ix-x.
3 Ibid., p. 198.
4 See Philip S. Foner, "Frederick Douglass," in Philip S. Foner, ed, *Life and Writings of Frederick Douglass, vol. 2* (New York: International Publishers, 1950), pp. 49–51 (hereafter cited as Foner II); Martin, *The Mind of Frederick Douglass*, pp. 182–4.
5 See John Blassingame, ed, *The Frederick Douglass Papers, Series One, vol. 1: 1841–46* (New Haven: Yale University Press, 1979), pp. xxi-lxix (hereafter cited as Blassingame I); see also Peter Walker, *Moral Choices: Memory, Desire, and Imagination in Nineteenth-Century American Abolition* (Baton Rouge: Louisiana State University Press, 1978), pp. 209–61; Ronald K. Burke, *Frederick Douglass: Crusading Orator for Human Rights* (New York: Garland Publishing, Inc., 1996); and Shelley Fisher Fishkin and Carla L. Peterson, " 'We Hold These Truths To Be Self-Evident': The Rhetoric of Frederick Douglass's Journalism," in E.J. Sundquist, ed, *Frederick Douglass: New Literary and Historical Essays* (Cambridge: Cambridge University Press, 1990), pp. 189–204; Henry L. Gates, Jr, *Figures*

in Black (New York: Oxford University Press, 1987), pp. 98–124; J. Saunders Redding, "Let Freedom Ring," in *Critical Essays on Frederick Douglass*, W. L. Andrews, ed (Boston: G. K. Hall, 1991), pp. 56–61.

6 Despite many scattered references and allusions, secondary literature concentrated on Douglass and moral suasion is very scant. See Howard H. Bell, "National Negro Conventions of the Middle 1840s: Moral Suasion vs. Political Action," in J. H. Bracey, A. Meier, E. Rudwick, eds, *Blacks in the Abolitionist Movement* (California: Wadsworth Publishing Comp., 1971), pp. 125–38; Bernard R. Boxill, "Fear and Shame as Forms of Moral Suasion in the Thought of Frederick Douglass," in *Transactions of the Charles S. Peirce Society*, 31 (4), Fall 1995, pp. 713–44.

7 Bernard R. Boxill, "Two Traditions in African-American Political Philosophy," in *The Philosophical Forum*, vols 1–3, Fall–Spring 1992–3, pp. 125–8.

8 Ibid., p. 126.

9 See Jerome Huyler, *Locke in America: The Moral Philosophy of the Founding Era* (Lawrence: University Press of Kansas, 1995).

10 "For God, the author of this law, has willed it to be the rule of our moral life, and He has made it sufficiently known, so that anyone can understand it who is willing to apply diligent study and to direct his mind to the knowledge of it." See John Locke, *Essays on the Law of Nature*, W. von Leyden, ed (Oxford: Clarendon Press, 1954), p. 187.

11 Quoted in Blassingame I, p. xxxiii.

12 See Frederick Douglass, *My Bondage and My Freedom* (New York: Dover, 1969), p. 253. Although this text was published in 1855, Douglass's statements regarding moral ignorance of enslaved Africans can be found in speeches given ten years earlier. For example, in a speech, delivered in Belfast, Ireland on December 11, 1845, Douglass asserts that slaves are regarded as inferior, because "[t]he Americans had darkened or bored out their [enslaved Africans] *intellectual* eyes . . . [and] blunted their moral feelings and perceptions." See Frederick Douglass, "The Slanderous Charge of Negro Inferiority," in Blassingame I, p. 99 [my emphasis and my addition].

13 Ibid., p. 253.

14 Frederick Douglass, "Is It Right and Wise to Kill a Kidnapper?," in Foner II, pp. 284–7.

15 Boxill, "Two Traditions," p. 129.

16 Ibid., p. 129.

17 See Frederick Douglass, "Is It Right and Wise to Kill a Kidnapper?," in Foner II, p. 287.

18 See Frederick Douglass, "Speech on John Brown," in Foner II, pp. 534–5.

19 See Blassingame I, p. xx. What is even more poignant is Douglass's attribution to his enslaved mother as the person who first provided him with his love of knowledge and literacy. According to Douglass, after his mother's death, he found out that she "could read, and that she was the

only one of all the slaves and colored people in Tuckahoe who enjoyed that advantage." How she acquired it, he does not know, but he recognizes the extraordinary character of his mother's feat given her slave status. This leads him "to attribute any love of letters [he] possesses, and for which [he] has got – despite of prejudices – only too much credit, *not* to my admitted Anglo-Saxon paternity, but to the native genius of [his] sable, unprotected, and uncultivated *mother* – a woman – who belonged to a race whose mental endowments it is, at present, fashionable to hold in disparagement and contempt." See *My Bondage and My Freedom*, pp. 57–8. This would be a fine start to a feminist or womanist reading of Douglass.

20 Ibid., p. xxiv.
21 Ibid., p. xxv.
22 Immanuel Kant, "An Answer to the Question: What is Enlightenment?" in H. Reiss, ed, *Kant's Political Writings*, trans. by H. B. Nisbet (Cambridge: Cambridge University Press, 1970), p. 54.
23 Ibid., p. 55.
24 Ibid., p. 55.
25 See Immanuel Kant, *Critique of Judgement*, trans. by J. H. Bernard (New York: Hafner Publishing Co., 1964), p. 136.
26 Kant's "Enlightenment" essay, too, was originally published as an opinion piece in the German newspaper, *Berlinische Monatsschrift*.
27 See Immanuel Kant, *Critique of Pure Reason*, trans. by N. K. Smith (New York: St. Martin's Press, 1965), pp. A820–1/B848–9.
28 This claim runs counter to certain remarks recently made about the relation of Douglass to certain German thinkers. The noted social and cultural theorist Paul Gilroy has drawn inferences from William McFeely's *Frederick Douglass* that Douglass had been familiar with the works of Goethe, Feuerbach, and the "German Idealist" tradition through his friendship with Ottilia Assing, who translated Douglass's *My Bondage and My Freedom* into German. Gilroy goes on to assert that, on the basis of that familiarity, Douglass's account of his struggle with Covey is a reconfiguration of Hegel's scheme of "Lordship & Servitude" in his *Phenomenology of Spirit*. But McFeely points out that Douglass's affiliation with Assing begins *after* 1855. If Hegel's "Lordship & Servitude" set the stage for Douglass's narrative of his fight with Covey, then Douglass would have had some familiarity with Hegel's work *prior to* 1855. But there is no evidence of Douglass being familiar with Hegel's or any other German philosopher's work prior to that year. Although it is possible for Gilroy to interpret cogently and favorably Douglass's fight with Covey in the light of Hegel's work, it does not appear likely that Douglass himself could be so inclined prior to 1855. See Paul Gilroy, *The Black Atlantic: Modernity and Double Consciousness* (Cambridge: Harvard University Press, 1993), p. 60; See also William McFeely, *Frederick Douglass* (New York: W.W. Norton & Company, 1991), p. 263.

29 See *My Bondage and My Freedom*, p. vii; my emphasis and additions in brackets.
30 See Frederick Douglass, *Narrative in the Life of Frederick Douglass, An American Slave* in *The Classic Slave Narratives*, H. L. Gates, Jr, ed (New York: New American Library, 1987), p. 326.
31 See Immanuel Kant, "An Answer to the Question: What is Enlightenment?," in Reiss, ed, *Kant's Political Writings*, p. 54.
32 See Douglass, *My Bondage and My Freedom*, p. 361.
33 Ibid., p. 360.
34 Frederick Douglass, "Letter to Hon. Chas. Sumner, 2 September 1852," in Foner II, p. 210.
35 For the uninitiated, besides the already mentioned *Critique of Pure Reason* (1781/1787$_3$) and *Critique of Judgment* (1790), there is also the *Critique of Practical Reason* (1788).
36 See Immanuel Kant, "An Answer to the Question: What is Enlightenment? ," in H. Reiss, ed, *Kant's Political Writings*, p. 55.
37 See Frederick Douglass, "Is It Right and Wise To Kill a Kidnapper?," in Foner II, pp. 284–7. The term "kidnapper" in the title refers even to a state-authorized individual (e.g., a federal marshal) charged with returning fugitive slaves to their owners.
38 See Frederick Douglass, "Letter to Samuel H. Cox," 1846, in Philip S. Foner, ed, *Life and Writings of Frederick Douglass, vol. 1* (New York: International Publishers, 1950), p. 192. (hereafter cited as Foner I)
39 See Emmanuel Eze, "The Color of Reason: The Idea of 'Race' in Kant's Anthropology," in K. Faull, ed, *Anthropology and The German Enlightenment* (London: Bucknell University Press, 1994), pp. 200–41. I cannot comment on Eze's very scholarly essay here. There are too many points he addresses for me to do his essay justice. However, allow me to make the following remarks. It is not Eze's intention to show that Kant has or subscribes to racist beliefs or that Kant's empirical theories on race classification are at the forefront in the early stages of scientific racism. These are points that have been previously raised by others, and he (and I) are in agreement with them. What is distinctive of Eze's views, however, is that he is of the mind that these beliefs and theories are built into the architecture of Kant's own transcendental philosophy. As a consequence, the idea of race assumes for Eze "transcendental" or *a priori* significance with respect to our mode of knowledge or to our being morally accountable. On this note, there is, I think, a major problem with Eze's position, which turns on his understanding of an *a priori* condition in Kant's sense. An *a priori* condition enables our cognitive representation of something to count discursively as objective. It does not enable the existence of something, independently of our cognitive representation of it, to count discursively as objective. Now if we assume that the idea of race is an *a priori* condition in the Kantian manner just defined, then it is clear that Eze makes a crucial error. He treats a racial representation, functioning as an *a priori* condition of our

experience or knowledge of a group, as something *gleaned* (intuitively) from a direct encounter with the *racial essence* of that group. Since the direct encounter with a racial essence, for Kant, is *not* discursively/cognitively a representation at all, racial or otherwise, and since a racial representation, for Eze, is derived from the encounter with a racial essence, the racial representation cannot be or function as a Kantian *a priori* condition as Eze claims. Unless Eze can show that there is an isomorphism between a racial representation as an *a priori* condition and a racial essence, which would be next to impossible, his claim that the idea of race is part of the architecture of Kant's transcendental philosophy is the victim of *ignoratio elenchi*.

40 Frederick Douglass, "Prejudice Against Color," in Foner II, pp. 127–30; bracketed words are my emendations.
41 See Douglass, *My Bondage and My Freedom*, pp. 361 and 362.
42 According to Blassingame, Douglass never actually gave speeches the way the Garrisonians wanted him to give them. He delivered them in his own manner and style. Still Douglass resented their demand and its implications, especially after his return in 1847 from his two-year speaking tour in the United Kingdom, and they resented his refusal to accept the place they had determined for him. See Blassingame I, pp. li-lii.
43 For Garrison's enlightenment view with a bit of Kantian flavor, see William Lloyd Garrison's "Free Speech and Free Inquiry," in *Selections from the Writings and Speeches of William Lloyd Garrison* (1852), reprinted (New York: Negro Universities Press, 1968), pp. 238–60.
44 For an exception, see Wylie Sypher, "Hutcheson and the Classical Theory of Slavery," in *Journal of Negro History*, 24 (3), July 1939, pp. 263–80.
45 The source of our digression is Francis Hutcheson's *Illustrations On The Moral Sense*, ed B. Peach (Cambridge: Harvard University Press, 1971).
46 See Francis Hutcheson, *An Inquiry into the Original of Our Ideas of Beauty and Virtue* [reproduced from 1725 edition] (Hildesheim: Georg Olms, 1971), p. 106.
47 Ibid., p. 140.
48 It would take Kant's formal analysis of the "good will" to avoid the conundrums that emerge in explaining how obligation and motivation are inherently connected. For an excellent discussion on this issue and on the philosophically historical context surrounding it, a discussion to which I am heavily indebted for my own digression, see Christine Korsgaard, "Kant's Analysis of Obligation: The Argument of *Foundations I*," in *The Monist*, 72 (3), July 1989, pp. 311–40.
49 "Address to the Anti-Slavery Women of Western New York," (Rochester) *Daily Democrat*, April 4, 1848. Cited in Nancy Hewitt's "The Social Origins of Women's Antislavery Politics in Western New York," in A. Kraut, ed, *Crusaders and Compromisers: Essays on the Relationship of the Antislavery Struggle to the Antebellum Party System* (Westport, Conn: Greenwood Press, 1983), pp. 205–33, especially, pp. 222–3.
50 William Lloyd Garrison, "Letter to the Editor of *The Emancipator*," May

31, 1839, in L. Ruchames, ed, *The Letters of William Lloyd Garrison, Vol. II* (Cambridge: Harvard University Press, 1971), pp. 464–86, especially pp. 473–4.

51 See William Lloyd Garrison, "Letter to Honorable Peleg Sprague" and "The Great Apostate," in his *Selections from the Writings and Speeches*, pp. 148 and 211.

52 Ibid., p. 148. "I am nevertheless bound to commence the work [of abolition], if no others will, and to cooperate with them if they have begun it. Why? Because he [the slave] is my neighbor, though occupying the remotest point of the earth; and I am charged by Him, 'who spake as never man spake,' to love my neighbor as myself."

53 See Frederick Douglass, "Emancipation Is An Individual, A National, and An International Responsibility" in Blassingame I, p. 257.

54 Admittedly Douglass calls for *British* abolitionists to make use of *non-moral/prudential* means to bring about the end of slavery in America. This may be an early signal not of Douglass's rejection of, but of his reservations about, the effectiveness of moral suasion.

55 See Frederick Douglass, "Too Much Religion, Too Little Humanity," in John Blassingame, ed, *The Frederick Douglass Papers Series One, vol. 2: 1847–54* (New Haven: Yale University Press, 1982), pp. 192, 180, and 189 (hereafter cited as Blassingame II).

56 Ibid., p. 193.

57 See Frederick Douglass, "Baptists, Congregationalists, The Free Church, and Slavery," December 23, 1845, in Blassingame I, p. 108.

58 See Burke, *Frederick Douglass: Crusading Orator*, p. 122.

59 See Frederick Douglass, "Love of God, Love of Man, Love of Country," in Blassingame II, p. 105.

60 Making discourse a moral principle for the establishment of a proceduralist and universalist morality is the position of Karl-Otto Apel and Jürgen Habermas. See Karl-Otto Apel, *Diskurs und Verantwortung* (Frankfurt: Suhrkamp Verlag, 1988) and "The Apriori of the Communication Community and the Foundation of Ethics: The Problem of a Rational Foundation of Ethics in the Scientific Age," in *Towards a Transformation of Philosophy*, trans. G. Adey and D. Frisby (London: Routledge, Kegan and Paul, 1980), pp. 225–301; see Jürgen Habermas, "Discourse Ethics: Notes on a Program of Philosophical Justification," in *Moral Consciousness and Communicative Action*, trans. C. Lenhart and S. W. Nicholsen (Cambridge: MIT Press, 1990), pp. 43–115.

61 A representative of this position is Nathan Huggins. See his *Slave and Citizen: The Life of Frederick Douglass* (Boston: Little, Brown and Company, 1980), pp. 59–68.

62 Representatives of this position are Benjamin Quarles and Peter Walker. See Quarles, "Abolition's Different Drummer: Frederick Douglass," in M. Duberman, ed, *The Antislavery Vanguard* (Princeton: Princeton University Press, 1965), p. 126; see Walker, *Moral Choices*, p. 245.

63 Most regard moral suasion₁ and the politics of abolition as antithetical to each other, because they understand the practice of politics to be guided not by morality, but by the *amoral* orientation of prudence, adjustment, and success. This is the gist of the prefatory epigraph from Booker T. Washington. However, it could be argued that what I have called moral suasion₁ has an intimate connection to the practice of politics of abolition. What that politics would have to be is one guided by, if not imbued with, a moral vision. This signifies that the politics of abolition must follow our benevolent moral sense unconditionally and leave the consequences of political action to God. Here the politics of abolition would exemplify unconditional trust in the ultimate victory of good in the world. And it would accept the negative consequences of its actions as either the expressions of the irrationality of the politics of everyone else or a test of the firmness of one's faith or convictions in one's morally guided politics. It could be argued that moral suasion₁, when closely related to some political action, no longer is a form of argumentation, but rather is a jeremiad. A representative of the intimate, not antithetical, relation between what I have called moral suasion₁ and the politics of abolition is Lawrence J. Friedman. See his *Gregarious Saints: Self and Community in American Abolitionism, 1830–1870* (Cambridge: Cambridge University Press, 1982), especially pp. 160–222.

64 See Frederick Douglass, "Change of Opinion Announced," May 23, 1851, in Foner II, pp. 155–6. However, Blassingame claims in an annotation that Douglass first announces this change of thought on the final day (May 9, 1851) of a three-day antislavery convention in Syracuse, New York. Douglass's "Change of Opinion Announced" subsequently appears in various newspapers and antislavery pamphlets throughout the rest of the month. See Blassingame II, pp. 330–1.

65 See Frederick Douglass, "What To The Slave Is The Fourth of July?," in Blassingame II, pp. 359–88.

66 See Frederick Douglass, "We Are In The Midst of a Moral Revolution," in Blassingame II, pp. 479–90. For two other good examples of moral suasion₂, see Frederick Douglass, "Bound Together in a Grand League of Freedom," June 21, 1854, and "The Claims of the Negro Ethnologically Considered," July 12, 1854, both in Blassingame II, pp. 490–7 and 497–525 respectively.

67 Ibid., p. 480.

68 Ibid, p. 481.

69 See Frederick Douglass, "Of Morals and Men," delivered May 8, 1849, in Blassingame II, pp. 170–4.

70 Ibid., p. 172.

71 This, too, runs counter to the position of Douglass-scholars who overemphasize the rhetorical dimension at the expense of the argument in Douglass's work. They would take the two speeches' rhetorical use of the metaphorical reference of "light" and "darkness" to morality and immor-

ality respectively and claim that the speeches are making similar, if not identical, arguments or claims. For an example of this kind of confusion, even in otherwise fine interpretations, see Shelley Fisher Fishkin and Carla L. Peterson, "We Hold These Truths To Be Self-Evident," in E. Sundquist, ed, *Frederick Douglass: New Literary and Historical Essays*, especially p. 195.

72 See Frederick Douglass, "We Are In The Midst of a Moral Revolution," in Blassingame II, pp. 487–8. These are the words of the following American statesmen: John C. Calhoun, Thomas L. Clingaman, George McDuffie, and John Pettit.

73 See Frederick Douglass, "What To The Slave is the Fourth of July?," in Blassingame II, p. 369.

74 See Frederick Douglass, "We Are in the Midst of a Moral Revolution," in Blassingame II, p. 489.

75 Besides political defenders of slavery, there are also "scholarly" defenders. What distinguishes the latter from the former is that the latter *do deny* the validity of the doctrine of natural law and, hence, deny the doctrine is self-evident to reason. Moreover, the "scholarly" apologists appear less likely to engage in the political suppression of antislavery speech and argument, since their aim is to show discursively that the antislavery argument is false. In short, however, their arguments are for the most part inflated techniques of manipulating theories to produce cognitive and moral distortions. Beyond these remarks, I am unable to offer any further digression into the extremely bizarre positions of the "scholarly" apologists Albert Taylor Bledsoe (*Liberty and Slavery: Slavery in the Light of Moral and Political Philosophy* in E. N. Elliott, ed, *Cotton is King*, Augusta: Prichard, Abbott and Loomis, 1860) and George Fitzhugh (*Cannibals All!: Or Slaves Without Masters*, reprinted from 1857 edition, Cambridge: Harvard University Press, 1960).

76 See Frederick Douglass, "Slavery The Live Issue," delivered April 11–13, 1854, in Blassingame II, p. 467.

77 See Frederick Douglass, "What to the Slave is the Fourth of July?," in Blassingame II, p. 369.

78 For an illuminating discussion of this issue, see Charles W. Mills's essay, "Whose Fourth of July?: Frederick Douglass and Original Intent" in this volume.

79 "I now hold, as I have ever done, that the *original intent and meaning* of the Constitution (the one given to it by the men who framed it, those who adopted it, and the one given to it by the Supreme Court of the United States) makes it a *pro-slavery instrument* such an one I cannot bring myself to vote under, or swear to support." See Frederick Douglass, "The Constitution and Slavery," in Foner I, p. 353.

80 "It should . . . be borne in mind that the intentions of those who framed the Constitution, be they good or bad, for slavery or against slavery, are to be respected so far, and so far only, as we find those intentions plainly

stated in the Constitution. It would be the wildest of absurdities, and lead to endless confusions and mischiefs, if, instead of looking to the written paper itself, for its meaning, it were attempted to make us search it out, in the secret motives, and dishonest intentions, of some of the men who took part in writing it . . . [W]here would be the advantage of a written Constitution, if, instead of seeking its meaning in its words, we had to seek them in the secret intentions of individuals who may have had something to do with writing the paper? What will the people of America a hundred years hence care about the intentions of the scriveners who wrote the Constitution? These men are already gone from us, and in the course of nature were expected to go from us. They were for a generation, but the Constitution is for the ages." See Frederick Douglass, "The Constitution of the United States: Is it Pro-Slavery or Anti-Slavery?," delivered in Glasgow on March 26, 1860, in Foner II, p. 469. Here we see Douglass appearing to shift from originalism exclusively to a theory of interpretation emphasizing the semantic content of the document, but also inclusive of the standpoint and background of future interpreters. We would only be a stone's throw away from a theory that includes with these the standpoint and background of the Framers. How this kind of interpretive theory would influence moral suasion$_2$ can only be the subject of another paper.

81 See note 63.
82 See note 1, note 61, and note 62.
83 Quoted in Foner II, p. 51.
84 See Frederick Douglass, "We Are In The Midst of a Moral Revolution," in Blassingame II, p. 489.
85 We already have argued above that moral suasion$_1$ is too ineffective.
86 See Frederick Douglass, "The Ballot and The Bullet," in Foner II, p. 458. Although a supporter for reading Douglass as a non-moral political abolitionist and as a critic of moral suasion would take this speech as proof positive for her position, it should be noted that the critique of moral suasion found here is extended exclusively toward the Garrisonians and, hence, only toward moral suasion$_1$, not moral suasion$_2$.
87 Ibid., p. 458.
88 Ibid., pp. 457–8.
89 I will not be discussing what is criterial for resistance generally. Nor will I be discussing a litany of the activities in which enslaved Africans were engaged that have become regarded as acts of resistance. For an excellent discussion of the former, see Howard McGary's "Resistance and Slavery" in his and Bill Lawson's *Between Slavery and Freedom: Philosophy and American Slavery* (Bloomington: Indiana University Press, 1992), pp. 35–54. For a fine discussion of the latter, see Raymond A. Bauer's and Alice H. Bauer's "Day to Day Resistance to Slavery," in *Journal of Negro History*, 27 (4), 1942, pp. 388–419.
90 See Frederick Douglass, "The Do-Nothing Policy," in Foner II, pp. 403–5, [my emphasis]. This claim is consistent with the following

delivered in August 1857: "The sin – the crime – the curse of slavery were all demonstrated in the light of reason, religion, and morality, and by a startling array of facts." See Frederick Douglass, "West India Emancipation," in Foner II, p. 428.

91 See Frederick Douglass, "Peaceful Annihilation of Slavery is Hopeless," in Foner II, p. 406. This claim is consistent with the following delivered in May 1857: "The world is full of violence and fraud, and it would be strange if the slave, the constant victim of both fraud and violence, should escape the contagion. He, too, may learn to fight the devil with fire, and for one, I am in no frame of mind to pray that this may be long deferred." See Frederick Douglass, "The Dred Scott Decision," in Foner II, p. 413 [my emphasis].

92 I have in mind, for example, Herbert Aptheker, *American Negro Slave Revolts* (New York: International Publishers, 1963); Allison Davis, *Leadership, Love, and Aggression* (New York: Harcourt Brace Jovanovich, 1983); Philip Foner, *Frederick Douglass* (New York: Citadel, 1969), L. F. Goldstein, "Violence As An Instrument of Social Change: The Views of Frederick Douglass (1817–1895)," in *Journal of Negro History*, 61, 1976; Richard Yarborough, "Race, Violence, and Manhood: The Masculine Ideal in Frederick Douglass' *The Heroic Slave*," in Sundquist, ed, *Frederick Douglass: New Literary and Historical Essays*.

93 I have in mind, for example, Frederic May Holland, *Frederick Douglass: The Colored Orator* (New York: Funk and Wagnalls, 1891); Benjamin Quarles, "Frederick Douglass: Bridge-Builder in Human Relations," in *Negro History Bulletin*, 29, (February 1966). It is not surprising that those who read Douglass as giving priority to moral suasion over violent resistance also take seriously into account the thoughts, reflections, and activities of the *postbellum* Douglass.

94 See *My Bondage and My Freedom*, p. 191, [my addition]. There are three other remarks reflecting this comparison. (1) "[The slaveholder] never lisps a syllable in commendation of the fathers of this republic, nor denounces any attempted oppression of himself, without inviting the knife to his own throat, and asserting the rights of rebellion for his own slaves." Ibid., pp. 269–70. (2) "A kidnapper [federally authorized marshal] has been shot dead, while attempting to execute the fugitive slave bill in Boston. The streets of Boston in sight of Bunker Hill Monument have been stained with the warm blood of a man in the act of perpetrating the most atrocious robbery which one man can possible commit upon another – even the wresting from him his very person and natural powers." From Douglass's, "Is It Right and Wise To Kill A Kidnapper?," in Foner II, p. 284, [my addition]. (3) "You call me a *black murderer*. I am not a murderer. God is my witness that LIBERTY, not malice, is the motive for this night's work. I have done no to those dead men yonder, than they would have done to me in like circumstances. We have struck for our freedom, and if a true man's heart be in you, you will honor us for the

deed. We have done that which you applaud your [white patriotic] fathers for doing, and if we are murderers, *so were they*." From the fictionalized voice of Maddison Washington in Douglass's novella, *The Heroic Slave*, in *The Oxford Frederick Douglass Reader*, edited by William L. Andrews (New York: Oxford University Press, 1996), p. 161, [my addition].

95 Eric J. Sundquist, *To Wake The Nations: Race in The Making of American Literature* (Cambridge: Harvard University Press, 1993), pp. 112–34.

96 This is why the San Domingo slave revolution led by Toussaint L'Ouverture, which is the only successful slave insurrection in the hemispheric Americas, could never be compared to the American Revolution. For a brilliant discussion of the San Domingo revolution, C. L. R. James's *Black Jacobins: Toussaint L'Ouverture and the San Domingo Revolution* (New York: Vintage Books, 1963) is still the representative text.

97 Yet both federal and state governments took the impendence of slave revolts very seriously as exemplified in Article I, Section 8 of the original Constitution of the United States giving state militias the right to quash slave insurrections.

98 See Sundquist, *To Wake the Nations*, p. 132.

99 See the fine text of Bernard R. Boxill, *Blacks and Social Justice* (Totowa: Rowman & Allanheld, 1984), pp. 186–204. On the matter of self-respect, I have been helped enormously by the following articles. Thomas Hill, "Servility and Self-Respect," in *The Monist*, 57, January 1973 and "Self-Respect Reconsidered," in O. H. Green, ed, *Respect for Persons* (New Orleans: Tulane University, 1982); Lawrence Thomas, "Self-Respect: Theory and Practice," in L. Harris, ed, *Philosophy Born of Struggle* (Dubuque: Kendall/Hunt, 1982); and most especially Michelle Moody-Adams, "Race, Class, and the Social Construction of Self-Respect," in J. P. Pittman, ed, *African-American Perspectives and Philosophical Traditions* (New York: Routledge, 1997).

100 It is usually a matter of course to invoke the name of Hegel and the well-known section in his *Phenomenology of Spirit* entitled "Independence and Dependence of Self-Consciousness: Lordship and Bondage," when discussing the notion of "struggle for recognition" and anchoring Douglass's fight with Covey or general issues about slavery to it. Douglass-scholars employ it constantly as the model for explaining the Covey incident or as the basis for enlarging the significance of Douglass's narration of the Covey incident to criticize Hegel's discussion of the relation between the lord and the bondsman. Paul Gilroy and Cynthia Willett are two contemporary scholars who take this route in their respective studies of Douglass. But they can take this interpretive path only if they presuppose that the 1806 *Phenomenology* is a social theory or consonant with broad existential matters. But if one interprets the notion of "struggle for recognition" in Hegel's *Phenomenology* as informed by the task of the book, viz., delineating and illustrating the problem of "Absolute Knowledge," then that notion can neither serve as a model for explaining the Covey fight nor serve as the basis

by which Douglass can criticize the alleged weakness of Hegel's account of the lord and the bondsman. I have critically addressed this matter in my "Comments on Cynthia Willet's *Hegel On Slavery And The African American Experience*," unpublished mss. presented in May 1994 at Central Division Meeting of the APA. See Cynthia Willet, *Maternal Ethics and Other Slave Moralities* (New York: Routledge, 1995), pp. 100–56; see Paul Gilroy, *The Black Atlantic*, pp. 46–71. For those who view general issues about slavery along the lines of "struggle for recognition" as presented in the "Lordship and Bondage" section of the *Phenomenology*, see David Brion Davis, *The Problem of Slavery in the Age of Revolution, 1770–1823* (Ithaca: Cornell University Press, 1975) and Orlando Patterson, *Slavery and Social Death* (Cambridge: Harvard University Press, 1982). For those, like myself, who are critical of treating the notion of "struggle for recognition" in the *Phenomenology* as part of a social-theoretical or existential reading, see Axel Honneth, *The Struggle for Recognition: The Moral Grammar of Social Conflicts*, trans. by J. Anderson (Cambridge: MIT Press, 1995), pp. 40–63; and Robert B. Pippin, *Hegel's Idealism: The Satisfactions of Self-Consciousness* (New York: Cambridge University Press, 1989), pp. 155–6. I am indebted to some of the insights raised in Honneth's fine book.

101 I draw my insights from Barbara Herman's marvelous piece, "Murder and Mayhem," in her *The Practice of Moral Judgement* (Cambridge: Harvard University Press, 1993), pp. 113–31.
102 See *My Bondage and My Freedom*, pp. 242 and 246–8.
103 See, for example, Douglass's discussion of the enslaved Nelly and her overseer Mr Sevier in *My Bondage and My Freedom*, pp. 94–5.
104 See Michele Moody-Adams, "Race, Class, and the Social Construction of Self-Respect," p. 256.
105 See Frederick Douglass, "Is It Right and Wise To Kill a Kidnapper?," in Foner II, p. 287.
106 Ibid., p. 287.
107 See Fredrick Douglass, "West India Emancipation," in Foner II, p. 437.
108 Ibid., p. 437 [my emphasis].
109 Ibid., pp. 434–6 [my emphasis].
110 See Kant, "An Answer to the Question: What is Enlightenment?," p. 59.
111 See Frederick Douglass, "West India Emancipation," in Foner II, p. 437.
112 See Bernard R. Boxill, "Fear and Shame as Forms of Moral Suasion in the Thought of Frederick Douglass," pp. 732–4.
113 See Robert S. Levine, *Martin Delany, Frederick Douglass and The Politics of Representative Identity* (Chapel Hill: The University of North Carolina Press, 1997), pp. 99–143.
114 I offer my utmost appreciation to Jorge Garcia, J. Everett Green, Howard McGary, Colin Palmer, Alfred Prettyman, and Steven Ross for their helpful and detailed critical comments on all parts of this essay. If I have not addressed specific remarks of theirs, I have certainly taken them to heart to prepare myself for the criticisms that will come down the road.

Part V

Incarcerating and Lynching Black Bodies

11
Frederick Douglass on the Myth of the Black Rapist

Tommy L. Lott

At a news conference following the O. J. Simpson trial, prosecution attorney Chris Darden predicted that affirmative action would suffer because of the "not guilty" verdict of the mostly black jury. Prior to the verdict, on CNN's Capitol Gang, a similar assessment had been voiced by a group of white male news commentators, all of whom agreed that Democrats would be hurt more than Republicans by a "not guilty" verdict. Why this expectation (expressed through mass media) that the crime of an individual black man will have such deleterious political consequences for African Americans as a group? Although revenge by white voters for the "not guilty" verdict is ostensibly the reason for this white backlash, the ever-present social taboo regarding interracial sexual relations cannot be ruled out as a factor.[1] We need only to recall George Bush's effective use of the image of convicted rapist Willie Horton to win his bid for president to see that the idea that all African Americans must pay a political price for the offense of a single black rapist continues to structure race relations in America.

Commentators have offered various interpretations of the social and political function of the historical practice of lynching black men for alleged sexual offenses against white women, yet they have not sufficiently considered the social and political significance of the figure of the black rapist in relation to the time-honored cultural norm proscribing interracial sexual contact between black men and white women.[2] One means of discerning the social and political significance of this proscription is by considering the manner in which the question of social equality for African Americans has been influenced by a racist myth.[3] Following the suggestion of several commentators I will be particularly interested in determining whether there is an economic basis for this proscription.

The idea that African Americans, as a group, are not entitled to full citizenship because of white fear that black men will ravish white women was called into question by Frederick Douglass. In 1894, a year before his death, he published his lecture on lynching as a pamphlet.[4] He argued that the basic aim of lynching was disfranchisement and attempted to expose the political motive underlying this practice by deconstructing the claim made by apologists that lynchings were necessary because *white women in the south were menaced by black rapists.* I shall refer to the view of black people on which the apologists' claim is grounded as the myth of the black rapist. According to this view, black men are prone to rape because black people *as a racial group* are bestial.[5]

Even with his added rhetorical flourish, Douglass's attempt to counter this claim, and the underlying myth that supplied its force, was deeply indebted to the view presented by Ida B. Wells-Barnett in 1892. 1 want to examine Douglass's account of the social and political function of the rape accusation to show its connection with Wells-Barnett's proposal to understand lynching in terms of the political economy of patriarchy and racism. I highlight certain elements of a very rudimentary political economic analysis that are present in their writings. Douglass misconstrued the origin and nature of the myth of the black rapist. Perhaps this was due to his tendency to conflate notions of race and class in his argument against lynching. Nevertheless, I indicate how this conflation reveals an important insight, available to Douglass, regarding the viability of an economic account of racism and patriarchy. The insight I attribute to Douglass, along with the political economic view suggested by Wells-Barnett, still applies to race and gender relations in America, if not more so. In highly publicized cases involving the alleged sexual violation of a white woman by a black male suspect there is a noticeable inclination by various representatives of the criminal justice system to circumvent due process.[6] This legal practice is historically tied to racially motivated lynchings. Often rationalized by moral outrage, legal lynchings continue to be justified by a tacit appeal to a racial myth about black people – a myth Wells-Barnett confronted and Douglass evaded.[7]

When Douglass published "Lessons of the Hour" as a pamphlet in 1894, he had already revised several earlier versions.[8] His lectures on this subject incorporated some of the white southern criticisms of his article "Lynch Law in the South," which had appeared in the *North American Review* in July 1892. Most of his revisions, however, were influenced by Wells-Barnett, including many of his embellishments of her basic strategy of presenting the political motivations of the white southern apologists. He aimed to expose the rape accusation as a recent "invention."[9] The lynching of black men accused of sexually assaulting white women had become such a common practice by 1892 that it was often referred to simply as the "Negro problem." When addressing this subject Douglass was well aware of the widespread acceptance of the white southerner's justification of lynching. The majority of his discussion was a critical examination of their arguments that aimed to dispel the myth southerners had used to win the support of progressive whites in the north. Although his counterarguments were forcefully delivered, he showed signs of awareness that, despite his sound reasoning, the myth that ultimately supplied the justification of lynching continued to operate subconsciously in the minds of many white Americans.

In his earlier writings on lynching Douglass placed a greater emphasis on the economic function of racial antagonism. He pointed out in "Lynch Law" that "the horror now excited is not for the crime itself," but rather is due to racial prejudice.[10] Nevertheless, he speaks of this "racial prejudice" in terms of an appeal "to the well-known hatred of one class towards another." These remarks set up two views of the cause of lynching. The analogy he drew between the persecution of Jews in Russia and Chinese Americans in California and the lynching of African Americans suggests an analysis based on class. But given that he also wanted to say that "race and color," and not the crime itself, is what arouses popular wrath, it is not clear how the class analysis he proposed can be sustained. He appealed to what he considered to be a sociological law to offer an explanation of the lynching of black people in the South – an explanation that combined overlapping notions of race and class. With explicit reference to the Memphis case that initiated Wells-Barnett's career as an antilynching activist, he stated: "The negro meets no resistance when on a downward course. It is only when he rises in wealth, intelligence, and manly character that he brings upon himself the heavy hand of persecution."[11] The point of Douglass's analogy between African Americans and other ethnic groups was to indicate an economic basis for the racial antagonism that frequently resulted in lynching.

The legacy of slavery was a central feature of many of the arguments Douglass marshaled to refute the apologists for lynching. He traced the continuity of the white southerner's lynching of black people with their treatment of slaves, noting that only a concern with loss of property had prevented the wholesale killing of slaves. In this regard emancipation had been an important factor contributing to an increase in lynching during and after reconstruction. A similar theme related to slavery and the Civil War is reviewed in his introduction to Wells-Barnett's pamphlet, *The Reason Why*.[12] After insisting that lynching, as a ritualized social practice, was logically consistent with the white southerner's former treatment of slaves, he again invoked, as a sociological law, the idea of the lowly class suffering the resentment of society for aspiring to rise. He wanted to present an account of lynching "on the same principle by which resistance to the course of a ship is created and increased in proportion to her speed" and cited class, not race, as the crucial factor.[13] "The Negro is just now under the operation of this law of society. If he were white as the driven snow, and had been enslaved as we had been, he would have to submit to this same law in his progress upward."[14] Here Douglass seems to view lynching as "simply an incident of a transitional condition" due to "the depravity, of human nature."[15] By deracinating slavery and employing it as a paradigm of economic exploitation, he wanted to account for lynching, even as a racist practice directed toward black people, in terms of political economy.

In a manner similar to the famous address Booker T. Washington would give a year later in Atlanta, Douglass presented the case for understanding the so-called Negro problem as a national problem and appealed to the self-interest of the nation as a whole to solve it. Washington, however, would have been reluctant to openly agree with Douglass's assertion that the reference to lynching as a "Negro problem" was a misnomer.[16] Washington's solution to lynching was essentially to accommodate the *de facto* repeal of the Fifteenth Amendment and to support miscegenation legislation. By contrast, Douglass criticized the racial views held by white southerners and appealed to whites in the north not to trust the southerner's claims regarding black people. As part of the solution to lynching, he insisted upon the legal enforcement of the human rights guaranteed by the constitution, especially the hard-fought right to vote.

For Douglass, the central issue was the accused black rapist's constitutional right to a fair trial. He highlighted the need of the southern mob to feed its vengeance by shooting, stabbing, and burning victims after they were already dead. "[W]hat is the special charge by which this ferocity is justified, and by which mob law is excused and defended even by good men North and South?"[17] Douglass's reference here to "the special charge" is important to consider in connection with the black rapist myth. He was concerned about the fact that a mere charge could justify such ferocious acts of vengeance. Showing no awareness of white mob reaction to a black man accused of raping a white woman as a ritualized cultural practice influenced by racial mythology he attempted to push through his constitutional rights argument for due process.[18]

Douglass's main line of attack in his defense of the reputation of black people against the "special" charge was to demonstrate, by counterargument, that the motive behind it was "nothing less than the Negro's entire disenfranchisement as an American citizen."[19] After noting the fact that this charge was not brought up in any prior period he suggested two possible reasons: first, there was no foundation for such a charge and, secondly, it was not necessary under slavery to justify lawless violence against black people. During slavery and the Civil War the old charges of insurrection, or insolence, were considered sufficient, but in the present period the new charge of assaulting white women "has now swallowed up all the other ones."[20] The aim of the new charge was "to blast and ruin the negro's character as a man and a citizen."[21]

Douglass believed that low esteem for the moral character of black people was a crucial factor inhibiting the social elevation of African Americans.[22] For this reason he proposed to meet the charge in the form in which it was presented. "I know that I cannot prove a negative; there is one thing that I can and will do. I will call in question the affirmative. I can and will show that there are sound reasons for doubting and denying this horrible charge of rape as the special and peculiar crime of the coloured people of the South."[23] Rather than deal with the "special and peculiar" nature of the rape charge, he instead interpreted the question of "negro character" and "manhood" more broadly – not once mentioning anything sexual.[24] His refutation, although well argued and quite logical, nonetheless was unconvincing precisely because he did not deal with the main thrust of the charge. He simply ignored a widely shared concern regarding interracial sexual relations and, consequently, failed to appreciate that his exposing the political objectives of the white southerner was consistent with the white southerner's claim that the charge was well grounded.

A rejoinder to this effect by a white southerner was cited by Wells-Barnett. In defense of lynching, he presented a quite different account of Douglass's claim regarding the relative absence of the rape charge under slavery and during the Civil War:

> The commission of this crime grows more frequent every year. The generation of Negroes which have grown up since the war have lost in large measure the traditional and wholesome awe of the white race which kept the Negroes in subjection, even when their masters were in the army, and their families left unprotected except by the slaves themselves. There is no longer a restraint upon the brute passion of the Negro ... The Negro as a political factor can be controlled. But neither laws nor lynchings can subdue his lusts.

Sooner or later it will force a crisis. We do not know in what form it will come.[25]

The point Douglass sought to establish regarding the white southerner's political motives, namely, his desire to disfranchise African Americans, is well represented by these remarks. But they also contain elements of the black rapist myth that Douglass failed to address adequately. Douglass cited the plantation rape of slave women by white masters to indicate that the white southerner's moral outrage was not a reaction to the crime of rape, but to the reversal of racial roles. As a counterargument this criticism was very lame, for it was only a further indication that Douglass failed to fully appreciate the power of the antiblack racism conveyed by the myth. He displayed a limited comprehension of the reason why sexual assaults by white men on black women were not viewed as rape by white southerners. He seemed completely unaware that the racist discourse that fostered the black rapist myth also subsumed black women, as members of the bestial race, under a twin myth as "sexual savages" incapable of being raped.[26]

One of the strongest objections to Douglass's argument along these lines came from a black southerner. Reverend E. K. Love, a Baptist pastor in Savannah, Georgia, delivered an impassioned sermon titled "Lynch-Law and Raping" that in effect condoned lynching.[27] He even proposed a modification of the criminal justice system to facilitate this. In what could have been a blueprint for the "justice" sought in the Central Park rape trial, Reverend Love asserted:

> The ravishers can be punished far more effectually by law and be killed just as dead by an officer of the law as by 500 masked outlaws. If shooting and hanging are not bad enough, then let the terrible penalty of Duillius be added to our statue books, that whosoever commits rape, "shall be burned alive" or any other barbarous or inhuman death. Only let our law say so. If there is a fear that the courts may be too slow in bringing the criminals to justice, let the law remedy that.[28]

The "law and order" Reverend Love contends for here is a far cry from that which Douglass wanted to uphold. Although Douglass also was not entirely opposed to lynching under special circumstances where there is no law enforcement, he argued that, given the white southerner's motives, there is sufficient reason to be skeptical of this practice in cases where black men are accused of raping white women.[29]

In what appears to be an endorsement of lynching, Reverend Love staked out a position that resonated more with the views of the white southerners Douglass had contested. Unlike Douglass, he recognized a commendable social and political purpose of lynching:

> There is such a healthy sentiment among the white people, that if the Negroes cross the line they must do so by force and this is rape, and for this they must die and this we must approve. It would be the same with white men forcing themselves on our side if we had the sentiment worked up among our women that it is death to cross the line. Be it said to our shame, that some of our girls and women can engage in this business and can even marry our best and hardest working young men. This is sometimes done even after they have become mothers. As long as this is the case, we cannot work up a healthy sentiment among us along this line. If for this state of things, the vile class of Negroes mean to get even with whites by raping their women, they should and must die, every guilty man of them. Not in one case out of a thousand is a colored woman raped by a white man and hence the raping of white women cannot be in retaliation.[30]

Reverend Love's refusal to admit that black women were often raped by white men is an indication that, like his white southern counterpart, he was more concerned with preventing consensual interracial sexual relations than with rape as such.[31] He aimed to invalidate the revenge motive often attributed to black men accused of raping white women by guilt-ridden white southerners.[32] His endorsement of lynching, as well as his acceptance of certain aspects of the black rapist myth, is accompanied by a strong commitment to the social norm prohibiting interracial sexual relations. His argument for law and order parallels the argument Douglass presented, but, contrary to Douglass, he shared the white southerner's fear of miscegenation as a threat to the social order. Rather than advocate the right of an accused black rapist to a fair trial, the main point of his sermon was to stipulate that the lynching in such cases be carried out legally.[33]

Wells-Barnett on Lynching and Miscegenation Laws

Wells-Barnett understood the need, to which Douglass referred in his lecture, to present a black perspective to correct the views of whites, both in the north and in the south, who had spoken on the topic. Having brought to Douglass's attention the political consequences of black leaders not speaking out against lynching, she persuaded him that a black voice was required to bring out the whole truth. The fact that Douglass was prompted by Wells-Barnett to lecture on the subject of lynching has been taken by some commentators as grounds for a more skeptical interpretation of his view. William McFeely takes Douglass to task for not including a discussion of the "scourge" of lynching in the last version of his autobiography.[34] With regard to Douglass's article for the *North American Review* McFeely claims that Douglass "did not fully disavow the widely accepted assumption that the victims of the horrible executions were to blame for their fate, that black men were indeed a sexual threat to Southern white women." He cites Wells-Barnett's remarks that Douglass "had begun to believe it true that there was increased lasciviousness on the part of Negroes."[35] Wells-Barnett's claim, however, is not warranted by anything Douglass states in his writings on this subject.[36] Indeed, the view McFeely wants to attribute to Douglass flies in the face of Douglass's attempt to show, in the light of the facts adduced by Wells-Barnett, that the black rapist myth was a politically motivated "invention."

When Douglass lectured on the subject of lynching he always made a point of distinguishing between his denial of the myth and a blanket denial of the offense. In "Lessons of the Hour," for instance, he claimed, "I do not pretend that Negroes are saints and angels. I do not deny that they are capable of committing the crime imputed to them, but I utterly deny that they are any more addicted to the commission of that crime than is true of any other variety of the human family."[37] According to Douglass, the charge falsely attributes to black men an "addiction" to ravish white women – a term that suggests an uncontrollable desire. It is worth noting that, as part of his denial of this charge, he invokes the membership of black people in the "human family." As I have already noted, the myth's attribution of a bestial nature to black men entails a parallel view of black women. Douglass recognized that the most important aspect of the sexual charge against black men was the social implication it carried for the race as a whole, yet it seems he did not recognize that both the lynching of black men, as well as the rape of black women, were rationalized and justified on the ground that the black race is not fully human.[38]

There is an important reason why Douglass's failure to address this implication adequately should not be taken as his capitulation to the myth. He was sharply focused on showing the political motives behind the white southerners' "invention" of the rape accusation without displaying any awareness of the issue of paramount concern to them, namely, the prevention of miscegenation. But the fear of miscegenation, shared by whites in the north as well as in the south, is what allowed the myth to operate so effectively as a justification in lynching cases, nearly two thirds of which involved no accusation of rape. Although I will suggest the opposite, Douglass's interracial marriage to Helen Pitts might be thought to have inhibited him from raising this issue.[39] There is sufficient reason to think that, even if this were true, his shortcomings in this regard need not be construed as due to his acceptance of the black rapist myth.

Support for the skeptical interpretation of Douglass nevertheless can be found in a letter he wrote to Wells-Barnett thanking her for her paper on lynching.[40] Douglass stated "There has been no word equal to it in convincing power. I have spoken, but my word is feeble in comparison." He seems to admit here that his attempt to refute the apologists for lynching had not been very effective. A similar tone of skepticism can be detected in some of his remarks in "Lessons of the Hour." For example, with regard to the charge against black people, he asserted "Now it is in this form that you and I, and all of us, are required to meet it and refute it, *if that can be done.*"[41] The reason he gave for thinking his attempt to counter the arguments of the supporters of lynching was "feeble" by comparison with Wells-Barnett's was that she spoke from a knowledge of the facts regarding lynching. But there were other reasons. Chief among them was the fact that Douglass could not speak as forcefully as Wells-Barnett on the subject of lynching because his interracial marriage was viewed by both blacks and whites as a violation of the social taboo that the practice of lynching aimed to enforce.[42]

When compared with Douglass's advocacy of law and order as a solution to lynching, some of the remedies proposed by Wells-Barnett rendered his view "feeble" in another important sense. His strong commitment to the enforcement of constitutional law made him reluctant to advocate violence, although he suggested that the mob rule of lynch law would eventually provoke retaliation.[43] He spoke of vengeance and anarchy as natural outcomes of lynching, but he never went as far as Wells-Barnett to advocate the use of armed self-defense against lynching. Conversely, on grounds of human rights and self-respect, Wells-Barnett presented a strong case for the use of violence by African Americans as a countermeasure:

> [T]he only case where the proposed lynching did not occur, was where men armed themselves in Jacksonville, Fla. and Paducah, Ky., and prevented it . . . The lesson this teaches and which every Afro-American should ponder well, is that a Winchester rifle should

have a place of honor in every black home, and it should be used for that protection which the law refuses to give. When the white man knows he runs as great a risk of biting the dust every time his Afro-American victim does, he will have greater respect for Afro-American life.[44]

The importance of armed self-defense was again championed by Wells-Barnett in her report of the killing of Robert Charles by a New Orleans mob.[45] Charles had become the target of an intense manhunt for killing a policeman in self-defense. Rather than allow himself to be captured and lynched Charles decided to fight to his death. Relying on details provided by several white New Orleans newspapers, Wells-Barnett tells this story with a deep sense of pride in the fact that Charles not only fought back, but also earned the respect of the white press for his excellent marksmanship. She was especially keen on reporting numerous acts of cowardice by the white men who pursued Charles.[46]

By comparison with Wells-Barnett, who always spoke with facts gleaned from white newspapers, Douglass only stated his position on armed resistance to lynching hypothetically. In a very important passage that criticizes the mortgage system in the south as a new form of slavery Douglass, somewhat facetiously, painted a pacifistic image of African Americans:

> Had he been a turbulent anarchist he might indeed have been a troublesome problem, but he is not. To his reproach, it is sometimes said that other people in the world would have invented some violent way in which to resent their wrongs. If this problem depended upon the character and conduct of the Negro there would be no problem to solve; there would be no menace to the peace and good order of Southern Society. He makes no unlawful fight between labor and capital. That problem, which often makes the American people thoughtful, is not of his bringing, though he may some day be compelled to talk of this tremendous problem in common with other laborers.[47]

Notice that Douglass's reference to an "unlawful fight between labor and capital" was in the context of a discussion of the so-called Negro problem. He of course wanted to establish that the real problem was not the moral character of the Negro, but the reconstitution of slavery in a new form. Lynching was a political counterpart to the economic exploitation of black labor in the south.[48] Sometimes he spoke of anarchy in connection with retaliation by African Americans for lynching, but he seems to have considered the dispute between labor and capital, if left unresolved, as having an even greater potential to produce this outcome.

In certain respects Douglass's remarks regarding economic matters were also feeble by comparison with Wells-Barnett's. His concern regarding the exploitation of black labor in the south was reformulated by Wells-Barnett as a remedy to lynching:

> To Northern capital and Afro-American labor the South owes its rehabilitation. If labor is withdrawn capital will not remain. The Afro-American is thus the backbone of the South. A thorough knowledge and judicious exercise of this power in lynching localities could many times effect a bloodless revolution. The white man's dollar is his god, and to stop this will be to stop outrages in many localities.[49]

What Douglass saw as the real cause of "the Southern trouble," namely, a host of economic issues pertaining to labor and capital, Wells-Barnett saw as a potential solution and advocated using as a mode of resistance.

For Douglass, the root cause of the so-called Negro problem was really economic and not social. Wells-Barnett's thorough investigation of reports on lynching had convinced him that lynching was a form of economic scapegoating.[50] Averring to Lincoln's blaming slavery for the Civil War as a cause of earlier riots in which large numbers of African Americans were killed, he maintained that once again African Americans were being blamed because of the present economic crisis facing the south. He compared the practice of calling this economic crisis a "Negro" or "race" problem with the former practice of blaming slaves. "In old slave times, when a little white child lost his temper, he was given a little whip and told to go and whip 'Jim' or 'Sal' and he thus regained his temper. The same is true to-day on a large scale." The point Douglass sought to illustrate with this example was that "He (the black man) has as little to do with the cause of the Southern trouble as he has with its cure."[51] The black rapist myth, according to Douglass, was invented after emancipation as a means of scapegoating African Americans for all of the south's troubles. It was created specifically to justify withholding citizenship from African Americans by representing black men as "moral monsters."

One rather puzzling aspect of Douglass's account of the origin of the black rapist myth is his convenient neglect of the history of a racist discourse used to justify colonial conquest and slavery. His contention that the *charge* did not exist prior to its post-Civil War invocation by white southerners implies, wrongly, that the myth was merely a creation by white southerners. He was right to the extent that the charge *per se* was a recent normative construction not required before emancipation. The white southerner's use of the legalistic lexicon of crime and punishment to legitimate lynching, however, was an expression of a long-standing racist ideology. In Western literature the idea of a dark villain threatening a white goddess can be traced to Greek mythology regarding the conquest of fair Persephone by Hades.[52] Similarly, in the modern era we can see the emergence of this figure in Shakespeare's plays *Titus Andronicus, Othello,* and *The Tempest.* And, as Douglass well knew, long before the end of the nineteenth century the idea that black people were more closely related to the lower primates had gained scientific support.[53] As I shall indicate shortly, this quite important lapse is consistent with Douglass's evasive treatment of miscegenation as an issue in his debate with the apologist for lynching.

Wells-Barnett directly addressed the white southerner's worry about miscegenation as the source of the black rapist myth. Unlike Douglass, she wanted to show that "The Afro-American is not a bestial race" by exposing the political motives of the supporters of lynching.[54] Douglass related the question of the African-American's moral character to earlier struggles, under slavery, to gain the right to such matters as baptism, marriage, and education. Both he and Wells-Barnett understood the debate about lynching to raise the question of justice in a manner that *presupposed* black people were not entitled to it. As in the case of animals who attack humans, lynch law applies to people who are considered beyond the pale of human sympathy.

In addition to identifying the white southerner's political motive of disfranchisement, Wells-Barnett went a step further than Douglass and identified a social function of the black rapist myth. She maintained that the lynching of black men accused of raping white women also functioned as a means of enforcing miscegenation laws that prohibited interracial sexual contact:

> The miscegenation laws of the South only operate against the legitimate union of the races; they leave the white man free to seduce all the colored girls he can, but it is death to the colored man who yields to the force and advances of a similar attraction in white women. White men lynch the offending Afro-American, not because he is a despoiler of virtue, but because he succumbs to the smiles of white women.[55]

If, as Wells-Barnett maintains here, one purpose of lynching was to prevent miscegenation, then Douglass's voice as spokesperson for the race was indeed compromised by his interracial marriage. Unbridled with the innuendo of social transgression that surrounded Douglass's interracial marriage, Wells-Barnett was free to attack the white southerner's view of lynching as a legitimate deterrent to consensual sexual relations between black men and white women. She endeavored to expose the black rapist myth by showing, with empirical evidence, that rape accusations were employed to enforce miscegenation laws that white women had violated. Citing the details of case after case of southern white women who had consensual sexual relations with black men, she argued that miscegenation laws were designed to enforce a social taboo that restricts the *desires* of white women. Needless to say, this claim infuriated both southern white men (who publicly threatened to lynch her), as well as her white women detractors in the north.[56]

The Politics of Rape and the Miranda Trap

Some commentators have interpreted Wells-Barnett's focus on revealing the truth about the willingness of white women to enter into consensual sexual relations with black men as counterfeminist. Alice Walker and Valerie Smith understood her to be defending the black male rapist at the expense of the white female victim, because of her emphasis on documenting admissions by white women that they were involved in consensual relationships with black men lynched for rape.[57] Smith questions Wells-Barnett's reference to the "willing victims" of an alleged black rapist. She points out that this expression is the opposite of an implied "unwilling victim." Taking this a step further, Walker understood Wells-Barnett to advocate silence in the latter case. This interpretation of Wells-Barnett seems to ignore her remarks regarding the guilty black rapist.[58] In the preface to *Southern Horrors* she stated very clearly that "This statement is not a shield for the despoiler of virtue, nor altogether a defense for the poor blind Afro-American Sampsons who suffer themselves to be betrayed by white Delilahs."[59] Wells-Barnett saw a clear difference between "willing" (white Delilahs) and "unwilling" victims. The point she insisted upon was that white southerners pretended to see no difference between them. Since miscegenation was the issue – not rape, she considered the white lynch mob's failure to respect this distinction to be an important factor that must be addressed by a consistent social policy.[60] Walker and Smith mistake Wells-Barnett's demand for justice for an accused black rapist with a commitment to remain silent when he is guilty.

Smith also seems worried that Wells-Barnett's apparent lack of concern for the "unwilling" white women victims indicates an unacceptable prioritizing of race over gender. Wells-Barnett's stated aim was to prove that black people are not a bestial race – an objective that included a concern with the reputation of black women as mythical whores incapable of being raped.[61] Smith and Walker overlook Wells-Barnett's black feminist challenge to white feminists, many of whom she openly criticized for granting race greater priority over gender. She urged white women to speak out when black women were raped by white men, as well as when black men were falsely accused of rape, because the word of a white woman carried greater weight in a court of law. Motivated by the general lack of response from white women, she acted in the interest of black women, which in this case intersected with the interests of African Americans as a group.[62]

The question of whether to give race priority over gender was also faced by Douglass in his clash with white feminists over their stance against the ratification of the Fifteenth Amendment.[63] Some of the feminists in the Equal Rights Association, including Susan B. Anthony and Elizabeth Cady Stanton, were against extending suffrage to black men if women were not included. With an eye to solving the problems posed by Reconstruction Douglass advocated support for the Fifteenth Amendment as a means of paving the way for extending the vote to women. This was opposed by some women who appealed to the white southerner's "ignorant Negro voter" argument, protesting that before black men are given the ballot intelligent and cultured white women should be enfranchised. The pernicious political consequence of this split in the Equal Rights Association surfaced when the argument was advanced that the enfranchisement of women would provide a bulwark in the south against "Negro rule."[64]

To garner support for the ratification of the Fifteenth Amendment Douglass attempted to distinguish the "Negro question" from the "women question" and cited the practice of lynching as sufficient warrant for granting race priority over gender:

> When women, because they are women, are dragged from their homes and hung upon lamp-posts; when their children are torn from their arms and their brains dashed upon the pavement; when they are objects of insult and outrage at every turn; when they are in danger of having their homes burnt down over their heads; when

their children are not allowed to enter schools; then they will have an urgency to obtain the ballot.⁶⁵

Douglass's eloquent oratory carried the measure, but some of the feminists at this meeting preferred to see it defeated. Soon after this convention the Equal Rights Association dissolved and was replaced by the National Woman's Suffrage Association, which divorced itself from the question of Negro suffrage.⁶⁶ At that time Douglass, of course, had no reason to think that the linking of lynching with black male suffrage later would be a source of latent racism in the women's movement. But once the association of rape with lynching was established the strained alliance between the women's movement and the antilynching movement was severely damaged.⁶⁷ The rise in support for the repeal of the Fifteenth Amendment among progressive white women lent credence to Douglass's assessment of the myth's political function. He interpreted their break with the antilynching movement as a clear sign of the success of the white southerner's campaign "to disfranchise the colored voter of the South in order to solve the race problem."⁶⁸

Miscegenation and Citizenship

From a political realist standpoint, white feminist opposition to the ratification of the Fifteenth Amendment was not entirely unwarranted given their concern that the enfranchisement of black men could shift the existing balance of power in some way unfavorable to their interests.⁶⁹ Bettina Aptheker supports the opposite position, taken by Douglass, on the ground of long-term gain for white women:

> Posed in terms of the priority of rights the debate over the Fifteenth Amendment was indeed insoluble . . . Black suffrage was a strategic question forced by the particularity of historical circumstances in the United States . . . Precisely because passage of the Fifteenth Amendment was intended to advance the cause of Afro-American freedom, it inevitably would have rebounded to the benefit of woman, but only a class-conscious element could have seen that point in 1869.⁷⁰

Aptheker underscores the historical circumstances that prevented white feminists from seeing this point regarding class. Douglass and Wells-Barnett cited economic competition between the races as an underlying cause of lynching, but given the legacy of slavery and Reconstruction, they were equally compelled to grant priority to the "Negro question."

To overcome the limitations of prioritizing gender and race Wells-Barnett and Douglass needed a more fully developed economic account of patriarchy and racism. Although she was critical of the complicity of white women, to her credit Wells-Barnett held white men responsible for lynching. She publicized the hypocrisy of miscegenation laws to bring to light the manner in which white women were being used by white men to oppress African Americans as a group. Her objective was to draw attention to the injustice of miscegenation laws by challenging the prerogative of white men to violate them with impunity. With full recognition that the myth of the sexual purity of white women was a correlate of the twin myths regarding the sexual savagery of African-American men and women, she wanted to reveal the manner in which this hypocritical sexual mythology served the interests of white men. Her indictment of white southern patriarchy was presented as a fundamental question regarding social policy: if such relations are illegal why are only black men punished for this violation?

Had Douglass chosen to address the political aim of using lynching as a means of enforcing the social taboo against interracial sexual relations perhaps he would have presented a more explicit economic account of miscegenation laws. Instead, he expressed a concern regarding the moral consequences:

> Depriving the Negro of his vote leaves the entire political, legislative, executive and judicial machinery of the country in the hands of the white people. The religious, moral and financial forces of the country are also theirs. This power has been used to pass laws forbidding intermarriage between the races, thus fostering immorality. The union, which the law forbids, goes on without its sanction in dishonorable alliances.[71]

These remarks may seem naive in a social context heavily infused with anxiety regarding miscegenation. Nevertheless, they were consistent with Douglass's political economic view of racism. His assertion that the "financial forces of the country" are in the hands of white people is particularly instructive.

Commentators have noted that since the early days of slavery miscegenation laws had been instituted to protect the property of white males.[72] Prior to the institution of these restrictive codes the offspring of interracial couples, being an intermediate caste, were deemed free citizens. In some of his earlier writings on emigration and colonization Douglass appealed to an American birthright and lineage as part of the African-American heritage, but without any reference to European ancestry. In his pamphlet on lynching, however, he claimed a right to American citizenship *by blood*, as well as by soil.[73] He advanced a mixed-race view of African Americans to argue against emigration as a solution to the race problem:

> The native land of the American Negro is America. His bones, his muscles, his sinews, are all American. His ancestors for two hundred and seventy years have lived and labored and died, on American soil, and millions of his posterity have inherited Caucasian blood.
>
> It is pertinent, therefore, to ask, in view of this admixture, as well as in view of other facts, where the people of this mixed race are to go, for their ancestors are white and black, and it will be difficult to find their native land anywhere outside of the United States.[74]

What appears to be an evasion of the miscegenation issue in Douglass's argument against the apologists for lynching turns out to have a profound political thrust. He cited the fact of miscegenation (albeit illegal) to set up his contention that European ancestry entitled African Americans to all of the rights guaranteed by the constitution. The so-called Negro problem is really a national problem in the sense that to disenfranchise African Americans in the south was "to surrender the constitution to the late rebels for the lack of moral courage to execute its provisions."[75]

One troublesome implication of Douglass's argument regarding the constitutional rights of African Americans is that the guarantee of due process allows the possibility, even if unlikely, that a guilty black rapist will escape punishment. In America, this guarantee of due process includes among other things an opportunity, as it were, for a guilty defendant in such cases to win acquittal. Given his somewhat agnostic remarks regarding the justification of lynching, Douglass leaves open the question of whether the lynching of a guilty black rapist would be justified in cases where this is likely to occur. He cites the fact that black voters had never exercised their political power in such a disloyal fashion, but what if they were to do so in judicial cases where racism is perceived to be a factor?[76]

> The only excuse for lynch law, which has a shadow of support in it is, that the criminal would probably otherwise be allowed to escape the punishment due to his crime ... But for it there is no

> foundation whatever, in a country like the South, where public opinion, the laws, the courts, the juries, the advocates, are all against the Negro, especially one alleged to be guilty of the crime now charged. That such a one would be permitted to escape condign punishment, is not only untenable but an insult to common sense. The chances are that not even an innocent Negro so charged would be allowed to escape.[77]

He clearly did not assume that due process would lead to justice, but rather expressed concern that the racism which justified physical lynchings would continue to justify legal lynchings as well.[78] The apologists maneuvered Douglass into accepting a view that excuses lynching when deemed necessary to prevent a guilty black rapist being set free. But there was no reason for Douglass to view the fact that a guilty black rapist may avail himself of the same legal means of avoiding punishment as a guilty white rapist as a justification of lynching. By not condemning lynching in principle he allowed the empirical possibility of cases in which mob action would be excused when such action expressed a legitimate public moral outrage. Although he realized that to suppose a need to deny that black men are ever guilty of raping white women would only reiterate the myth, he also understood that it was in the interest of African Americans for black leaders to condemn publicly both rape and lynching. When he proposed due process as a remedy, he never countenanced the thought that a guilty black rapist might escape punishment.

Notes

1 Toni Morrison raised a similar concern in her analysis of the media construction of O. J. Simpson during the trial: "The official story has thrown Mr Simpson into that representative role. He is not an individual who underwent and was acquitted from a murder trial. He has become the whole race needing correction, incarceration, censoring, silencing; the race that needs its civil rights disassembled; the race that has made trial by jury a luxury rather than a right and placed affirmative action legislation in even greater jeopardy. This is the consequence and function of official stories: to impose the will of a dominant culture." Toni Morrison, ed, *Birth of a Nation'hood* (New York: Pantheon Books, 1997), p. xxviii.

2 For a general discussion of antebellum southern sexual mores see John D'Emilio and Estelle Freedman, *Intimate Matters: A History of Sexuality in America* (New York: Harper and Row, 1988), pp. 85–108 and W. J. Cash, *The Mind of the South* (New York: Alfred Knopf, 1941). For first-hand

reports from black victims of rape in the post-Civil War era see Gerda Lerner, ed, *Black Women in While America: A Documentary History* (New York: Vintage Books, 1972), pp. 172–97. See also Robert Staples, "Violence and Black America," *Black World*, May 1972, pp. 17–34.

3 See, for instance, Susan Brownmiller, *Against Our Will: Men, Women and Rape* (New York: Harper and Row, 1975), chapter 7; Allison Edwards, *Rape Racism, and the White Women's Movement: An Answer to Susan Brownmiller* (Chicago: Sojourner Truth Organization, 1979); Angela Y. Davis, 'Rape, Racism and the Myth of the Black Rapist," in her *Women, Race and Class* (New York: Random House, 1983), pp. 172–201; Joy James, *Resisting State Violence* (Minneapolis: University of Minnesota Press, 1997), chapter 7; Trudia Harris, *Exorcising Blackness: Historical and Literary Lynching and Burning Rituals* (Bloomington: Indiana University Press, 1984).

4 I refer to Frederick Douglass, "Why is the Negro Lynched?" in Philip Foner, ed, *Life and Writings of Frederick Douglass*, vol. 4 (New York: International Publishers, 1952), pp. 491–523 as the pamphlet and "Lessons of the Hour" Address Delivered in Washington, D.C., on January 9, 1894, in John W. Blassingame and John R. McKivigan, eds, *The Frederick Douglass Papers*, vol. 5 (New Haven: Yale University Press, 1992), pp. 575–607 as the lecture. Also reprinted in William L. Andrews, *The Oxford Frederick Douglass Reader* (New York: Oxford University Press, 1996), pp. 340–65.

5 For a discussion of the early European view of black people as apes see Winthrop D. Jordan, *White Over Black: American Attitudes Toward the Negro 1550–1812* (Baltimore: Penguin Books, 1968), pp. 28–42.

6 Several commentators have pointed out this tendency in the O. J. Simpson trial. See David Goldberg, *Racial Subjects* (New York: Routledge, 1997), pp. 149–55 and A. Leon Higginbotham, Jr, Anderson Bellegarde Francois, and Linda Y. Such "The O. J. Simpson Trial: Who Was Improperly 'Playing the Race Card'?," in Morrison, ed, *Birth of a Nation'hood*, pp. 31–56.

7 In the trial following the Rodney King incident the police officers charged with the beating offered what some commentators refer to as the "King Kong" and "Mandingo" defenses. The officers bolstered their claim that King was a physical threat with the statement that he was also a sexual threat to a female officer. See Ishmael Reed, "Bigger and O. J.," in Morrison, ed, *Birth of a Nation'hood*, pp. 169–95.

8 Douglass often gave this lecture under the title "The Negro Problem." See Atchison, Kansas, *Blade*, October 7, 1893; Boston, Massachusetts, *Globe*, May 11 and 12, and October 26, 1894; Providence, Rhode Island, *New England Light*, November 10, 1894. See also his Address delivered at the Annual Meeting of the American Missionary Association on October 25, 1894, in Lowell, Massachusetts and published as a pamphlet entitled "A Defense of the Negro Race" (New York, 1894), cited in Blassingame and McKivigan, eds, *Douglass Papers*, vol. 5, p. 640.

9 Frederick Douglass, "Why is the Negro Lynched?," p. 503.
10 Frederick Douglass, "Lynch Law in the South," *The North American Review*, vol. 155, no. 428, July 1892, p. 19.
11 Ibid., p. 21
12 Trudier Harris, ed, *Selected Works of Ida B. Wells-Barnett* (New York: Oxford University Press, 1991), pp. 50–61.
13 Douglass, "Lynch Law," pp. 20–1.
14 Douglass, "Reason Why," in Harris, ed, *Selected Works of Ida B. Wells-Barnett*, p. 60.
15 Ibid., p. 60.
16 Despite their similar emphasis on economic self-help, Washington's accommodationist political orientation later became a source of great friction between his followers and Wells-Barnett. It should be noted that Washington was not completely unknown to have made public statements against lynching. See, for instance, his remarks in "Democracy and Education," September 30, 1896, in Howard Brotz, ed, *Negro Social and Political Thought 1850–1920* (New York: Basic Books, 1966), p. 370, "Address Delivered at Hampton Institute," February 19, 1898, in ibid., p. 374; "Is the Negro having a Fair Chance?," in ibid., pp. 446, 459–60.
17 Foner, ed, *Life and Writings*, vol. 4, p. 493.
18 Douglass often cited the horrid details of lynchings. My point here is that he considered economically motivated racism, more than the black rapist myth, to be a source of the vengeance expressed through the ritualistic killing of lynch victims. He believed the racism fostered by the black rapist myth was only a catalyst for lynching, the cause of which was class antagonisms between blacks and whites.
19 Foner, ed, *Life and Writings*, vol. 4, p. 503.
20 Blassingame and McKivigan, eds, *Douglass Papers*, vol. 5, p. 587.
21 Ibid., p. 589.
22 Douglass equated the exclusion of educated African Americans from the Chicago World's Fair with the silence about lynching. In a section of his pamphlet devoted to the unfairness of the American exhibition he raised the issue of misrepresentation and pointed out that the reputation of crime is added to an image of African Americans that is already negative. He accused the exhibitioners at the Chicago World's Fair of deliberate distortion. According to Douglass, "It says to the lynchers and mobocrats of the South, go on in your hellish work of Negro persecution. You kill their bodies, we kill their souls." Foner, ed, *Life and Writings*, vol. 4, p. 508. For an updated version of this critique of the black male image in mass media see Earl Ofari Hutchinson, *The Assassination of the Black Male Image* (New York: Touchstone, 1994/97).
23 Foner, ed, *Life and Writings*, vol. 4, pp. 496–7.
24 As was common in his time, Douglass often used the term "manhood" to speak of what we now would term "human." He has been criticized by Paula Giddings for having succumbed to this practice. See Paula Giddings,

When and Where I Enter: The Impact of Black Women on Race and Sex in America (New York: Bantam Books, 1985), p. 5. His discussion of the "manhood rights of the Negro" was ambiguous as between masculinity and humanity. See Foner, ed, *Life and Writings*, vol. 4, p. 521. But there are several distinct issues involved in his use of this expression. Hazel Carby quotes Pauline Hopkins's claim that "Lynching was instituted to crush the manhood of the enfranchised black" to show the connection between lynching and citizenship. Pauline Hopkins, *Contending Forces: A Romance Illustrative of Negro Life North and South* (1900; Carbondale, Ill., 1978), p. 270 cited in Hazel Carby "On the Threshold of Woman's Era: Lynching, Empire, and Sexuality in Black Feminist Theory," *Critical Inquiry*, 12, Autumn 1985, p. 314. But the denial of citizenship is to the group as a whole, not just to men. Since, at that time, only men had the franchise, such claims are sometimes taken also to raise the question of emasculation. For a discussion of this function of lynching and disfranchisement see Trudier Harris, *Exorcising Blackness: Historical and Literary Lynching and Burning Rituals* (Bloomington: Indiana University Press, 1994), chapter 2.

25 Quoted from the Memphis *Daily Commercial*: cited in " Southern Horrors,' Harris, ed, *Selected Works of Ida B. Wells-Barnett*, p. 33.
26 See D'Emilio and Friedman, *Intimate Matters*, p. xvi and Gerda Lerner, *Black Woman in White America: A Documentary History* (New York: Pantheon Books, 1972), p. 193, cited in Angela Y. Davis, *Women, Race and Class* (New York: Vintage, 1983), p. 174.
27 E. K. Love, "Lynch Law and Raping," November 5, 1893, (n.p.): 1–19 in *African-American Pamphlets*, 1820–1920, from the *Daniel A. P. Murray Collection*, Library of Congress.
28 Ibid., p. 6
29 Douglass, "Lynch Law," p. 19.
30 Love, "Lynch Law and Raping," p. 8.
31 Needless to say, Love's refusal receives little support from black women who have written on this subject. For example, in her novel, *Contending Forces*, Pauline Hopkins writes "The men who created the mulatto race, who recruit its ranks year after year by the very means which they invoked lynch law to suppress, bewailing the sorrows of violated womanhood! No, it is not rape." *Contending Forces*, pp. 270–1, cited in Carby, "On the Threshold of Woman's Era", p. 314.
32 For a discussion of the psychology of the guilt-ridden white southerner see Calvin C. Herton, *Sex and Racism in America* (Garden City, NY: Doubleday, 1965); Joel Kovel, *White Racism: A Psychohistory* (New York: Pantheon Books, 1970), chapter 4; Thomas F. Gossett, *Race: The History of an Idea in America* (New York: Schocken, 1963) p. 273, and Paul Hoch, *White Hero Black Beast* (London: Pluto, 1979), chapter 3. See also John W. Blassingame, *The Slave Community: Plantation Life in the Antebellum South* (London: Oxford University Press), pp. 10–11, 140, 163–4.

33 Reverand Love acknowledged cases of false accusations, but with little concern for the innocent victims in such cases. See Love, *Lynch Law*, p. 7.
34 Williain McFeely, *Frederick Douglass* (New York: Norton & Co., 1991), p. 360.
35 Ibid., pp. 361–2.
36 I propose an alternative to this strong reading of her remarks. In the same context she also spoke of herself as having believed the news reports were true, until her first-hand experience with the lynching of her friend, Thomas Moss, on a false rape accusation. See Alfreda M. Duster, *Crusade for Justice: The Autobiography of Ida B. Wells* (Chicago: University of Chicago Press, 1970), chapter 6.
37 "Lessons of the Hour" in Blassingame and McKivigan, eds, *Douglass Papers*, vol. 5, pp. 581–2. For parallel remarks see Douglass's introduction to "The Reason Why," in Harris, ed, *Selected Works of Ida B. Wells-Barnett*, p. 57 and Douglass, "Why is the Negro Lynched?" p. 496.
38 Douglass's ambivalence regarding his mother's relationship with her master may be a factor here. Jenny Franchot has argued that Aunt Ester, whom Douglass presented in his autobiography as the victim of a severe whipping by her master, was a surrogate figure for Douglass's mother. See "The Punishment of Ester: Frederick Douglass and the Construction of the Feminine," in Eric J. Sundquist, ed, *Frederick Douglass: New Literary and Historical Essays* (New York: Cambridge University Press, 1990), pp. 141–65.
39 See Wells-Barnett's comments regarding the negative reception of Douglass's interracial marriage. Duster, *Crusade for Justice*, pp. 71–5.
40 Harris, ed, *Selected Works of Ida B. Wells-Barnett*, pp. 15–16.
41 Italics added. "Lessons of the Hour," in Blassingame and McGivigan, eds, *Douglass Papers*, vol. 5, p.587.
42 In her autobiography Wells-Barnett remarked that, "I too, would have preferred that Mr. Douglass had chosen one of the beautiful, charming colored women of my race for his second wife. But he loved Helen Pitts and married her and it was outrageous that they should be crucified by both white and black people for so doing." Duster, *Crusade for Justice*, p. 73.
43 According to Douglass, "In warning the South that it may place too much reliance upon the cowardice of the negro, I am not advocating violence by the negro, but pointing out the dangerous tendency of his constant persecution . . . [H]e was not a coward at Harper's Ferry, with John Brown; and care should be taken against goading him to acts of desperation by continuing to punish him for heinous crimes of which he is not legally convicted." Douglass, "Lynch Law," pp. 22–3.
44 "Southern Horrors," in Harris, ed, *Selected Works of Ida B. Wells-Barnett*, p. 42.
45 Wells-Barnett describes the homicide, for which Charles was pursued and killed, as an act of self-defense against an unprovoked clubbing by a white

policeman. See *Mob Rule in New Orleans: Robert Charles and His Fight to the Death* (1900), in ibid., pp. 253–322.

46 Mary Helen Washington has discerned a number of fictional devices Wells-Barnett employed for rhetorical purposes. Presented at a colloquium sponsored by the Monroe Trotter Institute, University of Massachusetts/Boston, Spring 1988.

47 Foner, ed, *Life and Writings*, vol. 4, p. 519.

48 In "The Reason Why" Douglass pointed out that most southern states have " [a] convict lease system, the chain-gang, vagrant laws, election frauds, keeping back laborers' wages, paying for work in worthless script instead of lawful money, refusing to sell land to Negroes and the many political massacres where hundreds of black men were murdered for the crime(?) of casting the ballot." Harris, ed, *Selected Works of Ida B. Wells-Barnett*, p. 62.

49 In "A Red Record" she recommended a similar remedy to lynchings. She instructs her northern readers to "Bring to the intelligent consideration of Southern people the refusal of capital to invest where lawlessness and mob violence hold sway. Many labor organizations have declared the resolution that they would avoid lynch infested localities as they would the pestilence when seeking new homes." Ibid., p. 248.

50 See "A Red Record: Tabulated Statistics and Alleged Causes of Lynchings in the United States, 1892–1893–1894," in ibid., pp. 139–252.

51 Foner, ed, *Life and Writings*, vol. 4, pp. 518–19.

52 See Hoch, *White Hero Black Beast*, p. 44.

53 It is worth noting here that Douglass did not connect his earlier critique of racist ethnologists with the rapist myth. See Frederick Douglass, "The Claims of the Negro Ethnologically Considered" (1854), in Foner, ed, *Life and Writings*, vol. 2, pp. 289–309.

54 Harris, ed, *Selected Works of Ida B. Wells-Barnett*, p. 15. For arguments that parallel Douglass's see "Southern Horrors,' in ibid., pp. 18, 26–8, 44; "The Reason Why," in ibid., p. 74.

55 Ibid., p. 19.

56 Francis Willard responded with the assertion: "It is my firm belief that in the statements made by Miss Wells concerning white women having taken the initiative in nameless acts between the races she has put an imputation upon half the white race in this country that is unjust, and save in the rarest exceptional instances, wholly without foundation," cited in Wells-Barnett, "A Red Record," in ibid., pp. 226–7.

57 Alice Walker, "Advancing Luna and Ida B. Wells," in Mary Helen Washington, ed, *Midnight Birds* (Garden City, NY: Anchor Books, 1980), pp. 63–81 and Valerie Smith, "Split Affinities," in Marianne Hirsch and Evelyn Fox Keller, eds, *Conflicts in Feminism* (New York: Routledge, 1990), pp. 271–87. For a critical discussion of the Walker–Smith interpretation see Joy James, *Transcending the Talented Tenth: Black Leaders and American*

Intellectuals (New York: Routledge, 1997), chapter 3 and *Resisting State Violence*, chapter 7.

58 In her autobiography Wells-Barnett stated, "The many unspeakable and unprintable tortures to which Negro rapists (?) of white women were subjected were for the purpose of striking terror into the hearts of other Negroes who might be thinking of consorting with willing white women. I found that in order to justify these horrible atrocities to the world, the Negro was being branded as a race of rapists, who were especially mad after white women. I found that white men who had created a race of mulattoes by raping and consorting with Negro women were still doing so whenever they could, these same white men lynched, burned, and tortured Negro men for doing the same thing with white women; even when the white women were willing victims." See Duster, *Crusade for Justice*, p. 71

59 "Southern Horrors," p. 14. In a passage, from "A Red Record," that urges the law and order remedy proposed by Douglass she stated, "we demand a fair trial by law for those accused of crime, and punishment by law after honest conviction. No maudlin sympathy for criminals is solicited, but we do ask that the law shall punish all alike." In "A Red Record," published in 1895, Wells-Barnett cites Douglass's pamphlet and incorporated many aspects of his argument against lynching. See Harris, ed, *Selected Works of Ida B. Wells-Barnett*, pp. 140, 246–52.

60 She maintained "It is certain that lynching mobs have not only refused to give the Negro a chance to defend himself, but have killed their victim with a full knowledge that the relationship of the alleged assailant with the woman who accused him, was voluntary and clandestine . . . The defense has been necessary because the apologists for outlawry insist that in no case has the accusing woman been a willing consort of her paramour, who is lynched because overtaken in wrong." See "A Red Record," p. 200.

61 Wells-Barnett included cases of black women raped and lynched by white men. See especially "Southern Horrors," pp. 27–9, 45. As an activist in the women's movement she lectured in England to garner support for the antilynching campaign and considered herself a founder of the black women's club movement. The historical significance of Wells-Barnett's social activism is discussed in James, *Resisting State Violence*, chapter 7; Bettina Aptheker, *Women's Legacy* (Amherst: The University of Massachusetts Press, 1982), pp. 60–76, 107–14; Giddings, *When and Where I Enter*, pp. 26–31, 90–4.

62 See James, *Resisting State Violence*, p. 136 and Rosemarie Tong, *Women, Sex, and the Law* (Totowa, NJ: Rowman & Allanheld, 1984), p. 167.

63 At the Equal Rights Association convention in New York, May 1869.

64 In a letter to the editor of the *New York Standard* (December 26, 1925) Elizabeth Cady Stanton claimed, "The representative women of the nation have done their uttermost for the last thirty years to secure freedom for the negro, and as long as he was lowest in the scale of being, we were willing to press his claims, but now, as the celestial gate to civil rights is slowly

moving on its hinges, it becomes a serious question whether we had better stand aside and see 'Sambo' walk into the kingdom first . . . In fact, it is better to be the slave of an educated white man, than of a degraded, ignorant black one," quoted in Davis, *Women, Race and Class*, p. 71. For a satire of white feminist complicity with opponents of affirmative action see Ishmael Reed, *Reckless Eyeballing* (New York: Atheneum, 1988), pp. 26–7.

65 Foner, ed, *Life and Writings*, vol. 4, p. 43.
66 For a discussion of the history of the women's movement in relation to the earlier abolitionist and later antilynching movements see Aptheker, *Women's Legacy*; Davis, *Women, Race and Class;* Giddings, *When and Where I Enter;* Lerner, *Black Women in White America*.
67 Many commentators have noted that it was not until 1930 that Jesse Daniel Ames organized the Association of Southern Women for the Prevention of Lynching. See Tong, *Women, Sex and the Law*, pp. 167–9.
68 "Lessons of the Hour," in Blassingame and McKivigan, eds, *Douglass Papers*, vol. 5, p. 595.
69 Some black abolitionists such as Sojourner Truth and Robert Purvis also opposed ratification. See Aptheker, *Woman's Legacy*, p. 47.
70 Ibid., p. 48.
71 "Reason Why," in Harris, ed, *Selected Works of Ida B. Wells-Barnett*, p. 63. Douglass had remarked on miscegenation laws in connection with colonization as early as 1849, "The history of the repeal of the intermarriage law shows that the prejudice against color is not invincible." See Frederick Douglass, "The American Colonization Society," in Foner, ed, *Life and Writings*, vol. 1, p. 396. In 1862 he again addressed the subject of amalgamation and interracial marriage in a discussion of colonization. "And among those who denounce amalgamation most, you often find the fathers of mulatto and quadroon children, men mean enough to take advantage of their absolute power, as masters, to sustain a relation to their black slave women which can only be honorable in marriage, are the men who most loudly and coarsely denounce amalgamation." See Frederick Douglass, "The Spirit of Colonization," in Foner, ed, *Life and Writings*, vol. 3, p. 265. For Douglass's other remarks regarding miscegenation see "The Future of the Colored Race," in Foner, ed, *Life and Writings*, vol. 4, p. 195.
72 Giddings, *When and Where I Enter*, p. 38. Carby, *Reconstructing Womanhood*, chapter 2.
73 "Why is the Negro Lynched?," in Foner, ed, *Life and Writings*, vol. 4, p. 599. Douglass claimed, "But I *am* not only a citizen by birth and lineage, I am such by choice." See "The Future of the Negro People of the Slave States," in Foner, ed, *Life and Writings*, vol. 3, p. 213. In his other writings on emigration and colonization he only insisted upon citizenship by soil. See Foner, ed, *Life and Writings*, vol. 1, pp. 350–2; 387–99; vol. 2, pp. 167–9; 172–3; 243–54; 441–7; vol. 3, pp. 210–25; 60–6; vol. 5, pp. 111–25; 471–2.

74 "Why is the Negro Lynched?," in Foner, ed, *Life and Writings*, vol. 4, p. 512.
75 Ibid., p. 595.
76 See Andrew Ross, "If the Genes Fit, How Do You Acquit? O. J. and Science," in Morrison, ed, *Birth of a Nation'hood*, pp. 241–72 and Armond White, "Eye, the Jury," in ibid., pp. 339–66.
77 Foner, ed, *Life and Writings*, vol. 4, p. 500. See also Douglass, "Lynch Law," pp. 19–20.
78 For a discussion of "legal lynching" in connection with the Central Park Rape case see James, *Resisting State Violence*, chapter 7.

12

From the Prison of Slavery to the Slavery of Prison: Frederick Douglass and the Convict Lease System

Angela Y. Davis

"Slavery in the United States," wrote Frederick Douglass in 1846, "is the granting of that power by which one man exercises and enforces a right of property in the body and soul of another." Throughout his career as an abolitionist, his writings and speeches probed the contradictions of the legal definition of the slave as "a piece of property – a marketable commodity."[1] He used this definition of the slave as property, for example, as the basis for his analysis of theft by slaves as an everyday practice of resistance to slavery. The slave "can own nothing, possess nothing, acquire nothing, but what must belong to another. To eat the fruit of his own toil, to clothe his person with the work of his own hands, is considered stealing."[2] Because the slave "was born into a society organized to defraud him of the results of his labor ... he naturally enough thought it no robbery to obtain by stealth – the only way open to him – a part of what was forced from him under the hard conditions of the lash."[3] When Douglass himself escaped from slavery, he also stole property that belonged, in the eyes of the law, to his master. As a fugitive slave, both state and federal law constructed him as a criminal – a thief who absconded with his own body.

Throughout his life, Douglass periodically referred to the criminalization of the black population as a by-product of slavery. In 1877 President Rutherford Hayes appointed him US Marshall in the District of Columbia (over much criticism by both blacks and whites), which he said brought him into direct contact with black individuals stigmatized as criminals.[4] While he invariably contested the prevailing presumption of ex-slaves' natural proclivities toward crime, he nevertheless agreed that "they furnish a larger proportion of petty thieves than any other class,"[5] attributing this "thieving propensity" to holdovers from slavery. A central component in Douglass's philosophy of history was the assumption that over time, as the black population became increasingly removed from the era of slavery, these criminal propensities would recede accordingly:

> It is sad to think of the multitude who only dropped out of slavery to drop into prisons and chain-gangs, for the crimes for which they are punished seldom rise higher than the stealing of a pig or a pair of shoes; but it is consoling to think that the fact is not due to liberty, but to slavery, and that the evil will disappear as these people recede from the system in which they were born.[6]

More than a century after Douglass expressed his confidence that over time the black population would be transformed by material progress and spiritual enlightenment and would thus cease to be treated as a criminalized class, blackness is ideologically linked to criminality in ways that are more complicated and pernicious than Douglass ever could have imagined. The overwhelming numbers and percentages of imprisoned black men and women tend to define the black population as one that is subject *a priori* to incarceration and surveillance. In 1997, there were 1.8 million people in the country's jails and prisons, approximately half of whom are black. Almost one-third of all young black males are either incarcerated or directly under criminal justice surveillance.[7] Although women constitute a statistically small percentage of the overall prison population (7.4 percent), the rate of increase in the incarceration of black women surpasses that of their male counterparts.[8] Whereas the prison system established its authority as a major institution of discipline and control for black communities during the last two decades of the nineteenth century, at the close of the twentieth century, carceral regulation of black communities has reached crisis proportions.

Considering the central role race has played in the emergence of a contemporary prison industrial complex and the attendant expansion of incarcerated populations, an examination of Douglass's historical views on the criminalization of black communities and the racialization of crime may yield important insights. In this essay, I am especially interested in Douglass's silence regarding the post-Civil War southern system of convict lease, which transferred symbolically significant numbers of black people from the prison of slavery to the slavery of prison. Through this transference, ideological and institutional carryovers from slavery began to fortify the equation of blackness and criminality in US society.

When the Thirteenth Amendment was passed in 1865, thus legally abolishing the slave economy, it also contained a provision that was universally celebrated as a declaration of the unconstitutionality of peonage. "Neither slavery nor involuntary servitude, *except as a punishment for crime*, whereof the party shall have been duly convicted, shall exist within the United States, or anyplace subject to their jurisdiction" (my emphasis). The exception would render penal servitude constitutional – from 1865 to the present day. That black human beings might continue to be enslaved under the auspices of southern systems of justice (and that this might set a precedent for imprisonment outside the South) seems not to have occurred to Douglass and other abolitionist leaders. It certainly is understandable that this loophole might be overlooked amid the general jubilation with which emancipation initially was greeted. However, the southern states' rapid passage of Black Codes – which criminalized such behavior as vagrancy, breach of job contracts, absence from work, the possession of firearms, and insulting gestures or acts[9] – should have stimulated critical reconsideration of the dangerous potential of the amendment's loophole. Replacing the Slave Codes of the previous era, the Black Codes simultaneously acknowledged and nullified black people's new juridical status as US citizens. The racialization of specific crimes meant that, according to state law, there were crimes for which only black people could be "duly convicted." The Mississippi Black Codes, for example, which were adopted soon after the close of the Civil War, declared vagrant "anyone who was guilty of theft, had run away [from a job, apparently], was drunk, was wanton in conduct or speech, had neglected job or family, handled money carelessly, and . . . all other idle and disorderly persons."[10] Thus vagrancy was coded as a black crime, one punishable by incarceration and forced labor.

Considering the importance Douglass accorded the institution of slavery as an explanatory factor in relation to the vast numbers of "free" black people who were identified as criminal, it is surprising that he did not directly criticize the expansion of the convict lease system and the related system of peonage. As the premier black public intellectual of his time, he seems to have established a pattern of relative silence vis-à-vis convict leasing, peonage, and the penitentiary system, all of which clearly were institutional descendants of slavery. Douglass's most explicit denunciation of peonage did not occur until 1888, after a trip he made to South Carolina during which, according to Philip Foner, he "realized how little he had known about the true conditions of his people in the South."[11] In a speech on the occasion of the twenty-sixth anniversary of emancipation in the District of Columbia, Douglass said that the landlord and tenant laws in the south sounded like "the grating hinges of a slave prison" and kept black people "firmly bound in a strong, remorseless, and deadly grasp, a grasp from which only death can free [them]."[12] However, by the time he made this observation, tenant farming, peonage, and convict leasing had been in place for over two decades in some states. The Hayes-Rutherford Compromise of 1877 led to the expansion and strengthening of these systems throughout the South. Precisely at the time Frederick Douglass's voice was most needed to trouble the rise of this new form of slavery – experienced directly by thousands of black people and symbolically by millions – his political loyalties to the Republican Party and his absolute faith in principles of enlightenment seemed to blind him to the role the federal government was playing in the development of convict leasing and peonage. In fact, just as President Rutherford decided to withdraw federal troops from the South, he also decided to appoint Frederick Douglass as US Marshall of the District of Columbia.

According to Milfred Fierce, who has authored one of the few extended studies of the convict lease system within the field of African-American Studies, little is known about Douglass's views on convict leasing or those of other black leaders of his era.[13] Later, Booker T. Washington did occasionally speak out against convict leasing, and he integrated into his own project of industrial education some efforts to assist individuals caught up in the system of debt peonage. But he never developed an explicit strategy to abolish convict leasing. W. E. B. DuBois published an essay in 1901 entitled "The Spawn of Slavery: The Convict Lease System of the South" in a now obscure missionary periodical, and while it proposed a radical analysis, it seems that it was not widely read or discussed.[14] DuBois argued that not only was crime a "symptom of wrong social conditions," but that the entrenchment of convict leasing "linked crime and slavery indissolubly in [black people's] minds."[15] In 1907, Mary Church Terrell published an essay in *The Nineteenth Century* entitled "Peonage in the United States: The Convict Lease System and the Chain Gangs."[16]

Fierce explains the relative silence on the part of leaders like Frederick Douglass in part as a result of their limited knowledge of the atrocities connected with this system. However, it is difficult to believe that Douglass was unaware of the development of the lease system in the aftermath of emancipation or of its expansion at the close of Radical Reconstruction. While his speeches and writings suggest that he did not consider this an issue important enough to deserve a place on his agenda for black liberation, recurring references to presumptions of black criminality and evocations, albeit abstract, of chain gangs persuade me that Douglass must have been aware of the atrocities committed in the name of justice. I therefore tend to think that Fierce is more accurate when he contends that:

> in addition, Black leaders fell victim to the notion that "criminals" were getting what they deserved and, despite the cruelty of convict leasing, a crusade on behalf of prisoners was not seen as more important than fighting the lynching bee, opposing voting restrictions, or protesting the acts of racial bigotry that abounded. Those who accepted this analysis failed to fully appreciate how many of the convicts were kidnapped, held beyond their sentences, or actually innocent of the crimes, for which they were incarcerated, the total number of which will never be known.[17]

They also failed to recognize that black boys and girls were not exempt from the convict labor system. David Oshinksy, author of *Worse Than Slavery*, refers to a pardon petition for a six-year-old girl named Mary Gay, who was sentenced to thirty days "plus court costs" on charges of stealing a hat.[18]

The general impact of the convict leasing system was even more far-reaching than the horrors it brought to individual black lives. According to Oshinsky:

> From its beginnings in Mississippi in the late 1860s until its abolition in Alabama in the late 1920s, convict leasing would serve to undermine legal equality, harden racial stereotypes, spur industrial development, intimidate free workers, and breed open contempt for the law. It would turn a few men into millionaires and crush thousands of ordinary lives.[19]

By the time the National Committee on Prison Labor convened in 1911, a number of southern states had already abolished convict labor, and the abolitionist campaign had been rendered legitimate by the rising influence of the penal reform movement. The General Secretary of the National Committee on Prison Labor entitled his book on the Committee's findings *Penal Servitude* and introduced it with the following observation:

> The State has a property right in the labor of the prisoner. The 13th Amendment of the Constitution of the United States provides

that neither slavery nor involuntary servitude shall exist, yet by inference allows its continuance as punishment for crime, after due process of law. This property right the state may lease or retain for its own use, the manner being set forth in state constitutions and acts of legislature.[20]

Although the loophole in the Thirteenth Amendment was apparently missed by most at the time of its passage, in retrospect it is easy to see how the very limitation of "slavery" and "involuntary servitude" to "criminals" could facilitate the further criminalization of former slaves.

Throughout his post-Civil War writings and speeches, Frederick Douglass argued that vast numbers of black people discovered that crimes were imputed to them which carried no prison sentence for whites. Had he decided to examine this attribution of criminality to black people more thoroughly, he might have discovered a link between the leasing system and other institutions for the control of black labor. The Thirteenth Amendment putatively freed black labor from the total control to which it was subject during slavery. In actuality, new forms of quasi-total control developed – sharecropping, tenant farming, the scrip system, and the most dramatic evidence of the persistence of slavery, the convict lease system. Although Alabama and Louisiana had begun to use the lease system before the Civil War, it was only with the emancipation of the slaves that they and the other southern states began to use convict leasing on a relatively large scale. During the post-Civil War period, the percentages of black convicts in relation to white was often higher than 90 percent. In Alabama, the prison population tripled between 1874 and 1877 – and the increase consisted almost entirely of blacks.[21]

Radical Reconstruction did not abruptly end with the withdrawal of federal troops in 1877. However, as the first black recipient of a federal appointment that required Senate confirmation, Douglass failed to use his position to forcefully challenge the Republican Party's complicity with the repressive process of reestablishing control over southern black labor. "It was clear by inauguration day," Philip Foner contends, "that Hayes' agreement to remove the last remaining federal troops from the South had rendered meaningless his pledge to uphold the rights of the colored people. At this crucial moment, Douglass voiced no opposition to Hayes' policy."[22] Instead, Douglass continued to define freedom as access to political rights, thus prioritizing political progress over economic freedom. His argument that "slavery is not abolished until the black man has the ballot"[23] was transformed into intransigent – although not always uncritical – support for the Republican Party, which was combined with an enlightenment philosophy of history that emphasized inevitable future progress for the former slaves. Throughout his campaign for the Fifteenth Amendment and for the legislation necessary to enforce it, Douglass represented the ballot as the engine of progress for African Americans – even if these political rights were explicitly gendered as male and proscribed by the criminalization process to which all black people were vulnerable. However, after the fall of Radical Reconstruction and the solidification of the move toward disfranchisement, Douglass developed other arguments that revealed the Hegelian character of his unswerving belief in enlightenment and historical progress.

In an 1879 paper opposing the Exoduster movement, Douglass contended that black people were the only hope for progress in the South. He argued that "whatever prosperity, beauty, and civilization are now possessed by the South" could be attributed to the labor of black slaves. This dependence of the South on black people was no less the case in the aftermath of slavery: "[The Negro] is the arbiter of her destiny."[24] In addition, Douglass asserts:

> The Exodus has revealed to southern men the humiliating fact that the prosperity and civilization of the South are at the mercy of the despised and hated Negro. That it is for him, more than for any other, to say what shall be the future of the late Confederate States; that within their ample borders, he alone can stand between the contending powers of savage and civilized life; that the giving or withholding of his labor will bless or blast their beautiful country.[25]

That Douglass could represent black workers as already having achieved the status accorded white workers – that is they were free to sell or withhold their labor to southern employers – revealed his astounding failure to engage with the actual position of black labor in the South:

> The Negro . . . has labor, the South wants it, and must have it or perish. Since he is free he can now give it, or withhold it; use it where he is, or take it elsewhere, as he pleases. His labor made him a slave, and his labor can, if he will, make him free, comfortable and independent. It is more to him than either fire, sword, ballot boxes, or bayonet. It touches the heart of the South through its pocket.[26]

Ironically, Douglass's argument here foreshadows in starkly literal terms Booker T. Washington's admonition to "cast down your bucket where you are." If black labor was free at all, it was only in the formal sense that the economic system of slavery had been declared unconstitutional. Tenant farming, sharecropping, peonage, the practice of paying wages in scrip – and, for a vastly disproportionate number of black people, convict labor – militated against any assertion of economic freedom on the part of the masses of former slaves. Although a relatively small number of people were directly affected by the convict labor system, its symbolic importance resided in its demonstration to all black workers that incarceration and penal servitude were their possible fate. Convict leasing was a totalitarian effort to control black labor in the post-emancipation era and it served as a symbolic reminder to black people that slavery had not been fully disestablished.[27] That black women could be housed, worked, and physically and sexually abused by inmates and guards in camps that were largely male constituted a message that there was a fate even worse than slavery awaiting them. D. E. Tobias, one of the few black intellectuals at the turn of the century to prioritize the campaign against convict leasing, referred to the "immorality" abounding in the convict camps because of the co-correctional housing policies and because women were whipped nude in the presence of male convicts.[28] As long as it was possible to arrest and imprison black people (not only on serious charges, but also on petty charges that would never land a white person in jail) and lease out their labor under oppressive conditions that often surpassed those of slavery, black labor could not be said to be free.

In *Black Reconstruction*, W. E. B. DuBois would later argue that because there was no historical precedent for a black presence in southern prisons and because white convicts were released during the war to join the Confederate armies, the role of southern penitentiary systems was reconceptualized after the outbreak of the Civil War. "The whole criminal system," wrote DuBois, "came to be used as a method of keeping Negroes at work and intimidating them. Consequently there began to be a demand for jails and penitentiaries beyond the natural demand due to the rise of crime."[29] After the initiation of the convict lease system, one black member of the legislature presented a bill for the abolition of the penitentiary system.[30]

Douglass's argument against the Exoduster movement was thus based on a highly abstract construction of "free labor" that bore no relationship to black economic realities in the South and, in this context, served as a surrogate for the failed notion that the ballot promised full freedom and equality for the former slaves. However, to do Douglass's argument justice, it should be pointed out that he did not deploy it against emigration per se, but rather he focused his opposition on the organized Exoduster movement and its demands for federal financing. In light of the horrendous situation in the South, he suggested that "voluntary, spontaneous, self-sustained emigration on the part of the freedmen may or may not be commendable. It is a matter with which they alone have to do."[31] As long as emigration remained a private and individual matter, Douglass had no objections. However, when it was raised publicly and politically as a strategy for liberation, he strongly opposed it.

In summarizing the arguments in favor of emigration, he refers to Senate testimony by the emigrants themselves. He points to their contention "that a crime for which a white man goes free, a black man is severely punished" and "that the law is the refuge of crime rather than of innocence; that even the old slave driver's whip has reappeared, and the inhuman and disgusting spectacle of the chain-gang is beginning to be seen."[32] Douglass did not contest the truth of this testimony – in fact, he had and would continue to rely on the fact that the criminal justice system had become a sanctuary for racism of the cruelest sort – but he nonetheless chose to respond to it by maintaining that black labor was "free" and held a far greater promise than emigration.

But even though the violent racism that was at the core of restructured criminal justice systems in the South did not, in Douglass's opinion, furnish compelling arguments for a political strategy of exodus from the South, his speeches and writings for the rest of his life powerfully evoked ways in which crime was racialized and race criminalized. In an essay for *North American Review* in 1881, challenging essentialist constructions of race prejudice, he wrote that "the colored man is the Jean Valjean of American society. He has escaped from the galleys, and hence all presumptions are against him."[33] Although Douglass's contention that the social conditions of slavery and the persistence of racism during the post-slavery era were entirely responsible for the criminalization of black people led him to challenge these presumptions of criminality, they also steered him toward an analytical impasse. If slavery produced criminals, then black people had to be acknowledged as criminals. However, he argued against the imputation of guilt where none was present:

> If a crime is committed, and the criminal is not positively known, a suspicious-looking colored man is sure to have been seen in the neighborhood. If an unarmed colored man is shot down and dies in his tracks, a jury, under the influence of this spirit, does not hesitate to find the murdered man the real criminal, and the murderer innocent.[34]

As indicated above, Douglass often alluded to the fact that black people were punished for minor offenses as if they were hardened criminals, that "the crimes for which they are punished seldom rise higher than the stealing of a pig or a pair of shoes." In fact, the Mississippi legislature passed its notorious "Pig Law" in 1876, classifying the theft of any cattle or swine as grand larceny and carrying up to five years in the penitentiary. This law was in part responsible for a vast increase in the penitentiary population in that state.[35] In 1875, the Democratic legislature in Arkansas passed a similar law classifying the theft of property worth two dollars as a felony punishable by one to five years.[36] Several weeks after the Mississippi "Pig Law" was passed, the legislature legalized the leasing of convict labor to private companies. Prisoners, according to this act, would be permitted to "work outside the penitentiary in building railroads, levees or in any private labor or employment."[37] As David Oshinsky observes, "throughout the South, thousands of ex-slaves were being arrested, tried, and convicted for acts that in the past had been dealt with by the master alone . . . An offense against [the master] had become an offense against the state."[38] In 1875 Governor John Brown of Tennessee expressed his opinion that to imprison a black man who had stolen a pig with a white murderer was a gross injustice – to the white man. [39]

Because black people were more likely to be imprisoned for minor offenses than white people, in states like Florida, large numbers of black people convicted on charges of stealing were incarcerated alongside white men who had often committed appalling crimes. The author of an account on forced labor in the Florida turpentine camps pointed out that it was possible "to send a negro to prison on almost any pretext but difficult to get a white there, unless he committed a very heinous crime."[40]

Douglass was certainly conscious of the degree, to which crime was racialized, of the South's tendency to "impute crime to color."[41] With his usual eloquence, he said that "justice is often painted with bandaged eyes . . . but a mask of iron, however thick, could never blind American justice, when a black man happens to be on trial."[42] Not only was guilt assigned to black communities, regardless of the race of the perpetrator of a crime, white men, Douglass claimed, sometimes sought to escape punishment by disguising themselves as black:

> In certain parts of our country, when any white man wishes to commit a heinous offence, he wisely resorts to burnt cork and blackens his face and goes forth under the similitude of a Negro. When the deed is done, a little soap and water destroys his identity,

and he goes unwhipt of justice. Some Negro is at once suspected and brought before the victim of wrong for identification, and there is never much trouble here, for as in the eyes of many white people, all Negroes look alike, and as the man arrested and who sits in the dock in irons is black, he is undoubtedly the criminal.[43]

Douglass made these comments during an 1883 speech in celebration of the twenty-first anniversary of emancipation in the District of Columbia. Three years later on the same occasion, he referred to his previous remarks and produced a recent example of a white man in Tennessee who had been killed while committing a crime in blackface:

> Only a few days ago a Mr J. H. Justice, an eminent citizen of Granger County, Tennessee, attempted under this disguise to commit a cunningly devised robbery and have his offense fixed upon a Negro. All worked well till a bullet brought him to the ground and a little soap and water was applied to his face, when he was found to be no Negro at all, but a very respectable white citizen.[44]

Cheryl Harris argues that a property interest in whiteness emerged from the conditions of slavery and that "owning white identity as property affirmed the self-identity and liberty of whites and, conversely, denied the self-identity of blacks."[45] Douglass's comments indicate how this property interest in whiteness was easily reversed in schemes to deny black people their rights to due process. Interestingly, cases similar to the ones Douglass discussed have emerged during the 1990s – the case of Charles Stuart, who killed his wife in Boston and attempted to place the blame on an anonymous black murderer, and Susan Smith who killed her children in Union, South Carolina and claimed they had been abducted by a black carjacker.

The last period of Frederick Douglass's life coincided with the consolidation of Jim Crow segregation in the South. Within the penitentiaries and convict labor camps, the criminality imputed to blackness gave rise to ideologies of separation that, in comparison to those of the "free" world, were magnified and exaggerated. In the "free" world, school systems, transportation systems, hospitals, and neighborhoods were being subjected to strict laws of segregation. In some states there was the practice of incarcerating white convicts in penitentiaries and sending black convicts to labor camps.[46] While the prisons and labor camps were establishing lines of racial demarcation, black convicts who were incarcerated on charges of petty larceny were often treated as a danger to white convicts, even those in prison for murder. During the 1880s, meetings of the National Prison Association were replete with racist defenses of convict leasing, including arguments that the camps were a notch above black people's living conditions in freedom and that prison simply denied them "liberty, liquor and lust." White convicts, however, endured a much more trying ordeal, largely because they were compelled to live among black people.[47] It was claimed that the law "lays on the Caucasian a dreadful grief, which the African does not feel ... The fact remains, and will remain, that there is a psychological repulsion between races, horrible to one but not the other."[48] Southerners speaking before the NPA meetings called up such exaggerated comparisons as that between incarcerated whites with blacks and "the 'ancient torture' of tying up murderers with 'decaying corpses,' resulting in death to the living murderer."[49]

In light of Frederick Douglass's reticence regarding penal servitude, an analysis of his response to the prevailing discourses on race – which rendered criminality an obligatory ideological companion of blackness – might yield insights into the relative silence regarding penal servitude in black intellectual circles today. Douglass was quite outspoken on the issue of lynching and, in his many speeches and essays devoted to this subject, he was certainly required to address the criminalizing ideology of racism. But why speak out against lynching and remain silent on leasing? Lynching was outside the pale of the law. It could be opposed on the basis of its unlawfulness, of its seemingly chaotic and aberrant quality. The issue, as Douglass formulated it, was not so much the guilt or innocence of lynch victims, but rather that they were divested of their right to confront their accusers in an arena structured by law. To take on convict leasing would have required Douglass to relinquish some of his major enlightenment principles – and his vision of black liberation was too solidly anchored in the promise of legislated justice to permit him to ponder the possibility of the profound complicity of legal institutions in the continuation of this microcosmic slave system.

Consider this description of lynching from his well-known essay, "Why is the Negro Lynched?":

> It [mob-law] laughs at legal processes, courts and juries, and its red-handed murderers range abroad unchecked and unchallenged by law or by public opinion. If the mob is in pursuit of Negroes who happen to be accused of crime, innocent or guilty, prison walls and iron bars afford no protection. Jail doors are battered down in the presence of unresisting jailers, and the accused, awaiting trial in

the courts of law, are dragged out and hanged, shot, stabbed or burned to death, as the blind and irresponsible mob may elect.[50]

What Douglass fails to recognize is that the very iron bars that he looked to for security were as much a weapon of terror as the mob itself. "In a perverse way," according to Oshinsky, "emancipation had made the black population more vulnerable than before. It now faced threats from two directions: white mobs and white courts. Like the Ku Klux Klan, the criminal justice system would become a dragnet for the Negro."[51]

Perhaps Douglass's confidence in the law blinded him to ways in which black people were constructed, precisely through law, as only fit for slavery. This was the symbolic meaning of the convict lease system. By 1911, the National Prison Association openly acknowledged the links between the prison system and slavery:

> The *status of the convict* is that of one in *penal servitude* – the last surviving vestige of the old slave system. With its sanction in the common law, its regulation in the acts of legislatures, and its implied recognition in the Constitution of the United States, it continues unchallenged and without question, as a basic institution, supposedly necessary to the continued stability of our social structure.[52]

When Douglass wrote in 1894 about "the determination of slavery to perpetuate itself, if not under one form, then under another,"[53] he referred to the landlord tenant system as well as the practice of paying black laborers with store orders (instead of with money) as ways of perpetuating slavery. "The landowners of the South want the labor of the Negro on the hardest terms possible. They once had it for nothing. They now want it for next to nothing."[54] Interestingly, he suggests that landowners employ three strategies, yet he only mentions two (tenant farming and payment in scrip). Perhaps he originally meant to include convict leasing and/or peonage, but, on second thought, decided to remove references to these systems because they involved direct intervention or implicit sanction by the state.

Convict leasing and the accompanying laws permitting the criminal prosecution of people who did not fulfill their job contract were even more closely linked to slavery than the systems explicitly mentioned by Douglass. At the same time, all these legal and economic systems – leasing, peonage, tenant farming, sharecropping, and payment in scrip – mutually informed each other, all overdetermined by slavery in their techniques of controlling black labor. With respect to the fact that most people subject to these systems were black, Milfred Fierce points out that "for them, the distinction between antebellum de jure slavery and postbellum de facto slavery was close to being much ado about nothing."[55] Moreover, according to Fierce:

> Southern Blacks were trapped in [a] penal quagmire in excessive numbers and percentages of the total prison population of each southern state. For the victims, many of whom were ex-slaves, this predicament represented nothing short of a revisit to slavery. Those Blacks who were former slaves, and became victims of the convict lease system – especially those convicted and incarcerated on trumped up charges, or otherwise innocent of crimes for which they were imprisoned – must have imagined themselves in a time warp.[56]

Fierce argues – as indicated by the title of his study, *Slavery Revisited* – that the lease system established conditions that were tantamount to slavery, permitting plantation owners and industrialists to rent crews of mostly black convicts, using the same methods of coercion to guarantee their labor that had been practiced during slavery.

While Douglass may not have addressed the convict lease system because of its legal character, its elaboration under the auspices of criminal justice systems, had he examined this system more closely, he might have discovered that the authority of the state was not directly exercised through the lease system – rather the state served to mediate the privatization of convict labor. Alabama had already set a precedent for the privatization of convict labor before the abolition of slavery, which further affirms the historical link between slavery and leasing. The first penitentiary was constructed in Alabama in 1840 and by 1845 it was so much in debt the entire prison was leased for a period of six years to a J. G. Graham. Graham simply became warden and took the profits from the convicts' labor.[57]

When all the southern states established the system of convict leasing, it made overwhelmingly black convict labor forces available to planters and capitalists under conditions modeled along the lines of slavery, conditions that, in many ways, proved worse than the slave system. Matthew Mancini, author of *One Dies, Get Another*, proposes an analysis of the lease system that complicates the obvious connection with slavery. He persuasively argues that given the indisputable similarities and continuities, it is the differences and discontinuities that provide the most interesting perspective on convict leasing. He points out that the rate of economic exploitation – defined in marxian terms as the value of unpaid labor (and thus also the rate of profit) – was actually greater with the lease system than with slavery. Slaveholders were responsible not only for the maintenance of the laboring subjects, but were expected to guarantee the maintenance of the entire slave community – including children and elders who were not able to work.[58] Lessees, however, were only responsible for individual convicts, each of which represented a labor unit. Moreover, lessees purchased the labor of entire crews of convicts, not of individuals. According to Mancini:

> The individual convict as such did not represent a significant investment, and his death or release was, therefore, not a loss. When considered as a source of labor, then, slaves received a "wage" best thought of as aggregated, convicts one that was individual; as a form of capital, by contrast, slaves were individually significant, convicts collectively so. This does turn out to be a relevant distinction rather than a metaphysical exercise, for the consequence was an economic incentive to abuse prisoners. These two economic factors – the subsistence or lower-than-subsistence "wage" the convicts received and their status as aggregated capital – served to reinforce one another and to make leasing, from the point of view of the economic definition, "worse" than slavery.[59]

A small but significant number of black men and women were condemned to live out the worst nightmares of what slavery might have been had the cost of purchasing slaves been low enough to justify conditions of genocide, i.e., no man, woman, or child unable to work would be supported by the slave-owners. Under these conditions (which were not entirely unheard of during slavery), it also would have been profitable to literally work slaves to death, because the cost of purchasing new ones would not have interfered with profits. Precisely because of this, Mancini decided to entitle his study of convict leasing *One Dies, Get Another*. We can only speculate as to how Frederick Douglass might have responded to the convict lease system had he extricated himself from his faith in formal legalities and examined more closely this symbolic and malignant reincarceration of slavery. We can also only speculate about the impact his engagement with the lease system might have had on future agendas for black liberation and on the future relationship between black intellectuals and social movements against the US prison system.

Although Frederick Douglass did not enlist his communicative powers in an examination of convict leasing, three of his intellectual descendants did see fit to write about this issue.[60] D. E. Tobias, a self-taught researcher and organic intellectual in the Gramscian sense, published an essay in 1899, a significant portion of which was devoted to leasing. In 1901, W. E. B. DuBois published a relatively obscure article on convict leasing, and in 1907, Mary Church Terrell wrote about the subject in the same journal that had published Tobias's piece.

In his article, "A Negro on the Position of the Negro in America," D. E. Tobias described himself as a twenty-nine year old black man, son of slaves, who was studying the prison system in the US.[61] Unfortunately; this seems to be Tobias's only published writing. Interestingly, he positioned the campaign against convict leasing at the very top of his agenda for black liberation. In this sense, he directly contested the philosophical tradition initiated by Frederick Douglass – and later taken up by DuBois in his debate with Washington – according to which black political rights were the sine qua non of black liberation. Tobias did not deny the importance of the ballot. But he argued, in effect, that as long as convict leasing continued to exist, black people could never fully enjoy the franchise. Moreover, he suggested that the imprisonment of such large numbers of black people was tantamount to robbing them forever of their rights as citizens. "Once a Negro voter is sent to prison, he is forever thereafter disfranchised, and for this reason alone the whites have made thousands of negro convicts for the purpose of depriving them of their votes."[62] The use of incarceration as an explicit scheme to erode the potential political power of the black population reflected, in Tobias's view, what Frederick Douglass had referred to as "the determination of slavery to perpetuate itself." "The sole purpose of the South in going to war with the Nation," Tobias wrote:

> was to keep the black race as chattels, and having been defeated in that, ex-slaveholders were determined that the negroes should be held in bondage to serve them. Accordingly the remarkable ingenious scheme of making the negroes prisoners was soon devised, and at once scores and thousands of ex-slaves were arrested and convicted on any sort of flimsy charges, and farmed out to the highest bidders for human flesh. By reason of this new form of slavery, hundreds and thousands of black men and women have never known that they were emancipated.[63]

Tobias points out that southern authorities justified the institution of the convict lease system by evoking the Civil War destruction of most of the South's prison structures and thus by representing the lease plan as a "makeshift and an experiment until other means of caring for the large negro criminal population could be found."[64] However, after more than three decades, the lease system had become a critical component of southern criminal justice.

W. E. B. DuBois's 1901 article, "The Spawn of Slavery: The Convict-Lease System in the South" examines the lease system as a structural inheritance of slavery wherein black people accused of committing crimes were disciplined by the private imposition of labor, using "the slave theory of punishment – pain and intimidation."[65] He defined this system as "the slavery in private hands of persons convicted of crimes and misdemeanors in the courts."[66] This method of controlling black labor, DuBois argued, emerged alongside a juridical construction of black criminality in the chaos that followed emancipation when punishment was no longer the private purview of slavemasters, when black slaves were legally recognized as the property of their masters. "Consequently, so far as the state was concerned, there was no crime of any consequence among Negroes. The system of criminal jurisprudence had to do, therefore, with whites almost exclusively."[67] Although the Freedman's Bureau attempted to create innovative methods of mediating legal relationships, these new strategies failed and the state courts reestablished their authority:

> As the regular state courts gradually regained power, it was necessary for them to fix by their decisions the new status of the freedmen. It was perhaps as natural as it was unfortunate that amid this chaos the courts sought to do by judicial decisions what the legislatures had formerly sought to do by specific law – namely, reduce the freedmen to serfdom. As a result, the small peccadilloes of a careless, untrained class were made the excuse for severe sentences. The courts and jails became filled with the careless and ignorant, with those who sought to emphasize their newfound freedom, and too often with innocent victims of oppression. The testimony of a Negro counted for little or nothing in court, while the accusation of white witnesses was usually decisive. The result of this was a sudden large increase in the apparent criminal population of the Southern states – an increase so large that there was no way for the state to house it or watch it even had the state wished to. And the state did not wish to. Throughout the South laws were immediately passed authorizing public officials to lease the labor of convicts to the highest bidder. The lessee then took charge of the convicts – worked them as he wished under the nominal control of the state. Thus a new slavery and slave trade was established.[68]

I quote this long passage because it is such an insightful summary of the way the convict lease system served as a decisive lever for the transition from a bifurcated system of criminal justice – privatized punishment for blacks and public punishment for whites – to a system in which the state concentrated on the punishment of blacks and functioned as a mediator for punishment through privatized labor. In other words, "the state became a dealer in crime, profited by it so as to derive a net annual income for her prisoners."[69] DuBois would later write in *Black Reconstruction* that "[i]n no part of the modern world has there been so open and conscious a traffic in crime for deliberate social degradation and private profit as in the South since slavery."[70] DuBois's analysis of the convict lease system implicitly contested Douglass's construction of black labor as "free." DuBois made the astute observation that so-called "free" black labor was, in a very concrete sense, chained to black convict labor, for in many industries in which black people sought employment – such as brick-making, mining, road building – wages were severely depressed by the fact that convicts could be leased from the state at costs as low as $3 a month.[71] Moreover, DuBois pointed out that the very theory of work embodied in convict leasing would have to be radically transformed in order to establish a criminal justice system free of racial bias. Instead of convict labor serving as a scheme for both private and state profit, it would have to be reconstructed as a means of correction and reformation of the convict him/her self. With the abolition of the profit motive, DuBois seemed to imply, a powerful incentive for the racism at the core of the system would cease to exist.

Unfortunately, DuBois's contemporaries did not take up this insightful and radical analysis of the convict lease system. The relative obscurity to which it was relegated may be attributed to the fact that the essay appeared in a Protestant periodical devoted to writings on missionary projects, *The Missionary Review of the World*. As a result, its audience probably consisted largely of theologians and missionaries. Today, it is probably only read by students of religious studies and scholars researching convict leasing. However, DuBois did refer to convict leasing and peonage in his monumental study – *Black Reconstruction*.

Twelve years after Douglass's death, Mary Church Terrell remarked that "it is surprising how few there are among even intelligent people in this country who seem to have anything but a hazy idea of what the convict lease system means."[72] Her essay on convict leasing was published in the prestigious review, *The Nineteenth Century*, and although it is difficult to document how the essay was received, Milfred Fierce asserts that it "influenced many others, both Black and White."[73] Terrell, like Douglass in the preceding generation, was one of the major figures in the antilynching crusade. However, she wrote as passionately against the convict lease system as she had against lynching, meticulously documenting her allegations of untold cruelty with references to comments by southern legal authorities and official reports. "It is no exaggeration," Terrell wrote:

> to say that in some respects the convict lease system, as it is operated in certain southern States, is less humane than was the bondage endured by slaves fifty years ago. For, under the old *regime*, it was to the master's interest to clothe and shelter and feed his slaves properly, even if he were not moved to do so by considerations of mercy and humanity, because the death of a slave meant an actual loss in dollars and cents, whereas the death of a convict to-day involves no loss whatsoever either to the lessee or to the State.[74]

There are several references in the article to the way women were integrated into the convict lease system with little regard to their gender – they worked and were housed together with men. Focusing her examination on the state of Georgia, she quotes extensively from a report issued several years before by Colonel Alton Byrd, who had been appointed a special investigator into the conditions of Georgia's convict camps. In one passage he described a young black woman:

> Lizzie Boatwrignt, a nineteen-year old negress sent up from Thomas, Georgia, for larceny. She was clad in women's clothing, was working side by side with male convicts under a guard, cutting a ditch through a meadow. This girl was small of stature and pleasant of address, and her life in this camp must have been one of long drawn out agony, horror, and suffering. She told me she had been whipped twice, each time by the brutal white guard who had beaten McRay (an elderly Black convict at the camp) to death, and who prostituted his legal rights to whip into a most revolting and disgusting outrage. This girl and another woman were stripped and beaten unmercifully in plain view of the men convicts, because they stopped on the side of the road to bind a rag about their sore feet.[75]

It is probably the case that Terrell devoted her most extensive discussion of women in the labor camps to white women, because she assumed that the brutal treatment of white women would provoke more widespread expressions of outrage than would that of black women.

Although she did not indicate the source of her information, she wrote that in the preceding year, news was released about "one thousand white girls . . . [who] wear men's clothing and work side by side with coloured men who are held in slavery as well as the girls . . . In the black depths of [Florida] pinewoods, living in huts never seen by civilised white men other than the bosses of the turpentine camps, girls are said to have grown old in servitude."[76] Terrell concluded this section with the observation that "not only does peonage still rage violently in the Southern states and in a variety of forms, but that while it formerly affected only coloured people, it now attacks white men and women as well."[77] In this sense Terrell was probably influenced by the discourse of prison reform, which tended to equate the cruelty of peonage and convict leasing with its allegedly increasing impact on white people. For example, Richard Barry's 1907 article in *Cosmopolitan Magazine* emphasized the fact that employers in Florida had come under investigation because of the "monumental error" they made "in going beyond the black man with their slavery. Had they stuck to the racial division they might have escaped castigation, as they have for a decade. But, insatiate, and not finding enough blacks to satisfy their ambitious wants, they reached out and took in white men."[78]

Consequently, the movements to abolish convict leasing tended to reinforce notions of black criminality even as it emphasized the brutality of the leasing system. This abolitionist movement coincided with the increasing influence of discourses on eugenics and scientific racism. Although black leaders attempted to refute essentialist theories of innate criminality by emphasizing the historical conditions under which black criminality emerged, they did not openly examine the structural role of the expanding network of penitentiaries and convict labor camps in constructing and affirming these ideologies. Philosophically, this represented an engagement with the presumption of criminality, but not with the institutions that concretely structured this ideology of criminality.

If Douglass was consistently silent on the issue of convict leasing, then Terrell did not integrate her insights on leasing into her antilynching work and thus could not effectively challenge a criminal justice system that perpetuated notions of black criminality that still persist during the contemporary era. The same observation may be made of DuBois. This is particularly important in light of the popular historical memory of lynching that remains a critical component of African-American identity. If convict leasing and the accompanying disproportionality with which black people were made to inhabit jails and prisons during the post-emancipation period had been taken up with the same intensity and seriousness as – and in connection with – the campaign against lynching, then the contemporary radical call for prison abolition might not sound so implausible today.

Of course it is not fair to blame Douglass for over a century of failure to take on the pivotal role of the prison system in constructing and preserving ideological equations of blackness and criminality. And it certainly is not fair to hold him responsible for the "common sense" acceptance of the inevitability of prisons. However – and this is the conclusion of my examination of Douglass's silence vis-à-vis the convict lease system – scholars who rightfully criticize Douglass for the tenacity with which he embraced enlightenment principles and a philosophy of history that accorded the bourgeois state a foundational role in guaranteeing racial progress, also should acknowledge how this philosophy militated against an understanding of the prison system, and its specific role in preserving and deepening structures of racism. Moreover, by understanding Douglass's reluctance to directly oppose the penitentiary system of his era, we may acquire much needed insight into the difficulties activists encounter today in organizing movements against the contemporary prison industrial complex.

Notes

1 Frederick Douglass, "An Appeal to the British People," reception speech at Finsbury Chapel, Moorfields, England, May 12, 1846, in Philip Foner, ed, *Life and Writings of Frederick Douglass*, vol. 1 (New York: International Publishers, 1950), p. 155.
2 "Frederick Douglass Discusses Slavery," in Herbert Aptheker, *Documentary History of the Negro People* (New York: Citadel Press, 1969), p. 310.
3 Frederick Douglass, "The Condition of the Freedman," *Harper's Weekly*, Dec. 8, 1883, in Philip Foner, ed, *Life and Writings of Frederick Douglass*, vol. 4 (New York: International Publishers, 1955), p. 406.
4 In his speech on the occasion of the 24th anniversary of emancipation in the District of Columbia, he said: "Look at these black criminals, as they are brought into your police courts; view and study their faces, their forms, and their features, as I have done for years as Marshal of this District, and you will see that their antecedents are written all over them." Foner, *Life and Writings*, vol. 4, p. 435.
5 Ibid., p. 434.
6 Foner, *Life and Writings*, vol. 4, p. 406.
7 Marc Mauer, *Young Black Men and the Criminal Justice System: Five Years Later* (Washington, D.C.: The Sentencing Project, 1995).
8 Ibid., p. 12.

9 John Hope Franklin, *From Slavery to Freedom* (New York: Vintage, 1969), p. 303.
10 Milfred Fierce, *Slavery Revisited: Blacks and the Southern Convict Lease System, 1865–1933* (New York: Brooklyn College, CUNY, Africana Studies Research Center, 1994), pp. 85–6.
11 Foner, *Life and Writings*, vol. 4, p. 109
12 Ibid., p. 110.
13 Fierce, *Slavery Revisited*, p. 230.
14 W. E. B. DuBois. "The Spawn of Slavery: The Convict lease System of the South," *Missionary Review of The World*, vol. xxiv, no. 10, (New Series, vol. xiv, no. 10), October 1901.
15 Fierce, *Slavery Revisited*, p. 240.
16 Mary Church Terrell, "Peonage in the United States: The Convict Lease System and the Chain Gang," in *The Nineteenth Century*, vol. 62, August 1907.
17 Fierce, *Slavery Revisited*, p. 229.
18 David Oshinsky, *"Worse Than Slavery": Parchman Farm and the Ordeal of Jim Crow Justice* (New York: The Free Press, 1996), p. 47.
19 Ibid., p. 56.
20 E. Stagg Whitin, *Penal Servitude*, (New York: National Committee on Prison Labor, 1912), p. 1.
21 Fierce, *Slavery Revisited*, p. 88
22 Foner, *Life and Writings*, vol. 4, p. 101.
23 Frederick Douglass, "The Need for Continuing Anti-Slavery Work," speech at 32nd Annual Meeting of the American Anti-Slavery Society, May 9, 1865. in ibid., p. 166.
24 Douglass was invited to present this paper along with Richard T. Greener, the first black graduate of Harvard. Because he did not wish to engage in open debate around this controversial issue, he decided not to appear in person at the meeting but, to send his paper to be read by someone else. Greener, who had taught at the University of South Carolina during Reconstruction, now taught at Howard and was a prominent organizer of support for the emigrants. See William S. McFeely, *Frederick Douglass* (New York: W. W. Norton, 1991), p. 301; Douglass, "The Negro Exodus from the Gulf States," Address before Convention of the American Social Science Association, Saratoga Springs, September 12, 1879, *Journal of Social Science*, vol. XI, May 1880, pp. 1–21. Reprinted in Foner, *Life and Writings*, vol. 4, p. 327.
25 Ibid., p. 325.
26 Ibid., p. 327.
27 "Certainly the control of black labor was a leading motivation behind every significant effort to establish and maintain convict leasing for fifty years. Just as plain is the similarity between the brutal hardships of convict life and the oppression of slavery times. Finally, the racial character of convict leasing reinforced connections with the slavery regime." Matthew J. Man-

cini, *One Dies, Get Another: Convict Leasing in the American South, 1866–1928* (Columbia, S.C.: University of South Carolina Press, 1996), p. 20.
28 D. E. Tobias. "A Negro on the Position of the Negro in America," in *The Nineteenth Century*, vol. 46, no. 274, Dec. 1899, pp. 960–1.
29 W. E. B. DuBois, *Black Reconstruction* (New York: Russell and Russell, 1963), p. 506.
30 Ibid., p. 506.
31 Foner, *Life and Writings*, vol. 4, p. 332.
32 Ibid., p. 330.
33 Frederick Douglass, "The Color Line," *North American Review*, vol. CXXXII, June 1881, reprinted in ibid., p. 344.
34 Ibid., p. 345.
35 Fierce, *Slavery Revisited*, pp. 128–9, n. 16. Matthew Mancini argues that while the "Pig Law" may have been in part responsible for an immediate increase in the number of convicts, in 1877 the penitentiary population began to drop – but in fact began to soar immediately after the repeal of this law in 1888. Mancini, *One Dies, Get Another*, pp. 135–6.
36 Mancini, *One Dies, Get Another*, p. 120.
37 Mississippi Laws, 1876, c. 110, sec. 1, 3, pp. 194–5. Cited in Oshinsky, *"Worse Than Slavery,"* p. 41.
38 Oshinsky, *"Worse Than Slavery,"* p. 28.
39 Fierce, *Slavery Revisited*, p. 89
40 "Captain" J. C. Powell's *American Siberia* is quoted by Oshinsky, *"Worse Than Slavery,"* p. 71.
41 Frederick Douglass, "Address to the People of the United States," delivered at a Convention of Colored Men, Louisville, Kentucky, September 24, 1883, in Foner, *Life and Wrirings*, vol. 4, p. 379.
42 Frederick Douglass. "The United States Cannot Remain Half-Slave and Half-Free," speech on the Occasion of the Twenty-First Anniversary of Emancipation in the District of Columbia, April, 1883, in ibid., p. 357. Several months later at a Convention of Colored Men, he said, "Taking advantage of the general disposition in this country to impute crime to color, white men *color* their faces to commit crime and wash off the hated color to escape punishment." See "Address to the People of the United States," Louisville, Kentucky, September 24, 1883, in ibid., p. 379.
43 Ibid., p. 359.
44 Frederick Douglass "Southern Barbarism," speech on the occasion of the Twenty-Fourth Anniversary of Emancipation in the District of Columbia, Washington, D.C., 1886, in ibid., p. 434.
45 Cheryl Harris, "Whiteness As Property," Kimberle Crenshaw et al., eds, *Critical Race Theory: The Key Writings That Formed the Movement* (New York: The New Press, 1995), p. 285.
46 Oshinsky, *"Worse Than Slavery,"* p. 41.
47 Mancini , *One Dies, Get Another*, p. 92.

48 Ibid., p. 93. Mancini quotes the 1886 NPA proceedings.
49 Fierce, *Slavery Revisited*, p. 89
50 Frederick Douglass, "Why is the Negro Lynched?," in Foner, *Life and Writings*, vol. 4, p. 492.
51 Oshinsky, *"Worse Than Slavery,"* p. 29.
52 Whitin, *Penal Servitude*, pp. 1–2 (emphases added).
53 Douglass, "Why is the Negro Lynched?," p. 516.
54 Ibid., p. 516
55 Fierce, *Slavery Revisited*, p. 43.
56 Ibid., p. 78
57 Mancini, *One Dies, Get Another*, pp. 99–100.
58 Ibid., p. 22
59 Ibid., p. 23
60 I obtained references for these three essays from Milfred Fierce's *Slavery Revisited*.
61 Fierce indicates that "[n]ot much is known about Tobias except that his parents were illiterate former slaves and that he was born in South Carolina around 1870. He described himself as 'a member of the effete African race' and indicated that he was educated in the South and North, an education he financed by working with his hands." See *Slavery Revisited*, p. 243.
62 Tobias, "A Negro on the Position of the Negro in America," p. 960.
63 Ibid., p. 959.
64 Ibid., p. 960.
65 W. E. B. DuBois, "The Spawn of Slavery: The Convict-Lease System in the South," *Missionary Review of the World*, p. 743.
66 Ibid., p. 738.
67 Ibid., p. 738.
68 Ibid., p. 740.
69 Ibid., p. 741.
70 DuBois, *Black Reconstruction*, p. 698.
71 Ibid., pp. 744–5.
72 Mary Church Terrell, "Peonage in the United States," p. 303.
73 Fierce, *Slavery Revisited*, p. 231.
74 Terrell, "Peonage in the United States," p. 306.
75 Ibid., p. 317.
76 Ibid., p. 311.
77 Ibid., p. 313.
78 Richard Barry, "Slavery in the South To-Day," *Cosmopolitan Magazine*, March 1907. Reproduced in Donald P. DeNevi and Doris A. Holmes, eds, *Racism at the Turn of the Century: Documentary Perspectives, 1870–1910* (San Rafael, California: Leswing Press, 1973), p. 131.

Part VI

Douglass (1818–95): One Hundred Years Later

13
Frederick Douglass and African-American Social Progress: Does Race Matter at the Bottom of the Well?

Bill E. Lawson

Is social progress on racial matters possible? What is the social, political, and economic future of blacks in the United States? These questions are not new. They have been asked by blacks since the beginning of their presence in the United States. Thus it is not surprising that Frederick Douglass would ponder the fate of blacks in America. In 1863, Douglass addressed white concerns about what was to be done with the "Negro." He noted that the real question was:

> Can the white and colored peoples of this country be blended into a common nationality, and enjoy together, in the *same* country, under the same flag, the inestimable blessings of life, liberty and the pursuit of happiness, as neighborly citizens of a common country?[1]

Douglass has an unwavering answer:

> I answer most unhesitatingly, I believe they can. In saying this I am *not* blind to the past. I know it well. As a people we have moved about among you like dwarfs among giants – too small to be seen. We were morally, politically and socially dead. To the eye of doubt and selfishness we were far beyond the resurrection trump. All the more because I know the *past*. All the more, because I know the terrible experience of the slave, and *the* depressing power of oppression, do I believe in the possibility of a *better* future for the colored people of America.[2]

Frederick Douglass thought that in time blacks would be seen as full members of the state and that social progress on racial matters was possible. As full members, blacks would be able to rise or fall economically by their own efforts.

An important aspect of Douglass's vision for African-American social progress was his belief that, at some point in time, racial differences would not matter in the lives of the majority of Americans, black or white. While he understood that there might always be individual acts of racism, he hoped that the more widespread forms of societal sanctioned racism would end. The ending of societal sanctioned racism, he thought, would lessen individual acts of racism. In the end, there would just be Americans.[3]

While Douglass was disheartened with the Supreme Court's ruling in 1883 regarding the civil rights act and the backing away from the governmental protection of the legal rights of blacks by the Republican Party, he nevertheless remained steadfast in his belief that blacks would one day be seen as full members of the state. In 1889, Douglass restated the question: "The real question is whether American justice, American liberty, American civilization, American law and American Christianity can be made to include and protect alike and forever All American citizens. It is whether this great nation shall conquer its prejudices, rise to the dignity of its professions and proceed in the sublime course of truth and liberty [which Providence] has marked out for it."[4]

Douglass still thought that the answer to the question was yes. The United States, he thought, could and would live up to the principles articulated in the Declaration of Independence and the Constitution. His belief and faith that blacks would one day be seen as full members of the American polity anchored his theory of African-American social progress. Douglass believed that racism would not be a permanent feature in the lives of African Americans in the United States. Not everyone, however, shared Douglass' optimism about the political and social future of blacks in America.

One such thinker was Martin Delany (1812–85). Delany did not see a rosy future for blacks in America. Delany argued that whites would never recognize blacks as full and equal members of the state. Douglass and Delany disagreed about the nature of the problem and thus they offered different proposals concerning what was the best political and social strategy for blacks. Douglass saw racial assimilation as the most viable solution, while Delany proposed emigration.[5] Philosopher Bernard Boxill notes, however, that their disagreement was not over strategy only. Douglass and Delany also differed in their philosophical views about morality and human nature.[6] Douglass believed in the natural equality of humans. This equality extended to moral status and intellectual capacity. For Douglass all humans are rational creatures and it is the ability to reason correctly that would make the supposed distinctions between the races foolish. He thought that *reason* would one day compel whites to recognize the humanity of blacks.

Delany, however, did not think that appeals to reason or moral principles would "force" whites to see blacks as equals. There would always be, according to Delany, invidious racial distinctions in the United States. These racial distinctions would mark blacks off as being different from whites and not worthy of the same treatment. Delany thought that whites accepted these racial distinctions as natural and could not be convinced to think otherwise. Thus racism would be a permanent fixture in the United States. Douglass and Delany disagreed about the permanence of racism in the United States.

One hundred years after Douglass's death, the issue of the permanence of racism still resounds in black communities across the United States. In his book, *Double Exposure*, Chester Hartman has a chapter dedicated to this issue. Hartman notes that:

> *Double Exposure* starts with a number of short essays that respond to the provocative claim put forth by Derrick Bell, Richard Delgado, and others that racism is a permanent, non-eradicable feature of American life. Although a number of the contributors challenge the implication of this assertion, none of them claim that racism has been eradicated or will someday be eradicated in the United States. But conceding this point does not mean that racism as we know it is permanent.[7]

While there is no consensus by the contributors to Hartman's book, the issue raises a number of interesting questions on the current state of race relations for any racially classified group.

Even if we admit that there have been advances on the racial front since Douglass's death, the fact that the question of the permanence of racism is still being asked, "despite the gains of the civil rights era, raises serious concerns for all of us, making us reconsider our civil rights successes and wonder whether our lives have been, as Kenneth Clark reluctantly concludes, a 'series of glorious defeats' or the stuff of meaningful progress and victory."[8]

Currently the debate centers around two questions: Does racism still impact on the life chances of blacks? Is racism in the United States permanent?

While I will not attempt to answer these questions, what I want to suggest is that we find the modern-day equivalent of the Douglass/Delany debate in two widely read books: Cornel West's *Race Matters*[9] and Derrick Bell's *Faces at the Bottom of the Well*.[10] West and Bell take differing stances on the position of whether blacks will see a United States that is free of racism and racist social policy. West, I argue follows in the tradition of Douglass, while Bell carries on the tradition of Delany. I conclude that 100 years after his death the same issues regarding race that troubled Douglass still trouble black thinkers. There are, however, now black thinkers that argue that racism no longer adversely effects the life chances of blacks in the United States. How does the position of these thinkers differ from Douglass and Delany or West and Bell? I argue that their conceptions of justice and human nature set them apart.

Frederick Douglass and Cornel West

Douglass's program of social progress had as its goal full and unqualified citizenship for blacks. The moral principles of universal brotherhood and equality of human beings, coupled with the legal protections of the Constitution were the touchstones of Douglass's thought.[11] Cornel West's popular work *Race Matters* succinctly restates, I think, the basic tenets of Douglass's position on social progress.

It is interesting to note that West, like Douglass, enjoys a great deal of popular acclaim. Indeed, not since Douglass or King has a black public speaker drawn such an economically diverse interracial public following. People from various walks of life come to hear West speak about social reform. West, like Douglass and King, draws his audience from across the racial, gender, and class spectrum. Douglass gained and held the attention of the dominant race through his unsurpassed ability to articulate and relate to action the ethical contents of Christianity and the principles of the Declaration of Independence.[12] West holds the attention of members of both races through his ability to articulate the ethical principle of human equality and adherence to democratic principles. There is a great deal of ideological overlap in their positions. Importantly, West's and Douglass's positions about strategies for social progress also overlap.

But first let me note where they seem to differ. Douglass hopes for a time when it would be impossible to make racial distinctions. People of differing races would intermarry and racial distinctions would disappear. It is not clear that West holds or would support this position.

However, like Douglass, West argues that blacks should see themselves connected to the United States, as citizens. He constantly reiterates the interconnection between whites and blacks as citizens. Not only should the masses understand their positions as citizens, but also that any political and social leader should be bold in his or her declaration of the importance of citizenship as an ideal and practice. West, like Douglass, shares similar themes about the nature of political leadership. West, like Douglass, is forthright in his call for bold leadership. He writes:

> We need leaders neither saints nor sparkling television personalities who can situate themselves within a larger historical narrative of this country and our world, who can grasp the complex dynamics of our peoplehood and imagine a future grounded in the best of our past, yet who are attuned to the frightening obstacles that now perplex us.
> Our ideals of freedom, democracy, and equality must be invoked to invigorate all of us, especially the landless, propertyless, and luckless. Only a visionary leadership that can motivate "the better angles of our nature," as Lincoln said, and activates possibilities for a freer, more efficient, and stable America that leadership deserves cultivation and support.[13]

Douglass also constantly argued for bold leadership in solving the pressing problems of the day. He believed that the ideals set forth in the Declaration and Constitution set the moral standards by which Americans could live out the wishes of the founders. Bold and courageous leadership would adhere to these principles.

Yet, it is not only a belief in the value of these principles but also a belief that the struggle of blacks in America is tied to the struggles of other groups in America. Douglass realized that black social, economic, and political advancement would be a struggle. He appreciated the need for coalitions with other groups who were also struggling for progressive social recognition. In this regard, one can view Douglass's continual support of the women's movement as an example of his belief in the unity of struggle. Douglass always pushed for progressive coalitions.

West, like Douglass, is a believer in the ability of interracial coalitions to address the problems afflicting the country.[14] While he thinks that all groups should appreciate the value of coalitions, it is especially important that black leaders understand the importance of coalitions with other groups. According to West:

> To be a serious black leader is to be a race-transcending prophet who critiques the powers that be (including the black component

of the establishment) and who puts forth a vision of fundamental social change for all who suffer from socially induced misery.[15] . . . Rarely did we have a black leader highlight the moral content of a mature black identity, accent the crucial role of coalition strategy in the struggle for justice, or promote the ideal of black cultural democracy.[16]

Black leaders must recognize that blacks alone cannot win the struggle for racial justice and equality in the United States.

Black leaders are often mistrusting of interracial coalitions. This mistrust causes black leaders to adhere to racial reasoning as the panacea for black social progress. West discredits both viewpoints, but his attack on racial reasoning is striking. According to West, racial reasoning consists of making claims about black authenticity, that is what are the criteria that makes one black. These criteria are often set based on a closing rank mentality, in that one is to be concerned first and foremost with black people and the black community. This leads to "black male subordination of black women in the interest of the black community in a hostile white racist country."[17]

West understands why blacks would take such a stance regarding race, but still finds the position problematic in that it fails to take seriously the political realities of racial progress. Douglass would agree that a social and/or political strategy based on racial reasoning as a social policy for blacks is doomed to failure. Historian August Meier asserts that:

> Douglass then went on to specify, even though he ran "the risk of incurring displeasure," other errors committed by Negroes which contemporaries usually listed as virtues – race pride, race solidarity, and economic nationalism (or the advocacy of Negro support of Negro business). First among them was the "greater prominence of late" being given to the "stimulation of a sentiment we are pleased to call race pride," to which Negroes were "inclining most persistently and mischievously . . . I find it in all our books, papers and speeches."[18]

Meier notes that Douglass could see nothing to be either proud or ashamed of in a "gift from the almighty," and perceived:

> no benefit to be derived from this everlasting exhortation to the cultivation of race pride. On the contrary, I see in it a positive evil. It is a building on a false foundation. Besides, what is the thing we

are fighting against . . . but race pride . . .? Let us do away with this supercilious nonsense. Our policy should be to unite with the great masses of the American people . . .[19]

West's comments on the black community's response to the appointment of Clarence Thomas to the Supreme Court gives us a hint of his view of racial reasoning:

> Hence a grand opportunity for substantive discussion and struggle over race and gender was missed in black America and the larger society. And black leadership must share some of the blame. As long as black leaders remain caught in a framework of racial reasoning, they will not rise above the manipulative language of Bush and Thomas.[20]

Citing persons like Sojourner Truth, Tom Hayden, and Martin Luther King, Jr, West notes that:

> they understood the pitfalls of racial reasoning are too costly in mind, body, and soul especially for a downtrodden and despised people like black Americans. The best of our leadership recognized this valuable truth – and more must do so in the future if America is to survive with any moral sense.[21]

According to West, racial reasoning separates the races rather than uniting them. West is very critical of balck leaders that play the "race card." Needless to say, West is criticized for his comments about black leadership and the pitfalls of racial reasoning.[22] However, non-racial reasoning is not the only strategy needed.

The uniting of whites and blacks must involve the government playing a crucial role. For Douglass and West, the government should be involved in black advancement through the public policy it enacts. Both Douglass and West appreciate the role government has to play in the social, economic, and political advancement of blacks. One such governmental policy that has effected the lives of blacks is affirmative action.

West and Douglass make similar claims about affirmative action. West states that he would favor a class-based affirmative action program in principle. He notes, however, that given the history of racial and sexual discrimination an enforceable race-based and later gender-based affirmative action policy was the best possible compromise and concession.[23]

West endorses affirmative action as a means to abate discriminatory practices against women and people of color.[24] It may surprise some[25] to learn that in 1871, Frederick Douglass advocated a policy of affirmative action that gave special consideration to blacks because of the history of slavery and its aftermath. Douglass wrote:

> While I am for making no distinction, I am one of those who believe that whenever, and wherever, there is an office to be had, and a white applicant equally eligible, and equally available to obtain it; that while I am in favor of no distinctions on account of color, remembering the stripes, remembering the 250 years of bondage in this land, through which the colored man has been dragged, remembering that 250 years he has not had the right to learn to read the name of the God that made him, and that every man in the land has been at liberty to kick him, and to disregard his rights, he having no rights which a white man was bound to respect – I say, in view of that history, and the history of stripes, of tears, and of blood for the black man's track through this country for two hundred years I say, whenever the black man and the white man, equally eligible, equally available, equally qualified for an office, present themselves for that office, the black man, at this juncture of our affairs, should be preferred. That is my conviction.[26]

Needless to say Douglass did not foresee "affirmative action" for blacks as a permanent social policy. He envisioned a society in which race would one day play a minimal part in the life chances of any person. It would be by individual effort and intuitive that all Americans would advance. The role of the government is to provide the social and political environment in which such personal growth can be possible. In the end, the fate of each person would rise or fall on his or her own effort. West and Douglass want a society in which race does not matter, but both realize that we have not reached that point in American history.

The basic tenets of Douglass's program included, first, full adherence to the principles he saw espoused in the Declaration of Independence and United States Constitution, second, minimal reliance on racial categories, and, third, coalitions with other groups that suffered social and political injustice. Douglass also understood that while race should not matter, it does. Race-based policies may be needed for a time to advance black progress. But the goal nonetheless was to decrease the importance of race in the lives of all Americans. As I have said, Douglass realized blacks could not achieve full citizenship status without governmental assistance. These tenets for Douglass set the moral compass by which we were to plot strategies for black advancement in the United States.

Douglass was a believer in the enlightenment vision of full individual human equality. His view of social progress turns on his conception of man as a thinking being. As a thinking being, man is able to make moral judgments. These judgments should be based on facts. For Douglass, an important fact was the humanity of blacks, which meant that blacks are humans with the same mental capacities as whites. If it is true that all men (not just white men) are by nature endowed with the capacity to reason, it is unjust to devise a system that will limit that ability. Racial oppression limited the ability of blacks to full expression of their humanity. Douglass thought that whites failed to recognize the humanity of blacks because of faulty reasoning. This is why he preached the necessity of moral suasion. Douglass presented, until his death, arguments that attempted to counter racist claim about blacks. When whites saw the error of their reasoning about the humanity of blacks, Douglass thought, their opposition to blacks, as full citizens would cease. While Douglass, near the end of his life, became depressed about the social progress of blacks, he, nevertheless, thought that, in time, blacks would be seen as full members of the state. Douglass, with his view of the inherent equality and rationality of humans, thought that through moral suasion whites would come to accept blacks as equals.

Again West and Douglass meet. West writes that he wrote *Race Matters* to revitalize our public conversation about race.[27] A conversation that he hopes will be candid and frank about the problems facing America. One hundred years after the death of Douglass, he writes:

> We simply cannot enter the twenty-first century at each other's throats, even as we acknowledge the weighty forces of racism, patriarchy, economic inequality, homophobia, and ecological abuse on our necks. We are at a crucial crossroad in the history of this nation we either hang together or we hang separately. Do we have the intelligence, humor, imagination, courage, tolerance, love, respect, and will to meet the challenge? Time will tell.[28]

West, like Douglass, seeks an active respectful engagement with those persons who want to limit human rights. Douglass, as has been noted, thinks that humans are rational beings. They are able to understand arguments. Yet, they can be lead astray with erroneous facts, such as the false claims made about blacks. Whites have reasoned and do reason wrongly about the humanity of blacks. The goal is to get whites and some blacks to recognize their fallacious reasoning. Once they do, they will change their behavior and attitudes about racial justice.

Political and social leaders must take a bold stance and call for soul-searching discourse around the issues of race. Thus this strategy calls for open and honest conversation between the races. A conversation presupposes rationality of discourse and respect for the opinions of other. I believe that West, like Douglass, thinks that America will meet the challenge and become the type of nation envisioned by the founders – a nation based on mutual respect and democratic principles. West, I am sure, would not agree with all that Douglass claims. Nonetheless, there is a ringing similarity between the two positions. Again, this is not to imply that West is a racial assimilationist. It is, however, to assert that an important part of the Douglass legacy, a firm belief that the American dream will one day become a reality, still lives.

For West and Douglass, the goal is to ensure full state membership for blacks. But is it possible for blacks to be accepted as full members of the polity? It seems clear that for both Douglass and West the answer is yes. Is racism permanent? If my reading of Douglass and West is correct, their answer to this question is no.

Martin Delany and Derrick Bell

Is it possible for blacks to be accepted as full members of the United States? Is racism permanent? Martin Delany would answer no to the first question and yes to the second.

In 1854 Delany argued that white racism would prevent the full inclusion of blacks into the republic. He noted that the major problem facing Afro-Americans was not "a question of rich against poor, nor the common people against the higher classes; but a question of whites against blacks every white person, by legal right, being held superior to a black person or colored person." He could not envision an end to black subjugation in the United States because "[t]he rights of no oppressed people have ever been obtained by a voluntary act of justice on the part of the oppressor."[29] Delany concluded that blacks would never achieve full equality in the United States.

Delany argued that since whites never accepted blacks as social equals in the United States, whites would always oppress blacks. Delany gives two basic reasons for why this is the case. First, it was in white self-interest to oppress blacks. The strong always use the weak when it is in the self-interest of the strong. Second, the differences in physical appearances prevent whites from having the sympathies to concern themselves with the plight of blacks.[30] Delany thought that whites lacked the necessary feeling of sympathy toward blacks that would force them to be concerned with the maltreatment of blacks. Once again Bernard Boxill is worth citing at length:

> Two points about Delany's account of sympathy are especially important. First the absence of sympathetic ties is not in itself a motive for aggression. It only removes the constraints on aggression when aggression serves self-interest. Thus Delany specifically denied that it was "on account of hatred to his color, that the African was selected as the subject of oppression." He insisted that Africans were enslaved because this served the self-interest of Europeans; the difference in color between Africans and Europeans only dampened European sympathy for Africans. He even believed that the powerful would help the weak that were foreign to their sympathies when doing so served their self-interest.[31]

Boxill continues:

> The second important point about Delany's accounts of sympathy concerns those apt to be bound by sympathetic ties. David Hume thought that these ties mainly depended on the degree of contiguity and familiarity between the persons involved; thus he wrote in the *Enquiry* that "sympathy with persons remote from us [is] much fainter than that with persons near and contiguous," and in the *Treatise* that, concerning the attention we give to others, "'tis only the weakest which reaches to strangers and indifferent persons." In particular, he did not remark that the strength of sympathetic ties also seemed to depend on the degree of resemblance between the persons involved, although his cruel and dismissive disparagement of "negroes" suggests that this dependence may not be insignificant.[32]

Boxill notes that Delany could not have failed to appreciate this fact about how our sympathies run. He saw everyday that white sympathy for black misfortune was faint and weak, though the races were, by that time, no longer strangers to, nor remote from, one another.[33] Delany reasoned that racism was permanent in the United States. Unlike Douglass, Delany did not think that whites would be moved by moral suasion to accept blacks as full members of the state. For Delany, black assimilation of white manners and customs would not matter. A realistic look at race relations would reveal, according to Delany, that racism in the United States is permanent.

Following in Delany's tradition, the legal scholar Derrick Bell wrote *Faces at the Bottom of the Well* (1992). In this book, Bell offers his thesis that racism will remain a permanent fixture in the lives of blacks in the United States. While Bell's conclusion about the permanence of racism is identical to Delany, it must be noted that Bell's position relies on his understanding of the history of race relations in the United States. Bell's argument rests on historical determinism. That is, whites have generally disrespected blacks in the past. Whites generally disrespect blacks today. There is no reason to believe that whites will not disrespect blacks in the future. While Bell relies on history to prove his point, what he does say about the nature of the sympathetic feeling in whites is telling and *reminiscent of* Delany.

Bell notes that we simply cannot prepare realistically for our future without assessing honestly our past. It seems cold, accusatory, but we must try to fathom with Professor Linda Myers:

> the mentality of a people that could continue for over 300 years to kidnap an estimated 50 million youth and young adults from Africa, transport them across the Atlantic with about half dying unable to withstand the inhumanity of the passage, and enslave them as animals.[34]

Still citing Myers, Bell continues:

> "What," she wonders, can be understood about the world view of a people who claim to be building a democracy with freedom and justice for all, and at the same time own slaves and deny other basic human rights?"[35]

> Few whites, [Bell writes] are able to identify with blacks as a group the essential prerequisite for feeling empathy with, rather than aversion from, black's self-inflicted suffering. Unable or unwilling to perceive the "there but for the grace of God, go I," few whites are ready to actively promote civil rights for blacks. Because of an irrational but easily roused fear that any social reform will unjustly benefit blacks, whites fail to support the programs this country desperately needs to address the ever-widening gap between the rich and the poor, black and white.[36]

Bell, like Delany, thinks that whites lack the sympathy to be concerned with the plight of blacks and that the overall behavior of whites is self-interested. These themes form the background for Bell's view of the permanence of racism. But he turns quickly to the role of history and notes:

> We must see this country's history of slavery, not as an insuperable racial barrier to blacks, but as a legacy of enlightenment from our enslaved forbears reminding us that if they survived the ultimate form of racism, we and those whites who stand with us can at least view racial oppression in its many contemporary forms without underestimating its critical importance and likely permanent status in this country.[37]

Bell then sets forth a proposition that he thinks is easier to reject than refute. He writes:

> Black people will never gain full equality in this country. Even those Herculean efforts we hail as successful will produce no more than temporary peaks of progress, short-lived victories that slide into irrelevance as racial patterns adapt in ways that maintain white dominance. This is a hard-to-accept fact that all history verifies. We must acknowledge it not as a sign of submission, but as an act of ultimate defiance.[38]

Bell seems to think that many white Americans have a fixed attitude about blacks and it is not likely that their attitudes will be changed by arguments[39] or by seeing successful blacks.[40] He leaves us to ponder whether racism is permanent because of some innate psychological disposition whites have about blacks or "others." Does he think that the history of race relations has shaped fixed attitudes about blacks in the minds of whites that will not change? I think that Bell, like many blacks, feels the pressure of the innate disposition thesis, but he moves to support his claim by relying on the history of race relations rather than trying to expound some psychological thesis. But does he really believe that racism is permanent?

In *Faces at the Bottom of the Well*, Bell argues for the permanence of racism and black inequality. If we focus on the "likely permanence of racism," Bell thinks that it is logically possible to overcome racism, but he doubts whether this is a practical possibility. Bell leaves us to ponder his apocalyptic tale of "The Space Traders," which comes at the end of the book. In this story, aliens from outer space make the people of the United States a very seductive offer. The space traders will give the United States a source of unlimited energy, enough gold to erase the national deficit, and they will clean up the environment. All of these items will be given in exchange for all of the African Americans who live in the United States. Bell's tale follows the debate as to whether people (white) of the United States would accept the deal. In the end, the offer is accepted and blacks are traded to the space traders. Blacks are then removed from the United States. It is difficult to imagine that such a tale hints at the possibility of good future relationships between blacks and whites in the United States. Bell, nevertheless, thinks that the tale should not engender despair. He argues that to understand the permanence of racism is to be a realist. In this regard, blacks have to shape their policies and actions accordingly. Bell writes:

> Perhaps those of us who can admit we are imprisoned by the history of racial subordination in America can accept – as slaves had no choice but to accept – our fate. Not that we legitimate the racism of the oppressor. On the contrary, we can only *de*legitimate it if we can accurately pinpoint it. And racism lies at the center, not the periphery; in the permanent, not in the fleeting; in the real lives of black and white people, not in the sentimental caverns of the mind.
>
> Armed with this knowledge, and with the enlightened, humility-based commitment that it engenders, we can accept the dilemmas of the committed confrontation with evils we cannot end. We can go forth to serve, knowing that our failure to act will not change conditions and may very well worsen them.[41]

Even if it is true, according to Bell, that blacks will never gain full equality, blacks have to work to make their lives in the United States tolerable. Bell, unlike Delany, does not endorse emigration, although the Afrolantica story has emigrationist overtones. Nonetheless, Bell, like Delany, thinks that blacks should accept that racism is a part of what it means to be in America. While, as noted, Bell does not directly appeal to some psychological predisposition to explain the continuation of racism, he does follow Delany's lead in assenting that appeals to justice and moral principle will do little to improve the plight of blacks. Racism is a permanent feature of the United States.

Does Race Matter at the Bottom of the Well?

If my reading of West and Bell is correct, we find the continuation of an age-old debate in the black community. Douglass and Delany represent a nice historical perspective from which to review the debate over race relations, while West and Bell represent its contemporary manifestation. In the case of all of these writers, we find black thinkers who take differing positions on the future of blacks in the United States. Cornel West and Derrick Bell are carrying on this important debate with the same deep and thoughtful reflections that marked the work of Delany and Douglass.

The debate over the permanence of racism, nevertheless, gives us a continuum on which to place and to examine the position of various black leaders over time. Indeed, how one answers the question of the permanence of racism seems to bear directly on the strategies he or she selects for achieving black progress. On the permanence end of the continuum, we find Paul Cuffe, Marcus Garvey, The Nation of Islam, and the Republic of New Africa. On the other side, we find Martin Luther King, Jr, the NAACP, and other civil rights groups. I would suggest that the debate over the focus of black studies going on between Harvard University and Temple University is a continuation of this debate.

However, the most provocative participants in this debate are the black conservatives who think that 100 years after Douglass's death racism has diminished to the point where it no longer plays a significant role in the social, economic or political advancement of black people.

If these writers are correct, the position put forth by Delany, and later articulated by Bell, has been proven to be false. Racism is not a permanent feature in the lives of blacks in the United States. If this is true, then race no longer matters and it would appear that Douglass was right. Is this the case?

Stan Faryna, editor of the book *Black and Right: The Bold New Voice of Black Conservatives in America*,[42] describes this work as addressing these questions about race relations in the United States: "Is America a hopelessly racist nation? Do most white people want to see blacks fail? Is it impossible for black people to be racists?" He answers:

> The angry rhetoric of mainstream black leadership in America today suggests that the answer to each of these questions is "Yes!" ... But black conservatives, an often-neglected voice in media presentations of race in America are fighting back and speaking for themselves and by themselves. They are declaring that the Ameri-

can dream for blacks is alive and well, that most non-blacks are not racists, that the evil of racism comes in all colors, and that racism is no excuse for unacceptable behavior.[43]

While much of this is hyperbole, the basic gist is that racism no longer plays a significant role in the life chances of blacks. Let me quickly note that one does not have to be a conservative to advance the position that there has been a significant decline in racist attitudes. William Julius Wilson ascribes to this position.[44] Wilson and the conservatives would agree that many blacks are still at the bottom of the social well, but reject the claim that race is the cause of their predicament.

This line of reasoning has its ideological roots in the writings and practices of Booker T. Washington.[45] Washington developed his view of racial progress during a period when there was no hint of equality between the races. It did not appear that even formal equality was in the offering. Remember that in 1896, the Supreme Court ruled in *Plessy v. Ferguson* that "separate but equal" was the law of the land. Washington understood that things were "separate but not equal." In this political climate, Washington discerned a basic understanding of the psychology of whites. They were basically egoistic. As Robert Factor notes:

> Booker Washington's total approach to the race question turned on a theoretical complex including a theory of human nature, of society, and of action. Human nature was seen as egoistic rather than altruistic, and materially rather than spiritually motivated. The springs of social intercourse were fed by economic considerations above all others. Tactically, social action must be fluid. Therefore, Washington created a highly tractable and variegated system of operations resting on an intuitive mastery of social psychology. He sought at all times to locate and work with the directing forces in the constellation of social groups. The logic of his controlling assumptions pointed him toward cooperation with men whose primary interest in the Negro was economic. This was most natural. He also recognized the advantages to be had in working with men whose interest in the Negro was primarily humanitarian. Often their particular interest coincided with those of the entrepreneur.[46]

If this is true then appeals to morality or to claims of poor treatment of blacks as citizens were doomed to failure. Accordingly, if humans are basically egoistic, the best strategy for blacks was to appeal to the self-interest of whites. Thus, blacks should not push for social equality or political equality, since these were not in the interest of whites. Washington thus thought that it was in the best interest of blacks to appeal to the economic self-interest of whites.

Factor notes that:

> At the lower and higher levels of economic activity, Washington counted on his theory of human nature to hold true. Prejudice would wither and die before the perennial gale of self-interest. Man has an instinct to truck, barter, and trade, and to get the best deal for his money. He has no instinct to prejudice.[47]

Citing Washington, Factor writes:

> In any conflict between the two, Washington was certain of the outcome, and drew two implications therefrom. The race problem would disappear: "Two races are good friends in proportion as the one has something of value that the other wants." And, economic development would settle the question of civil and political rights: "The individual or race that owns the property is going to exercise the greatest control in government . . . whether he lives in the North or South."[48]

For Washington, the economics of race relations was treated as the ultimately determining factor. According to Washington, the social interactions of humans are shaped by economic structures. "This general line set the broad limits of Washington's strategy, and determined his tactical position from day to day and from issue to issue."[49] Clearly Washington was a complex thinker and thus made alliances with whites that had, as Factor noted, a more humanitarian approach for the social advancement of blacks as well as those who only had an economic interest in blacks. While, for Washington, race matters, it need not play a significant role in individual advancement.

Washington thought that through economic advancement the day would come when blacks would be respected as functioning productive members of the state. In this regard, there would be no white resistance to the social strivings of any black. One hundred years later, we find some black thinkers arguing that this day has arrived.

There are, at least, two approaches that attempt to understand why some blacks would think that race does not matter at the bottom of the well. The first approach looks at how individuals evaluate what they take to be the empirical sociological data. Law professor John A. Powell correctly notes that there "is a difficulty in defining a racial baseline and comparing the African American circumstance during two different periods of time." He continues that "one would have to ignore history to assert that conditions and status of blacks in America have not improved since slavery."[50] But have the political, economic, and social conditions changed to such a degree that we can proclaim that race no longer matters?

Powell then gives two possible reasons for the belief that racial equality has been achieved. "One reason is that many people are *not* aware of the racial disparity. If they see disparity at all, they see economic disparity that just happens to disproportionately affect blacks."[51] Clearly, this is not the position of neo-accommodationists. They constantly note the differing social and economic disparities between blacks and whites. They cite the various ways the life conditions of blacks differ from that of whites. Obviously, they are aware that the disparity is not just economic. Like Washington, these modern-day accommodationists think that the disparities are the fault of blacks. As early as 1894, Washington shifted the blame for the social and economic plight of black to blacks. He insisted that the lack of black progress be tied to the values they held. There is, it seems, a belief by Washington and his followers that the culture of poverty thesis is true. That is, social disparity is a result of poor family values. These early values were formed, according to Washington, by the slavery experience.[52] His modern-day followers would claim that these values have become intergenerational. Negative values are passed from one generation to the next. If an individual changes his or her values from "ghetto specific" to "middle class," there will be a marked difference in the overall social standing of that individual.

It is not only a belief about values, but also an interesting understanding of the value of formal equality that supports the accommodationist view that racial equality has been achieved. According to Powell:

> [this] reason hinges on the way we think about equality. Many people believe that inequality is determined by formal laws and intentional individual practices. The removal of explicitly racial barriers during the civil rights era, such as laws prohibiting blacks from living in certain neighborhoods or going to certain schools engendered a belief that the vast majority of racial inequality had been corrected because of the advance in the level of formal equality.[53]

In this regard, a primary reason for black social disparity is the failure by blacks to appreciate that their progress is tied to the free market system. That is, blacks must take on the values that will make them successful in the current economic climate. Accordingly, there are, at this time, no racial barriers that prevent blacks from becoming successful within the current economic arrangements. Bernard Boxill has argued for the unsoundness of this argument[54]. Truly the neo-accommodationists cannot think that formal equality translates into actual or substantive equality. If this is so, then their understanding of justice and their understanding of the permanence of racism must be reviewed.

It is easy to understand why it would be thought that the issue turns on the accumulation of empirical data. In this case, each side tries to marshal enough evidence to support its claim that racism is or is not still a factor in the lives of blacks. While this approach is insightful, the more philosophically interesting problem concerns their understanding of social justice.

Justice and Social Progress

Douglass, Delany, and Washington differ on certain issues, but they share a common bond. They start with different views of human nature and thus derive different strategies for black advancement, but as I shall argue they all share a libertarian conception of justice.

As political philosopher John Hospers notes:

> The political philosophy that is called libertarianism (from the Latin word *libertas* – liberty) is the doctrine that every person is the owner of his own life, and that no one is the owner of anyone else's life: and consequently every human being has the right to act in accordance with his own choices, unless those actions infringe on the equal liberty of other human beings to act in accordance with their choices.[55]

Douglass, Delany, and Washington being drawn to this conception of justice should come as no surprise.

All three of these thinkers understood how legal sanctions impeded the social and economic liberty of blacks. It was clear at that point in history that if American citizens were left free to guide their lives as they saw fit, they could prosper. But they had to have the liberty to act freely without unjust intervention into their affairs. Indeed, all of these thinkers understood that the legal constraints of slavery were liberty restricting. The Jim Crow Laws after slavery had the same effect. They limited the liberty of blacks. The goal then, for these thinkers, was to bring about a civil society that provided the greatest amount of personal liberty for all. Douglass and Washington thought that this could be achieved in the United States. Delany thought that blacks could find this freedom, but not in the United States.

Douglass fought all of his life for the right of personal liberty for all humans. He understood the power of the state to restrain the liberty of individuals. In 1869, when asked what should be done for the negro, Douglass replied:

> My politics in regard to the negro is simply this: give him fair play and leave him alone, but be sure you give him fair play. He is now a man before the law. I rejoice at it. What we want, what we are resolved to have, is the right to be men among men; men everywhere.[56]

Douglass goes on to state that the government is bound to see, not only that the negro has the right to vote, but that he has fair play in the acquisition of land; that when he is offered a fair price for the land of the south, he shall not be deprived of the right to purchase, simply because of his color.[57] Douglass admitted that it might seem inconsistent to ask for government help and to leave the Negro alone. But he noted that it was consistent with what should be the first proposition – give him fair play, and leave him alone. This view is rooted in the libertarian tradition. Black social advancement should be handled through the free market, but people deserve compensation when their rights are violated. While Douglass believed that there should be group compensation, Thomas Sowell and other contemporary black conservatives, while citing Douglass's notion of fair play, call for compensation of wrongs done to individuals only.

Douglass's view of human nature is compatible with his libertarian conception of justice. All humans were defined as rational beings. And as such, they should be accorded all the liberties consistent with their powers of reasoning. Given that there were no natural differences between blacks and whites as rational beings, slavery and Jim Crow Laws placed unfair limitations on the liberty of blacks. These restrictions were unjust, as Howard McGary notes, not because they were placed on blacks, but because these restrictions limited the liberty of rational beings. According to Douglass and McGary, these restrictions are unjust no matter what group is subjected to them.

Douglass thought that persons could be moved by moral suasion to change their views. Thus Douglass attempted to change the negative opinions of whites about blacks by argumentation. Douglass's appeal was to the rational side of human understanding.

Washington and his followers also hold a libertarian conception of justice. However, they believed human behavior is motivated by self-interest. The proper role of the government is to ensure that each person has the liberty to pursue his or her interest, without undue interference. Washington did not think that moral suasion would move whites to treat blacks fairly. Blacks had to convince whites that it was in their self-interest to treat blacks justly. Black progress was tied to the self-interest of whites.

However, there is an important difference between Washington and his modern-day disciples. Washington was willing to use political means to achieve his ends. Modern-day conservatives claim to want to avoid politics and focus on the market. The invisible hand of the market solves the problem rather than politics. According to them, the government needs to let the free market work. The free market will be just, but not as some means to a social good. The just government allows transactions to take place according to the principles of fair exchange. The rub is that these contemporary conservatives believe that the social conditions exist now that allow blacks the freedom to participate fully in the free market.

Finally, Delany would agree with Douglass's and Washington's libertarian conception of justice, but he would disagree with their conclusion that justice for blacks could be achieved in the United States. Delany also thought that whites were self-interested but their lack of empathy for blacks prevents them from feeling any sense of solidarity with blacks. Delany also believed that individual liberty was very important, but it would not be possible for blacks to be free in the United States.

We have a common conception of justice at work here, but Douglass, Delany, and Washington have different conceptions of human nature. If my reading of these three writers is correct, then the primary question for these black thinkers was not over how to define justice, but how to achieve it. For them it was clear that justice requires that personal liberty is respected and protected.

There is a tension between protecting individual liberty and pushing a certain conception of good. Should we give more weight to liberty or to the good? Derrick Bell appreciates the problem this tension raises for the ending of racism. Bell understands that the libertarian tradition is rooted in the American way of life. If strong weight is given to personal liberty, then persons should be allowed to associate with whom they please. If some whites only want to associate with other whites, it is unjust according to the libertarian perspective to force them to do otherwise.

There is ongoing debate about what the state can do to bring about ends that most members of the state would consider good, e.g., the elimination of racism. Bell gives us a unique way to resolve the tension between liberty and the good, as it is manifested in the debate over racism. In *Faces*, he proposes what he calls the Racial Preference Licensing Act:

> Under the new act, all employers, proprietors of public facilities, and owners and managers of dwellings places, homes, and apartments could on application to the federal government, obtain a license authorizing the holders, their managers, agents, and employees to exclude or separate persons on the basis of race or color.[58]

Bell admits that license would be expensive, but not prohibitively so. Bell writes:

> Far from being a retreat into our unhappy racial past . . . the new law embodies a daring attempt to create a brighter racial future for all our citizens. Racial realism is the key to understanding this new law. It does not assume a nonexistent racial tolerance, but boldly proclaims its commitment to racial justice through the working of a marketplace that recognizes and seeks to balance the rights of our black citizens to fair treatment and the no less important right of some whites to an unfettered choice of customers, employees, and contractees.[59]

Bell understands that libertarianism will not have the desired effect that Douglass and Washington wanted. The state has to balance the liberties of whites with the welfare of blacks. The state should not force whites to be accepting of blacks. Many whites will never see blacks as social equals. If we allow for personal liberty, we must allow for the continuation of racism unless the individual willingly finds a reason to change. Douglass thought that moral suasion could do it, while Washington appealed to white self-interest. Delany, however, thought that whites would never accept blacks as social equals. But with all these thinkers, liberty trumps the good.

Cornel West, though, does not seem to give adequate weight to the tension between liberty and the good. West seems to think that the state should be concerned with the good over certain personal liberties, for example, the accumulation of wealth. West thinks that black poverty will be eliminated not by affording blacks more liberty, but by the redistribution of wealth. He writes:

> Affirmative action is not the most important issue for black progress in America, but it is part of a redistributive chain that must be strengthened if we are to confront and eliminate black poverty.[60]

The problem for West is not one of lack of personal liberty, but the economic structure of the state. Whether or not people can be persuaded to give up liberty for the good of blacks by moral suasion is questionable. West fails to fully appreciate that the libertarian perspective has deep roots in black and white communities. Blacks have long claimed that what they needed was more personal liberty. This view, as we have seen, harkens back to Douglass, Delany, and Washington. Douglass indeed thought that appeals to morality would change people's opinions about blacks, but, unlike West, he never asked them to forgo their personal liberty to disassociate from people that they did not like.

In the final analysis, how one answers the question of the permanence of racism draws on conceptions of justice and his or her understanding of human nature. One's understanding of these important concepts[61] will determine how one answers the question: does race matter at the bottom of the well?

Douglass One Hundred Years Later

One hundred and fifty years ago, the dispute about the biological and intellectual capacities of blacks was at the core of the slavery controversy. At the time of Douglass's death, there were debates about the intellectual and criminal nature of blacks. Today with works like the *Bell Curve* and *The End of Racism* the dispute about the biological and intellectual capacities of blacks is at the core of the education, crime, and welfare controversy. Perhaps this is why questions about the permanence of racism have endured.

One hundred years after Douglass's death the debate around race is as furious as it was during his times. Indeed, some of the views that dominated racial reasoning in his day are articulated today. Consider that there is now a strident interest in Afro-centric ideology by a significant number of blacks. How does this differ from the racial pride movement that Douglass criticized? On the other side, there are deep-seated views of black inferiority and criminality held presently by many whites. Douglass had critiqued these positions before the Civil War and again before his death in 1895. The continued restating of these views is a sad commentary on the state of race relations in the United States.

However, what Douglass could not have foreseen was that 100 years later some blacks could look at the plight of less fortunate blacks and still think that racism had ended or declined. One hundred years later his words have a force of truth:

> Can the negro be a citizen? was the question of the Dred Scott decision. Can the negro be educated? Can the negro be induced to work for himself, without a master? Can the negro be a soldier? Time and events have answered these and all other like questions. We have amongst us, those who have taken the first prizes as scholars; those who have won distinction for courage and skill on the battlefield; those who have taken rank as lawyers, doctors and ministers of the gospel; those who shine among men in every useful calling; and yet we are called "a problem;" "a tremendous problem;" a mountain of difficulty; a constant source of apprehension; a disturbing force, threatening destruction to the holiest and best interests of society.[62]

Douglass resisted the idea of defining blacks as a problem. But he understood that as long as blacks were collectively seen as a problem, this was a clear sign that antiblack racism had not declined and blacks were not full members of the state. One hundred years later, blacks are still considered a social problem. (Of course, neo-accommodationists would claim that they are still a problem because they have not taken advantage of the declining impact of racism.)

The current state of race relations would be very disheartening to Douglass. Would he give up hope that the American dream would become a reality for all blacks?[63] I am not sure. But an important part of Douglass's legacy is his insistence that all Americans come to grips with the reality of race and racism and the role of each in the fulfillment of the American dream. When full equality of opportunity is achieved, Douglass would conclude that social justice has been achieved.

Given the interesting juxtapositions between justice and the permanence of racism, Douglass's insights about the nature of race relations in the United States are still provocative. Reflecting on the state of race relations today, we must agree with Douglass when he writes:

> Strange things have happened of late and are still happening. Some of these tend to dim the luster of the American name, and chill the

hopes once entertained for the cause of American liberty. He is a wiser man than I am, who can tell how low the moral sentiments of the Republican may yet fall. When the moral sense of a nation begins to decline, and the wheels of progress to roll backward, there is no telling how low one will fall or where the other will stop. The downward tendency, already manifest, has swept away some of the most important safeguards. The Supreme Court has surrendered. State Sovereignty is restored. It has destroyed the civil rights Bill, and converted the Republican Party into a party of money rather than a party of morals, a party of things rather than a party of humanity and justice. We may well ask what next?[64]

Indeed with the memory of Douglass's insights and fortitude, we too must ask 100 years later, what next?[65]

Notes

1. Frederick Douglass, "The Present and Future of the Colored Race in America: An Address Delivered in Brooklyn, New York, on 15 May 1863," John Blassingame, ed, *The Frederick Douglass Papers*, vol. 3 (New Haven: Yale University Press, 1985), p. 576.
2. Ibid., p. 576.
3. Douglass, "The Negro Problem," an Address delivered in Washington, D.C., on October 21, 1890, John Blassingame and John R. McKivigen eds, in *The Frederick Douglass Papers*, vol. 4 (New Haven: Yale University Press, 1991), p. 455
4. Ibid., p. 409.
5. Bernard R. Boxill, "Douglass Against the Emigrationists," in this volume.
6. Bernard R. Boxill, "Two Traditions in African-American Political Philosophy," in *The Philosophical Forum*, vols 1–3, Fall–Spring 1992–3, p. 119.
7. Chester Hartman, ed., *Double Exposure* (Armonk, New York: M. E. Sharpe, 1997), p. 4.
8. Ibid., p. 6.
9. Cornel West, *Race Matters* (New York: Vintage House, 1993).
10. Derrick Bell, *Faces at the Bottom of the Well* (New York: Basic Books, 1992).
11. Robert L. Factor, *The Black Response to America: Men, Ideals, and Organization from Frederick Douglass to the NAACP* (Reading: Addison-Wesley Publishing Company, 1970), pp. 104–5.
12. Ibid., p. 105.
13. West, *Race Matters*, p. 13.
14. Howard McGary, "Racism, Social Justice, and Interracial Coalitions," in *The Journal of Ethics*, vol. 1, no. 3, 1997.
15. West, *Race Matters*, p. 70.

16 Ibid., p. 47.
17 Ibid., p. 24.
18 August Meier, "Frederick Douglass' Vision for America: A Case Study in Nineteenth-Century Negro Protest," in Harold M. Hyman and Leonard W. Levy, eds, *Freedom and Reform* (New York: Harper & Row, Publishers, 1967), p. 145.
19 Ibid., p. 145.
20 West, *Race Matters*, p. 49.
21 Ibid., p. 49.
22 Possibly one of the most negative attacks on West has been Adolph Reed's article in *The Village Voice*. See, Adolph Reed, "What are the drums saying, Booker?" The Current Crisis of the Black Intellectual," in *The Village Voice*, April 11, 1995, pp. 31–6.
23 West, *Race Matters*, p. 95.
24 ibid., p. 96.
25 For example, Supreme Court Justice Clarence Thomas and Harvard Law Professor Randall Kennedy make constant reference to Douglass's rejection of the role of race in public policy. See Clarence Thomas, "Toward a 'Plain Reading' of Constitution – The Declaration of Independence in Constitutional Interpretation," in *Howard Law Journal*, 30, 1987, pp. 691–703; and Randall Kennedy, "My Race Problem-and Ours," *The Atlantic Monthly*, www.theatlantic.com/atlantic/issues/97may/kennedy.htm.
26 Frederick Douglass, "We Need a True, Strong, and Principled Party," Address delivered in Washington, D.C., on March 29, 1871, in Blassingame and McKivigen, eds, *The Frederick Douglass Papers*, vol. 4, p. 284.
27 West, *Race Matters*, p. 158.
28 Ibid., p. 159.
29 See Alphonso Pinkney, *Red, Black and Green: Black Nationalism in the United States* (Cambridge: Cambridge University Press, 1976), pp. 25–6.
30 See Bernard R. Boxill, "Two Traditions", p. 121.
31 Ibid., p. 121.
32 Ibid., p. 121.
33 Ibid., p. 121.
34 Bell, *Faces*, p. 11.
35 Ibid., p. 11.
36 Ibid., p. 4.
37 Ibid., p. 12.
38 Ibid., p. 12.
39 Ibid., p. 28.
40 Ibid., p. 26.
41 Ibid., pp. 197–8.
42 Stan Faryna, ed., *Black and Right: The Bold New Voice of Black Conservatives in America* (Westport, Connecticut: Praeger, 1997).
43 This description of *Black and Right. The Bold New Voice of Black Conservatives in America*, was given as part of a review of the book

on the following website: http//www.labridge.com/msbooks/opinions/MoreonBlackandRight.html.

44 William J. Wilson, *The Declining Significance of Race* (Chicago: University of Chicago Press, 1980) and *The Truly Disadvantaged* (Chicago: University of Chicago Press, 1988).
45 Bernard R. Boxill, "The Race/Class Debate," in Bill E. Lawson, ed, *The Underclass Question* (Temple University Press, 1991) pp. 19–32.
46 Factor, *Black Response to America*, p. 193.
47 Ibid., p. 193.
48 Ibid., p. 193.
49 Ibid., p. 193.
50 John A. Powell, "Is Racism Permanent," in Hartman, ed, *Double Exposure*, pp. 37–8.
51 Ibid., p. 38.
52 Frank M. Kirkland, "Modernity and Intellectual Life in Black," in *The Philosophical Forum*, vols 1–3, Fall–Spring 1992–3, p. 146.
53 Powell, " Is Racism Permanent," p. 38.
54 Bernard R. Boxill, *Blacks and Social Justice* (Lanham, MD.:Rowman and Littlefield, 1992).
55 John Hospers, "The Libertarian Manifesto," in James Sterba, ed, *Justice: Alternative Political Perspectives* (Belmont Ca.: Wadsworth Publishing Company, 1992), p. 41.
56 Douglass, "Let the Negro Alone: An Address Delivered in New York, New York on May 11, 1869," *The Frederick Douglass Papers*, vol. 4, 202.
57 Ibid., pp. 202–3.
58 Bell, *Faces*, p. 49.
59 Ibid., p. 47.
60 West, *Race Matters*, p. 65.
61 Douglass, "Lessons of the Hour: An Address Delivered in Washington, D.C. on January 9, 1894," in John Blassingame and John R. McKivigen, eds, *The Frederick Douglass Papers*, vol. 5 (New Haven: Yale University Press, 1991), p. 607.
62 Douglass, *The Frederick Douglass Papers*, vol. 4, p. 607.
63 Bill E. Lawson, "Social Disappointment and the Black Sense of Self," in Lewis R. Gordon, ed, *Existence in Black* (New York: Routledge, 1997), pp. 149–56.
64 Douglass, "Lessons of the Hour", p. 596.
65 I want to thank Howard McGary for his comments, time, and support in the writing of this essay. I also benefited from discussions with my son, William Lance Lawson and my wife, Renee Sanders-Lawson.

Selected Bibliography on Frederick Douglass

Andrew, William L., ed., *To Tell A Free Story: The First Century of Afro-American Autobiography, 1760–1865.* Urbana: University of Illinois Press, 1986.
——, ed., *The Oxford Frederick Douglass Reader.* New York: Oxford University Press, 1996.
——, *Critical Essays on Frederick Douglass.* Boston: G. K. Hall, 1991.
Bassham, Gregory, *Original Intent and The Constitution.* Lanham: Rowman Allanheld and Littlefield, 1992.
Bell, Derrick, *Faces at the Bottom of the Well.* New York: Basic Books, 1992.
Blassingame, John, et al., eds, *The Frederick Douglass Papers*, 1–5 vols. New Haven: Yale University Press, 1979–94.
Blight, David W., *Frederick Douglass' Civil War: Keeping Faith in Jubilee.* Baton Rouge: Louisiana State University Press, 1989.
Bogin, Ruth and Lowenberg, Bert, eds, *Black Women in Nineteenth Century American Life.* University Park: The Pennsylvania State University Press, 1976.
Bontemps, Arna, *Free at Last: The Life of Frederick Douglass.* New York: Dodd, Mead, 1971.
Boxill, Bernard R., *Blacks and Social Justice.* Lanham: Rowman Allanheld and Littlefield, 1984 and 1992 (2nd edition).
Brotz, Howard, ed., *African-American Social and Political Thought: 1850–1920.* New Brunswick: Transaction Publishers, 1991; formerly entitled *Negro Social and Political Thought: 1850–1920.* New York: Basic Books, 1966.
Burke, Ronald K., *Frederick Douglass: Crusading Orator for Human Rights.* New York: Garland Publishing, 1996.
Davis, Allison, *Leadership, Love, and Aggression.* New York: Harcourt Brace Jovanovich, 1983.
Davis, Angela Y., *Women, Race and Class.* New York: Vintage Books, 1983.
Factor, Robert L., *The Black Response to America: Men, Ideals, and Organization from Frederick Douglass to the NAACP.* Reading: Addison-Wesley Publishing Company, 1970.

Faryna, Stan. ed., *Black and Right: The Bold New Voice of Black Conservatives in America*. Westport, Connecticut: Praeger, 1997.
Fehrenbacher, Don E., *The Dred Scott Case: Its Significance in American Law and Politics*. New York: Oxford Univeresity Press, 1978.
Foner, Philip S., ed., *Life and Writings of Frederick Douglass*, 5 vols. New York: International Publishers, 1950–75.
——, *Frederick Douglass*. New York: Citadel, 1969.
Foster, Frances Smith, *Written By Herself: Literary Production By African-American Women, 1742–1892*. Bloomington: Indiana University Press, 1993.
Franklin, John Hope, *From Slavery to Freedom*. New York: Alfred Knopf, 1974.
—— and McNeil, Genna Rae, eds, *African Americans and the Living Constitution*. Washington, D.C.: Smithsonian Institution Press, 1995.
Friedman, Lawrence J., *Gregarious Saints: Self and Community in American Abolitionism, 1830–1870*. Cambridge: Cambridge University Press, 1982.
Gordon, Lewis R., ed., *Existence in Black: An Anthology of Black Existential Philosophy*. New York: Routledge, 1997.
Harris, Leonard, ed., *Philosophy Born of Struggle: Anthology of Afro-American Philosophy from 1917*. Dubuque: Kendall/Hunt, 1983.
Hartman, Chester, ed., *Double Exposure*. Armonk, New York: M. E. Sharpe, 1997.
Higginbotham, A. Leon, *In the Matter of Color: Race and the American Legal Process*. New York: Oxford University Press, 1978.
Huggins, Nathan I., *Slave and Citizen: The Life of Frederick Douglass*. Boston: Little, Brown, 1980.
Jaffa, Harry V., ed., *Original Intent and The Framers of the Constitution: A Disputed Question*. Washington, D.C.: Regnery Gateway, 1994.
Lawson, Bill E., ed., *The Underclass Question*. Temple University Press, 1991.
Levine, Robert S., *Martin Delaney, Frederick Douglass, and The Politics of Representative Identity*. Chapel Hill: University of North Carolina Press, 1997.
Martin, Waldo E., *The Mind of Frederick Douglass*. Chapel Hill: University of North Carolina Press, 1984.
McFeely, William S., *Frederick Douglass*. New York: W. W. Norton, 1991.
McGary, Howard and Lawson, Bill E., *Between Slavery and Freedom: Philosophy and American Slavery*. Bloomington: Indiana University Press, 1992.
Moses, Greg, *Revolution of Conscience: Martin Luther King, Jr and the Philosophy of Non-Violence*. New York: Guilford Press, 1997.
Moses, Wilson J., *Alexander Crummell: A Study of Civilization and Discontent*. New York: Oxford University Press, 1989.
Oshinsky, David, *"Worse Than Slavery": Parchman Farm and the Ordeal of Jim Crow Justice*. New York: The Free Press, 1996.
Peterson, Carla L., *"Doers of the Word": African-American Women Speakers and Writers in the North (1830–1880)*. New York: Oxford University Press, 1995.
Pinkney, Alphonso, *Red, Black and Green: Black Nationalism in the United States*. Cambridge: Cambridge University Press, 1976.

Pittman, John P., ed., *African-American Perspectives and Philosophical Traditions*. New York: Routledge, 1997.

Quarles, Benjamin, *Frederick Douglass*. Washington, D.C.: Associated Publishers, 1968.

Rogers, William B., *"We Are All Together Now:" Frederick Douglass, William Lloyd Garrison, and The Prophetic Tradition*. New York: Garland Press, 1995.

Stuckey, Sterling, *Slave Culture: Nationalist Theory and the Foundations of Black America*. New York: Oxford University Press, 1987.

Sundquist, Eric J., ed., *Frederick Douglass: New Literary and Historical Essays*. Cambridge: Cambridge University Press, 1990.

——, *To Wake the Nations: Race in the Making of American Literature*. Cambridge: Harvard University Press, 1993.

Walker, Peter F., *Moral Choices: Memory, Desire, and Imagination in Nineteenth Century American Abolition*. Baton Rouge: Louisiana State University Press, 1978.

West, Cornel, *Race Matters*. New York: Vintage House, 1993.

Willett, Cynthia. *Maternal Ethics and Other Slave Moralities*. New York: Routledge, 1995.

Index

Aaraleff, Hans   189
abolition of slavery   187–8;
  benevolence   266; Constitution
  85–6; moral/physical struggle
  291, 293–4; moral relevance
  247; moral suasion   228–9,
  243–4, 246, 305n63; politics
  267, 268–9, 275–8; scholars'
  role   153
Adams, Abigail   117
affirmative action   5, 15n8, 313,
  371–2, 387
Africa   26, 27, 29; languages
  171n38, 191
African Americans: *see* blacks
Afro-centric ideology   387
Agassiz, Professor   151, 157
Alabama, convict leasing   344, 352
alienation of blacks   25, 30, 33, 45,
  126, 211
A. M. E. Zionist church   149,
  169n19
Amendments to Constitution:
  Thirteenth   341, 344; Fifteenth
  316, 326–7
America, Central   26, 27
America, South   26, 27, 46n35
American Colonization Society   22,
  45–6n6, 27
Anderson, M. D.   149, 158
Anglo-conformity   75
animal rights   59
anomaly theorists   117, 140n82
Anthony, Susan B.   326
anti-slavery political action   277,
  278, 292; *see also* abolition of
  slavery
anti-white supremacy   109, 111
Appiah, Kwame Anthony   62–3n16,
  194
Aptheker, Bettina   327
Aquinas, Saint Thomas   93, 106
Aristotle   106, 122, 146, 147
assimilation   76–7, 78–9, 123; as
  adaptation   74–5; black
  institutions   61; Boxill   64, 79;
  Douglass   11, 50, 64–5, 69,
  75–6, 78–9, 104–6, 365, 366;
  end of racism   11–12, 13; and
  integration   75; self-segregation
  50, 53
Augustine, Saint   211
Auld, Hugh   67
Auld, Sophia   186, 214, 249
Auld, Thomas   67, 218, 220
Austin, John   108, 167

Banneker, Benjamin 168n13, 236–7
Barry, Richard 358
Bassham, Gregory 110
Batchelder incident 289, 290
Bauer, Bruno 69–70
Bell, Derrick: desegregation of schools 44; interest convergence thesis 132; libertarianism 385–6; Racial Preference Licensing Act 386; racism 367, 376–8; Space Traders 21, 171n39, 377–8
benevolence 258–9, 260–1, 262–3, 266, 303n48
Bentham, Jeremy 108, 190, 199
bestiality 314, 317–18, 320, 324
bible 66, 147, 159, 194
Bingham, Caleb 103, 249
biography, moral/mental 174
biological determinism 57, 122, 127, 162, 387
biological evolution 156
Black Codes 341
black consciousness 208–9
black conservatism 379–80
black emigration: black supporters 21; Crummell 21, 45n6; Delany 21, 26, 60–1, 366–7, 374, 384; Douglass 21–2, 29–30, 42–4, 60–1, 347; Jefferson 21, 22–3; Walker 232
black leadership 369–71
black nation-state 26, 27, 28, 35–6, 44
black power 35–7, 106
black studies 379
Black Theology 213
black thinkers xiii, 173, 210
blacks: alienated 25, 30, 33, 45, 126, 211; American nationality 31–4, 102; bestiality 314, 317–18, 320, 324; children 343; citizenship rights 65, 105, 115–16, 118–19, 132, 365, 366, 368–9, 372–3, 388; colonization 21, 22–3, 185, 337n71; criminalized 339–40, 347, 350–1, 358–9, 387–8; exclusion 118, 121, 235, 332n22; English language 183–4, 190–2, 193–4; exodus to north 42, 49n73; humanity 120, 121, 154–7, 373–4; identity 33, 77; impudence 128, 256–7; inequality of punishments 115, 273, 344, 348, 349–50, 356; inferiority 67, 125, 126, 128, 387–8; labor 356, 360–1n27; lived experience 217; middle-class 59, 62–3n16, 140–1n87; as nation within nation 24; oppression 58, 71–2; personhood 100, 121–2, 154–7; political participation 13–14; self-conception 15n12; successes 130; violence against lynching 321–2; women 318, 319, 326, 346
Blackstone, Sir William 91
Blassingame, John 149, 244, 246, 247, 249, 257, 264
Blight, David 2
Boatwright, Lizzie 357
Bok, Sissela 233
Bork, Robert (Judge) 87, 88, 91, 109
Boxill, Bernard: assimilation 64, 79; continuation thesis 294, 296–7; Douglass/Delany 367–8; economics of race 383; injustice 233; moral suasion 60–1, 244, 247, 281; racial pride 52; resistance 222, 247, 281, 284–5; sympathy 375
brotherhood of man 5–6, 65, 260
Brown, John: Harpers Ferry 227, 236, 237, 239–40, 334n43; insurrectionary force 237; resistance 40, 41, 291

Brown, John (Governor)   348
Brown, John, Jr   246
Brown v. Board of Education   106
Brutus, anti-Federalist critic   114
Burke, Ronald   257, 264
Bush, George   313
Butler, Broadus   210
Byrd, Alton (Colonel)   357

Canada, black emigrants   26–7
capital and labor   322, 323
categorical imperative (Kant)   54
Chambers, William   280
Charles, Robert   322, 334–5n45
Chinese Americans   315
Christianity: ethnology   157; Judaism   71; moral suasion   220; polygeny   159; slavery   261; trial/maturation   222; Walker   238
Cicero   107, 122
citizenship: active   11; birthright   25; for blacks   65, 105, 115–16, 132, 365, 366, 368–9, 372–3, 388; miscegenation   327–30
civil disobedience   44
civil rights   366, 379
civil society, and state   73
civilization   23–4, 175, 191
Clark, Kenneth   106, 367
class: lynching   315; middle-class blacks   59, 62–3n16, 140–1n87; suffrage   327
Clay, Henry   21, 22, 262, 269
colonization   21, 22–3, 185, 337n71; *see also* black emigration
color, metonym for slavery   73
colorblind laws   11
Commentaries on the Constitution of the United States (Story)   87–9, 94
Commentaries on the Laws of England (Blackstone)   91
common ancestry   165, 170n25
communication   192–3, 195–6
consciousness: black   208–9; double   48n56, 103, 208; false   210; white domination   129–30
Constitution: Douglass   85–6, 115–16, 366; Fifteenth Amendment   316, 326–7; Fugitive Slave Clause   93; Garrison   87, 112; liberty   113; nationhood   44; natural law   85, 86, 87, 97, 107–8, 117–18, 119, 267–8, 269; Preamble   90, 93–4, 95; pro-slavery   112, 275; slavery   85–6, 92, 93, 104, 111, 114; as social contract   86; strategic use   113; textual interpretation   115; Thirteenth Amendment   341, 344; 3/5 clause   159; *see also* original intent
Continental Congress   101
convict camps   346; *see also* labor camps
convict leasing   340, 342–3, 344, 346, 351–4, 355
Cooper, Anna Julia   218
Covey, Edward   38–9, 40, 41, 67, 68, 210–11, 216, 218–21, 223, 286, 287, 297
Cox, Samuel H.   255
criminal justice systems   347
criminalization of blacks   339–40, 347, 350–1, 358–9, 387–8
Crummell, Alexander: benighted blacks   49n63; black emigration   21, 45n6; ideas   199–200; knowledge/morality   174; language   185–6, 190–2, 193–4; new era   173; slavery/progress   183
Cruse, Harold   75
Cuffe, Paul   379
cultural pluralism   75

Darwin, Charles   156, 170n26
Davis, Angela Y.   207, 209–10, 218
debt peonage: *see* peonage

Declaration of Independence 93, 366; dignity 159; equality 120, 272; natural law 117, 269; natural rights 94
decoding of meaning 187–8, 193
degeneracy 113, 183
degradation: dependency 16n20; slavery 27, 67, 72–4, 78, 128, 230–1; thought 184–5
Delany, Martin Robson 162; black emigration 21, 26, 60–1, 366–7, 374, 384; black nationality 31–4; black power 35–6; *Blake* 27, 28; Boxill 367–8; elitism 48–9n63; emigration 384; equality 374; "nation within nation" 24–5; permanent racism 376; rights 24; separatism 105; sympathy 23, 25, 32, 34–5, 46n17, 374–5
Delgado, Richard 367
DeMott, Benjamin 130
Denon, Vivant 163
d'Entreves, A. P. 106, 108
dependency 16n20, 67, 68, 130
Derrida, Jacques 172n41
desegregation of schools 44
determinism: intelligence 162, 387; Providence 233; race 57, 127; slaves 122
dignity 50, 159; moral convictions 40; and power 38, 39, 40; through struggle 221, 222
discrimination 8–9, 371–2
disenfranchisement 314, 317, 318, 328
double consciousness 48n56, 103, 208
double endorsement, Douglass 295–7
Douglass, Frederick 145; affirmative action 371–2; black emigration 21–2, 29–30, 42–4, 60–1, 347; black exodus from South to North 42, 49n73; black institutions 5–6, 7–8, 51–2, 59, 60, 61, 65, 133; blacks' role 255–6; and Brown 237, 239; citizenship 388; Constitution 85–6, 115–16, 366; convict leasing 342–3; criminalization of blacks 339–40, 350–1; dignity 50, 159; do nothing policy 290, 298; double endorsement 295–7; and Enlightenment 243, 244–5, 248, 254–5, 359; existentialism 147, 208; and Fanon 215–16; freedom 344; Garrisonians 16, 243–4, 252, 256–7, 266–7, 303n42; German thinkers 301–2n28; grammar/communication 195–6; humanity 213, 215, 366–7; and Kant 251–2; lynching 314–16, 329–30, 332n18; moral sentiments 261, 389; moral suasion 228–9, 244–5, 246, 248, 257; nationhood 365; natural law 106–9; patriotism 47–8n48; power 38; racial pride 51, 52; racism 139n68; religious liberalism 169n20; representativeness 2, 14n2; self-respect 286, 287–8, 291, 295, 298–9; slave system 71–3, 179–82; slavery 86–7, 197–9, 207, 209, 261–2; and Walker 229; women's movement 326–7, 369; *see also* original intent
Douglass, Frederick, biographical details: fight with Covey 38–9, 40, 41, 210–11, 216, 218–21, 223, 286, 287; interracial marriage 321, 325, 334n42; literacy 186, 187; mother 300–1n19, 334n38; as mulatto 139n68, 334n38; as slave 67–8, 103

Douglass, Frederick, qualities: confidence in law 351; identification with whites 101, 123; as self-made man 1, 6–7, 68–9; texts/anti-texts 148, 166–7, 172n41

Douglass, Frederick, roles: as assimilationist 11, 50, 64–5, 69, 75–6, 78–9, 104–6, 365, 366; as federalist 88; as moral sentimentalist 261; as orator 249–50; as politician 167–8n6, 243; as Republican 344–5; as thinker 2–4, 145–6, 160

Douglass, Frederick, works: "The Ballot and The Bullet" 307n86; "The Claims of the Negro Ethnologically Considered" 8, 146, 148–66, 168n15, 169n18, 171n35; "The Do-Nothing Policy" 279–80, 308n90; "The Heroic Slave" 238; "Is It Right and Wise To Kill a Kidnapper?" 40, 288, 289, 290, 308–9n94; "Lessons of the Hour" xvi, 314, 320, 388, 389; *The Life and Times of Frederick Douglass* 222; "Let the Negro Alone" 384; "Love of God, Love of Man, Love of Country" 265; "Lynch Law in the South" 314, 315; "The Meaning of July Fourth for the Negro" 100, 101–4, 113, 124, 269, 273, 283; "Of Morals and Men" 269–70; *My Bondage and My Freedom* 145, 149, 214, 218, 245, 251–2, 283, 308n94; "The Negro Problem" 365; "Peaceful Annihilation of Slavery is Hopeless" 308n19; "The Present and Future of the Coloured Race in America" 365; "The Reason Why" 335n48, 337n71; "Self-Made Men" lecture 236; "We are in the Midst of a Moral Revolution" 269, 270, 277; "We need a True, Strong, and Principled Party" 372; "Why is the Negro Lynched?" 350–1

Dred Scott v. Sanford 86, 90, 92, 96–7, 113, 118–19, 120, 159, 266, 388

D'Souza, Dinesh 4, 8–9, 10, 11, 12

DuBois, W. E. B.: alienation of blacks 45; *Black Reconstruction* 346, 356; color line 100; convict leasing 342, 354, 355; double consciousness 48n56, 103, 208; identity 33, 48n56, 218; race 57; whiteness 129

Dunbar, Paul Laurence 115

duty 177

Dworkin, Ronald 93, 124

education: desegregation 44; segregation 106

Egyptians 161, 163

elitism, Delany 48–9n63

emancipation problems 351

Emerson, Ralph Waldo 147

emigration of blacks: *see* black emigration

end of racism thesis 4, 8, 9–10, 12–13

Engels, F. 74, 80n12

English language 183–4, 190–2, 193–4; Caribbean 194; plantation 193, 195–6

Enlightenment: Douglass 243, 244–5, 248, 254–5, 359; equality 121; Founding Fathers 103; humanity 121; Kant 248, 250–1, 254, 294; liberal state 111; Locke 103; natural law 106; self-interest 23–4

Equal Rights Association 326, 327

equality: Declaration of Independence 120, 272; Delany 374; Enlightenment 121; Jefferson

168n13; law   105; Lincoln 168n13; natural law   107, 119–20, 121; and separateness   380; West   368
equality of opportunity   130–1, 367
ethics   106–7
ethnological science   8, 147, 148, 153, 157
etymology   189
European thought   210
evolutionary theory   156
exclusion of blacks   118, 121, 235, 332n22
existentialism   147, 207–8, 211, 215–16, 219
exodus to north   42, 49n73
Exoduster movement   345, 346–7
exploitation   352–3
Eze, Emmanuel   302–3n39

Factor, Robert   380–1
false consciousness   210
Fanon, Frantz   208, 211, 212–13, 215–17
Faryna, Stan   379–80
Federalists   87–8
Fehrenbacher, Don   124
Feinberg, Joel   56
feminism   122, 326
Fierce, Milfred   342–3, 352, 356, 362n61
Flemming, Chief Justice   87
Foner, Philip   244, 246, 341, 344
force   37–8, 91, 107, 218, 222
foundationalism   169–70n22
Founding Fathers   103; *see also* original intent
Franklin, John Hope   135–6n8, 139, 139–40n72
Frederickson, George   125, 126, 128
Freedman's Bureau   355
freedom: existentialism   207–8; and humanity   181, 217; language of   191; political rights   344; public speaking   252–3; self-determining   253–4
Frege, G.   192
Fugitive Slave clause, Constitution   93
Fugitive Slave Law (1851)   266
Fuller, Lon   93

Garnet, Henry Highland   21, 291
Garrison, William Lloyd: American Colonization Society   45n6; Constitution   87, 112; legal positivism   85; moral suasion   229, 243, 260; Republican   88; rhetoric   103
Garrisonians   16, 85, 86, 96, 243–4, 252–3, 256–7, 266–7, 291, 303n42
Garvey, Marcus   379
Gates, Henry Louis, Jr   14n2, 198, 246
Giddings, Paula   332–3n24
Gilroy, Paul   301–2n28, 309–10n100
Gliddon, George R.   157, 163
Godwin, William   160
Goodell, William   86, 113
Gordon, Milton M.   74–5
Graham, J. G.   352
grammar: and communication   192–3, 195–6; Crummell   188, 189, 190–2, 193–4; decoding   187–8; Humboldt   188–9; literacy   186–7; natural language   188; universal   175
Greek mythology   324
Green, Shields   237, 240
grief, slave songs   197–9
Griggs v. Duke Power Co.   132

Hacker, Andrew   129
Hare, R. M.   55, 58
Harpers Ferry   227, 236, 237, 239–40, 334n43
Harris, Cheryl   131, 349

Harris, Nellie 38, 39, 40, 41, 42
Hartman, Chester 367
Hayden, Tom 371
Hayes, Rutherford 339
Hayes-Rutherford Compromise 342
Hegel, G. W. F. 230, 309–10n100, 345
Heidegger, Martin 172n41
Herder, J. G. 184, 194
Higginbotham, A. Leon, Jr (Judge) 115
Hobbes, Thomas 122
Holly, James 21
Holmes, Oliver Wendell 109
honor 235
Hopkins, Pauline 333n24, n31
Horsman, Reginald 125
Horton, Willie 313
Hospers, John 383
human rights 245, 374
humanism 103–4, 105, 188, 210
humanity: American experiment 3; and bestiality 320, 324; blacks 120, 121, 154–7, 373–4, 377–8; brotherhood 5–6, 65, 260; Cicero 122; common ancestry 165, 170n25; denied 65, 223, 229, 271; Douglass 213, 215, 366–7; Enlightenment 121; existentialism 211; freedom 181, 217; and religion 262; self-evident 245, 246; suffering 58–9; sympathy 324; Washington 380–1
Humboldt, W. K. von 185, 188–9
Hume, David 192, 258, 375
Hutcheson, Francis 229, 258

idealism 111–12
identity: blacks 33, 77; double 48n56; DuBois 33, 48n56, 218; national 42–3, 194, 232–3; racial 257; social 3, 73–4, 77–8; struggle 218
ignorance 179, 180

ill-treatment of slaves 236
immigrant-assimilation 76–7
impudence 128, 256–7
inclusion 118, 122, 130–2
independence 16n20, 24–5, 101, 283–4
individualism 130
inequality of punishments 115, 273, 344, 348, 349–50, 356
injustice 43–4, 229, 233–4
institutions, black 5–6, 7–8, 51–2, 59, 60, 61, 65, 133
insurrectionists 227–8, 237
integrationism 75, 105, 117
integrity, slaves 285–6, 293
intelligence 162, 387
interest-convergence thesis 132
interracial coalitions 370
interracial liaisons 217, 313; Douglass 321, 325, 334n42
Irish 161–2, 164

Jaffa, Harry 120
Jansberry, Lorraine 218
Jefferson, Thomas: Banneker 168n13, 236–7; blacks 125, 237; colonization 21, 22–3; Constitution 87; English language 194; equality 168n13; immigration 29; self-evident truths 117
Jews 69–70, 71, 77, 315
Jim Crow laws 57–8, 60, 105, 132, 349, 383–4
Johnson, Samuel 117
Jones, William R. 208, 211
Judaism 69–70, 71
jurisprudence 108, 133
Justice, J. H. 349
justice 41–2, 92, 103–4, 162, 265, 383–6

Kahn, Paul 90–1
Kansas-Nebraska Bill (1854) 266
Kant, Immanuel: categorical

imperative 54; Enlightenment 248, 250–2, 254, 294; good will 303n48; moral reasoning 176–7; personhood 122–3; race 255, 302–3n39; universalism 176
Kennedy, Randall 4, 5, 6
Kierkegaard, S. 147, 211–12
King, Martin Luther Jr 44, 289, 371, 379
King, Rodney 331n7

labor: black 356, 360–1n27; capital 322, 323
labor camps 357–8; *see also* convict camps
labor division, moral 299
language: civilizing power 175; Crummell 185–6, 190–2, 193–4; freedom 191; and ideas 199–200; of modernity 185–6; national character 189–90; race 195; systems 199
languages: African 171n38, 191; English 183–4, 190–2, 193–4; natural 188
law: equality 105; as force 91; and morality 100, 106, 108, 114, 116, 268; positivism 85, 108–9, 119, 120, 224n9, 267–8; reason 91–2, 96; will-centred 96; *see also* natural law
Lawson, William Lance 391–65
Ledewitz, Bruce 110
legal activism 113
Levine, Robert 294, 297–8
liberalism 111, 124, 169n20
liberation struggles 207, 216, 218
Liberator 112
Liberia 22, 45n6, 27, 183, 193
libertarianism 383, 384, 385–6
liberty 94, 97, 101, 104, 113, 207, 386–7; *see also* freedom
life chances 146, 147, 367
Lincoln, Abraham 21, 22, 168n13

linguistics, historical 163
literacy: Douglass 186, 187, 249; Douglass's mother 300–1n19; grammar 186–7; power 174–5; for slaves 188, 213, 214–15
literary theory 1–2, 283
Lively, Donald 133
Locke, John 93, 103, 122, 133, 189–90, 192, 244, 245–6
Lott, Tommy 75
Louisiana, convict leasing 344
L'Ouverture, Toussaint 309–96
Love, Rev E. K. 318–19, 333n31, 334n33
lynch law 324, 329–30
lynching 313; class 315; disenfranchisement 314, 317, 318, 328; Douglass 314–16, 329–30, 332n18; legal 314–15; patriarchy/racism 314; press reports 236; and slavery 315–16, 322; violence against 321–2

McFeely, William 320
McGary, Howard 384
Malcolm X 218
Mancini, Matthew 352–3
marooning 228, 238, 240–1
Marshall, Chief Justice 87
Marshall, Thurgood 105, 113
Martin, Waldo E., Jr 105, 243, 244, 294
Marx, Karl: "On the Jewish Question" 69–71, 74, 78; proletarians 74; as social assimilationist 78
masking behavior 115, 151
materialism 111–12, 134, 232–3
meaning, decoded 187–8, 193
Meese, Edwin (Attorney General) 109, 136–7n26
Meier, August 370
Melting Pot theory 75

memory, and recollection 184
might: *see* force
Mills, Charles W. 1
mind 176, 181–2
mind-language-morals thesis 175, 178, 179–80, 183–4, 186, 195–200
miscegenation 320–1, 325–6, 327–30
Mississippi: Black Codes 341; Pig Law 348
mixed-race solution 329
modernity 184, 185–6
monogenism 156, 157–9, 161, 163, 165
Moody-Adams, Michele 287
moral community 234–5
moral realism 107
moral sentiments theory 248, 258–66, 389
moral suasion: abolition 228–9, 243–3, 246, 305n63; Boxill 60–1, 244, 247, 281; Christianity 220; Douglass 228–9, 244–5, 246, 248, 257; Garrison 229, 243, 260; methods 42, 104, 248; and moral sentiment 258–63, 264–5; natural law 264, 266, 271–9, 281–2, 294, 295; public use of reason 262–3; racism 61, 128, 384–5; resistance 292, 294; rhetoric 257–8, 264; and violent resistance 246, 292, 294
morality: communication 192; dignity 40; Kant 176–7; knowledge 174; law 100, 106, 108, 114, 116, 268; mind 176; natural law 100, 104, 267–8; objectivity 112; politics 50, 276; purity 176; race 52–3, 56–7, 58, 124, 131–2; slavery 52, 179, 222–3; struggle 247, 248, 291, 293–4; universality constraint 53, 54–6

Morrison, Toni 330n1
Morton, Samuel 151, 157–8, 161
Moses, Greg 224n9
motivation 248, 259–60
mulattoes 139n68, 162, 171n37, 333n31, 336n58
Murray, Pauli 240
Myers, Linda 376
Myrdal, Gunnar 117, 126, 131, 140n82

NAACP 105, 379
Nation of Islam 379
national character, language 189–90
National Committee on Prison Labor 343–4
national identity 194, 232–3
National Prison Association 350, 351
National Woman's Suffrage Association 327
nationality 32–3, 46n22
nationhood 25, 365
"nations within nations's" 23, 24, 25
Native Americans 122, 123, 125
nativism 194
natural justice 92, 103–4
natural law 106–9, 249; absolutist 107; Constitution 85, 86, 87, 97, 107–8, 117–18, 119, 267–8, 269; Declaration of Independence 117, 269; Enlightenment 106; equality 107, 119–20, 121; moral suasion 264, 266, 271–9, 281–2, 294, 295; morality 100, 104, 267–8; original intent 274–5; race 122; scientifically correct political order 91, 92–3, 96, 98; slavery 96, 100; Story 95; Vattel 123
natural rights 53, 65–6, 87–8, 92, 94, 95, 107, 125–6
negative theology 172n41
negritude 217
Negroes: *see* blacks

Negro problem   315, 316, 323; *see also* blacks
neo-accommodationists   382–3, 388
Nochlin, Linda   146, 166
North American Review   320, 347
Nott, Josiah Clarke   157, 163
Nussbaum, Martha C.   233–4

obligation   248, 260–1, 265, 272
ontology   208, 216
opportunity: equality of   130–1, 367; merit-based   9; for scholarship   146, 147
oppression   58, 71–2, 185, 373
original intent, Constitution   109–16, 307n80; antislavery   134; general/specific   110; interpretations   89–90; liberty   94, 104; majoritarian   124–6; natural law   274–5; natural rights   87–8, 95; normative foundation   111; pro-slavery   275, 306n79; social dynamics   111–12; Taney   88, 91, 96, 113–14, 124–5, 139–40n72; textual intent   110
Oshinsky, David   343, 351
the Other   212, 223, 377–8
Outlaw, Lucius T.   208

Pagden, Anthony   122
Parent Society   260
parents and children   56, 177–8
paternalism   253
patriarchy   314, 328
patriotism   47–8n48
Peirce, C. S.   198
Peller, Gary   127
penitentiaries   346
peonage   341–2, 346, 358
personhood   100, 121–2, 154–7; denied   270–1, 272; Kant   122–3; legal status   114; Walker   238
Philadelphia Convention   114

Phillips, Wendell   115
philosophy xiii, 1, 146–7
phrenologists   162
Pig Law   348
Pitts, Helen   321, 334n42
pity   35; *see also* sympathy
plantation English   193, 195–6
Plato   106, 146–7, 161
Plessy v. Ferguson   100, 129, 380
political leadership   369–71
political order, scientifically correct   91, 92–3, 96, 98
political rights   344
politics: abolition   267, 268–9, 275–8; action   282, 292; black participation   13–14; culture of   278; morality   50, 276; romanticism   266, 267; welfare   10
polygeny   147, 151, 159
positivism: legal   85, 108–9, 119, 210, 224n9, 267–9; nativism   194; natural law   124
postmodernism   147–8, 172n41
poverty culture   130, 382
Powell, John A.   381–2
power: dignity   38, 39, 40; and force   37–8; literacy   174–5; respect   35–6, 43
Preamble to Constitution   90, 93–4, 95
prejudice   126–7, 128, 161–2, 315, 347
Prichard, James   163, 170n28
pro-slavery sentiment   112, 157–8, 270, 275, 306n79
proletarians   74, 80n12
Prometheus   216
property   212, 349; slaves as   210, 212, 339
proto-racism   125
Providence, determinism   233
public discourse   114–15, 252–3
public use of reason   250, 251–2, 254, 262–3, 271–2

punishment inequalities   115, 273, 344, 348, 349–50, 356

race: biologically determined   57, 127; classified   50; differences between   162, 163, 164; Douglass   255–6; DuBois   57; economics of   383; identity   257; jurisprudence   133; Kant   255, 302–3n39; language   195; morality   52–3, 56–7, 58, 124, 131–2; natural law   122; realism   386; social construction   57, 59, 127; social progress   365, 366, 368; sympathy   23, 25, 32
race relations   379, 381
racial assimilation: *see* assimilation
racial cryptography   115, 124
racial neutrality   11, 122
racial polity   100, 124, 126–7, 132, 147
Racial Preference Licensing Act   386
racial prejudice: *see* prejudice
racial pride   4, 51, 52, 387
racism   15–16n15, 324; Bell   367, 376–8; black nation-state   44; in decline   380; dehumanizing   222–3; Douglass   139n68; end of   4, 8, 9–10, 12–13; life chances   367; lynching   314; moral suasion   61, 128, 384–5; myth of black rapists   313, 316, 318, 320, 323; patriarchy   328; permanence   376, 378, 387; scientific   125, 185, 302n39, 358; *see also* miscegenation
Radical Reconstruction   344, 345
rapists, alleged: black   313, 314–15, 316, 318, 320, 323; fair trial   316, 329–30; white   319, 326
reason: and law   91–2, 96; public use of   250, 251–2, 254, 262–3, 271–2
recognition   296, 309–10n100
recollection, and memory   184

Rehnquist, William   109
religion   70, 262
religious liberalism   169n20
Renan, E.   32
representation   228
representative heuristics   232, 233, 234–5
Republic of New Africa   379
Republicans   87, 88, 344–5
resistance: Boxill   222, 247, 281, 284–5; dignity   40; justification   246, 247, 289, 290, 307–8n89; and moral suasion   292, 294; slave's right   282–3, 285, 286–7, 288–9; theft   339; violent   246, 247, 281–2, 292, 294
respect   35–6, 43, 378
revolution   280, 282, 284, 297–8, 309n96
rhetoric   103, 249–50, 257–8, 264, 269
Rights, Bill of   44
rights: Delany   24; fighting for   38–9; human   245, 374; natural   53, 65–6, 92, 94, 107, 125–6; political   344; to revolt   280, 282; violated   24, 98
Rousseau, Jean-Jacques   210

San Domingo slave revolution   309n96
Sandel, Michael   4–5
Sanders-Lawson, Renee   391n65
Sartre, Jean-Paul   211, 215, 217
Saxton, Alexander   126
scholars, abolition of slavery   153
scientific racism   125, 185, 302n39, 358
scrip system   344, 346, 351
segregation   9, 50, 53, 106, 132–3
self   4–5, 217; *see also* identity
self-defense   286–7, 289, 322
self-determination   68, 73, 253–4
self-help, economic   332n16

self-improvement 176
self-interest 23–4, 374–5, 376–7, 381, 385
self-reliance 7, 9, 10
self-respect 238, 260, 285, 286, 287–8, 290, 291, 295, 298–9
self-segregation 50, 53
Senghor, Léopold 208
sentencing: *see* punishment inequalities
separate but equal ruling 380
separatism 105, 106, 127–8
serfdom 355
Sevier, overseer 38, 39, 40, 41, 42
sharecropping 344, 346
Simpson, O. J. 313, 330n1
Slaughter, Thomas 208
slave revolution, San Domingo 309n96
slave system 71–3, 154–7, 179–82
slaveholders: fear 40, 41; honor 235; moral blindness 245, 246–7
slavery 211–12; as categorical evil 222; Christianity 261; Constitution 86–7, 92, 93, 104, 111, 114; and criminality 347; degradation 27, 67, 72–4, 78, 128, 230–1; denial of humanity 65; Douglass 86–7, 207, 209, 261–2; Douglass's personal experience 67–8, 103; essentialism 209–10; exclusion 235; and the Fall 211–12; injustice 229; and justice 4, 265; and knowledge 186–7; and liberty 97, 207; and lynching 315–16, 322; mind 181–2; and morality 52, 179, 222–3; natural law 96, 100; political defenders 306n75; and progress 183; as violation of rights 98; *see also* abolition of slavery
slaves: biological determinism 122; Hegel 230; historical experiences 208; honor 235; ignorance 179, 180; inferiority 67, 235–6; integrity 285–6, 293; literacy 188, 213, 214–15; as property 210, 212, 339; resistance 282–3, 285, 286–7, 288–9; right to revolt 280, 282; singing 197–9; treatment of 236, 315–16
slaves of the community 67, 72, 74
Smith, Adam 258
Smith, Charles H. 163
Smith, Gerrit 86, 113
Smith, Susan 349
Smith, Valerie 325–6
social-assimilation 76–7, 78–9
social construction 57, 59, 127, 287
social criticism, insider/outsider 167n5
social identity 3, 73–4, 77–8
social justice 383; *see also* equality
social progress, race 365, 366, 368
society 74–5, 78
sociogeny 217
sociology, race 381–2
Socrates 146–7, 233
songs of slaves 197–9
Southern states: black labor 344, 345; criminal justice systems 347; penitentiaries 346; *see also* Jim Crow laws
Sowell, Thomas 8, 9, 384
Space Traders (Bell) 21, 171n39, 377–8
specificity, and universality 55
speech act theory 193
Spooner, Lysander 86, 91–2, 113
Stanhope, Samuel 170n28
Stanton, Elizabeth Cady 326, 336–7n24
states: black participation 13–14; civil society 73; intervention 28; and nations 25
Steinberg, Stephen 140n82

Stewart, Maria W.   173–6, 240
Stoics   106, 107
Storing, Herbert   167–8n6
Story, Justice Joseph   87–9, 94, 95
Stowe, Harriet B.   238
struggle: dignity   221, 222; identity   218; liberation   207, 216, 218; morality   247, 248, 291, 293–4; physical   291, 293–4; unifying   369
Stuart, Charles   349
suasionists: *see* moral suasion
sub-persons   122, 123; *see also* humanity
subjectivity   213
suffering, and humanity   58–9
suffrage, class   327
Sumner, Charles   253
Sundquist, Eric J.   283–4
Sunstein, Cass   110
symbiosis thesis   127
sympathy: Bell   376; Boxill   375; Delany   23, 25, 32, 34–5, 46n17, 374–5; and humanity   324
syntax   189
system-centrism, European thought   210

Takaki, Ronald   44, 168n13
Taney, Roger (Chief Justice): *Dred Scott v. Sanford*   86, 92, 118–19, 159; legal positivism   85; original intent   88, 91, 96, 113–14, 124–5, 139–40n72
Taylor, Zachary   262, 269
teleology   208
temperance thesis   294, 297–8
temperate revolutionism   297–8
tenant farming   342, 344, 346, 351
Terrell, Mary Church   342, 354, 356–7
textual interpretation, Constitution   115
theft, as resistance   339

Thomas, Clarence   371
Thoreau, Henry D.   231–2
3/5 Clause, Constitution   93, 159
Tobias, D. E.   346, 353–4, 362n61 309n96
truth   117, 169–70n22
Truth, Sojourner   371
Turner, Nat   240
turpentine camps   348

United Kingdom   23, 25
United States v. Fisher   92
United States Supreme Court   85, 92
universal grammar   175
universality   55, 103–4, 173, 176
universality constraint   53, 54–6, 57–8

vagrancy   341
Van den Berghe, Pierre   126
Vattel, Emer de   123
Volney, C. F. C.   163

Walker, Alice   325–6
Walker, David: Christianity   238; colonization societies   232; insurrection   227–8, 229–30, 240; Providential determinism   233; racial slavery   230–1; representative heuristics   232, 233, 234–5
Walker, Peter   244
Walzer, Michael   167n5
Washington, Booker T.: convict leasing   342; on Douglass   14, 243; humanity   380–1; labor   345; libertarianism   385; lynching   316; moral suasion/abolition   305n63; slavery   218
WASP ideal   75
Wayland, Henry   149
Webster, Daniel   103
Webster, Noah   91
welfare state   10, 16–17n21

Wells-Barnett, Ida B.: Douglass's interracial marriage 334n42; lynching 314, 317, 319–20, 327–8; miscegenation 320–1, 324–5, 328; rapists 336n58; *The Reason Why* 315, 335n48; "Red Record" 335n49, n56; violence against lynching 321–2
West, Cornel 208, 368–74, 386–7
West Indies, black emigrants 26
white backlash 132, 133, 313
white supremacy claims 126, 127, 129, 273
Whitefield, J. M. 21, 29
whiteness: as American norm 140n84; degeneracy 113, 114; myths 324; privilege 131; property 349; wages of 129
whites: blacks' humanity 373–4, 377–8; criminals, black disguises 348–9, 361n42; domination 125, 129–30; equal opportunities 130–1; rapists 319, 326; self-interest 374–5, 376–7, 381, 385; women 325, 336n58; workers, and slaves 73–4
Wiecek, William 114
Willett, Cynthia 309–10n100
Wilson, William Julius 380
Wittgenstein, Ludwig 198
women: black 318, 319, 326, 346; in labor camps 357–8; white 325, 336n58
women's movement 326–7, 369
women's rights convention 245
words, use/meaning 191–2
Wright, Richard 208, 211, 218
Wynter, Sylvia 217

Yahweh 211, 213, 224–5n11, n15